IRISH UNIONISM: ONE
THE ANGLO-IRISH AND THE NEW IRELAND
1885–1922

IRISH UNIONISM: ONE

The Anglo-Irish
and the New Ireland
1885-1922

PATRICK BUCKLAND

Gill and Macmillan · Dublin
Barnes & Noble Books · New York
a division of Harper & Row Publishers, Inc.

First published in Ireland in 1972

Gill and Macmillan Ltd
2 Belvedere Place
Dublin 1
and in London through association with the
Macmillan
International Group of Publishing Companies
Published in the U.S.A. in 1972 by
Harper & Row Publishers, Inc.
Barnes & Noble Import Division

Jacket designed by Hilliard Hayden

Gill & Macmillan SBN: 7171 0595 4
Barnes & Noble ISBN: 06 4907503

Printing history
10 9 8 7 6 5 4 3 2 1

Printed and bound in the Republic of Ireland by
Cahill and Co. Limited Dublin

To Pat

To Pat

Contents

Contents

Preface

THE story of southern unionism is the story of how the Anglo-Irish in the south of Ireland reacted to the advent of democratic nationalism. At first they opposed and helped to thwart the new Ireland, but eventually they came to terms with it and helped Irish nationalists to realise at least some of their aims after the first world war. Hitherto, southern unionism has been as neglected by historians as it used to be criticised by contemporaries. Though a rebuttal of the worst that such criticisms implied forms a useful theme, this book is not intended as an *apologia* on behalf of the southern unionists. Nor does it claim to be a definitive history of southern unionism. Rather, by using a clearly defined and representative body of source material, it hopes to provide an overall picture of the movement, a narrative framework, which may be of general interest and which may provide the basis for further discussion and research.

Acknowledgements

I AM most grateful to Professor J. C. Beckett for his advice and encouragement at every stage of this work; to Mr P. M. H. Bell for reading and commenting upon the Ph.D. thesis from which this book emerged; to Dr D. G. Boyce for many stimulating hours spent discussing the Irish question in British politics; and to Professor R. B. McDowell for talking so freely about the Irish convention. I am also grateful to Professor D. W. J. Johnson, Professor D. B. Quinn and Mr J. Parker for their encouragement.

Extracts from Crown copyright material in the Public Record Office and elsewhere appear by kind permission of the Controller of Her Majesty's Stationery Office. Extracts from the Lloyd George and Bonar Law papers are printed with the permission of the First Beaverbrook Foundation, while extracts from the papers of Joseph and Austen Chamberlain are printed with the permission of the librarian of Birmingham University. I am grateful to the Earl of Midleton for allowing me to quote from the various papers of the first Earl; to the Trustees of the British Museum for permission to use the Balfour and Bernard papers; to the Council of Trustees of the National Library of Ireland for permission to publish extracts from the Redmond and Daunt papers; to the University of Dublin for permission to quote from the Lecky papers; and to Mr Mark Bonham Carter for permission to use the Asquith papers. For permission to use material in the Public Record Office of Northern Ireland I am indebted to the Deputy Keeper and to Captain Peter Montgomery.

Finally, I must express my thanks to the staffs of the libraries and record offices in which I have worked, and record my special debt to Mr Kenneth Darwin, former Deputy Keeper of the Public Record Office of Northern Ireland, to Mr Brian Trainor, the present Deputy Keeper, and to two members of their staff, Dr Anthony Malcomson and Mr James Boston.

Abbreviations

A.P.L.	Unionist Anti-Partition League.
B.L.	Beaverbrook Library (figures prefaced by a letter denote the Lloyd George papers; those without such a prefix denote the Law papers).
B.M., Add. MS	British Museum, Additional Manuscripts.
Bodleian	Bodleian Library, Oxford.
Bt	Baronet.
B.U.L., AC	Birmingham University Library, the Austen Chamberlain papers.
B.U.L., JC	Birmingham University Library, the Joseph Chamberlain papers.
D.L.	Deputy Lieutenant.
H.M.L.	His Majesty's Lieutenant.
H.S.	High Sheriff.
I.B.M.C.C.	Irish Business Men's Conciliation Committee.
I.L.P.U.	Irish Loyal and Patriotic Union.
I.R.A.	Irish Republican Army.
I.U.A.	Irish Unionist Alliance.
N.L.I.	National Library of Ireland.
Parl. Deb.	*Parliamentary Debates.*
P.C.	Privy Councillor.
P.R.O.	Public Record Office, London (where these letters are followed immediately by figures, a classification prefix of P.R.O. should be understood).
P.R.O.I.	Public Record Office, Dublin.
P.R.O.N.I.	Public Record Office of Northern Ireland, Belfast.
R.I.C.	Royal Irish Constabulary.
S.I.L.R.A.	Southern Irish Loyalists Relief Association.
T.C.D.	Trinity College, Dublin, manuscript department.
U.A.I.	Unionist Associations of Ireland.
U.U.C.	Ulster Unionist Council.
Vt	Viscount.

N.B. Except for pamphlets which were published in Dublin, and unless otherwise stated, all works cited were published in London. Letters in named collections to persons other than those after whom the collections of papers are named are usually copies which were forwarded to the person after whom the collection is named.

Introduction

BY the last quarter of the nineteenth century there was emerging a new Ireland chafing at the restrictions imposed by a social system dominated by Anglo-Irish landowners and a political system based upon direct British rule. It was the product of years of economic, social and educational change and religious tolerance. Such developments, eroding the traditional deference of the Irish peasantry, fostered instead independent attitudes, a desire for a higher standard of living, and a deeper appreciation of things Irish. The clearest expression of this new Ireland was political, the nationalist movement. Nationalists tended to be Celtic and Catholic, and the movement drew its strength from the southern Irish democracy. Dating from 1870 as an effective movement, with the formation of Isaac Butt's Home Government Association, it soon dominated the Irish political scene. Though for many years involved with the land and Catholic university questions, its main aim was the restoration of the Irish parliament abolished by the Act of Union of 1800. By the second decade of the twentieth century the Irish Parliamentary Party's demand for a limited form of home rule within the British empire had been replaced by the Irish Republican Brotherhood's demand for an independent Irish republic, a demand expressed constitutionally through Sinn Fein and violently through the Irish Volunteers and the Irish Republican Army.

As soon as it had gathered momentum with the Land and National Leagues under Charles Stewart Parnell, Irish nationalism provoked a counter movement, unionism. As an organised and distinctive movement, Irish unionism dates from 1885. It was a reaction against the development of the nationalist movement on class and sectarian lines and a response to the extension of the franchise in 1884. It drew its strength from the Protestant Anglo-Irish and Scotch-Irish, the products of successive plantations, and enabled former liberals and conservatives to co-operate in attempting to maintain minority, ascendancy, interests and influence. Unionists opposed the demand for an Irish parliament and argued that Ireland's interests could be best served by preserving the legislative union between Great Britain and Ireland, by preserving rule by the Westminster parliament. Despite an impressive record of endeavour, unionism remained a minority movement in Ireland. Whereas nationalists were able for many years to return over eighty M.P.s to Westminster, unionists could only hope to return at most twenty-six (in 1918).

The Irish unionist movement was divided into two groups. There were the unionists of the historic nine-county province of Ulster, strongest in the six counties that now comprise Northern Ireland, and there were the unionists of the three southern provinces. In Ulster, unionists represented an almost self-contained society, ranging from landowners and businessmen to tenant farmers and industrial and agricultural labourers. Among this community there developed a fierce and aggressive unionism, often though unfairly equated with Orangeism. The attitude of these Ulster unionists, prepared if necessary to resist Dublin rule by armed force, contrasted markedly with that of their fellow unionists in the southern provinces who were fewer and less self-contained. For instance, in Ulster, in 1911, there were 890,880 Protestants (a substantial number of whom were Presbyterians) out of a population of 1,581,969, and Ulster unionists could usually count upon winning half of the parliamentary representation of that province. In the three southern provinces, however, where there were only some 256,699 Protestants (belonging mainly to the Church of Ireland) scattered among a Roman Catholic population of 2,551,854, unionists could barely rely on returning three members to parliament. These census and electoral returns are important. They indicate not only the relative strengths but also the different social and political situations of unionists in Ulster and in the south of Ireland. Whereas Ulstermen represented a social pyramid, the southern unionists formed the tip of the social pyramid in the south.

TWO

The backbone of the southern unionist movement was the old landed Anglo-Irish Protestant ascendancy. Although they might almost be described as White Anglo-Saxon Protestants, these landowners were by no means homogeneous. Apart from questions of temperament and intelligence, they fell into three broad, though not watertight or mutually exclusive, categories. Firstly, there were those like James MacKay Wilson, who were prominent in Ireland at a local level. James Wilson was born in 1863, the first son of a fourth son of an average family, descended from John Wilson of Rashee, Co. Antrim, who was supposed to have landed at Carrickfergus in the suite of William III. Nationally the Wilsons do not appear to have been an important family: they were distinguished if at all in the army, the height being reached by James's brother, Henry, the field marshal assassinated in 1922 by Irish republicans. They were, however, active locally. In 1878 James's father owned 1,158 acres valued at £835 a year in Co. Longford, and this slender basis supported a civilised life for James. Having been educated at Harrow and Trinity College, Dublin, and having married the daughter of the Speaker of the House of Keys, James lived in the family mansion, Currygrane, Co. Longford, which was burned down in the civil war. He involved himself in local life, being Deputy Lieutenant and a justice for the county, becoming High Sheriff in 1887, and contesting the county in the unionist interest in the general elections of 1885 and 1892. He died in exile in England at the age of seventy, a bitter critic of Irish self-government.[1]

Secondly, there were men like Dermot Robert Wyndham, seventh Earl of Mayo, who had large interests in Ireland and whose families could be said to have developed a tradition of prominence in Irish life at a national level. Born in 1851, educated at Eton, serving in the Hussars and Grenadier Guards, and marrying a grand-daughter of the fourth Earl of Bessborough, he owned, in 1878, 7,834 acres in the counties of Kildare, Meath and Mayo, valued at £7,690. His principal residence was Palmerston House, near Straffan, Co. Kildare, in which county he owned 4,915 acres and for which he was Deputy Lieutenant and a justice. (Palmerston House was also burned in the civil war.) Dermot was a notable huntsman, writing a history of the famous Kildare hunt, and in several respects his situation was similar to that of

1. *Burke's Landed Gentry of Ireland* (1958), pp. 766–7; U. U. H. de Burgh, *The Landowners of Ireland* (Dublin 1878), p. 479; *Dod's Parliamentary Companion 1886 and 1893*; obituaries in *Irish Times*, 9 Sept. 1933, and *The Times*, 12 Sept. 1933.

J. M. Wilson. There was, however, a large difference. Dermot's family, the Bourkes, was a very old Norman-Irish family, claiming descent from William Fitzadelm de Burgo, Strongbow's successor as governor of Ireland, and the family had developed a tradition of public service nationally as well as locally, providing a number of representatives for the Irish and united parliaments.[2] Perhaps the most distinguished of the public men was the sixth Earl, Dermot's father, Richard Southwell, the Viceroy of India assassinated in 1872 while on a tour of inspection at the Andaman Islands. His son, Dermot, was also a man of wide experience and interests with a lively and adaptable mind. *Sport in Abyssinia* was a lively account of his adventures there, yet he was also a collector of English china and miniatures. Though a conservative in politics, he had strong nationalist sympathies in the broad sense of the word, being anxious to promote the agricultural and industrial welfare of Ireland. Maintaining his family's tradition of public service, he became in 1890 an Irish representative peer, and later a senator of the Irish Free State.[3]

Lastly, there was that group of Irish landowners with much wider horizons, such as Henry Charles Keith Petty Fitzmaurice, fifth Marquess of Lansdowne,[4] Spencer Crompton Cavendish,

---

2. Contemporary comments on the first two Earls include the following. When recommending the first Earl for the barony of Naas, Earl Harcourt wrote, 'He is of an ancient and respectable family, has a very large estate. He has been fifty years in parliament, a constant supporter of the king's government. . . . His eldest son is a man of understanding and ability, a very good speaker in parliament'. Sir John Blaquiere, after detailing offices which the second Earl and his father had obtained for themselves, their relatives and friends, added, 'He is a very zealous friend to government, but not inattentive to his own interests'.

3. *Burke's Peerage* (1967), pp. 1678–80; G.E.C., *Complete Peerage,* viii. 610–11; de Burgh, *Landowners of Ireland,* p. 314; obituaries in *Irish Times* and *The Times,* 2 Jan. 1928.

4. (1845–1927); ed. Eton and Oxford; liberal Junior Lord of the Treasury (1869), Under-Sec. for War (1872–4) and for India (1880), but resigned owing to lack of sympathy with Gladstone's Irish policy; Gov.-Gen. of Canada, 1883–8; Viceroy of India, 1888–94; Sec. of State for War, 1895–1900, and for Foreign Affairs, 1900–5; leader of conservatives and unionists in House of Lords, 1903; Minister without Portfolio, 1915–16; excommunicated from conservative and unionist party because of his peace proposals, 1916–17. In 1883 he owned 142,916 acres in the U.K., worth £62,025 a year. Of these about 122,000 acres worth about £32,000 a year were in Ireland: 94,983 in Co. Kerry; 12,995 in Co. Meath; 8,980 in Queen's Co.; 2,132 in Co. Dublin; 1,642 in Co. Limerick; and 617 in King's Co. His Irish residence was Derreen, Kenmare, Co. Kerry. Lord Newton, *Lord Lansdowne. A Biography* (1929).

eighth Duke of Devonshire,[5] and William St John Fremantle Brodrick, ninth Viscount Midleton, having large interests in Great Britain and becoming prominent in British public life. Born in 1856, educated at Eton and Balliol College, Oxford, and married into an English aristocratic family, Midleton was descended from a Surrey family, the Brodricks, a branch of which had settled in Ireland during the troubles of 1641 and which had greatly profited by the forfeitures of the seventeenth century. Although his principal residence was Peper Harow, Godalming, Surrey, the greater part of the family estates were in Co. Cork, where Midleton had a seat, The Grange, Midleton. In 1883 his father was said to have owned 9,580 acres in the U.K., valued at £10,752; of these 6,475 worth about £6,018 a year were in Co. Cork. There was some family tradition of public service, but it was largely through his own efforts that Midleton raised himself to prominence in British politics. From 1880 to 1905 he sat in the House of Commons, for the West Surrey division until 1885 and then for the Guildford division, where he made such an impact with his criticism of Gladstone's Irish policy that he was made Financial Secretary to the War Office in Salisbury's ministry in 1886. He held this post until the ministry's resignation in 1892, and back in opposition he was active, inspiring the motion that caused Rosebery's fall in 1895. On the unionists' return to power, Midleton became successively Under-Secretary for War, then for Foreign Affairs, Secretary of State for War, 1900–3, and finally, between 1903 and 1905, he was Secretary of State for India. In 1907 he succeeded his father and entered the House of Lords where he became an active member of the

5. (1833–1908); better known between 1858 and 1891 as the Marquess of Hartington; ed. Cambridge; M.P. for N. Lancs. (1857–68), New Radnor (1869–80), N.E. Lancs. (1880–85), Rossendale division of Lancs. (1885–91), when succeeded father; liberal Under-Sec. for War, 1863–6; Sec. of State for War, 1866; Postmaster General, 1868–70; Chief Secretary for Ireland, 1870–74; Sec. of State for India, 1880–2, and for War, 1882–5; broke with Gladstone over home rule and founded with Joseph Chamberlain the liberal unionist party; declined premiership, 1886 and 1887; independently supported Salisbury's government, 1887–92; Lord President of the Council, 1895–1903. In 1883 his father owned 198,572 acres in the U.K., valued at £180,750. Of these about 60,000 acres worth over £34,000 a year were in Ireland: 32,550 in Co. Cork; 27,483 in Co. Waterford; and three in Co. Tipperary. His Irish residence was Lismore Castle, Co. Waterford. B. Holland, *Life of Spencer Crompton, 8th duke of Devonshire*, 2 vols (1911).

unionist opposition. He took a special interest in the Irish question, becoming leader of the Irish peers in 1908 and presenting the southern unionist case against home rule to the party leaders. Eventually as leader of the southern unionists, he began to work for some form of Irish self-government and was rewarded in 1920 with an earldom. Yet although he played a large role in the establishment of a second chamber for the Irish Free State, he refused to serve in it.[6]

Southern unionism was not exclusively landed, Protestant and 'British'. Some Catholics of 'substance and repute'[7] descended from old Irish families supported the union, such as The O'Conor Don of Co. Roscommon,[8] while some Protestant unionists, such as the limbless Arthur MacMurrough Kavanagh of Borris House, Co. Carlow,[9] had almost impeccable Irish pedigrees. Many Protestant businessmen were unionists: some, like the ardent Daniel Williams, a Cork city councillor and carriage builder, had purely local interests, but generally they were connected with substantial firms and enterprises, being brewers like the Guinness brothers[10] or distillers like Andrew Jameson.[11] Civil servants

6. Lord Midleton, *Records and Reactions 1856–1939* (1939) and *Ireland—Dupe or Heroine* (1932); *Dictionary of National Biography, 1941–50*, pp. 108–10; G.E.C., *Complete Peerage*, viii. 701–6; J. Bateman, *The Great Landowners of Great Britain and Ireland* (1883), p. 309. De Burgh (*Landowners of Ireland*, p. 317) puts the Cork acreage at 6,188 and the value at £6,588 a year.

7. Midleton, letter in *The Times*, 21 Oct. 1912.

8. Charles Owen (1838–1906); descended from Conor, king of Connaught who d. 971; ed. Downside; M.P. for Co. Roscommon, 1860–80; commissioner of intermediate education; P.C.; H.M.L., J.P., H.S. (1884), Co. Roscommon; J.P., H.S. (1863), Co. Sligo; Belanagare and Clonalis, Co. Roscommon.

9. (1831–1889); descended from Dermot MacMurrough, last king of Leinster who d. 1170; conservative M.P. for Co. Wexford (1866–8), Co. Carlow (1869–80); P.C.; H.M.L., J.P., H.S. (1857), Co. Carlow; D.L., J.P., H.S. (1856), Co. Kilkenny. Despite only having stumps for arms and legs, Kavanagh enjoyed a full life, sailing, hunting, etc. S. D. Steele, *The Right Honourable Arthur MacMurrough Kavanagh. A Biography* (1890).

10. Arthur Edward Guinness, 2nd bt and 1st Baron Ardilaun (1840–1915); ed. Eton and Trinity College, Dublin; head of Guinness's brewery, 1868–77; conservative M.P. for Dublin City, 1868–9; 1874–80; baron, 1880; St Anne's Clontarf, Co. Dublin, and Ashford, Cong, Co. Galway. Edward Cecil Guinness, 1st Earl of Iveagh (1847–1927); ed. Trinity College, Dublin; shared in management of the brewery, chairman, 1886; bt, 1885; baron, 1891; vt, 1905; earl, 1919; 80 St Stephen's Green, Dublin, and Farmleigh, Castleknock, Co. Dublin. Both brothers were generous philanthropists. P. Lynch and J. Vaizey, *Guinness's Brewery in the Irish Economy, 1759–1876* (Cambridge 1960).

11. (1885–1941); ed. London International College and Cambridge; chairman

found themselves in a difficult position,[12] but unionism did attract other professional men, particularly those rising rapidly to the top of their chosen professions: lawyers such as John Blake Powell, the solicitor who became a high court judge,[13] or James Henry Campbell, the second last Lord Chancellor of Ireland and first chairman of the Free State Senate;[14] and land agents such as George Francis Stewart, a long-serving vice-chairman of the southern unionist association and for a short time chairman.[15] Less support was forthcoming down the social scale, but unionism did attract Protestant tenant farmers, especially in such counties as Leitrim and Queen's, and the more substantial working men in and around Dublin who belonged to the City and County of Dublin Conservative Workingmen's Club.[16] Finally, unionism found favour among established academics at Trinity College, Dublin, a Protestant foundation. Some were only passive supporters of the unionist movement, but the active and public support of men such as Edward Dowden, Professor of English Literature,[17] was welcomed as proof that unionism flourished

---

of John Jameson and Sons Ltd; director of Bank of Ireland, governor, 1896–8; chairman of Irish Lights Commissioners; P.C.; senator of the Irish Free State and leader of the independent group; J.P., D.L.; Sutton House, Sutton, Co. Dublin.

12. W. Goaby to I.U.A., 4 Mar. 1893, P.R.O.N.I., D 989A/8/2.

13. (1870–1923); a Roman Catholic said to have been a Parnellite in his early days; K.C., 1905; senior crown prosecutor for Cos Leitrim and Sligo; Solicitor-General for Ireland, 1918; judge of High Court of Justice in Ireland, 1918; 41 Fitzwilliam Place, Dublin.

14. 1st Baron Glenavy (1851–1931); ed. Kingstown School and Trinity College, Dublin; Q.C., 1892; unionist M.P. for St Stephen's Green (1898–1900) and Dublin University (1903–16); Solicitor-General for Ireland, 1901–5; Attorney-General, 1905, 1916; Lord Chief Justice of Ireland, 1916; bt, 1917; Lord Chancellor of Ireland, 1918–21; baron, 1921; chairman of Irish Free State Senate, 1922–8; Glenavy, Milltown, Co. Dublin.

15. (1851–1928); ed. Marlborough and Trinity College, Dublin; senior partner in J. R. Stewart and Sons, with extensive agencies in Co. Leitrim; director of Bank of Ireland, governor, 1914–15; active in Irish Landowners Convention; P.C.; D.L., J.P., H.S. (1892), Co. Leitrim; Summerhill, Killiney, Co. Dublin.

16. I.L.P.U. and I.U.A., *Annual Reports*.

17. (1843–1913); ed. Trinity College, Dublin; Professor of English Literature, 1867; a leading Shakespearean authority much honoured in the U.K. and Germany; commissioner of national education in Ireland, 1896–1901; a president and vice-chairman of the I.U.A., being an enthusiastic unionist whose delightful turn of phrase endeared him to audiences at anti-home rule demonstrations; Rockdale, Orwell Road, Rathgar.

intellectually as well as materially.[18] In sum, southern unionists tended to be not only Protestant and anglicised but also aristocratic and landed, with a leavening of Roman Catholic landowners, intellectuals from Trinity College and prominent businessmen.

This mixture and the divergence within groups were to have important consequences for southern unionism, but they should not obscure essential unity on two points. In the first place, all groups shared ascendancy attitudes, revelling in a traditional pattern of life and authority based upon their own, largely landed, ascendancy. Since the plantations and confiscations, the Anglo-Irish had enjoyed a full life in Ireland based upon the ownership of landed estates. The estate was much more than a source of income, it was a social institution and gave the landlord and his entourage a commanding position in Irish life. The landlord was a king among his tenants, his relations his aristocracy, so to speak. The 'big house' was the court and all its ancestral portraits and ornaments were symbols of social continuity and cohesion, forcing on the occupants a recognition of a traditional and distinctive way of life.[19] Perhaps one of the best representatives of this paternalist tradition was A. M. Kavanagh. Succeeding to the family estates in 1852, he continued the Kavanagh custom of holding an unofficial court from the stone mounting block which surrounded an old oak in the courtyard of Borris House:

There, like a chieftain in the midst of his vassals, he would sit patiently listening to all who came from far and near, with their tales of perplexity or grievance, to seek counsel or redress. All were received, men and women alike, with the same unfailing sympathy, and many a curious piece of family history or story of impending feud could that old tree reveal![20]

This commanding position in a localised and paternalistic society inculcated in the Anglo-Irish certain attitudes which were slow to die. The Anglo-Irish equated Ireland's best interests with their own, and they saw their own political ascendancy as essential to

18. *Dublin Daily Express*, 9 Jan. 1886.
19. G. Cummins, *Dr E. Œ. Somerville. A Biography* (1952), pp. 39, 66, 67; E. Hamilton, *An Irish Childhood* (1963), pp. 19, 45, 49–50, 69, 74–5; and E. Bowen, *Bowen's Court* (1942, 1964), *passim*.
20. Steele, *Arthur MacMurrough Kavanagh*, pp. 134–5.

Irish well-being. Movements or institutions which did not seek
or win their support were regarded as unrepresentative, irresponsible and inimical to Ireland's best interests. Their high view of
their historical significance was magnificently expressed by
William Butler Yeats in 1925:

We are no petty people. We are one of the great stocks of Europe.
We are the people of Grattan; we are the people of Swift, the people
of Emmet, the people of Parnell. We have created the most of the
modern literature of this country. We have created the best of its
political intelligence.[21]

One of the most interesting features of the Anglo-Irish is the
way in which they maintained ascendancy attitudes well into the
twentieth century, when, objectively speaking, Irish society had
ceased to be localised and paternalistic. Despite the changes
helped along by the home rule movement, the introduction into
Ireland of democratic local government, and land legislation, the
Anglo-Irish continued to believe in their own importance and
indispensability. As J. M. Wilson put it during the first world war:

No greater disaster could, in my opinion, overtake a country such
as Ireland than the total elimination of its resident gentry—a process
which, alas, is already far advanced.
As one travels through the country one is astonished to see so many
derelict houses, and neglected demesnes, the houses formerly in many
cases of an independent and virile section of the body politic, not free
from faults indeed—as what section is?—but, taken as a whole, forming
I venture to assert oases of culture, of uprightness and of fair dealing,
in what will otherwise be a desert of dead uniformity where the poor
will have no one to appeal to except the priest or the local shopkeeper
(rapidly becoming a local magnate)—whence the rich will fly, and
where lofty ideals, whether of social or imperial interest, will be
smothered in an atmosphere of superstition, greed, and chicanery. As
in local, so in national administration there can be no more hope
for a country from which the cultured element has been divorced, and
the helpful friend of the poor and the protector of the weak driven to
seek new surroundings and new occupations. It is surely the duty,
wherever possible, of the so-called English garrison in Ireland to retain

21. Quoted in F. S. L. Lyons, 'The minority problem in the 26 counties',
in *The Years of the Great Test 1926-39*, ed. F. MacManus (Cork 1967), p. 94.

its hold, to leaven society with its hopes and aspirations that their common country may never become the plaything of a base political clique, whose ambition would be—in spite of all their protests—to see an Ireland in the grip of a Tamany [*sic*] Hall administration, where mendacity would flourish, corruption would be rampant and industry would decay. I believe in my heart that even in these days of dreadful crisis with the enemy at our gates if a perfectly secret plebiscite could be taken, a large majority would be [easily?] in favour of retaining those members of the landlord class in Ireland, a class whose blood is so freely shed for the empire, who for years have done their best to discharge their onerous and often thankless duties by their humble neighbours all over Ireland.[22]

No respectable Anglo-Irishmen or women, not even the younger ones, would have disagreed with this high view of their role in Ireland.[23]

22. P.R.O.N.I., D 989A/11/9.
23. There is a charming illustration of the persisting belief in the landlords' social role, despite land purchase, in one of the R.M. stories of Somerville and Ross. A purchasing tenant, Stephen Casey, about to be distrained for debt by the local shopkeeper, sought Mrs Knox's protection, because, as he said, he knew she would never be satisfied to see one of her own tenants wronged. Mrs Knox replied tartly, 'I have no tenants . . . the government is your landlord now, and I wish you joy of each other!' 'Then I wish to God it was yourself we had in it again!' lamented Casey; 'it was better for us when the gentry was managing their own business. They'd *give* patience, and they'd *have* patience.' 'Well, that will do now', said Mrs Knox; 'go round to the servants' hall and have your tea. I'll see what I can do.' There was a silence when Casey withdrew and then Mrs Knox, flinging a sod of turf on the huge fire with practised aim, said to Major Yeates, 'When those rascals in parliament took our land from us . . . we thought we should have some peace; now we're both beggared and bothered!' Needless to say, she dealt with the exacting shopkeeper (*In Mr Knox's Country* (1915), pp. 28–51).
Despite their exposure to the Gaelic revival or to socialist ideas, younger members of the Anglo-Irish ascendancy, like Bryan Cooper and Sir Christopher Lynch-Robinson, could not avoid accepting the traditional view of life. On Cooper, see below, pp. 47–8, 299–300. Lynch-Robinson (1884–1958), ed. at Wellington and R.M.C., Sandhurst, serving in the Royal Fusiliers (1903–12), and exposed to socialist ideas when private secretary to the Governor of Jamaica (1910–12), was an Irish R.M. from 1912 to 1922, when he retreated to England and took a managerial post with Crosse and Blackwell; see his *The Last of the Irish R.M.s* (1951). Some, like Francis Macnamara and Constance Gore-Booth, the Countess Markievicz, did reject the conventions of Anglo-Irish life, but the very vehemence of their rejection is significant of the pressures to conform even in the late nineteenth and early twentieth centuries. See N. Devas, *Two Flamboyant Fathers* (1966, Readers Union ed. 1967) and A. Marrecco, *The Rebel Countess. The Life and Time of Constance Markievicz* (1967).

Nor, at least until 1922, would they have disagreed about the desirability of the British connection, the second point upon which the Anglo-Irish were united. Many loved Ireland and the Irish and regarded themselves as Irish. They even accepted the violence of agrarian outrage as adding to the quality of life there:

From youth to manhood [wrote one land agent], and from manhood to the verge of age, it has been my lot to live surrounded by a kind of poetic turbulence and almost romantic violence, which I believe could scarcely belong to real life in any other country in the world.[24]

Nevertheless, as a result of their origins, their contributions to the imperial exchequer, and their service in the British empire, the Anglo-Irish did share a predisposition to favour the British connection, to put Ireland in a larger imperial context.[25]

THREE

As a distinctive society, it is not surprising that the Anglo-Irish in the south took up a distinctive attitude towards the Irish nationalist movement. Most obviously, the differences between them and the Ulstermen overrode what may be called a common Protestant ethic and determined that Ulster and southern unionism should exist as separate and often competing movements. Although on occasion they co-operated for propaganda purposes, they maintained separate organisations. Ulster unionist energies were eventually mobilised through the Ulster Unionist Council.[26] The southern unionists were organised into the Irish Loyal and

24. R. Steuart Trench, *Realities of Irish Life* (5th ed. 1870), pp. v–vi.

25. Dismissing the electoral argument about the expense of land purchase, Lord Castletown held that 'as long as any landlord pays taxes which reach the imperial exchequer he is entitled to the credit which his contribution to the general fund of the empire confers upon him. I contribute about £3,000 a year to the imperial funds and my ancestors for generations before me also contributed in like manner. Why am I to be deprived of the share in the imperial credit which the money of my family has helped to build up? I do not desire to worry you on this point but I mention our right to imperial credit is patent though our power of obtaining it may be nil' (to Joseph Chamberlain, 3 June 1887, B.U.L., JC 8/6/3A/7).

26. For the history of Ulster unionism, see P. J. Buckland, *Irish Unionism 1885–1923: Select Documents* (Belfast 1972); D. C. Savage, 'The Origins of the Ulster Unionist party, 1885–6', *Irish Historical Studies,* xii (1961), pp. 185–208; A. T. Q. Stewart, *The Ulster Crisis* (1967).

Patriotic Union (founded in 1885 and known after 1891 as the Irish Unionist Alliance) and the Unionist Anti-Partition League (formed in 1919 by a breakaway group of the I.U.A.).

To many contemporaries, southern unionism seemed an inadequate and inconsistent response to the challenge of the new Ireland. Southern unionists were derided by nationalists,[27] scorned as timid and unreliable by Ulster unionists,[28] and dismissed almost out of hand by British politicians such as Winston Churchill, in whose lengthy review of the Irish situation and treaty negotiations in 1921 southern unionists are noticed only by a somewhat slighting allusion to their inability to support the British government by force.[29] To cap it all, such derogatory opinions have been endorsed in the writings of their former leader, Midleton. He wrote that southern unionists lacked leaders and with rare exceptions political insight and cohesion:

Contented to air their feelings at intervals, they restricted themselves to the easy task of attending meetings in Dublin, and voting strong resolutions, which they expected the British government to respect.... I remember a special meeting at Londonderry House, at a crisis, when after vigorous attacks on the government, of which I happened to be a junior member, the meeting adjourned to a sumptuous luncheon, without defining any policy they might accept.[30]

There is some substance to these criticisms. Southern unionists did set themselves politically against the mass of the Irish nation; they never resorted to force; they did at times lack cohesion and appear to content themselves with voting strong resolutions. Moreover, they did not achieve all their aims. They could not prevent the repeal of the union; nor as a second best could they persuade nationalists to adopt an aristocratic constitution for the new southern Irish state and to accept close imperial ties. They did secure for the Free State legislature a second chamber, but

27. See below, p. 9.
28. See below, pp. 17, 103, 175, 178, 196-7.
29. W. S. Churchill, *The World Crisis. The Aftermath* (1929), p. 301: 'The 300,000 loyalists in southern Ireland, perfectly helpless in the fighting, raised a lamentable cry in the parley.'
30. Midleton, *Records and Reactions*, pp. 226-7 and his comments in *A Page from the Past. Memories of the Earl of Desart*, by the Earl of Desart and Lady Sybil Lubbock (1936), pp. 241-2.

even this, a shadow of the Senate they desired, was abolished in 1936 and replaced in the following year by an even shadowier one. Whereas Irish nationalists and Ulster unionists still have the Republic of Ireland and the state of Northern Ireland as testimonies to the albeit limited success of their movements, the southern unionists have none.

Nevertheless, these criticisms and contrasts should not be carried too far, for they obscure the importance and essential consistency of southern unionism. Judged from a southern Anglo-Irish viewpoint, it was valid and consistent. The Anglo-Irish in the south could not afford to be as single minded and as adamant as their Ulster counterparts. A scattered minority, they relied for the maintenance of their position either upon the good will of their fellow countrymen or upon the protection of the British government. Their response to nationalism thus depended upon how threatening or promising they regarded Irish national-ism, and how useful or otherwise the British connection seemed. Southern unionism was almost a frame of mind, a delicate and finely-balanced movement registering southern Anglo-Ireland's reaction to the new Ireland through eight phases.

The initial phase of confident opposition was prolonged. From 1885 until the outbreak of the first world war in August 1914, suspicions about the nature of Irish nationalism and a confidence in the British connection made the Anglo-Irish staunch upholders of the union. They contributed to the rejection of the first two home rule bills in 1886 and 1893 by the House of Commons and House of Lords respectively, and they played a significant role in holding up the third home rule bill between 1912 and 1914 and in preventing a compromise on the basis of partition, the exclusion of Ulster from the operation of the bill. Thereafter, in face of changes in British and Irish politics, and with the decline in the number of Anglo-Irish families in the south, southern unionists tried to come to terms with the new Ireland. This *rapprochement*, growing out of co-operation between unionists and nationalists in the war, was a gradual one and not without periods of reaction and doubt, after the Easter Rising in 1916 and the conscription crisis in April 1918. It was nonetheless a sure process, as southern unionists became less suspicious of Irish nationalism, realising that they would not necessarily be an oppressed minority under an Irish government, and as they became increasingly suspicious of the utility of the union and the willingness of the British people and government to maintain it. They began to consider the virtues of having an Irish parliament, and then to work positively for some form of Irish self-government which would reconcile nationalist aspirations with minority and imperial interests. The new viewpoint emerged publicly at the Irish convention of 1917-18, when the southern unionist representatives produced a characteristic solution to the problem of Irish self-government, emphasising the British connection and the importance of a united Ireland with generous safeguards for minorities. This new departure was fiercely criticised and split southern unionism, but with the onset of the Anglo-Irish war, more and more southern unionists were willing to accept a settlement which conceded wider powers to an Irish parliament and contained fewer safeguards. They accepted the partition of Ireland by the Government of Ireland Act of 1920 which established the state of Northern Ireland; and their leaders helped to shape an even wider settlement for the south of Ireland, playing a part in the negotiations that preceded the Anglo-Irish treaty of 6 December 1921, and in the discussions about the Free State constitution in the following year. By the end of 1922 the southern unionist movement had petered out, as the Anglo-Irish who remained in southern Ireland abandoned separate political activity and accepted the Free State as the form of government desired by the majority of their countrymen.

In short, southern unionists showed energy and initiative in organising themselves over a long period and made southern unionism a significant factor in British and Irish politics. Indeed, it can be argued that an appreciation of southern unionism provides a missing link in the history of the Irish question, helping to explain why British governments were slow in coming to terms with the new Ireland. The present partition of Ireland seems a sensible solution to the problem of reconciling the claims of Irish nationalism with the apprehensions of Ulster unionism; and this reflection prompts the question why did such a settlement have to wait until 1920-21. The answer is provided by the southern unionists who obscured the issue for contemporaries and who influenced both the timing and to a lesser extent the content of a settlement of the Irish question. Their opposition to home rule, particularly in the years 1912-14 and in 1916, helped to delay a

settlement, while their later willingness to work for the establishment of an Irish parliament eventually facilitated a settlement.
Having helped to thwart Irish nationalists for so long, southern
unionists finally helped them to realise at least some of their
ideals after the first world war.

I

Phase One: Confident Opposition, 1885-1914

THE southern unionist movement emerged in 1885 to express Anglo-Ireland's opposition to the political aspirations of the new Ireland. Divided politically into liberals and conservatives, the Anglo-Irish had previously shown little energy in combatting the developing home rule movement and had taken for granted the legislative union between Great Britain and Ireland. In 1885, however, they began to take a more considered stand on both. Deciding that there could be no half-way house between the government of Ireland by the imperial parliament and the complete separation of the two countries, they plumped firmly for the former. On 1 May a group of landowners and academics tried to sink old party differences and combat home rule by founding a new organisation, the Irish Loyal and Patriotic Union. 'Entirely unsectarian in its character, and . . . composed of members of both great political parties in the state', the new association had but one single plank, maintenance of the union.[1]

1. Manifesto, *Irish Times*, 16 Oct. 1885. The leading organisers appear to have been: William Lygon Pakenham, 4th Earl of Longford, of Pakenham Hall, Co. Westmeath (1819–87), conservative, a general, served in Crimean war and Indian mutiny, Under-Sec. for War 1866–8; Sir Thomas Butler, 10th bt, of Ballinatemple, Co. Carlow (1836–1909), a conservative, ed. Cheltenham College, served in the Crimean war, and active member of the Irish Landowners Convention; Richard Bagwell of Marlfield, Clonmel, Co. Tipperary (1840–1918), the historian, a liberal, ed. Harrow and Oxford, special local government commissioner (1898–1903) and commissioner for national education (1905–18); Henry Bruen of Oak Park, Co. Carlow (1828–1912), conservative M.P. for Carlow (1857–80); A. M. Kavanagh; Dr John Hewitt Jellett (1817–88), liberal and Provost of Trinity College, Dublin (1881–8); and Professor John Pentland Mahaffy (1839–1919), first Professor of Ancient History (1869) and later Provost of Trinity College (1914–19). Bernard Edward Barnaby Fitzpatrick, 2nd Baron Castletown, of Grantstown manor, Queen's Co. (1848–1937), ed. Eton and Oxford and liberal-conservative M.P. for Portarlington (1880–83), and John Robert William Vesey, 4th Vt de Vesci, of Abbey Leix, Queen's Co. (1844–1903), formerly a lt-col. in the Coldstream Guards, were particularly active. Most had worked on behalf of landlordism in the Land League crisis and were members of the Representative Body of the Church of Ireland.

This re-alignment of parties was prompted by the prospect of a general election, the first following the third and what southern unionists regarded as almost the final Reform Act. The extension of the franchise in 1884 and the redistribution of seats in 1885 led some opponents of home rule to hope that Parnellism might be checked if all loyalists sunk their differences and co-operated in contesting the election. Others were less optimistic of electoral success. They were not a little piqued that the Westminster parliament had permitted the extension of the Irish franchise which they thought tantamount to handing Ireland over to the nationalists. They wanted loyalists to organise to show that loyalism was not dead in Ireland and that the traditional ruling class was still a significant force in Irish life and politics.[2] The immediate object of the I.L.P.U. was, therefore, to fight the general election of 1885 in the three southern provinces of Ireland. From May onwards enrolment was carried on quietly, and it was not until 16 October, about a month before the start of the elections, that the I.L.P.U. revealed itself to the public in a manifesto urging the loyal sections of the population of both the liberal and conservative parties to co-operate in forthcoming elections, and offering to help finance such contests.[3] Meeting a widely felt need for loyalist combination,[4] such manifestos stimulated unionist organisation throughout the south of Ireland, as preparations were made to contest the elections.

These preparations could have been speedier and more thorough,[5] but at least the nationalists, who had had an easy passage in 1880, found themselves opposed in fifty-two constituencies in the south. In contrast to the average home rule candidate, the unionist candidates tended to be drawn from the Anglo-Irish ascendancy—Protestants, landowners, or sons of

---

2. For this mixture of pique and optimism leading to the formation of the I.L.P.U., see J. W. Good, *Irish Unionism* (1920), pp. 177-8; E. W. O'Brien to W. E. H. Lecky, 30 Oct. 1885, T.C.D., Lecky correspondence, no. 37; and the report of the first a.g.m., *Irish Times,* 9 Jan. 1886.

3. Manifestos and notices appeared in the press on 16, 23, 24, 26 Oct. 1885.

4. See the correspondence columns of the *Irish Times* for Sept. and Oct. 1885 and the formation of local defence unions.

5. See e.g. the complaints in the *Irish Times,* 5 Dec. 1885, which found some justification in the tardiness of the conservative candidate for N. Sligo who issued his election address towards the end of November and regretted that 'owing to the short time between this and the election, it is impossible for me to visit you and solicit your votes' (*ibid.,* 23 Nov. 1885).

landowners; and all but eight were conservatives. Nevertheless, they did not fight on a narrow party platform: all agreed upon the need to lay aside traditional party designations and to maintain the union.[6] True to its word, the I.L.P.U. played a significant role in the elections. A 'goodly sum' had been subscribed, enabling the new association to give financial aid in forty-eight of the contests, and to supplement local efforts with vigorous propaganda in the shape of some 14,000 pamphlets and roughly 270,000 anti-home rule leaflets.[7]

These efforts did not result in the return of any unionist candidate. Anti-home rule candidates received on average only ten per cent of the poll, the number of votes cast for them ranging from thirty in East Co. Kerry to 3,736 in South Co. Dublin, and the only conservatives returned for the three southern provinces were the unopposed and sitting members from Dublin University. Nevertheless, this loyalist protest had not been entirely wasted. Liberals and conservatives had shown themselves capable of co-operating in a common cause; the activities of the I.L.P.U. had received favourable attention in Great Britain;[8] and some comfort could even be found in the fact that, taking Ireland as a whole, the number of votes cast in favour of home rule barely exceeded one-half of the electorate, one quarter having voted against, the remaining quarter having abstained.[9] The experience thus encouraged further action and inaugurated a period of thirty-eight years of consistent Anglo-Irish political activity, the first twenty-seven of which were devoted to outright opposition to home rule.

6. For the election manifestos, see *ibid.* for Oct. and Nov. 1885.
7. I.L.P.U., *Prospectus* (1886); report of the executive committee, *Irish Times*, 9 Jan. 1886.
8. *The Times*, 16 Oct. 1885; *The Globe*, 26 Oct. 1885; George Joachim Goschen, reported in *The Times*, 6 Nov. 1885. Goschen, 1st Vt (1831–1907), ed. Ripon and Oxford, and M.P. for city of London (1863–80), Ripon (1880–85), East Edinburgh (1885), St George's, Hanover Square (1887–1900), was a leading liberal until 1885–6, having held ministerial posts in liberal governments between 1865 and 1874, and having refused the Speakership in 1883. A strenuous opponent of home rule, he helped to found the liberal unionist party and became Chancellor of Exchequer (1886–92) and First Lord of the Admiralty (1895–1900) under Salisbury, being created vt in 1900.
9. *Irish Times*, 19 Dec. 1885, commenting on the I.L.P.U.'s analysis of the polling figures.

TWO

This re-alignment of parties had been occasioned by the extension of the franchise in 1884 and the general election of 1885; but what underlay it was Anglo-Ireland's assessment of its own substantial interests in the light of the British and Irish political situations. What caused them to sink old party differences in a new unionist movement in 1885 was not only a deep-seated fear and suspicion of the home rule movement; but also the hope that the union could and would provide continued protection. The new Ireland seemed menacing; the old system safe and reliable.

The Anglo-Irish opposed the home rule movement because they thought that the re-establishment of a parliament in Dublin would destroy abruptly the traditional pattern of life. Obviously with the social and economic changes taking place in Ireland after the Famine, some adjustment of social and political power was necessary. This re-adjustment could have taken place gradually, but, as far as Anglo-Irish ascendancy was concerned, the Land League crisis quickened the tempo of change disastrously. Until then it had been possible for many of the Anglo-Irish to support or be indifferent to the home rule movement, the political manifestation of this process of adjustment. Admittedly, the tendency of the Home Government Association in the early 1870s to take up the tenant right question had alienated some landed proprietors; and the identification of the newly formed Home Rule League in 1873 with the Roman Catholic hierarchy, and its subsequent development on denominational lines, had alienated even more of the Protestant ascendancy from the new movement.[10] Nevertheless, the movement under Butt was never sufficiently threatening to cut across old party lines and to unite the ascendancy into one political organisation. The Land League crisis of 1879–81 and the 'new departure' under Parnell, however, threatened to overthrow the old ascendancy abruptly.[11] Although the Land League was suppressed in the autumn of 1881, the Anglo-Irish, failing to discern the rightward shift in Parnell's

10. D. Thornley, *Isaac Butt and Home Rule* (1964), *passim*, and 'The Irish conservatives and home rule, 1869–73', *Irish Historical Studies*, xi (1959), pp. 200–22.

11. N. D. Palmer, *The Irish Land League Crisis* (New Haven 1940); C. C. O'Brien, *Parnell and his Party* (Oxford 1957, revised impression 1964).

policy,[12] regarded the National League formed in 1882 as a resurrected Land League in disguise.

It is almost impossible to exaggerate the impact of the Land League crisis upon the ascendancy. Such concentrated class antagonism Ireland had scarcely ever known. Agrarian outrage had been lived with, but what was new with the advent of the Land League was that not only 'bad' landlords but all landlords were the object of hatred. The League, under the socialistic influence of the former Fenian, Michael Davitt, aimed at the extirpation of landlords and landlordish influence, and in the general election of 1880 few landlords, even those with a long record of parliamentary service behind them, were returned in face of the opposition of the League.[13] Irish parliamentary representation ceased to be the preserve of the propertied classes, and became instead the province of the Irish democracy. For example, of the 86 home rule M.P.s returned in the general election of 1885, over half, 44, can be described as 'lower class'— members of the lower professions, shopkeepers, farmers, wage earners: of the remainder, the 'upper class', 15 were merchants, industrialists, bankers or rentiers; 22 belonged to the higher professions; and only 6 owned over 1,000 acres of land.[14] The class composition of the 1885 Irish Parliamentary Party thus contrasted markedly, in nineteenth-century eyes, with that of their unsuccessful opponents in the south of Ireland. Of the 52 southern unionist candidates (there were 54 separate candidatures, but two candidates each contested two seats), 51 were 'upper class', including 23 landowners; the odd man out being a tenant farmer. These results reflected the association of the home rule movement with the levelling attitudes of the Land League. This association made the home rule issue a vital internal problem for

12. Arthur Hugh Smith-Barry, *Irish Times,* 30 Jan. 1886. 1st Baron Barrymore (1843–1925); ed. Eton and Oxford; conservative M.P. for Co. Cork (1867–74), S. Huntingdonshire (1886–1900); active opponent of the plan of campaign, vice-president of Irish Landowners Convention; baron, 1902; P.C., J.P., D.L.; Fota Island, Co. Cork.

13. J. H. Whyte, 'Landlord influence at elections in Ireland, 1762–1885', *English Historical Review,* lxxx (1965), pp. 740–60. For instance, after fourteen years in parliament, Kavanagh was overwhelmingly defeated in the Co. Carlow election and burned in effigy. What rankled with him was the fact that 'the majority of my own men broke their promise to me. . . That is the poisoned stab.' (Steele, *Arthur MacMurrough Kavanagh,* pp. 202–3).

14. O'Brien, *Parnell and his Party,* p. 152.

Ireland, and not just a simple conflict between the mother country and a dependency. It turned the issue of home rule or union into a conflict between two opposed concepts of government and society in Ireland and allowed people to interpret the home rule movement as a conspiracy against the landlord and ascendancy class.

As the debate developed, many detailed objections to home rule and to particular home rule schemes were advanced. Moreover, each unionist might have his own particular nightmare about home rule, but there were two broad objections to it. Firstly, the restored Irish parliament would be dominated not by men of property, either Protestant or Roman Catholic, but by 'lower class' Roman Catholics, or, as southern unionists liked to put it, agitators and others misguided by their clergy and spurred on by the Anglophobe Irish-Americans who subscribed freely to nationalist funds.[15] Secondly, such a parliament would be the first step towards severing the valued British connection[16] and would very likely penalise the old ascendancy and undermine Irish prosperity and social harmony. Substantial businessmen thought that an Irish parliament deprived of their services and the resources of the British exchequer would be incapable of handling Ireland's economic, commercial and financial affairs.[17] Educationalists at Trinity College feared that control of education including higher education would pass to the Roman Catholic clergy with the result that Ireland would become as 'intellectual as Ashantee'.[18] Above all, landowners felt that the Land League crisis had given them every reason to fear that an Irish parliament would confiscate and redistribute, either directly or by discriminatory taxation, landed property in favour of the tenantry.[19] Furthermore, they were all concerned about the position of the Roman Catholic church which they credited with an all-pervasive influence in Ireland; if they did not initiate movements, the

15. See e.g. the I.L.P.U. pamphlets, *Union or Separation* (1886) and *A Guide to the 'Eighty-six'* (1886).

16. *Ibid.*

17. See e.g. the criticism of the financial proposals of the third home rule bill, organised by the I.U.A. and bearing '151 signatures of leading men engaged in trade and commerce south of Ulster', published in *The Times,* 27 Nov. 1913.

18. T. Maguire (Professor of Moral Philosophy), *The Effects of Home Rule on Higher Education* (1886).

19. See e.g. Smith-Barry, *Irish Times,* 30 Jan. 1886.

hierarchy and priesthood did guide them, moulding people's wishes and making them vote as they, the clergy, desired. According to Mayo:

They watched the current and dug dykes and directed it, and with it irrigated the political soil of Ireland, if it suited their purpose to do so. The peasantry grew up and flourished under that irrigation, and were influenced in every possible way by the priesthood.[20]

Few southern Protestants were so bigoted as to fear actual persecution in a self-governing Ireland or to believe literally that home rule meant Rome rule; but most unionists in the south did fear discrimination on religious grounds in administrative and political matters and that Protestantism would be a disqualification from public life.[21] In fact, the whole concept of home rule was alien to the Anglo-Irish in the 1880s. The traditional fabric of Irish society would be dissolved if an Irish parliament were re-established: power would be transferred to a misguided, 'communistic', and priest-ridden democracy.

The case of the historian William Edward Hartpole Lecky provides a convenient example of the relationship between opposition to home rule and unionism on the one hand, and the Land League crisis on the other.[22] In his early days Lecky was a severe critic of the union and advocated the restoration of the Irish parliament. Fenianism had caused him a shadow of doubt as to the capacity of his countrymen to govern themselves, but the Land League crisis caused him to oppose the re-establishment of an Irish parliament and to become one of the most articulate champions of the unionist cause. Parnell, Davitt, and company had demonstrated how radically and profoundly unfit Ireland was for self-government. As Lecky's own historian has com-

20. *Parl. Deb.*, 4 ser., xvii, 6 Sept. 1893, col. 268.
21. Walter Edward Guinness, *Parl. Deb. (Commons)*, 5 ser., xxxix, 13 June 1912, col. 1129. 1st Baron Moyne (1880–1944), son of 1st Baron Iveagh; ed. Eton; served in South African and 1914–18 wars; conservative M.P. for Bury St Edmunds, 1907–31; Under-Sec. for War, 1922–3; Financial Sec. to Treasury, 1923–4, 1924–5; P.C., 1924; Minister of Agriculture, 1925–9; baron, 1932; Colonial Sec., 1941–2; Minister of State, Cairo, Jan. 1944, assassinated Nov.; Knockmaroon, Castleknock, Co. Dublin.
22. D. McCartney, 'Lecky's *Leaders of Public Opinion in Ireland'*, *Irish Historical Studies*, xiv (1964–5), pp. 119–41. Lecky (1838–1903) was unionist M.P. for Dublin University, 1896–1903.

mented, 'People who find in Lecky's *England in the Eighteenth Century* a scrupulous impartiality, the judicial statement for and against, a philosophic calm, would never recognise their Lecky in his private letters of the late seventies or early eighties.'[23] He had become horrified at the 'criminal turbulence' evoked by the land agitation, the 'new communism' as he often called it.[24] Reminding one of his home ruler correspondents of the fate of the Girondins, he wrote, 'I hope we may both keep our heads and something at least of our Irish properties!'[25] He found the very rudiments of political morality absent from Ireland and never expected Ireland to be really quiet again: rather he expected at any moment a 'regular outbreak'.[26] Lecky would have been willing to entrust the government of Ireland to its Catholic or Protestant gentry; but he did not believe that the government could be safely entrusted to the National League—'to priests, and Fenians, and professional agitators, supported by the votes of an ignorant peasantry' and 'subsidised from America by avowed enemies of the British empire'.[27] To Lecky, it was absurd to argue that, because a parliament of Irish Protestant landlords was abolished in 1800, a parliament of Land Leaguers should be established in 1886. Lecky, along with others of the Anglo-Irish ascendancy, took his stand against democratic home rule and had 'little doubt that Henry Grattan himself would have been on my side'.[28]

Southern unionist suspicions of the malevolent exclusiveness of Irish nationalism were slow to die. They survived the split in the nationalist movement, the death of Parnell in 1891, and the eventual re-uniting of the movement in 1900 as the United Irish League under the moderate and mild John Redmond. They even outlasted the co-operation between unionists and nationalists in the Recess committee of 1896, in the agitation over the financial relations report of the same year, and in the land conference of

23. *Ibid.*, p. 128.
24. O'Neill Daunt's journal, 30 Sept. 1881, N.L.I., MS 3042, f. 1170; Lecky to Daunt, 14, 22 Dec. 1879, T.C.D., Lecky correspondence, nos. 179, 183.
25. Lecky to Daunt, 16 Jan. 1886, quoted in E. Lecky, *A Memoir of W. E. H. Lecky* (1909), pp. 185–6.
26. Lecky to Daunt, 14 Dec. 1879, 11 Dec. 1880, T.C.D., Lecky correspondence, nos. 179, 214.
27. Lecky, letter in *The Times*, 5 May 1886.
28. *Ibid.*, 9 June 1886.

1902-3.[29] The success of the land conference in providing the basis for Wyndham's Land Purchase Act of 1903 did encourage the landlord representatives to seek further accommodation with Irish nationalists. Through the newly formed Irish Reform Association, Lord Dunraven and his associates suggested in September 1904 a compromise between union and home rule, a scheme of devolution by which a central Irish council of representative Irishmen would exercise, within the framework of the union, a measure of local authority. Causing a furore when it was launched,[30] the idea was taken up by the liberal government in its abortive Irish councils bill in 1907, nationalists rejecting this half-way house as inadequate, and southern unionists finding it no consolation to be told that their 'mangled limbs' would find a half-way ledge to rest on momentarily before plunging to their final descent.[31] That southern unionists should have remained so suspicious of nationalism is, at least, understandable. On the one hand, nationalists, dismissing the Irish gentry as 'destitute of the slightest sense of national honour or national dignity'[32] and likening their efforts to halt Parnellism to those of a 'bull on the prairies charging a railway train',[33] in general made no attempt to win over the southern unionists or to assuage their fears.[34] On the other hand, unionist memories of the early 1880s were frequently fed by later developments. Recurrent agrarian agitation closely associated with nationalist M.P.s, in 1886-91, 1899-1903 and 1906-7, reinforced doubts as to the security of life and property in Ireland once the controlling hand of the union was removed.[35] Moreover, the Roman Catholic

29. F. S. L. Lyons, *The Irish Parliamentary Party, 1890-1910* (1951); H. Plunkett, *Ireland in the New Century* (1904); Earl of Dunraven, *Past Times and Pastimes*, 2 vols (1922).

30. F. S. L. Lyons, 'The Irish Unionist Party and the devolution crisis of 1904-5', *Irish Historical Studies*, vi (1948), pp. 1-22.

31. Dowden, *Dublin Daily Express*, 3 Jan. 1906.

32. O'Neill Daunt's journal, 6 Apr. 1885, N.L.I., MS 3042, f. 1262.

33. Quoted by 'A Cork loyalist', letter in *Irish Times*, 2 Oct. 1885.

34. See e.g. the inconclusive exchange over possible minority safeguards in the third home rule bill between Lord MacDonnell, Walter Kavanagh (A. M. Kavanagh's son and home rule M.P. for Co. Carlow, 1908-10) and Redmond, Sept. 1912, N.L.I., MS 15199 (3).

35. In 1907, one southern unionist, Frederick William Pennefather (of Rathsallagh, Colbinstown, Co. Wicklow, formerly judge of the Supreme Court of New Zealand), wrote that the Irish situation was far worse than people realised: cattle driving had spread as far as Co. Carlow and 'though my immediate

hierarchy's blatant intervention in Irish politics following Parnell's involvement in the O'Shea divorce case,[36] and the introduction into Ireland of democratic local government in 1898, confirmed apprehensions that Protestants and unionists would be excluded from public life under home rule. Only a handful of unionists and Protestants were elected to the new county councils which unionists came to regard as 'mere hand-maidens of the National League . . . an example of what we might expect from a parliament in College Green'.[37]

In sum, southern unionists refused to regard the demand for home rule as a manifestation of a deep national consciousness. They flatly refused to accept that the consistent return of over eighty home rule M.P.s reflected any widespread real demand for home rule. Such M.P.s southern unionists dismissed as representative only of the opinion of the Roman Catholic hierarchy, Fenians, Clan-na-Gael and the tyrannous Land League, elected on the orders of a clique by less than half the electorate through 'power of combination, or through clerical influence'.[38] They thus explained away the nationalist movement in terms of an extended agrarian conspiracy theory: self-seeking or misguided individuals, financed by the Irish in America and playing on the greed of an ignorant and semi-literate Irish peasantry. As Lord Donoughmore put it on one occasion, the home rule movement was becoming 'less and less Irish, and more and more American'.[39] Home rule would give the part of Ireland which was worst mastery over the best.

This interpretation of the home rule movement almost forced the Anglo-Irish to take a more positive attitude towards the union. Their fear of the consequences of the home rule movement

---

neighbourhood is still perfectly quiet, I never know when I may be attacked . . . to "protect our own property", as Birrell sneeringly tells us to do, is out of the question; I have 250 head of cattle, besides sheep, scattered over a large farm, how can I keep a private army ready to ward off the attacks of 100 men who may come at any time of the day or night?' (Pennefather to Lord Tennyson, 12 July 1907, N.L.I., MS 3249).

36. For some southern unionist reactions, see I.U.A., *The Irish Priest in Politics . . . the Meath Election Petitions* (1893).

37. Carson, *Dublin Daily Express*, 8 Dec. 1906.

38. Castletown, *Parl. Deb.*, 4 ser., xvii, 6 Sept. 1893, col. 257.

39. *Dublin Daily Express*, 23 Apr. 1910.

turned them into active unionists, defining and championing the
value of the union to Ireland and to themselves. Faced with a
democratic and social revolution, the ascendancy looked to the
maintenance of the union to protect them and to regulate social
and political tension in Ireland. In a sense they had no alternative.
A scattered and isolated minority among a potentially hostile
tenantry, they could not take steps on their own behalf to resist
any large movements on the part of the tenantry. They could
only maintain their special position in Ireland with the aid of the
British connection; and they did not find this fact humiliating or
unusual. Their origins, ties through kinship and marriage, their
traditional attachment to the British connection, led the Anglo-
Irish to expect help from Great Britain. They felt they deserved
help from Great Britain and did not expect the English people
to allow any minister or government

. . . to barter away, for the venal votes of the representatives of Irish
disaffection, the property, liberties, the lives of the loyalists of Ireland
—men whose only offence is that they have been friends of England
through evil report and good report, and that they have steadfastly
endeavoured to maintain the unity of the British empire.[40]

Gladstone's conversion to home rule in 1886 shocked them, but
they took comfort from the liberal unionist secession and the
imperialism of the conservative party,[41] and vented their spleen
by writing learned pamphlets condemning Gladstone[42] and by
hanging cartoons of him in their lavatories.[43] In retrospect, this
reliance upon British goodwill seems naïve and pathetic; but it
was not without justification. Of the various groups in Ireland,
they were the most attractive and acceptable to large sections of
English opinion. Suspicious of the 'Celtic Irish' and uneasy with
the extremism and intolerance of Ulstermen, many Englishmen
and women were attracted by the southern Anglo-Irish who
'though they have acquired much of the surface gaiety of the
Celts, have not lost the sense of logic and proportion which they

40. I.L.P.U., *Union or Separation*, p. 29.
41. L. P. Curtis, jun., *Coercion and Conciliation in Ireland, 1880-1892. A Study
in Conservative Unionism* (Princeton 1963).
42. See e.g. below, pp. 25-6.
43. Lynch-Robinson, *Last of the Irish R.M.s*, p. 27.

owe to their Scandinavian ancestors. Just enough of fancy to please without the distortion of fact that is so bewildering.'[44]

Moreover, the more southern unionists thought about the union, the greater the advantages it seemed to have for Ireland. In fact, they built up a unionist view of Irish history, whereby Irish economic, social and cultural advancement depended upon rule by the Westminster parliament. According to southern unionists, Ireland had so benefited from the union that

in every detail which goes to make up the sum of civilised life, the Irish people are at this moment [1886] very far in advance of the condition of their ancestors at the time of the union. They are better housed, better clad, better fed; they receive better prices for the produce of their farms, and higher wages for their labour; they have greater liberty and better protection in health; abundant provision for sickness, and facilities for the education and advancement in life of their children, such as were undreamt of eighty years ago.[45]

This view of the beneficial effects of the union was a recurrent theme of the opponents of home rule, but it was most forcefully and fully expressed in a statement submitted by the I.L.P.U. to the Prime Minister in 1886, part three of which was issued as a pamphlet. This pamphlet (from which the last quotation was taken) was subtitled *The Union Vindicated* and was a unionist re-interpretation of Irish history, particularly economic history, up to 1886, designed to refute the nationalist notion that the union had retarded Ireland's progress. A mass of statistical evidence was produced to show that prior to the union Ireland's prosperity was declining owing to the mismanagement of the so-called Irish parliament, whose members' time was

almost entirely taken up with fierce party conflicts, enlivened by personal attacks and recriminations, from which they were sometimes diverted by the irruption of armed mobs into the chamber, and, on one memorable occasion, by the malicious burning of the senate house over their heads.[46]

44. Col. Sir Thomas Montgomery-Cuninghame, *Dusty Measure. A Record of Troubled Times* (1939), p. 81. As a captain he was stationed at Holywood, the Curragh and Tipperary between 1907 and 1912.

45. I.L.P.U., *Statement Submitted to the Prime Minister by the I.P.L.U.: Part III. The Union Vindicated. Ireland's Progress 1782-1800-1886* (1886), p. 39.

46. *Ibid.*, p. 7.

Not all supporters of the union would have agreed with the belittling of Grattan's parliament, but few would have disagreed that since the union Ireland had prospered. The case was supported by statistics showing increases in the tonnage of ships owned and registered at Irish ports, in the number of ships built, in the value of Irish imports and exports, in gross Irish revenue, in savings and the number of small depositors, in the value of sheep, pigs and cattle, in the amount raised by excise duties and in the number of first and second class houses. Moreover, all sections of the community had benefited from the union, especially the Catholics, despite the fact that Great Britain was Protestant. Denying that there could be any genuine religious grievance behind the home rule movement, another pamphlet explained that all substantial Catholics supported the union. 'And why should they not?' it asked:

Is there a country in the whole world where the Roman Catholic church has such complete immunity from state interference, such perfect liberty, as in Ireland under the British crown? From the day that Catholic emancipation was granted by the Protestant parliament of England, the history of Irish legislation has been a history of redress of grievances and concessions to Roman Catholics.[47]

Legislative achievements apart, southern unionists did not claim that the union had produced all the good results which succeeded it, any more than they admitted that it had caused the evils ascribed to it by 'agitators'. They acknowledged that nineteenth century prosperity was the result of many causes— social changes consequent on the Famine, the establishment of free trade, the extension of the railway system, the development of cross-channel traffic. But they did claim that the union had enabled Ireland to avail herself more readily and more advantageously of the benefits of 'the enlightened principles of legislation and of the marvellous results of scientific research, which have placed the latter half of the nineteenth century so far in advance of any previous epoch'.[48] The fact that Ireland had also on occasion suffered serious setbacks in the nineteenth century did not dampen unionist optimism. On the contrary, southern

47. I.L.P.U., *Union or Separation*, p. 7.
48. I.L.P.U., *The Union Vindicated*, p. 24.

unionists held that such setbacks afforded proof of the virtues of the union: the occasional distresses of the first half of the century and the final calamity of the Famine had been produced by wholly local causes and would have been infinitely worse had it not been for the union. During the Famine, for instance, the union had proved of the greatest advantage to Ireland:

Who, that remembers that awful time, can doubt that but for the active sympathy and assistance, both public and private, offered by the English people, the sufferings of the poor in Ireland would have been immeasurably greater than they were?[49]

Neither did they consider the depression of the 1880s any argument against the union: it was general throughout Europe and not attributable to the union; it was temporary and should be seen against the background of the enormous strides taken since 1800. It was nonsense, southern unionists argued, to say that in the 1880s Ireland was on the brink of ruin which could be averted only by the re-establishment of an Irish parliament. Statistics and personal experience showed that there was still a good deal of prosperity. All Ireland had to do was to wait patiently for the return of 'good times', and such a return would only be hindered by the establishment of home rule.[50]

Southern unionists reckoned that what Ireland needed was not legislation but government, not new laws but the steady enforcement of existing ones. They, therefore, had an ambivalent attitude towards the reforming legislation of liberal and unionist governments in the late nineteenth and early twentieth centuries. Such reforms did emphasise the value of the union to Ireland and the Irish,[51] but local government reform and land legislation also whittled away the remaining power of the ascendancy.[52] Nevertheless, the union on these terms was preferable to anything that might follow home rule:

49. *Ibid.*, pp. 37–8.
50. *Ibid.*, 40–1.
51. Bowen, *Bowen's Court*, p. 398; B. Cooper to J. O. Hannay (G. A. Birmingham, the novelist), 10 Mar. 1911, N.L.I., MS 8271, no. 48.
52. See e.g. the complaints in I.U.A., *Annual Report* (1899), and the unionist split in South Co. Dublin in the 1900 general election which resulted in the defeat of the sitting unionist member and the return of the nationalist candidate.

So sure as parliament is led by any infatuation to sanction the revival of an Irish parliament in any shape or form, so sure will the scenes of the closing years of the last century be re-enacted. Ireland will again become the theatre of outrage and crime, before which the worst days of the Land League will sink into insignificance. 'Right-boys', the 'Assassins', the 'Tarring and feathering committees', the 'Houghers', the 'Defenders', the 'Revolutionists', will again appear on the stage; they are only waiting till the strong hand of England is withdrawn to issue from their hiding-places. And then will come rebellion and civil war. . . .[53]

While willing to admit that this state of affairs might not last for ever, southern unionists were not willing to risk it or to pay the price of change. As one honest unionist said in 1906, arguing for the *status quo*:

It might be well enough to say that fifty years of home rule would develop a healthier element, but I confess myself selfish enough to wish to live the remainder of my life in peace and liberty rather than to sacrifice both to a nebulous future.[54]

THREE

Up until 1914, therefore, southern unionists fought against home rule. On 8 January 1886 a meeting of the members and sub-scribers of the I.L.P.U. decided to extend its scope.[55] Though largely attended, the meeting typified the limited social basis of southern unionism. There were few working, business or com-mercial men; it was essentially a meeting of landed southern Protestants. Only 2 of the 28 speakers were Roman Catholics but 18 were peers, sons of peers, or landed gentry from the south. The organisers did their best to obscure this preponderance of property, but could hardly succeed. One speaker got into diffi-culties when he referred to the executive committee as men of property:

When I say property I do not refer to any special class of property;

---

53. I.L.P.U., *The Union Vindicated*, p. 66.
54. Rev. Canon J. W. Tristram (Killeen, Killiney, Co. Dublin), in *Dublin Daily Express*, 8 Dec. 1906.
55. *Irish Times*, 9 Jan. 1886.

but when I say property I refer to the property of all men, whether it might be in land or money or muscle. The association was for the protection of him whose property consisted in the health and strength which God has given him, but . . . which he is not allowed to use to his advantage.

Nevertheless, the tone of the meeting was optimistic. Particularly encouraging was the support received from the Ulster conservative members of parliament. Since there was a sizeable unionist vote in Ulster, the I.L.P.U. could be represented as a more effective protest against Parnellism; and since Ulster returned sixteen unionist M.P.s to the southern provinces' two, southern unionists could feel better represented in British politics. When one southern unionist entreated the Ulster members to rise above the notion of provinces, Edward James Saunderson, the leading Ulster unionist M.P., responded generously on their behalf.[56]

Thus encouraged, the southern unionists determined to extend their activities and to work on two fronts. On the one hand, they decided that one unionist association for all Ireland should be formed with local branches organised to carry out the objects of the association and to secure a proper representation of unionist strength. On the other hand, proper arrangements were to be made for supplying accurate information to M.P.s and others interested in Irish affairs; and to form a sound public opinion by the spread of literature and the organisation of public meetings throughout the United Kingdom 'to properly represent the condition of Ireland and the true character of the so-called nationalist movement'. Immediately after the meeting, the I.L.P.U., with the help of paid organisers, set out to make itself the leading unionist association for all Ireland with branches in every county.[57]

Eventually, however, it had to recognise two limitations. In the first place, the I.L.P.U. (or as it became in 1891, the I.U.A.) became increasingly a southern unionist organisation. There were

56. Usually known as Colonel Saunderson (1837–1906); ed. privately; commanded 4th Batt. Royal Irish Fusiliers; whig M.P. for Co. Cavan, 1865–74; after 1882 took great interest in Orange Order; conservative M.P. for N. Armagh, 1885–1906; one of the originators of Irish unionist movement and leader of Irish unionist M.P.s; H.M.L., Co. Cavan; Castle Saunderson, Belturbet, Co. Cavan. R. Lucas, *Colonel Saunderson, M.P. A Memoir* (1908).

57. I.L.P.U., Executive council minute book, 1886–9; Organising subcommittee minute book, 1886, P.R.O.N.I., D 989/A/13, 2.

organisational links and personal ties with the north, and the
I.L.P.U. and I.U.A. gave crucial financial aid to Ulster unionist
registration societies and provided propaganda material for
Ulster unionist M.P.s.[58] But the southern unionists found the
Ulstermen becoming increasingly more exclusive and independent. Once they had woken up to the threat of home rule,
Ulstermen preferred to fight it in their own way. Gradually the
northern advocates of close co-operation between unionists in the
north and south were overborne by the Ulster businessmen and
democracy.[59] While willing to co-operate with southern unionists
for propaganda purposes Ulster unionists preferred to maintain
their own separate policy-making organisation. Considering the
later origins of effective unionist organisation in Ulster and its
early indebtedness to southern unionists, it is ironic that Ulster
unionism should eventually obscure the existence of southern
unionism. Perhaps, too, it is understandable that southern
unionists should at times have resented the growing exclusiveness
of Ulster unionism; but it was a fact that they had to accept by
1892–3, the time of the second home rule bill and the Ulster
Convention League.[60] The essentially southern character of the
I.U.A. was made more obvious during the devolution crisis by
the reorganisation of Ulster unionism and the formation of the
U.U.C. in 1904–5; and it was confirmed beyond all doubt by
the crisis over the third home rule bill, 1912–14, when, ironically,
Ulster unionists were led by a Dublin lawyer, Sir Edward Henry
Carson, an orator of passionate and uncomfortable sincerity.[61]

58. I.L.P.U. and I.U.A., *Annual Reports*; I.L.P.U., Executive council minute
book, 1886–9, 11, 18 June, 23 July, 1886; Parliamentary consultative committee
minute book, 1894–1900, *passim*, P.R.O.N.I., D 989A/1/7. The southern unionist
association was frequently approached by the Ulster registration societies, for
the central Ulster unionist associations were unable or unwilling to subsidise
local registration work, or at any rate were quite willing to allow southern
unionists to do so.

59. Good, *Irish Unionism*, pp. 221–30.

60. I.U.A. manifesto, Apr. 1893, copy in P.R.O.N.I., D 989A/1/4.

61. Baron Carson (1854–1935); b. Dublin; ed. Portarlington School and
Trinity College, Dublin; junior counsel to Attorney-General, 1887; Q.C., 1889;
involved in prosecutions connected with plan of campaign; Solicitor-General for
Ireland, 1892; M.P. for Dublin University, 1892–1918; English Q.C., 1894;
acknowledged a leading advocate after Oscar Wilde's libel action against
Queensbury; Solicitor-General for England, 1900–5; knighted, 1900; P.C., 1905;
leader of Irish unionists in House of Commons, 1910, and subsequently Ulster
unionist leader; Attorney-General, 1915–16; First Lord of the Admiralty,

By then, however, southern unionists were becoming reconciled to the existence of separate organisations in view of the Ulstermen's extreme religious objection to home rule and advocacy of force as an instrument of policy. Some unionists in and around Dublin did emulate the Ulster Volunteer Force and practise drilling;[62] but in the main southern unionists, scattered and defenceless, resented 'Carsonism' and Carson's 'silly proposals for Ulster to march on Cork etc.'[63] Moreover, many disagreed with Ulster unionists over the question of exclusion. Ulster unionists thought that in the event of home rule being forced upon Ireland, they had a right to opt out if they could, whereas many southern unionists believed that their own and Ireland's best interests would be served by a united Ireland containing the substantial Ulster minority. In so far as they publicly supported the Ulster case, many southern unionists did so for tactical reasons, believing that home rule without Ulster would be unworkable and unacceptable to nationalists.[64]

Not only was it impossible for the I.U.A. to represent the views of Ulster unionists, it also proved impossible to establish a conventional mass party organisation even in the three southern provinces. This failure was due to the limited social basis of southern unionism and to political apathy on the part of the Anglo-Irish. In some respects political apathy was a function of the limited social basis, for the scattered Anglo-Irish were reluctant to take any action that might antagonise the nationalist majority among whom they lived and upon whom they partly depended. This was especially true of businessmen. Even the largest tended to be shy of unionism: as the I.U.A. was told in 1892, 'You should recollect that we business men in Dublin live by the nationalists in the country towns and there is no use in *abusing* them.'[65] Only in certain areas, therefore, such as Dublin

---

1916–17; member of war cabinet, July 1917–Jan. 1918; M.P. for Duncairn division of Belfast, 1918–21; resigned leadership of Ulster unionists, 1921; Lord of Appeal in Ordinary, 1921–9. E. Marjoribanks and I. Colvin, *The Life of Lord Carson,* 3 vols (1932–6); J. C. Beckett, 'Carson—unionist and rebel' in *Leaders and Men of the Easter Rising: Dublin 1916,* ed. F. X. Martin (1967), pp. 81–94.

62. Hamilton, *An Irish Childhood,* p. 162; minute book of the Kingstown and District Unionist Club (founded 13 Feb. 1911), P.R.O.N.I., D 950/1/147.

63. Midleton to A. J. Balfour, 5 Oct. 1911, B.M., Add. MS 49721, ff. 291–2.

64. See below, pp. 86, 134, 176, 178, 198–9.

65. T. Pim jnr (a director of Pim and Sons, one of the largest commercial concerns in Ireland) to I.U.A., 27 Apr. 1892, P.R.O.N.I., D 989A/8/2.

and Cork where the Anglo-Irish were more concentrated, did branches of the I.U.A. become almost textbook examples of how local branches of political organisations should function; elsewhere they tended to be weak and dependent upon the energy and initiative of a single individual. Energetically promoted reorganisations in 1891 and 1893 did not remedy this situation, and by 1906 the I.U.A. recognised its limitations. In that year it abandoned ambitious schemes of constituency branches with multiple sub-branches and contented itself with the formation of county committees. The intention was merely to maintain sufficient organisation in Ireland to sustain a campaign in Great Britain against home rule.[66]

These limitations should not obscure the achievements of the I.U.A. If it did not become a mass party organisation, it did at least become the effective and recognised medium for southern unionist opinion and propaganda. It could rely on the enthusiasm of dedicated individuals, and wealth and social cohesion meant that the association was adequately financed and closely knit.[67] Above all, it was always strongly organised at the centre in Dublin, with offices first in Dawson Street and then at 109 Grafton Street. In general terms, the governing body consisted of a general council of all, or a representative section of, subscribers, with an executive committee, partly elected, partly co-opted, responsible for the day to day administration of the affairs of the association. In practice, the general council and the elective element of the executive committee had little say in the running of affairs, partly because the nature of the fight against home rule meant that the association required the advice of its political experts and most experienced men of affairs, partly because the cost and inconvenience prevented elected members in remote country parts from attending meetings in Dublin or London. The affairs of the association thus tended to fall into the hands of

---

66. Buckland, *Irish Unionism*, ch. V.

67. *Ibid.*; and I.U.A., Finance committee minute book, 1907–12, and Subscription book, P.R.O.N.I., D 989A/1/10 and D 989A/3/3. The Guinness brothers were particularly generous, but many members responded to appeals for funds in times of home rule crises. In 1914, when at the height of the campaign against the third home rule bill the I.U.A. issued an appeal for funds, £5,075.16.6d. was subscribed in two months, as compared to £1,529.8.0d. throughout 1909 when politics were concerned with the 'people's budget' and the home rule issue was not pressing.

its chief officers—the chairman, two vice-chairmen, three honorary secretaries and a paid secretary, who consulted with the more substantial Dublin or London based members of the committee, most notably the Irish peers. The administrative structure expanded and contracted according to the vicissitudes of the political situation. In 1893, when Gladstone was toying with his second home rule bill, there existed six separate sub-committees, each with a paid secretary and staff. In addition to these committees and the Dublin office, there was a London office which organised the association's propaganda in Great Britain. Financial pressure and the defeat of the home rule bill meant that this elaborate structure was not long maintained and the number of committees was reduced; but as the struggle over the third home rule bill developed, there were again established six committees, three of which had their own paid secretaries or accountant.[68]

The central organisation kept in touch with unionist opinion in the country not only through the branches but also through other unionist bodies. Such organisations as the Primrose League, Orange Body, Liberal Union of Ireland, Unionist Clubs Council, local conservative and constitutional clubs and unionist registration societies, were given representation on the general council of the I.U.A. and were sometimes affiliated.[69] Unlike the north, there was in the south no definite link with the Protestant churches. However, individual clergymen were active in the I.U.A., and the executive committee liked to prod the churches into action in times of emergency and to take advantage of church organisation to mobilise unionist opinion in the south. Since religious antagonism was not as intense in the south as in the north, this policy was not without its critics. In 1910 the I.U.A. asked clergymen of various Protestant denominations to assist it in obtaining the signatures of those members of their congregations who were opposed to the policy of home rule. This idea had been mooted in 1886[70] but the crisis had not lasted long enough for the suggestion to be acted upon. In 1910 the decision provoked some criticism, a number of prominent clergymen writing to the

---

68. I.U.A., *The Irish Unionist Alliance: its Work and Organisation* (1893); *Annual Report 1910–11*, appendices.

69. *Irish Times,* 9 Jan. 1886; I.L.P.U. and I.U.A., *Annual Reports.*

70. I.L.P.U., Executive council minute book, 1886–9, 23 Mar. 1886.

Irish Times and accusing the I.U.A. of seeking to turn the clergy into its agents. This outcry could have been serious for the I.U.A., which could not afford to lose a friend, still less make an enemy. However, not only had such critics difficulty in publicising their views, the other unionist daily, the *Dublin Daily Express,* refusing to publish letters of protest; but Protestant clergymen in the main were in agreement with the objects of the I.U.A. They seem to have responded to being approached as 'our fellow workers in the cause of those scattered Protestants throughout the rural districts of Ireland whose interests and welfare' were 'more at stake at the present moment than those of any other class of our fellow-countrymen'. Accordingly, long lists appeared in the Irish press during the general election of December 1910, and the vice-chairman of the I.U.A. felt that these 'long lists, columns in length . . . testified to the fact that our services are not un-appreciated.'[71]

By these methods of organisation, the I.U.A. became the leading unionist association in the south of Ireland. With its nucleus of members, some 683 in 1913,[72] it acted as an effective rallying point in time of crisis and could utilise and mobilise the resources of the ascendancy. In Ireland it sought to give evidence of the existence of opposition to home rule in the south. At first it had hoped to do so by fighting elections, but too few unionists were returned and this policy had to be abandoned. Between 1885 and 1914, unionists were returned regularly only for Trinity College and Dublin Co. South, though they were successful in the St Stephen's Green division of Dublin on occasion and in Galway City in 1900.[73] Instead, southern unionists relied in-creasingly upon the organisation of manifestos, petitions and demonstrations, particularly in Dublin, to prove to the outside world that they existed.

The Dublin demonstrations, held at least annually and addressed by leading British politicians, were always a great spectacle, thoughtfully organised. In 1887 two liberal unionists, George Goschen and Lord Hartington, visited Dublin, and Professor Dowden abandoned his academic pursuits for some time to

71. Stewart, *Dublin Daily Express,* 25 Apr. 1911.
72. I.U.A., *Annual Report 1912–13,* appendices.
73. *Dod's Parliamentary Companion 1885–1918*; I.L.P.U. and I.U.A., *Annual Reports.*

assist in organising what were usually impressive displays of 'large and heated' masses of 'human creatures', enlivened on this occasion by nationalist trouble makers with forged tickets who were quickly run out of the side door into the street.[74] Visitors were as satisfied as their hosts with such demonstrations. On 7 December 1906 Austen Chamberlain, Joseph's eldest son, addressed a superbly stage-managed meeting in the Rotunda. The balconies and windows were tastefully draped and festooned with red, white and blue. Across the platform ran a dainty border of flowering plants and exotics, while at the back were elaborate and artistic arrangements of flags and banners surmounted by mottoes such as 'No Home Rule'. The enthusiasm of the waiting audience was whipped up by a band playing such patriotic airs as 'Rule Britannia' and 'Hearts of Oak', and between the instrumental selections hundreds of voices sang unaccompanied the national anthem and 'Soldiers of the Queen'.[75] Chamberlain, received with a prolonged standing ovation, told his step-mother that 'as a unionist demonstration it was a great success. The Rotunda was crowded. So was the overflow, and many were turned away, unable to get admission to either. It has given the unionists there the tonic they needed and I hear they are all very happy and pleased.' Moreover, Chamberlain himself, though unhappy with his speech, was pleased that 'its reception was all I could desire'.[76]

The advent of the third home rule bill and the dominating position of Ulster unionism required further demonstration of the existence of unionism in the three southern provinces. This evidence was provided not only by a series of county demonstrations organised in 1912 in such centres as Cork, Waterford, Tralee, Sligo, Limerick and Kilkenny,[77] but also by tours of Ireland for

---

74. E. D. Dowden (ed.), *Fragments of Old Letters. E.D. to E.D.W. 1869–1892* (1914), i. 181; E. D. and H. M. Dowden (eds), *Letters of Edward Dowden and his Correspondents* (1914), p. 230.

75. *Dublin Daily Express,* 8 Dec. 1906. (Joseph) Austen (1863–1937); half brother of Neville Chamberlain; ed. Rugby and Cambridge; liberal unionist M.P. for E. Worcestershire (1892–1914), W. Birmingham (1914–37); Civil Lord of the Admiralty, 1895–1900; Financial Sec. to Treasury, 1900–2; Postmaster-General, 1902–3; P.C., 1902; Chancellor of the Exchequer, 1902–5; unsuccessful contender for unionist leadership, 1911; Sec. of State for India, 1915–17; member of war cabinet, 1918; Chancellor of Exchequer, 1919–21; Lord Privy Seal and leader of unionist party in House of Commons, 1921–22; Foreign Sec., 1924–29; knighted, 1925; First Lord of the Admiralty, 1931.

76. A. Chamberlain to Mary, 8 Dec. 1906, B.U.L. AC 4/1/127.

77. *Notes from Ireland* (1912), *passim.*

British electors. By July 1914 one or two deputations of between ten and fifteen electors were arriving weekly to inspect certain areas supposedly illustrating nationalist incompetence or terrorism.[78] The success of such work depended upon the enthusiasm and self-sacrifice of local unionists in the small towns of Ireland who had to give a great deal of time and trouble to the tours, interviewing visitors and asking other unionists to do so. One such self-sacrificing unionist, selected for commendation by the secretary of the I.U.A.,[79] was a Roman Catholic. He was Michael M'Cann of Newtownforbes, Co. Longford, who with his wife had 'done as much as anybody in Ireland to convert the radical visitors'. A big farmer and the Longford branch representative on the general council of the I.U.A., he had entertained a very great number of tourists at his house and frequently fed them. For his pains he was severely boycotted. Another organiser was Henry Valentine ('Vee') Macnamara of Ennistymon House, Co. Clare, honorary secretary of the Clare branch of the I.U.A. Despite living in 'one of the worst districts in Ireland', he showed 'the very greatest pluck', making 'admirable arrangements for the reception of tours in Ennis' and doing 'splendid work in Co. Clare during the last year'.[80] Thus the exhortation (given at the first annual meeting in 1886 to loud cries of 'Hear, Hear') that 'those who had leisure should give up their amusements, their hunting, and devote themselves heart and soul to this great cause', was not mere rhetoric.[81]

FOUR

This work in Ireland served to support an almost continuous campaign in British politics against home rule. Unable to contain the nationalist movement within Ireland, southern unionists fought it within the whole field of British politics. They had to ensure that a bill dissolving the union would not be passed by the Westminster parliament or approved by the British electorate, and the only constitutional means open to them was to carry on,

78. *Ibid.* (1913–14), *passim.*
79. R. Shaw to P. Wicks, 15 June 1914, P.R.O.N.I., D 989A/8/4.
80. *Ibid.* Macnamara (1861–1925); ed. Harrow and Cambridge; capt. Royal Carmarthen Artillery Militia; unsuccessful attempt to assassinate him, 1919, when shooting party was ambushed.
81. *Irish Times*, 9 Jan. 1886.

mainly through their association, a campaign in British politics against home rule.

Owing to the liberal commitment on home rule, the campaign had to be organised through the unionist party of Great Britain. It was waged in two spheres. In the more restricted sphere of parliamentary and party politics, the southern unionists relied upon action in both houses of parliament. In 1886, for example, of the 144 peers with Irish interests, no less than 116 had land in, or were sons of families in, the three southern provinces; and even though these provinces returned only 2 unionist M.P.s, 17 southern Anglo-Irishmen sat as unionists for British constituencies.[82] The number varied from time to time, but whenever home rule was considered in parliament such southern unionists would present a reasoned case against it, with all the appearance of disinterestedness.[83] Moreover, southern unionist activity behind the scenes, through deputations and letters to party leaders and conferences,[84] was assisted by the fact that prominent unionist leaders, such as Lansdowne, had substantial interests in the south of Ireland.

The campaign in the constituencies was fourfold: the production and distribution of literary propaganda—leaflets, maps, posters and pamphlets; the organisation of demonstrations; canvassing; and the maintenance of a 'follow-up service'. This work concentrated on marginal seats and crystallised around elections, when all the I.U.A.'s resources were thrown behind the unionist candidates, and was sometimes carried on in conjunction with Ulster unionists. Of course, the amount of work depended upon the state of home rule politics, but at times of home rule crises it was prodigious, as the following figures show. In 1886, the year of the first home rule bill, the I.L.P.U. prepared and circulated one million copies of 164 leaflets, half a million copies of larger publications—posters, pamphlets and maps, and 91,500

82. *Dod's Parliamentary Companion, 1886;* and below, Appendix B.

83. See e.g. W. Guinness on the Ulster question, *Parl. Deb.* (*Commons*), 5 ser., xxxix, 13 June 1912, col. 1131, and Barrymore on the amending bill, *Parl. Deb.* (*Lords*), 5 ser., xvi, 1 July 1914, cols 595–8.

84. For deputations to leaders and conferences, see e.g. *Notes from Ireland* (1907), when southern unionists spoke to leading unionists against devolution and condemned, at the annual conference of the National Union of Conservative and Constitutional Associations, the liberal government's apathy in face of growing Irish lawlessness.

copies of a weekly bulletin of Irish affairs, *Notes from Ireland*; and
in the general election of that year the association had 43 speakers
in 86 of the most important English and 12 of the most important
Welsh constituencies, with a separate staff of 10 speakers working
through the Scottish constituencies. A similar effort was made in
1892–3 and at the time of the third home rule bill. Since late
in 1907 the southern unionists had been co-operating for propaganda purposes with the Ulster unionists, through the Joint
Committee of the Unionist Associations of Ireland. From
September 1911 to the middle of July 1914 this joint committee
bombarded British voters with propaganda. In England the
committee organised over 5,000 meetings, canvassed 1,246,225
doubtful voters in over 200 constituencies, and assisted at twenty-
three contested by-elections; in Scotland 3,843 meetings were
held, 205,654 doubtful voters were canvassed, and aid was given
to unionist candidates in ten by-elections; moreover, an estimated
six million booklets, leaflets and pamphlets all pointing out the
folly of home rule were distributed throughout Great Britain.[85]

Some of this work was carried out by full-time and paid
workers, but more often than not the I.L.P.U. and the I.U.A.
relied upon volunteers. Lecky appeared on an I.L.P.U. platform
in 1886,[86] and the novelists Edith Somerville and Martin Ross
enjoyed a stint as canvassers in East Anglia in the general election
of 1895, their task being to convert the East Anglian professional
classes to unionism and the unionist candidate. Though they
found the work unexpectedly arduous, Somerville ever remem-
bered with pride that 'our man got in, and that a radical poster
referred directly, and in enormous capital letters, to Martin and
me as "Irish locusts" '.[87] With such literary talent at their disposal
it is not surprising that southern unionist publications were of a
high standard. They avoided outright bigotry[88] and were so
varied as to cater for most levels of intelligence and interest,
though many of the pamphlets must have been above the heads

---

85. For this campaign in the constituencies, see I.L.P.U. and I.U.A., *Annual
Reports;* and Buckland, *Irish Unionism,* ch. VIII.

86. Lecky, *A Memoir,* p. 190.

87. Somerville and Ross, *Irish Memories* (1917), pp. 253–4.

88. When Dowden was collecting 'songs for unionist Ireland', he had to
explain to Swinburne, who had responded to his appeal, that the phrase 'black
as . . . creed of priest' would not do 'for our catholic unionists'. Swinburne oblig-
ingly substituted 'beast' for 'priest' (Dowden, *Letters of Edward Dowden.* p. 383).

of most of the working class voters in Great Britain. Some
southern unionists seem to have taken advantage of the opportunity offered by political pamphleteering to air their knowledge.
For instance, in 1886 in a very learned pamphlet criticising
Gladstone's conversion to home rule, Thomas E. Webb, LL.D.,
Q.C., Regius Professor of Law and Public Orator in the University of Dublin, wrote thus: 'The nationalism of Mr Parnell
stands to the home rule of Mr Butt in much the same relation as
the differential calculus of Leibnitz stands to the fluxions of
Sir Isaac Newton—the one was a development and simplification
of the other'; and 'Mr Gladstone has undergone as many trans-
formations as Proteus, as many transmigrations as Indur, as many
stages of evolution as a protoplasmic cell.'[89]

FIVE

The distinguishing features of this campaign were its insistence
and sweet reasonableness. It paid dividends, making southern
unionism a significant factor in any discussion of the Irish
question. Unable to kill the home rule movement, southern
unionists at least managed to thwart it temporarily and to delay
the repeal of the union. They were able to do so because their
activity established close links between them and the unionist
party of Great Britain, stiffening that party's resistance to home
rule. This is not to say that British unionists opposed home rule
solely on account of southern unionism. British unionists objected
to home rule on a number of grounds, imperial, constitutional,
anti-socialist, and out of concern for the Protestants of Ulster;
but it can be argued that southern unionist pressure on, acceptability to, and contacts in, the party activated and kept alive
prejudices against home rule despite changing conditions. By the
twentieth century many Englishmen were coming round to the
view that the only way to settle the Irish question was to partition
Ireland, to allow Ulster unionists to opt out of a Dublin parliament; but the southern unionists hindered such a compromise
solution over the third home rule bill.[90]

89. Webb, *The Irish Question: a Reply to Mr Gladstone* (1886), pp. 7, 16.
90. On the crisis in general, see R. Blake, *The Unknown Prime Minister* (1955);
D. Gwynn, *The Life of John Redmond* (1932); Stewart, *Ulster Crisis*. For an
examination of the role of southern unionists, see Buckland, 'The southern Irish
unionists, the Irish question and British politics, 1906–14', *Irish Historical Studies*,
xv (1967), pp. 228–55.

The liberal government, headed since 1908 by Herbert Henry Asquith, introduced the third home rule bill on 11 April 1912. The bill offered to Ireland only a narrow measure of autonomy in that it proposed to establish a Dublin parliament of two chambers but reserved to the imperial parliament wide powers and retained Irish representation at Westminster. Nevertheless, it was fiercely denounced by Irish unionists and the unionist party in Great Britain. It was not just that the bill contained inadequate safeguards for minorities, providing, for instance, only an elective second chamber which, it was argued, would simply reproduce the nationalist majority in the lower house. It was the whole concept of home rule that unionists opposed. The bill was thus obstructed all along the line by the unionist party which took full advantage of the delaying powers left to its majority in the Lords under the 1911 Parliament Act. The bill, which passed smoothly through the House of Commons, was rejected, as in 1893, by the Lords and thus condemned to three prolonged parliamentary circuits. Meantime, tempers were rising, particularly in Ulster where unionists, with the connivance of leading British unionists, were putting their organisation on a paramilitary basis and preparing to set up a provisional government in the event of the bill becoming law. By the autumn of 1913 suggestions for a compromise on the basis of the exclusion of Ulster were floated in an attempt to calm the situation. They were to no avail, because they failed to take into account the influence of southern unionism. Although southern unionists recognised that the Parliament Act made some form of home rule for the south at least almost inevitable and were considering what safeguards would in that event be desirable,[91] they were as opposed as ever to the concept of home rule and were determined to put off the evil day as long as possible.[92] They put increasing pressure on the unionist party and thus prevented the unionist leadership from seriously and constructively considering compromise proposals and from abandoning opposition to home rule. Any compromise would have been construed as the desertion of the loyal minority in the south and could have sparked off a party revolt. Thus, when in September 1913 the King's secretary

91. R. B. McDowell, *The Irish Convention, 1917–18* (1970), pp. 39–40.
92. I.U.A. to Carson, 7 May 1914, P.R.O.N.I., D 989A/8/4.

suggested a conference on the basis of the exclusion of Ulster, Andrew Bonar Law, the unionist leader in the House of Commons, could only refuse on the ground that 'there would be a wild outburst of resentment against us in the south of Ireland which would be reflected with almost equal violence in England.'[93] Unionists continued to oppose the third home rule bill and prevented it from becoming operative before the first world war. It was put on the statute book only on 18 September 1914, under the provisions of the Parliament Act, and remained a dead letter. Southern unionists had contributed largely to this delay in granting home rule. A settlement of the Irish question and the realisation of the political ambitions of new Ireland thus depended to some degree on a change of heart on the part of the Anglo-Irish.

93. Quoted in Blake, *The Unknown Prime Minister*, p. 159.

II

Phase Two: The First World War
Rapprochement

THIS change of heart began with the outbreak of the first world war. In many instances the 1914–18 war may be regarded as a solvent to many of the themes of the old pre-war society. It is so in respect of southern unionism. There were, of course, exceptions, but in the main the Anglo-Irish in the south threw themselves as wholeheartedly into the war effort in 1914 as they had done at the time of the South African war.[1] This response had important consequences for the unionist movement in the south of Ireland.

The Anglo-Irish contributed to the war effort in a number of ways. Most obviously, they joined the colours, and many, like William M'Neil, the secretary of the Cork Defence Union, argued that they did so to a greater degree than Roman Catholics and nationalists. Commenting in March 1916 on the large proportion of unionists from Cork Protestant young men's associations who had joined the colours, M'Neil held that the percentage of recruits from Roman Catholic young men's institutions 'would be very small', though he excused them ironically on the ground that 'they are retained with a good plausible object, "To guard the shores of Ireland", a very sure place to mount guard so long

---

1. For an amusing instance of the effects of this wholehearted southern unionist response to the call to arms on social life in Ireland, see E. Œ. Somerville and M. Ross, *Some Irish Yesterdays* (1906), pp. 43–5: 'If an instance of all that is worst in a picnic be required I may lightly record some of the features of an entertainment which, one summer, I was, by Heaven's help and a little lower diplomacy, enabled to evade. The drag-net of the African war had gone heavily over the neighbourhood, and to the forty women who had unflinchingly accepted, but two men were found to preserve the just balance of the sexes. These numbers are not fictitious. They are to be found seared upon the heart of the hostess. . . . The two men faced the position. Through smoke and bees they did their duty, carting back and forth the eighty cups of tea which the occasion demanded; but they said afterwards that more than patriotism barbed the regret that their country deemed them too old for active service.'

as the British navy are outside!'[2] Whatever the rights and wrongs
of the debate over the relative contributions of Catholics and
Protestants, nationalists and unionists, to the new army, the fact
of the wholehearted Anglo-Irish response to the need for recruits
is beyond question. Owing to the practice of drafting Englishmen
into Irish regiments, the number of Protestants in any Irish
division is no reliable indication of the Anglo-Irish contribution.
However, some idea of the degree to which they were committed to the war effort may be gleaned from a study of the
service of those southern unionists (and certain of their relatives)
who are listed in the appendix of the I.U.A.'s *Annual Report* for
1912–13 as officers of the association or as members of the general
council, and who can be traced in the 1958 edition of *Burke's
Landed Gentry of Ireland.*

The sample is very small: there are only 114 who fulfil these
two conditions; but they do illustrate a point. Only twenty-nine
appear to have provided neither sons, nor grandsons, nor brothers,
nor nephews for the war effort; and these twenty-nine were in
the main too old to serve, or unmarried, or without sons, or
without sons of military age. Statistically speaking these figures
are scant, but more important is the impression they convey;
and often they underrate the involvement of the Anglo-Irish in
the war. Often there is little or no information about the activities
of the offspring of the female relatives of the southern unionists;
and, if the figures are extended to include cousins, brothers-in-
law and sons-in-law, the impression of a class of people firmly
committed to the war is confirmed. For instance, Acheson
Ffrench of Monivea, a member of the Galway branch of the
I.U.A., had neither sons nor brothers nor nephews serving in the
war. His only brother had died in 1896 leaving only one daughter,
and, although Acheson himself was married, he had only two
daughters. Nevertheless, according to *Burke's,* he had five relatives
serving in the war, one of whom was killed in action and two
others died in subsequent engagements. One cousin, the grandson
of Acheson's uncle, seemed a particular glutton for punishment.
That branch of the family had emigrated to Australia, but had
kept up a tradition of service on behalf of the British empire.
Evelyn Alexander Wilson Ffrench, a captain in the R.F.A., R.F.C.

2. W. M'Neil to J. M. Wilson, 22 Jan. 1916, P.R.O.N.I., D 989D/6.

and R.A.F., served in both the South African war and in the first world war and was severely wounded in both. Nevertheless, on both occasions he appears to have bounded back to service, only to be killed on active service on 23 December 1918.[3]

The impression thus gained of a class intimately involved in the war is underlined when inter-family relationships are taken into account. As Douglas Hyde, writing from the west of Ireland to an American friend a year after war had broken out, said:

Nearly everyone I know in the army has been killed. Poor Lord de Freyne and his brother were shot the same day and buried in one grave. The MacDermot of Coolavin, my nearest neighbour, has had his eldest son shot dead in the Dardanelles. All the gentry have suffered. *Noblesse oblige.* They have behaved magnificently.[4]

Of course, this contribution to the war effort was in no way decisive and it is impossible to generalise about the conduct of southern unionists in the war, although some examples of outstanding gallantry can be selected. Loyalists and their families who did not go to the front contributed to the war effort as best they could. The Irish peers, in particular, played an important role in home affairs;[5] the gentry played a role in recruiting;[6] while the women-folk were active on all manner of committees and engaged in charitable works, especially in connection with hospitals and the comfort of returning, wounded soldiers.[7] On this home front, too, the Anglo-Irish were prepared to argue that they were making the greater sacrifices. Thus in February 1917, John Henry Bernard, the Protestant Archbishop of Dublin, complained to Viscount Devonport, the Minister of Food, that

a large number of the upper classes are doing their best to limit their consumption of flour, and meat, as well as of sugar; but no effort whatever is being made, or will be made without compulsion, by too many of the public institutions or by the ignorant poor. It is freely alleged, and I believe with good reason, that the amount of these things consumed in the union workhouses and kindred establishments

3. *Burke's Landed Gentry of Ireland*, pp. 272–3.
4. Quoted in Lennox Robinson, *Bryan Cooper* (1931), p. 88.
5. See below, pp. 36–7.
6. See below, pp. 44–6, 49–50.
7. See e.g. the diary of Lady Alice Mary Howard for 1915–16, N.L.I., MS 3622.

is excessive even in time of peace, and is not being diminished appreciably.[8]

Why the southern unionists responded so readily to the war effort is not a difficult question to answer. There may have been political motives. Perhaps they hoped to win the gratitude of the British people who would thus be persuaded to maintain the union. Certainly, after the war (and in 1916) loyalists were ready to emphasise their services to the empire and the debt it owed them.[9] Perhaps others hoped to lead a new departure in Irish politics, and joined the National Volunteers to keep them loyal to the British connection. Perhaps they hoped to retrieve their deteriorating position in Irish politics and Irish life by putting themselves once more at the head of the tenantry.[10] Perhaps, too, there may have been a sort of death-wish: some of the young and not so young men of Anglo-Ireland may have thrown themselves into Flanders and Gallipoli impelled by a kind of despair, because the habits of Ireland no longer fitted the country gentry, and their position and great houses had become straitjackets.[11]

8. J. H. Bernard to Vt Devonport, 14 Feb. 1917, B.M., Add. MS 52782, f. 141. Bernard (1860–1927); ed. Trinity College, Dublin; ordained, 1886; fellow of Trinity College, 1884–1902; Archbishop King's Lecturer (afterwards Professor) in Divinity, 1888–1911; Dean of St Patrick's cathedral, 1902; Bishop of Ossory, 1911; Archbishop of Dublin, 1915; Provost of Trinity College, 1919; works include commentaries on and translation of Kant and a commentary on St John's gospel. R. H. Murray, *Archbishop Bernard, Professor, Prelate and Provost* (1931).

9. See e.g. below, 59–60, 277.

10. *Irish Times* 5 (leader), 6 (Lord Desart's letter) Aug. 1914. See also the comments of Dawson Bates to Montgomery, 11 May 1918, and Montgomery to Bates, 13 May 1918, P.R.O.N.I., D 627/432.

11. See e.g. W. B. Yeats, making an Irish airman foresee his death:

> I know that I shall meet my fate
> Somewhere among the clouds above:
> Those that I fight I do not hate,
> Those that I guard I do not love;
> My country is Kiltartan Cross,
> My countrymen Kiltartan's poor,
> No likely end could bring them loss
> Or leave them happier than before.
> Nor law, nor duty made me fight,
> Nor public men, nor cheering crowds,
> A lonely impulse of delight
> Drove to this tumult in the clouds;
> I balanced all, brought all to mind,
> The years to come seemed waste of breath,
> A waste of breath the years behind
> To balance with this life, this death.

Perhaps those who stayed at home and helped had more selfish, more mixed, motives, like the widowed Aunt Brenda in *Mad Puppetstown,* who did work for remounts and went to dances at the Curragh:

She had forgotten that it was important to marry again. She was conscientious and efficient in her work and tired sometimes to a contentment past belief. Partly she felt the war *must* be over before Evelyn [her favourite son] was old enough to go—and Basil, of course, too—and with a delightful microscopity of vision she saw her work, as an important cog in the great machine called Winning this War. The solace and fortification this lent to her spirit was as deep as it was calming.[12]

Probably, all these motives, political, personal and selfish, were present, but they are insufficient to explain the spontaneity and near unanimity of the southern unionist response to the war. Nor are they sufficient to explain the almost unthinking attitude taken by Anglo-Irish novelists to the war. The male characters of military age of M. J. Farrell, for instance, invariably join up, almost automatically, and their dependants and relatives accept it unquestioningly.[13] Not even Asquith's policy of putting the home rule bill on the statute book despite the party truce, or the advice of their mentors in British politics (who thought that southern unionist support for Redmond would weaken the case against home rule), could alter the determination of southern unionists to support the war effort and, in the first instance, the National Volunteers. Although cool reflection and pressure from their British allies made some cautious, the enthusiasm for the war effort was difficult to contain, since it was a spontaneous reaction governed only partly by political considerations, by political tactics.[14] Indeed, the southern unionist response to the war effort should, perhaps, be seen as the natural response of the Irish

12. M. J. Farrell, *Mad Puppetstown* (1931), p. 82.

13. See e.g. Major Chevington in *Mad Puppetstown* and Desmond French-McGrath in *The Rising Tide* (1937).

14. Shaw to Carson, 7 Aug. 1914, P.R.O.N.I., D 989A/8/4, discussing the advisability of the I.U.A. publishing a resolution welcoming 'the patriotic spirit which has actuated Sir Edward Carson and Mr John Redmond in this crisis in our country's history' and calling on 'all unionists in Ireland, in the imperial spirit which they have always shown, to co-operate with their fellow-countrymen in the defence of Ireland and the empire'.

territorial aristocracy with their traditions of military and political service and leadership.

This point needs no stressing for men such as Lansdowne and Midleton who saw themselves as, and were seen to be, natural rulers of the British empire, and who quite naturally put the war effort above all else. But it applies equally to southern unionists who were not primarily politicians. In a sense, the southern unionist society was a military one, and this military tradition had been built up in the service of the British government in Ireland and in the empire at large. Of the unionist families who appear in the 1958 edition of *Burke's Landed Gentry of Ireland*, the majority may be said to have had a well-established military tradition. The consequences of this tradition were accepted almost unconsciously by southern unionists. Just as in fiction Flurry Knox, devoted to horses and hunting, fought unquestioningly in the South African war,[15] so in real life did the fifth Earl Longford, devoted to bravery as well as to horses and hunting, distinguish himself in the first world war.[16] His family, which hitherto had produced only one Catholic and few politicians, were mainly landowners, huntsmen and especially soldiers or sailors. The fifth Earl proved no exception to the general rule. In 1883 the family estates were said to have consisted of some 19,900 acres in counties Dublin, Westmeath and Longford, worth £47,198 a year; the fifth Earl lived comfortably at Pakenham Hall, County Westmeath; and was H.M.L. of County Longford where he had town property. A 'natural' unionist and president of the Longford branch of the I.U.A., he was once Master of Foxhounds for Westmeath and lived for horses and soldiers, showing phenomenal courage on huntfield and battlefield. Joining the Life Guards as second lieutenant in 1887, he served as captain of the 45th Imperial Yeomanry and with the 2nd Life Guards in the South African war, where he distinguished himself, being wounded at Lindley Hill and being awarded the Queen's medal and four clasps. In the first world war he was commissioned as brigadier of the Yeomanry and achieved his life's wish to take

---

15. E. Œ. Somerville and M. Ross, *Experiences of an Irish R.M.*, Everyman ed. (1944), incorporating *Some Experiences of an Irish R.M.* (1899) and *Further Experiences of an Irish R.M.* (1908); and *In Mr Knox's Country*.

16. F. Pakenham, *Born to Believe* (1953), pp. 12–14.

part in a charge at the Dardanelles, where he led his group gallantly and died fighting at Hill 70, Suvla Bay, Gallipoli.[17]

TWO

Whatever the motives of the Anglo-Irish, there can be little doubt about the effect of their support for the war effort on unionism in the south of Ireland. It began a process that broke down the stereotyped Irish political situation that had existed since the 1880s, and did so in two ways. In the first place, unionist organisation in the south was adversely affected, as the big houses were emptied of able men of fighting age and those remaining concentrated on the war effort. Although the 1916 crisis was to show that southern unionists were still capable of prompt and decisive action, the general effect of the war was to weaken southern unionist organisation.

With the outbreak of war the political activities of the I.U.A. virtually ceased. The executive committee continued to meet, but no longer engaged in political controversy. With the party truce its propaganda activities ceased and the Joint Committee of the Unionist Associations of Ireland was wound up.[18] So concerned was the I.U.A. to concentrate upon the war effort and to preserve national unity that it did not agitate vigorously against Asquith's successful attempt to put the home rule bill on the statute book. Although the publication of *Notes from Ireland,* suspended in August owing to the war, was revived in October as a protest against an action they regarded as deceitful and as a betrayal, it is doubtful whether the mass of the supporters of the I.U.A. would have countenanced anything other than a statement of their views. Indeed, it is probable that the I.U.A. would have been repudiated had the committee tried to bargain with the government.[19] A few members thought that the association

17. G.E.C., *Complete Peerage,* viii. 125 (The Dublin estate was held jointly with Vt de Vesci); Pakenham, *Born to Believe,* pp. 12–14; I.U.A., *Annual Report 1912–13,* appendices.

18. Minute book of the Joint Committee of the Unionist Associations of Ireland, 15 Jan. 1915; Bates to Montgomery, 11 May 1918, P.R.O.N.I., D 627/432.

19. *Notes from Ireland* (1914); Shaw to Carson, 7 Aug. 1914, P.R.O.N.I., D 989A/8/4. On 16 September, the executive committee of the I.U.A. passed a resolution condemning 'the flagrant breach of faith by the government', but at the same time it added another pointing out 'the duty of Irishmen to undertake

should be doing more by way of propaganda and pressure in
British politics,[20] but, owing to the necessities of the war and
public opinion, most southern unionists thought that they could
do little.[21]

Midleton's activities during the war conveniently illustrate the
self-denying ordinance passed by southern unionists, their concern for national unity and concentration on the war effort.
Before the war Midleton had been active in and out of parliament
on behalf of southern unionists; but during the first years of the
war the Irish question slid into the background for him, and he
was not willing to oppose vigorously the putting of the home
rule bill on the statute book. Though protesting against the
government's policy, Midleton refused to enter into a controversy, for

it would be indecent for us to enter upon a domestic controversy when
our whole energy should be devoted to the furtherance of the war.[22]

Midleton's main concern was that the maximum national effort
should be achieved in war-time, and, owing to his experience at
the War Office in previous conservative governments, he
regarded himself as peculiarly qualified to give advice to the
government on war matters. And he did, despite constant setbacks. Earl Kitchener, the hero of Khartoum made War Minister
on 5 August 1914, soon dissolved a committee set up early in
August 1914 with which Midleton was to have organised the New
Army; Kitchener resisted for a long time the need to form a
special department for the supply of munitions, and refused to
accept the advice of the Defence Committee and of Midleton
about the use of territorials. Nevertheless, Midleton persevered,
and, as he says in his reminiscences,

practically every civilian of experience found himself called upon to
assist the government in some capacity, and I was no exception. Those
four years of war were, consequently, as fully occupied as any period
in my life.

---

their full share of imperial responsibility in the present national emergency', and
calling upon its supporters to continue their efforts to secure recruits for the
army. (W. A. Phillips, *The Revolution in Ireland 1906–1923* (1923), pp. 83–4.)

20. Wilson to Carson, 6 May 1915, P.R.O.N.I., D 1507/1/1915/15.
21. Rice to I.U.A., 13 Mar. 1916, *ibid.*, D 989A/8/6.
22. *Parl. Deb.* (*Lords*), 5 ser., xvii, 15 Sept. 1914, col. 636.

Apart from agitating in parliament and behind the scenes on such matters as the treatment of recruits, information about fighting in France, repatriation allowances, the differences between Field-Marshal Sir John French and Kitchener, the munitions difficulty and government expenditure, Midleton served on many important committees. These included the committee for apportionment of man-power between munitions and combatant service, a committee for regulating new government departments 'which sprang up like mushrooms', and, later on, he had to attend to the 'unpleasant weekly work of a conscription tribunal at Guildford'. The Irish question thus came as a tedious interruption to the larger issue of winning the war; and whenever Midleton was forced to face Irish affairs, he tried to avoid talking in a controversial manner. Before the Rising he did try to draw the attention of government and politicians in Britain to the growth of lawlessness in certain parts of Ireland, to the danger of the Irish Volunteers, and to warn of the possibility of a rising (especially by passing on information received from friends in Ireland and from the I.U.A.). But all this was done discreetly, behind the scenes or by speeches in the House of Lords, without a campaign in the constituencies and without arguing for the union or against home rule.[23]

If the central organisation of the I.U.A. was merely kept ticking over, the local unionist organisations were gradually fading out of existence. There is interesting evidence of this process in the writings of J. M. Wilson, who made a tour of certain Irish counties during the war and reported his findings to Walter Long. Since Wilson was a staunch unionist, and always anxious to emphasise the strength of unionist opinion and feeling in the south of Ireland, his observations on the weakness of unionist organisation there may be taken at their face value; unless, of course, it may be objected, he was anxious to show how patriotic were southern unionists. Nevertheless, he was on good terms with Long and little needed to make propaganda in this quarter; his reports

23. See e.g., apart from Midleton's activities in the House of Lords, Midleton, *Records and Reactions 1856–1939*, pp. 218–19, 228–9, 277–87; copy of a report on arming and drilling in Ireland sent by the I.U.A. to Barrymore and Midleton, 6 Mar. 1916, and communicated by them to the government, P.R.O.N.I., D 989A/9/8; Midleton to Law, 14 Sept., 9, 13 Nov. 1914, 11, 16 Jan., 6, 8, 25 Apr., 19 Nov. 1915, B.L., 33/1/47, 35/2/17, 28, 36/1/12a, 24, 37/1/14, 37/5/16, 37/1/60, 51/5/33.

make interesting reading and bear out statements made at a later date as to the decline of unionist organisation.[24]

There were two reasons for flagging unionist organisation in the south: enlistment deprived the localities of their active unionist population; and concentration on the war effort at home led southern unionists to abandon purely political activities. In Leitrim (where the bulk of the members of the I.U.A. appear to have been smaller Protestant farmers), it was reported by a local landowner that unionists had held no meetings since the war; and a Protestant farmer with 400 acres in a 'wild district' alleged that the underlying object of the present movement was to get rid of all unionists by persuading them to enlist and go to the war, and then give their positions to those who remained.[25] In County Sligo a less sinister picture was painted. Since the war all unionist activity had ceased, for all parties were working in harmony with regard to war work, and some doubted whether unionists could ever be galvanised into life again.[26] The story was the same in the east as it was in the west. In Wexford it was reported that 'everything is dormant', and in Waterford it was said that 'every unionist has gone to the war'.[27]

THREE

The second effect of the unionist concentration upon the war effort was to weaken unionist sentiment in Ireland. This point is hard to illustrate precisely and quantitatively: often the evidence of, say, Wilson's reports is conflicting. On the one hand, it is reported that, despite the lapse of organisation, unionists 'have not weakened in their faith', that 'the same fighting spirit as ever exists', that 'they have not thrown up the sponge but are firmer than ever.'[28] On the other hand, there is evidence of a drift away from unionism. In Limerick a land agent and farmer

24. J. M. Wilson's notes on his tour of Ireland, reporting, on a county by county basis, local feeling with regard to the war, conscription, politics, etc., 1915–17, P.R.O.N.I., D 989A/9/7. Wilson's conclusions about the ebbing of party feeling are confirmed by police reports which held that 'the outbreak of war worked a revolution in the state of party feeling' (Phillips, *The Revolution in Ireland,* p. 86).
25. Wilson's tour, Leitrim, 3 Jan. 1916.
26. *Ibid.,* Sligo, 24 Feb. 1916.
27. *Ibid.,* Waterford, 14–16 Jan. 1916, Wexford, 13 Jan. 1916.
28. Wilson's tour, Clare, 23 Jan. 1916, Cork, 19–20 Jan. 1916.

told Wilson that unionists were 'practically submerged. Hardly a hundred now on the Register. If the issue was raised again, very hard to say if [they] would bow to the inevitable.'[29] A solicitor who had a large practice in County Mayo and who was a controller of recruiting and Lieutenant commander in the Royal Naval Volunteer Reserve, thought that unionists were 'very, very few indeed. Many feel [they] must bow to the inevitable, but there is no talk now.'[30] In Wexford another of Wilson's informants reported that

unionists around this district are growing less and less and those that remain are not as staunch in their opposition to home rule as they formerly were. Many of those would now fail to raise objections to home rule, apparently being complacent and they have not got the fear of it they used to have.[31]

Wilson's evidence of this tendency, the weakening of unionist sentiment in the south of Ireland, is confirmed by the reaction of certain southern unionists to the home rule proposals in 1916. Then some southern unionists said they would be prepared to consider home rule at the end of the war.[32] A more reliable confirmation of this drift than the public declarations of the I.U.A. are the private opinions of 'mild' Dublin unionists (some of whom had been among the most vigorous opponents of the third home rule bill), as expressed to Cecil Harmsworth just after the Rising.[33] One of the unionists Harmsworth interviewed was G. F. Stewart, vice-chairman of the I.U.A., 'a broad minded Dublin unionist' who 'unionist as he is he holds that we have travelled beyond the stage' where the union could be regarded as a permanent solution of Irish government, and looked to federation for the 'ultimate solution'. 'Another mild Dublin unionist', Sir Alfred Callaghan, late secretary of the City of Dublin Steam Packet Company and proprietor of the *Church of Ireland Gazette*, thought that 'the old regime would have worked well enough if it had been given a chance and if administration

29. *Ibid.*, Limerick, 25 Jan. 1916.
30. *Ibid.*, Mayo, 26 Feb. 1916.
31. *Ibid.*, Wexford, 13 Jan. 1916.
32. See below, p. 65.
33. Cecil Harmsworth's report on the views of Dublin unionists, May 1916, B.L., D/14/1/45.

had been in strong hands' and that southern unionists were
reconciled to home rule and 'as long as Redmond himself were
in control would feel tolerably safe and happy.' At first glance,
it is tempting to see some pattern in this evidence of the decline
of unionism in the south of Ireland: there seem to be regional
variations: in some counties unionism remained strong, while in
others it weakened. But, on closer investigation, this pattern
disappears and the tendency for unionism to decline seems a
fairly general and widespread one—geographically speaking.
There were even staunch unionists among the 'mild' Dublin
unionists, as the future rift in southern unionist ranks was to
underline. In Tipperary, though one of Wilson's informants
(apparently a recruiting officer) reckoned that 'feelings are just
as bitter as ever', another, a large land agent, thought that
unionists were 'very weak here' and 'lying low'.[34] The same
discrepancy appears in Waterford. While a naval officer said that
unionists 'are dormant, but they have not thrown up the sponge',
a controller of recruiting reported that unionists are 'very few
and very scattered and very half-hearted. Most of them do not
wish to take any part and wish to let things slide.'[35]

There are several possible explanations for this weakening of
unionist sentiment. The basis of southern unionism was a particular interpretation of the Irish and British situations in relation
to Anglo-Irish interests. It could, therefore, be argued that the
action of Asquith's government in putting the home rule bill on
the statute book caused southern unionists to lose confidence in
the utility and efficacy of the British connection. Certainly some
southern unionists regarded the government's action as a betrayal,
and their sense of grievance may have been confirmed by the
government's refusal to take a firm line with the Irish Volunteers
and by 'a bitter feeling engendered owing to little or no acknow-
ledgement by anyone in the House that the bulk of recruiting in
the south and west has been from the two classes, landlord and
the lowest'.[36] One landowner in the extreme west of Clare felt
'too disgusted for words at times', for although the landlords
claimed 'no special kudos', he thought, 'the fact ought to be

34. Wilson's tour, Tipperary, 16–18 Jan. 1916.
35. *Ibid.*, Waterford, 14–16 Jan. 1916.
36. See e.g. Wilson's tour, Tipperary, 16–18 Jan., Clare, 23 Jan. 1916; Sir
Malby Crofton to I.U.A., 11 Mar. 1916, P.R.O.N.I., D 989A/8/6.

mentioned and rubbed in'.[37] However, too much should not be made of this point. On the whole, southern unionists, though initially angry, were not on reflection too perturbed by the 1914 Home Rule Act, for they came to regard it as a dead letter. Moreover, between 1914 and 1916 they never gave up hope of protection from the British government.

More significant for the weakening of unionist sentiment in the south of Ireland was the effect of the southern unionist concentration upon the war effort on their interpretation of the Irish situation and of Irish nationalism. Two things may be said in explanation of southern unionist willingness to accept Redmond as the first Irish Prime Minister.

In the first place, concentration on the war effort enabled some, though not all, southern unionists to see the Irish question in a different perspective. It was true that the Home Rule Act had been put on the statute book, but the circumstances and conditions surrounding the action encouraged southern unionists to discount the act. Asquith's manoeuvre was regarded as so deceitful and morally wrong as to detract from the moral force of an act of parliament: and the condition that the bill would operate only if an agreement should be reached on Ulster seemed incapable of fulfilment. Moreover, concentration on the war effort meant that neither the Irish question nor the Home Rule Act was a matter for constant discussion or even regarded as an important live issue. Perhaps the euphoria of war affected the judgement of southern unionists, but for this reason they can be excused for regarding home rule as a dead issue. In a sense, the struggle over the union, as they had known it since the 1880s, was over and resolved in their favour. Home rule had been foiled again: the Home Rule Act was never likely to operate. The old controversy seemed dead, and concentration on the war effort meant that the issue slid into the background. This is not to say that southern unionists had changed their minds on the question of the union: what it does suggest is that they had other things to occupy their minds and that any revival of the question of home rule had to be viewed from a different and broader standpoint. One of the main factors in keeping unionism alive in the south of Ireland had been the constant reiteration of the need for unionism, for unionists to

37. Wilson's tour, Clare, 23 Jan. 1916.

organise, but now the danger of imminent home rule was past
and southern unionist energies were absorbed elsewhere. To put
it melodramatically, perhaps with banality, one old battle had
been fought out; honour had been satisfied; and in future the old
protagonists *could* meet on different ground and upon more
equal terms.[38]

In the second place, not only did concentration upon the war
effort *enable* southern unionists to see the Irish question in a
different perspective, it also *encouraged* them to look more
favourably upon the Irish situation and upon Irish nationalists.
Redmond's declaration of support for the war effort and his
endeavours, and those of some of his followers, to get recruits
in Ireland did much to bridge the gulf that had existed since the
1880s between unionists and nationalists in the south. In the first
instance it did so dramatically. On 3 August 1914 Redmond,
speaking in an emotionally charged House of Commons, pledged
Ireland's support for the war. He urged the government forthwith
to remove its troops from the country leaving the defence of the
Irish coasts to the Irish nationalist Volunteers, formed in
November 1913 and since May 1914 controlled by Redmond,
and to the Ulster unionist Volunteers, formed in January 1913.[39]
This speech evoked a warm response among many southern
unionists. It is only a slight exaggeration to say that an emotional
wave swept Ireland. 'From southern unionists expressions of
personal gratitude to Redmond, and of a desire to forget all
former differences, henceforward, were forthcoming at once'.[40]
The idea of regularising both forces of Volunteers, northern and
southern, appealed to many, and several members of the loyalist
class joined the Irish Volunteers and tried to encourage fellow
unionists to do likewise. The list of inspecting officers for the
Irish Volunteers included a prominent liberal unionist peer, the
Earl of Fingall;[41] and one of the most active members of the
I.U.A., Captain Bryan Cooper, came out quickly in support of
Redmond in August 1914. Though he had been unionist M.P.
for Dublin County South in 1910 and one of the I.U.A.'s most

38. This argument is based on a reading of *Notes from Ireland* and speeches on
Ireland in the House of Lords, Sept. 1914–April 1916.

39. D. Gwynn, *Life of John Redmond*, pp. 356–7.

40. *Ibid.*, pp. 365, 374.

41. *Irish Independent*, 7 Aug. 1914.

enthusiastic propagandists between 1912 and 1914, he was a broad minded, intelligent and imaginative man and responded readily to Redmond's patriotism. On 5 August he telegraphed to Redmond 'Your speech has united Ireland. I join National Volunteers today, and will urge every unionist to do same'; and he wrote to the *Irish Times:*

Our response to Mr Redmond's magnificent speech must be an immediate one. I am this day joining the National Volunteers, and I urge every unionist, who is physically fit, to do the same, and show the world that Irishmen can forget their quarrels and stand united against a common danger.[42]

Not only did prominent southern unionists declare their gratitude to Redmond in the national press;[43] action was also taken at a local level. For instance, a public meeting, held in Carlow on 4 August to advocate the fusion of unionists and National Volunteers for the defence of the realm, resulted in the formation of a mounted corps, thirty strong, representing all shades of political opinion;[44] on 5 August a representative meeting of Protestants held at Athlone decided to join the Volunteers; and on the same day the Blackrock and Urban District Council unanimously passed a resolution, proposed by a unionist and seconded by a nationalist, congratulating Redmond and Carson for sinking their differences and for having tendered the services of the Irish and Ulster Volunteers for the defence of the country against the common enemy.[45]

The split in the nationalist Volunteers in September into the National Volunteers, the majority who followed Redmond, and the Irish Volunteers, who, objecting to Irish participation in the war, tried to discourage recruiting, caused some slight waning of this initial enthusiasm,[46] and others were slower to respond; but gradually Redmond's patriotism led to a *détente* between unionists and nationalists. At first, unionists like the twelfth Earl of Meath, the enthusiastic philanthropist and imperialist,[47] and 'Lord F', a

---

42. Lennox Robinson, *Bryan Cooper, passim*; *Irish Times,* 5 Aug. 1914.
43. See e.g. *Irish Times,* 5–8 Aug. 1914.
44. B. Mac G. Choille (ed.), *Intelligence Notes 1913–16* (Dublin 1966), p. 82.
45. *Irish Times,* 6 Aug. 1914.
46. *Intelligence Notes 1913–16*, p. 83.
47. Reginald Brabazon (1841–1929); styled Lord Brabazon, 1851–87; ed. Eton; Foreign Office clerk, 1863, transferring to diplomatic service, 1866; sec.

large landowner and employer of labour in Mayo (probably the
third Baron Oranmore and Browne),[48] saw in the war an opportunity for all parties in Ireland to co-operate in defence of Ireland
and the empire; but they were bewildered 'at finding that
Redmond really was an imperialist who meant to give effect to
his constant professions of friendship towards the empire', and
were suspicious of his good faith.[49] This suspicion of nationalist
good faith was almost traditional, but, owing to the exigencies of
the war, most unionists were willing to be convinced.[50] Thus,
following Redmond's repeated declarations of good faith, his
early attempts to encourage recruiting in Ireland, his tactful
handling of unionist fears and reservations, and the resultant
social peace in Ireland in 1914–15,[51] southern unionists soon began
to co-operate with their former opponents, formally and in-
formally, for recruiting and other purposes. For instance, Lord
Oranmore and Browne wrote to Redmond, telling him of his
pleasure that Redmond was to address a recruiting meeting in the
west of Ireland, and took the opportunity to express his

keen appreciation of the attitude you have taken up with regard to this
question and to assure you that I have taken every opportunity in
talking to the nationalists amongst whom I live to express my eagerness
to assist you in the object you have at heart of persuading Irishmen to
join with Englishmen and Scotchmen in defence of the empire;[52]

to the legation at Athens, 1873; militia a.d.c. to Queen Victoria and Edward VII;
Chancellor of Royal University of Ireland, 1902–6; alderman of London County
Council, 1889–92, 1898–1901; H.S., Co. Wicklow, 1883; H.M.L., Co. Dublin;
founded Empire Day and Hospital Saturday fund; Kilruddery Castle, Bray,
Co. Wicklow.

48. George Henry Browne (1861–1927); ed. Cambridge; sometime lt in 4th
Batt. Royal Scots Fusiliers; Irish representative peer, 1902–27; commissioner of
Congested Districts Board, 1919; senator of Southern Ireland, 1921; Castle
Macgarrett, Claremorris, Co. Mayo.

49. D. Gwynn, *Life of John Redmond*, p. 370; Wilson's tour, West Mayo,
12–14 Apr. 1917. For a good example of initial southern unionist confusion, see
R. Wandesforth to Bernard, 12 Oct. 1914, B.M., Add. MS 52782, ff. 31-2.

50. See e.g. the leader articles in the *Irish Times*, 4 Aug., and *Dublin Daily
Express*, 4, 14 Aug. 1914.

51. Phillips, *The Revolution in Ireland*, pp. 82–6.

52. Oranmore to Redmond, 13 Nov. 1914, N.L.I., MS 15219 (6). He said that
he would have liked to have been on the platform as well, but did not ask since
he recognised that the nationalist leader would have to refer to controversial
issues which he did not agree with and because a strong unionist on the platform
would injure the case.

while, perhaps, the new spirit was testified to more formally by the existence of organisations such as the City of Cork Volunteer Training Corps, with the fourth Earl of Bandon (a unionist and staunch conservative) and the Mayor of Cork (a nationalist) as patrons.[53]

As was to be expected, unionists and nationalists still found room for disagreement, this time over the best way to utilise Irish resources of manpower. Most obviously, they disagreed over the desirability and feasibility of conscription.[54] Yet, as certain southern unionists (and people who may be said to represent their views) argued that

a well-regulated compulsory service would not only obtain the men who ought to be in the fighting ranks, but would prepare the way for a home rule made much less dangerous by the discipline which all the young men of the country would have to pass through,

even this disagreement showed how quickly diminishing were the differences between unionists and nationalists.[55] Moreover, their differences were probably obscured, for practical purposes at any rate, by the common difficulties facing their efforts for recruiting in Ireland. Both suffered from the anti-recruiting activities of the extreme nationalists, and, it seems, a good deal of unionist dismay on this count was directed not against the nationalist leaders but against the British government. 'I do not know', wrote one Sligo unionist in March 1916, 'how the government can go on urging us to use every means to get recruits, while they do nothing to put down a movement which is directed against recruiting, and is I fear doing a great deal to

53. Leaflet of the rules of the City of Cork Volunteer Training Corps, copy in P.R.O.N.I., D 989D/6. This, of course, is only a local example of a national trend, epitomised, perhaps, by the great recruiting meeting at Warrenpoint in Co. Down, 7 July 1915. James Francis Bernard, 4th Earl of Bandon (1850–1924); ed. Eton; a.d.c. to Lord Lieutenant of Ireland, 1874–77; Irish representative peer, 1881–1924; president of the County and City of Cork Unionist Association and of the Cork Defence Union; H.S., Co. Cork, 1875; H.M.L., 1877; Castle Bernard, Bandon, Co. Cork.

54. See e.g. F. Wrench to Carson, 2 July 1915, P.R.O.N.I., D 1507/1/1915/22. He wrote 'we all welcomed the introduction of your registration bill, but we are deeply disappointed that Ireland should be singled out as usual for special treatment'.

55. *Ibid.*

stop it.'[56] The difficulty of the unhelpful and slighting attitude taken by the War Office towards Irish recruitment was an even more potent factor in driving together Irishmen of different political creeds. For instance, Redmond's enthusiasm overcame the initial suspicions of Lord Meath, who, on 15 August, had asked Redmond for an assurance that 'by giving official support and encouragement to the nationalist Volunteers as H.M.L. for the county and city of Dublin I shall in no way fail in any loyal duty to His Majesty the King'.[57] Meath decided to assist Redmond in his recruiting campaign, and their co-operation seems to have been consolidated in face of the War Office's delay in forming an Irish army corps.[58]

It was the same with unionists who went to the front. All classes of Irishmen rubbed shoulders in the trenches, and the experience liberated the thoughts of many unionists from traditional grooves. Before the war they had been prepared to accept, almost unthinkingly, every unionist and anti-nationalist platitude; but the common experience of Irishmen in the war made many of the ascendancy class look upon nationalism and nationalists in a new light. The diminishing significance of long and bitter memories and inherited animosities as a result of the war is seen in the formation of the Irish Division. The war-time army was not a professional one, but an army of officers and men who had themselves, or whose relatives had, played an active part in the agrarian and political struggles of pre-war Ireland. Old social and political barriers, all too often coincident, were thus broken down. Whole units had grown up together. The men in the ranks had watched young officers, who had joined ignorant of the rudiments of drill, acquire knowledge and self-confidence; and in the process had learned to trust them. In training there were many common memories: 'wet days on the Curragh, long treks in the Hampshire dust, scuffles in the hedge-rows during a field-day, bivouacs in a twilight meadow'.[59] All these experiences combined to cement a feeling of friendship between officers and men; and the common experience of action and death made these ties deeper. As Cooper has remarked,

56. Crofton to I.U.A., 11 Mar. 1916, P.R.O.N.I., D 989A/8/6.
57. Gwynn, *Life of John Redmond*, p. 370.
58. *Ibid.*, p. 396; Meath to Redmond, 10, 14, 17 Oct. 1914, N.L.I., MS 15206 (3).
59. Bryan Cooper, *The Tenth Irish Division in Gallipoli* (1918), p. 251.

It was not merely number so-and-so Private Kelly who was killed, it was little Kelly, who had cooked (very badly) for the mess at Basing-stoke, or Kelly who had begged so eagerly not to be left behind with the first reinforcements, or Kelly, the only son of a widowed mother, who lived on the Churchtown road, three miles from home.[60]

How far these soldiering days broke down old barriers is well testified by Cooper, in his vivid history of the 10th Division. All the bitter memories 'went for nothing', as Irishmen united for a common purpose:

. . . the bond of common service and common sacrifice proved so strong and enduring that Catholic and Protestant, unionist and nationalist, lived and fought and died side by side like brothers. Little was spoken concerning the points on which we differed, and once we had tacitly agreed to let the past be buried we found thousands of points on which we agreed. To an Englishman this no doubt seems natural, for beneath all superficial disagreements the English do possess a nature in common and look on things from the same point of view, but in Ireland up to the present things have been very different.[61]

The potential effect of such a *détente* on the unionism of ascendancy soldiers must have been enormous; and thus the case of Bryan Cooper should be seen as only an outstanding example of the weakening effect of the war upon the unionism of the Anglo-Irish serving at the front. He was not the best of soldiers, being temperamentally and constitutionally unsuited for such a tough life; but he did join the Connaught Rangers (part of the 10th Division) and threw himself wholeheartedly and enthusias-tically into the war effort, as his mentions in despatches testify.[62] This experience weakened his unionism: on the one hand, it removed him from the environment and tradition which caused and required his mind to run on conventional tracks; and, on the other hand, it brought him more and more into contact with ordinary Irishmen, the common experience of hardship and particularly death breaking down old barriers of Irish life. Before the war Cooper had been a staunch unionist and his life had been a little sheltered. As a young boy at Eton, Cooper had been influenced by the Gaelic revival, particularly Douglas Hyde's

60. *Ibid.*, pp. 251–2.
61. *Ibid.*, p. 253.
62. Lennox Robinson, *Bryan Cooper*, pp. 91–107.

Love Songs of Connaught; but tradition and the influence of his forceful grandfather, 'the last of the line of benevolent despots',[63] had forced him to accept the role of a country gentleman and master of Markree Castle. Despite his electioneering which brought him into contact with a few people who were not of his own way of thinking, Cooper had mixed mainly with his own class. His soldiering, however, altered this: his experience in the wartime army brought him into contact with the ordinary man and he acquired and never lost 'a deep sympathy for the ordinary man, above all for the soldier'.[64] As his history of the 10th Division shows, his soldiering days indelibly coloured his future and his views, giving him a more tolerant and appreciative attitude to Irish nationalism and completing the process fired off by Redmond's patriotic declaration.[65] Cooper was a unionist in transition. On occasion, it showed itself in humorous ways: he bore chaff with an unfailing good temper, as on one march, when, with his company leading, the band played 'A nation once again', not once but three times. But after the war it revealed itself in more serious ways, for he came back to Ireland in 1919 a changed man. No longer was he content to throw 'on the counter every used coin of unionism', but he put himself in the most advanced line of southern unionism: advocating a settlement of the home rule issue; willing to appreciate the ideals and attitudes of Irish nationalists, particularly of the Sinn Fein variety; and as a press censor in Dublin in 1919–20, interpreting regulations so as to get a 'square deal' for Ireland.[66]

Much detailed and local work needs to be done on the question of recruitment in Ireland, but it does seem reasonable to suggest that this co-operation between unionists and nationalists over recruitment and at the front enabled and encouraged southern unionists to revise their estimate of the Irish situation and of the Irish nationalists. Not surprisingly, some southern unionists were never able to do this, and men like Wilson and D. Williams, the coach builder in Cork, found their worst suspicions of Redmond and the nationalists confirmed by what they regarded as nationalist hypocrisy in supporting the war effort. They saw sinister motives

63. *Ibid.*, pp. 27–8.
64. *Ibid.*, p. 94.
65. See also Lennox Robinson's comments, *ibid.*, pp. 93–4.
66. *Ibid.*, pp. 92–3, 110, 114–23.

behind the demand to arm the National Volunteers and regarded Redmond's recruiting activities as a covert attempt to foster and to keep alive nationalism. What they wanted was firm and aggressive government to put down the Irish Volunteers and to implement a vigorous measure of conscription. They wanted to exalt Ireland's status, her patriotism, by the extension of British war measures to Ireland, and the refusal of Irish nationalists to countenance conscription only activated and increased their suspicions of and their contempt for nationalists.[67]

Nevertheless, despite this strong feeling on the part of some southern unionists, there are indications that unionists were pleased and surprised that they could work smoothly with the nationalists, and saw the possibility of further co-operation in the future. Perhaps these contradictory and divisive tendencies can best be illustrated by a quotation from a letter which Williams wrote to Wilson, explaining indignantly that recruiting drives in Cork relied upon green flags with yellow harps, military bands playing Irish airs including very frequently 'A nation once again' and 'For the wearing of the green', and, on one occasion, a large white banner with the words 'Home Rule' and 'Ireland freed from Conscription and Compulsion'.[68] Williams tried to follow up the matter, but found little satisfaction when he took it up with a staunch unionist member of the recruiting committee. Williams reported to Wilson that:

. . . I went yesterday to see a prominent and active member of [the] recruiting committee, whom I knew to be a staunch unionist, and I caught him today at his business place and had a word with him . . . I knew my man, but was sure *he* would *think* of this banner as I do. Well, he told me, he really did not bother to read this . . . I said ' . . . is it not *playing the game very low* to put "home rule" out. You know it is unlikely, [the] present bill, and this practically says "you are getting it".

He replied—'I don't say we will get *that* bill, but we will get *some form* of home rule. I believe matters will be much altered and politics much dead after the war . . . And there is a *great change*, and I, personally, see nothing in playing these airs, in green flags, banner or anything else, for recruiting purposes. I thought it wonderful for me, differing

67. Wilson to Carson, 6 May, 19 Oct., 3 Nov. 1915, P.R.O.N.I., D 1507/1/1915/15, 46, 63; D. Williams to Wilson, 15 Feb. 1916, *ibid.*, D 989A/8/7.
68. Williams to Wilson, 15 Feb. 1916, *ibid.*

both ways, to be on platforms in the county at meetings with parish priest on one side and the biggest of nationalists on [the] other side of me'.

I said—'What was wonderful in it? Surely you realise they all know *their* skins are in danger as well as *yours* and *mine*. It is to *their interest* as well as ours to save the country. What thanks is due. As to the here-after, I disagree with you as to *no politics* and present unanimity prevailing. . . .'

He said—'Oh, the Shin [*sic*] Fein men *must* be put down, and whatever *you* may think of Irish National Volunteers, you will find very soon now the government will *recognise* them; they will take the oath, be armed, put on *home defence,* and then the *Irish* volunteers will be *dis*armed or put in jail if caught with arms, as, when we have the National Volunteers under [the] war office [and] recognised, there will be an order "no arms allowed only to men having taken the oath of allegiance".'

I replied—'They will be useful (?) if they guard the bridges as they did before for [a] few weeks they were recognised without the oath, and it would be better business on [the] government's part, and [a] safer test, to get all these young men in [the] National Volunteers to join [the] army and go across from here. The police can do the home defence. Otherwise the volunteers are *armed* for *another* war, "nearer home", after the German war is over . . .'

FOUR

The drift of southern unionism in the war was thus away from the old policy of negative unionism. There were still southern unionists who remained hostile to nationalists and Irish national-ism, but unionist organisation in the south was disintegrating, and whereas the overshadowing of the Irish question by the war enabled southern unionists to look again at the Irish situation, their experience of co-operation with the nationalists in the war effort enabled and encouraged them to re-appraise in a favourable light the claims of Irish nationalism. Perhaps, sooner or later, the conscription issue would have once more erected barriers between nationalists and unionists. More probably, had the atmosphere of 1914–16 been allowed to continue, southern unionist opinion would have acquiesced in home rule. Or rather, such a large body of southern unionists would have accepted the necessity for some form of home rule that even a determined, die-hard minority would have been discouraged.

III

Phase Three: The Rising and Reaction, May–July 1916

THIS happy tendency was interrupted by the Easter Rising. It is ironic that southern unionist views of Redmond were being revised just when he and the Irish Parliamentary Party were about to be seriously challenged by extreme nationalists. Discontent with Redmond's policies of parliamentary agitation and a limited form of home rule had been voiced by such bodies as Arthur Griffith's Sinn Fein party, formally established as such in 1905, the Irish Republican Brotherhood, which had been behind the formation of the Irish Volunteers in November 1913, and James Connolly's Irish Citizen Army, founded in October 1913; but such critics had made little headway. Redmond appeared supreme in the first years of the war. In April 1916, however, the Irish Republican Brotherhood and the Citizen Army enacted a blood sacrifice to re-awaken Irishmen to a sense of their nationality. On 24 April 1916, Easter Monday, a section of the Irish Volunteers and the Citizen Army occupied part of the city of Dublin and proclaimed the Irish republic.

As a military uprising with only some 2,000 men in the field, the Easter Rising was a failure. It was soon crushed once the government had recovered from its surprise, and Padraic Pearse surrendered at 3.30 p.m. on Saturday, 29 April, after 1,000 had been killed or wounded and Dublin had suffered £3 million worth of damage. Nevertheless, the men of 1916, with the aid of the British government who swiftly executed fifteen of the leaders, were not without their successes. If their aim was to discredit the Irish Parliamentary Party and to prevent a moderate settlement of the Irish question, they certainly succeeded. Not only did the Rising and its aftermath create sympathy for Sinn Fein; it also caused a southern unionist reaction which helped to thwart a limited settlement in July 1916.

TWO

Although southern unionists had repeatedly warned the government of the possibility of a rising, and had been ignored,[1] the actual outbreak still came as a shock to them. Some of their correspondents enjoyed the experience and the excitement,[2] but for the majority the Rising was a traumatic experience. The fighting, the breakdown of communications, the rumours, the ignorance of what was actually happening, all had an effect upon southern unionists that far outlasted the actual events of the Rising.[3] Apprehension and anger should not be confused with cowardice, for a man such as Midleton showed great energy, initiative and courage in protecting his property in Cork;[4] but most loyalists were apprehensive and angry. It is true that few unionists were wounded, like Bagwell of Clonmel, and not many seem to have lost much property.[5] It is also true that southern unionist propaganda exaggerated the extent of disorder in Ireland. But these very exaggerations are significant of the state of mind of southern unionists in 1916; the exaggerations reflected the insecurity they felt. In Dublin the houses of some of the unionist class stood, like Archbishop Bernard's, near to the chief points seized by the rebels: and the situation was felt to be as bad outside of Dublin. Sir William Joshua Goulding, who had been under fire for two days at Kingsbridge, wrote to Law, the unionist leader and Secretary of State for the Colonies, that newspaper reports (that the rebellion had been confined to Dublin and that the rest of Ireland was believed to be quiet) were 'absolutely false'. He continued

In my own county Kildare three fourths of the people were waiting for news of a success of the rebels to at once join in, so-called National Volunteers and others—and I have met every train from the country

1. Copy of a report on arming and drilling in Ireland sent by the I.U.A. to Lords Barrymore and Midleton, 6 Mar. 1916, and communicated by them to the government, P.R.O.N.I., D 989A/9/8; Midleton, *Records and Reactions*, pp. 228–9.
2. J. A. Maconchy to Bernard, 6 May 1916, B.M., Add. MS 52782, f. 59.
3. For the daily reactions of a Wicklow unionist to the events and rumours of the Rising, see the diary of Lady Alice Mary Howard, 1915–16, N.L.I., MS 3622.
4. Midleton, *Records and Reactions*, pp. 230–2.
5. William Ridgeway to Bernard, n.d., B.M., Add. MS 52782, ff. 57–8.

and friends from all parts of the south and west have told me that it was
exactly the same in every county.[6]

The Rising was not so highly organised or so widely supported
as people like Goulding believed, but it is interesting to see how
common were his fears among men of his ilk. For instance, the
Bishop of Tuam, County Galway, felt unable to attend a meeting
of Church of Ireland bishops on 17 May, because 'things are in a
very unsettled state here in the west' and 'my place is for the
moment among my clergy and people and so I am not leaving
home this week'.[7] According to the bishop,

Public opinion is moving in the direction of open sympathy with the
rebels and is showing itself by every kind of anti-English feeling and
expression.

Our western rebels are still at large and with the people now aiding
them in their efforts at evading the police, it will be some time before
we will feel secure.

Only last Saturday the Tuam train was attacked with stones and
fire-arms a few miles outside of the town.

I confess to feeling very anxious about the immediate future and if
I diagnose the under current of feeling correctly we may be on the
verge of great trouble in the west.

The National Volunteers are well armed and they only wait to see
what attitude Redmond and co. assume and they are ready to lead
an anti-British crusade.

It is possible also that even Redmond will not long be able to hold
them in control.

The total disarmament of north and south seems to be the only
possible solution.[8]

The effect of the Rising was thus to drive out from the minds of
even the most mild southern unionists thoughts of home rule in
1916, for they saw the need of the moment to be firm govern-

6. Goulding to Law, 4 May 1916, B.L., 53/2/5. Goulding, 1st bt (1856–1925);
chairman, W. and H. M. Goulding Ltd, chemical manufacturers; director,
National Bank; chairman, Great Southern and Western Railway of Ireland;
deputy chairman, Fishguard and Rosslare Harbours and Railway Co.; chairman,
Irish Railways Clearing House; chairman, Property Losses (Ireland) Commission,
1916; bt, 1904; P.C., 1917; senator for Southern Ireland, 1921; J.P., D.L.;
Millicent, Sallins, Co. Kildare; Luttrellstown, Clonsilla, Co. Dublin.
7. Bishop of Tuam to Archbishop of Armagh, 16 May 1916, B.L., D/14/1/45.
8. *Ibid.*

ment.[9] Even the usually restrained Bernard called for severe and relentless action on the part of the government.[10] On the whole the extreme and the mild unionists urged and supported the execution of the ringleaders of the Rising and demanded the continuance of martial law, the total disarmament of north and south, the appointment of a strong government representative in Ireland, and were disappointed that conscription was not applied to Ireland in May.[11] Bernard's demand for severely drastic measures has been described as proceeding 'from the wounded pride of a member of the caste the dominance of which was threatened', and this may be taken as a fair description of the southern unionist attitude in 1916.[12] They did feel threatened, and what they feared most in 1916 (next to another rebellion) was weakness on the part of the British government. One unionist wrote to Carson,

There is no use in blinking the fact that the greatest apprehension is felt here that too much indulgence will be granted by the cabinet to the *ad misericordiam* of Redmond and co.

No one asks for vengeance, but weakness now would be fatal.[13]

THREE

The southern unionists were therefore in no mood to accept without protest proposals for a compromise settlement of the Irish question made in May 1916 by Lloyd George, then Minister of Munitions, supposedly on behalf of the coalition government in power since 25 May 1915. Asquith, the Prime Minister, after visiting Irishmen whom he considered representative of all shades of political opinion in Ireland, reckoned that the Rising provided

9. See e.g. Cecil Harmsworth's report on the views of Dublin unionists, including those of Sir William Goulding, B.L., D/14/1/45. Harmsworth reported Goulding as being 'one of the most important business men in Ireland. A unionist of the usual mild Dublin type who is reconciled to the eventual coming of home rule but earnestly deprecates any immediate instalment of home rule on the novel ground among others that Redmond has lost too much power to be able to govern Ireland.'

10. Bernard's letter in *The Times*, 5 May 1916; Murray, *Archbishop Bernard*, pp. 235–6.

11. See e.g. Balfour to Bernard, 11 May 1916, B.M., Add. MS 52782, f. 72; Wilson to Carson, 11 May 1916, P.R.O.N.I., D 1507/1/1916/19; C. Harmsworth to Baron Northcliffe, 23 May 1916, B.L., D/14/1/8.

12. Murray, *Archbishop Bernard*, p. 236.

13. Wilson to Carson, 11 May 1916, P.R.O.N.I., D 1507/1/1916/19.

an opportunity to effect a settlement, and he persuaded the cabinet, which included eight unionists, to agree to Lloyd George's seeing if he could bring the various Irish parties to agree upon a settlement that could be implemented after the war.[14]

Lloyd George soon discovered that Redmond would not agree to any settlement that did not include immediate home rule, and, therefore, he proceeded, without cabinet consent, on that basis to persuade Carson to accept home rule. Evidently, he misled Carson by giving the impression that the cabinet supported the proposals which he put forward for the operation of the 1914 act suitably modified to meet Ulster unionists' objections, and Carson was persuaded that a settlement was necessary.[15] The failure of the Lloyd George negotiations to bring Redmond and Carson to ultimate agreement on the basis of home rule plus exclusion is too well known to need recounting here in all its detail. What is less well known is the role played by the southern unionists in these negotiations, and the failure of Lloyd George to win over the southern unionists. Not that he did not try. The 1916 negotiations show Lloyd George's methods well. He identified the parties to be dealt with and refused to allow himself to be distracted by deputations from Ulster liberals and from the Irish labour movement.[16] He saw that the problem lay in getting the three major political groupings in Ireland to agree: in persuading Carson and Redmond to agree upon a settlement, and in keeping quiet the southern unionists and inducing them to accept the Redmond-Carson agreement.

Having persuaded Redmond to consider home rule and exclusion Lloyd George set about winning over the southern

---

14. Jenkins, *Asquith*, pp. 395–402; Asquith's report on his visit to Ireland, 19 May 1916, B.U.L., AC 14/5/22, 23. For the terms on which Lloyd George was supposed to meet the several Irish parties, see a cabinet memorandum by Lord Lansdowne on 'The proposed Irish settlement', 21 June 1916, *ibid.*, AC 14/5/26. (The cabinet papers relating to the Irish question in 1916 were first consulted in the Austen Chamberlain and Asquith collections, and these are the references given below. Since this chapter was first drafted, the cabinet papers have become available in the P.R.O., reference Cab. 37/148, 150, 151, 152.)

15. D. Gwynn, *Life of John Redmond*, ch. XIV; Colvin, *Life of Lord Carson*, iii. chaps XVII and XVIII. For the unionist ministers' ignorance of the way in which negotiations subsequently developed, see e.g. Austen Chamberlain to Asquith, 22 and 23 June 1916, and Asquith to Chamberlain, 22 June 1916, B.U.L., AC 15/1/4, 9, 10.

16. B.L., D/14/3/23, 30.

unionists to the scheme. To judge from the way he refused Carson's offer to represent them, it seems that Lloyd George thought that his task would not be difficult.[17] He had isolated the three major parties and was to negotiate separately with each of them. Thus, on 26 May, he wrote to Midleton that he was anxious to talk with him and, say, Barrymore in the next week about the position of the 'Irish Protestant unionists in the south of Ireland' and their attitude towards a settlement of the problems of Irish government.[18] On 29 May he met Midleton and, it seems, (owing to the illness of Barrymore and the advice of Walter Long, president of the Local Government Board) Stewart, the vice-chairman of the I.U.A., and put his proposals to the anxious pair.[19] Southern unionists had become worried about rumours of an impending settlement, and were determined to get to the bottom of them. Stewart's arrival in London and the activities of other southern unionists, such as Midleton and Wilson, underlined for Lloyd George the importance of obtaining the consent of southern unionists to any proposals aiming at a settlement of the Irish question, and the need to persuade them to accept the settlement. On the one hand, it became clear that southern unionists were not to be easily convinced; on the other hand, it was clear that the attitude of certain cabinet ministers to a settlement depended very much upon the willingness of southern unionists to submit to a settlement.[20] Thus Lloyd George became even more anxious to discuss the situation with them, and devoted a considerable part of his time in June interviewing them.[21] In the week preceding 8 June, he spent mornings and afternoons discussing the possibility of a settlement with southern unionists, and received deputations from the I.U.A. on 23 and 27 June.[22]

17. Colvin, *Life of Lord Carson*, iii. 165.
18. Lloyd George to Midleton, 26 May 1916, B.L., D/14/1/25.
19. Memorandum of meeting with Lloyd George, 29 May 1916, P.R.O., 30/67/31, ff. 1618–24; memoranda by Long on 'The Irish situation', 15 June 1916, B.U.L., AC 14/5/13, 14; Long to Lloyd George, 29 May 1916, B.L., D/14/1/37; G. F. Stewart to Long, 31 May 1916, *ibid.*, D/14/1/45.
20. See below, pp. 71–5.
21. Midleton to Lloyd George, 30 May, 2 June 1916, B.L., D/14/1/40 and D/14/2/4; Lloyd George to Carson, 3 June 1916, P.R.O.N.I., D 1507/1/1916/25; Wilson to Midleton, 22 June 1916, *ibid.*, D 989A/8/10.
22. Lloyd George to John Dillon, 9 June 1916, B.L., D/14/2/20; notes of appointments for interviews between Lloyd George and various Irish represen-

Lloyd George seems to have handled the southern unionists with his accustomed skill, appearing, as was his wont, all things to all men. He put his case for a settlement to the southern unionists with charm and courtesy: on the one hand, he emphasised the imperial necessity for a settlement, the need to win over opinion in the United States, and the position taken up by the British cabinet; on the other hand, he suggested certain safeguards for the loyal minority in such a way that some southern unionists believed he was making definite offers instead of (as it turned out) putting forward some points as the basis for discussion.[23] Lloyd George's efforts were not wholly unsuccessful, for the southern unionists were persuaded by the end of June to suggest what safeguards they would require in the event of home rule becoming law.[24] But they did so grudgingly and without abandoning the principle of union, and in the main, with one or two exceptions, southern unionists proved less tractable than either Carson or Redmond. As Lloyd George wrote to John Dillon, Redmond's second in command, on 9 June, he had been interviewing southern unionists all week and found them 'very irreconcilable' with only a few reasonable.[25]

Lloyd George was not exaggerating the extent of southern unionist hostility to a settlement in 1916. They refused to accept

tatives, *ibid.,* D/15/1/13; Wilson to D. Davies, 22 June 1916, *ibid.,* D/14/3/32; memorandum of the southern unionist deputation's views to lay before the ministers, with a list of names of the deputation, 19 and 23 June 1916, P.R.O.N.I., D 989A/9/5; *Notes from Ireland* (1916), pp. 33–4.

23. See e.g. Memorandum of meeting with Lloyd George, 29 May 1916, P.R.O., 30/67/31, ff. 1618–24; Stewart to Long, 31 May 1916, B.L., D/14/1/45; Stewart to Lloyd George, 12 June 1916, *ibid.,* D/14/2/34; Stewart's telegram to Lloyd George, and Lloyd George's reply, 16 June 1916, *ibid.,* D/14/3/6, 7; Wilson to Lloyd George, 6 June 1916, P.R.O.N.I., D 989A/8/10 and B.L., D/14/2/15. The safeguards he suggested were: special representation in the Irish senate and executive (two ministers in a cabinet of seven); two changes in the 1914 act (allowing appeals from the lowest courts and a supreme court in London, and providing that whatever statutes were to be subsequently law in Ireland should be re-enacted after the war); and a continuation of martial law for the present.

24. Memorandum on the interview between the southern unionist deputation and the Prime Minister and Lloyd George, 27 June 1916, P.R.O.N.I., D 989A/9/8. The southern unionists' suggestions for possible safeguards were circulated in July among the cabinet together with the damning comments of Sir Arthur Thring, an expert parliamentary draftsman, B.U.L., AC 14/5/41. This memorandum is reproduced in Appendix C.

25. Lloyd George to Dillon, 9 June 1916, B.L., D/14/2/20.

his view of the need for agreement and were impervious to his coaxings. One member of a deputation that waited on Lloyd George at the beginning of June, after placing on record 'my appreciation of your great courtesy and candour', ventured 'a word or two of warning'. Safeguards were 'quite immaterial and would be utterly worthless', but Lloyd George's appeal 'to us of patriotism would not have fallen on deaf ears had we been persuaded that the fate of the war, conceivably if not probably, depended on a "settlement" in Ireland, but, sir, we are absolutely convinced that no settlement at such a moment as this would have anything but the opposite effect which you surmise'.[26] In fact, the southern unionists decisively rejected all the arguments in favour of a settlement in 1916.

They refused to accept the assertion that the system of government under the union had broken down and that a settlement was necessary for the success of the war effort. They scathingly denied the validity of the American argument, and reckoned that any concession in 1916 would hinder the war effort.[27] As a deputation from the I.U.A. told Asquith and Lloyd George, they failed to see

how it would benefit the empire in the prosecution of the war, to give a section of the community hostile to England free scope for their operations, enabling them to give assistance to her enemies, in a country which from every point of view, strategic and otherwise, it is vital for England to control.[28]

As has been said, according to southern unionists what Ireland needed in 1916 was firm government to protect loyalists, to hinder disloyalists, and to assist the war effort; and they were quite convinced that these things could be achieved only under the union honestly operated. Nothing Lloyd George could say would move them from that position.

Apart from objections to the details of the proposed settlement, there were two broad reasons that led southern unionists to reject Lloyd George's arguments in favour of a settlement and to re-

26. Wilson to Lloyd George, 6 June 1916, P.R.O.N.I., D 989A/8/10 and B.L., D/14/2/15.

27. *Ibid.*; Midleton, *Records and Reactions*, pp. 233-4; see also the resolutions passed by various unionist organisations in the south of Ireland in June 1916, *Notes from Ireland* (1916), pp. 35-6.

28. *Ibid.*, p. 34.

affirm their faith in the union, though both were rooted in the effect of the traumatic experience of the Rising on southern unionists. In the first place, they were vexed that the government should try to break the party truce and reward sedition at the expense of loyalty, and this sense of betrayal made them ill-disposed to listen to arguments in favour of home rule in 1916. Later on the fact that the U.U.C. had consented to partition in 1916 weighed heavily with some southern unionists; but, though they did hope that all unionists in Ireland would be able to unite in opposition to home rule, the fact that Ulster unionists decided in favour of a settlement was only of marginal significance for the sense of betrayal and desertion felt by southern unionists in 1916.[29] The southern unionists were more indignant with the British government than with the Ulster unionists. For instance, the Cork Junior Unionist Alliance

viewed with horror and shame the breach on the part of the government of the compact by which the vexed question of home rule was to be postponed until after the war;

and the executive council of the more sedate Unionist Registration Association of South Co. Dublin, 'a constituency containing many of the most representative property owners and professional and commercial and business men in Ireland, as well as a very large number of loyalists of the artisan and other classes', protested

in the strongest manner against the breach of the political truce involved in the action of the coalition government in bringing the home rule question again into controversy, and attempting to rush through great constitutional changes in Ireland in the midst of the war.[30]

It would be unfair and incorrect to say that southern unionists gave their support for the war effort only on the understanding that home rule would be dropped, but many southern unionists did believe that their loyal and enthusiastic support for the war gave them claim for better and more considerate treatment from

29. Stewart to Long, 31 May 1916, B.L., D/14/1/45; Stewart to Montgomery, 18 June 1916, Montgomery to G. de L. Willis, 15, 17 June 1916, P.R.O.N.I., D 627/429.
30. *Notes from Ireland* (1916), pp. 35–6.

the government. And it is because it is significant of the extent to which southern unionists felt that they were being betrayed, that a pathetic letter written in protest by one southern loyalist to Law is worth quoting at length:

With all respect I write to you as the leader of [the] unionist party to beseech of you to think before committing such a gross breach of trust as to be a party to the breaking of the *truce* entered into at the outbreak of war . . . On the strength of assurances given to loyalists in this country they have given their all for the empire . . . Have you no thought of what you have got by these assurances? Do you not intend to make good your promises on the strength of which you got the blood and bone of loyalist Ireland? . . . Is the tearing of the solemn truce or covenant you made not as bad as the Kaiser's tearing of the treaty with Belgium? I say it is worse. You are a Briton. You are aiding and pleasing Germany if you assist or please Casement's friends . . . In God's name, I ask you to think of the after consequences of any breach of faith with parents of men who have given their lives on guarantees by you. I myself have given 2 sons being assured that home rule would not come on till after [an] amending bill was considered and passed *after* the war. How can you say 'I am an honest man' if this pledge is broken. Yours in trouble . . .[31]

In different circumstances, the southern unionists' sense of outraged loyalty might have completed the decay of unionism in the south of Ireland, in train since the beginning of the war. In the middle of 1916, however, this was unlikely. Not only did the close links that southern unionists had in British politics encourage them to believe that the British connection was still a living thing and that they could, by exploiting these contacts, defeat Lloyd George's scheme:[32] but, more importantly, the southern unionists' interpretation of the Irish situation made them cling more closely to the union.

This was the second reason why southern unionists rejected any settlement in 1916. They were once again apprehensive about the future of Ireland and this apprehension enabled them to reject Lloyd George's rosy view of the future of Ireland under home rule. The Rising and the subsequent growth of Sinn Fein

31. David Turner (1 Mount Pleasant Square, Rathmines, Dublin) to Law, 9 July 1916, B.L., 53/3/8.
32. See below, pp. 62–3, 69, 77–8.

had come as a shock to southern unionists who feared for the future peace of Ireland in the event of home rule being conceded in 1916. They explained this revulsion in favour of Sinn Fein and against constitutional nationalism in prosaic terms. According to Goulding, Redmond's weakness arose not only from his having alienated extreme men by his patriotic attitude during the war, but also from the fact that the Irish farmers had hardened off into conservatism and had lost interest in home rule. Although tradition, loyalty, the sense of past favours, the party machine, kept the farmers faithful to the nationalist party, and although the farmers were unlikely to run to any extreme, their lukewarmness for Redmond created an unstable political situation in Ireland.[33] Orderly government under a Dublin parliament seemed an impossibility. It was not only that southern unionists still thought that they would be excluded from office and would not receive 'fair play and toleration' under home rule. Admittedly, that was still likely, especially as events since the Rising had shown that Redmond could not control the people of Ireland, and Sinn Fein would soon become the dominant power in the country.[34] But what weighed more heavily with southern unionists was the fact that concessions in 1916 would be regarded as a triumph for those who brought about the rebellion, and would put a premium on revolutionary and violent methods in Ireland. According to the vice-chairman of the I.U.A., in a very sensible memorandum to Long at the end of May 1916, the strongest objection to home rule was

the fact that the proposed change in the government of Ireland would practically justify the recent Sinn Fein rebellion. The Sinn Feiners rebelled against what was known as Castle rule, now it is to be swept away, root and branch, and a nationalist government established in its place. Therefore it will be said that the Sinn Feiners were right and the next time a change of government is desired the methods of 1916 will be preached and followed.[35]

33. See e.g. Harmsworth's report on Goulding's views on the Irish situation, May 1916, B.L., D/14/1/45.

34. See e.g. J. H. Scott to Law, 27 June 1916, B.L., 53/3/8, and the resolution passed at a meeting of members of both houses of parliament with interests in the south of Ireland, 6 June 1916, *ibid.*, 53/3/3.

35. Stewart to Long, 31 May 1916, B.L., *ibid.*, D/14/1/45. For an interesting article by a 'Southern Presbyterian' who tries to adjust the old arguments against home rule to the new situation in 1916, see *The Witness*, 26 May 1916.

This combination of outraged loyalty and apprehension galvanised southern unionists into action once more, with the result that Lloyd George's failure to win them over had a twofold effect. Not only did he fail to convince them of the need for a settlement in 1916; he also failed to prevent them from working against his proposals; for, having learnt what he intended, they set themselves and their organisation to defeat the Lloyd George scheme.

FOUR

That, with one or two exceptions, the southern unionists should prove less tractable than either Redmond or Carson must have come as a shock to Lloyd George. Nevertheless, it was quite understandable. Whereas both Redmond and Carson had something definite to gain from such a settlement as Lloyd George proposed, the southern unionists considered that they had everything to lose. Moreover, the southern unionists, who, unlike the Ulster unionists, had strong connections in British politics, were little inclined to accept lightly Lloyd George's view of the cabinet's attitude and had no hesitation in discussing the situation with the leaders of the unionist party, and especially with Lord Lansdowne, Minister without Portfolio but in the cabinet, and Long.[36] Though the importance of these contacts for the success of southern unionist agitation can scarcely be overemphasised, their significance should not be misunderstood. In 1916 British contacts did not cause southern unionists to oppose a settlement; indeed, as will be shown later on, the reverse was the case. The existence and knowledge of these contacts did, however, give southern unionists more confidence in the acceptability of their independently determined views and a wider range of political manoeuvre than was possible for either Redmond or Carson. Moreover, the advice of men such as Lansdowne and Long not only helped to direct southern unionist agitation to where it would be most effective, but also strengthened the resolve of waverers, such as Stewart and the Irish (unionist) government officials who

36. Lansdowne, 'The proposed Irish settlement', 21 June 1916; Long, 'The Irish situation', 15 June 1916.

were in danger of being overawed by the attention paid to them by erstwhile and skilful opponents such as Asquith and Lloyd George.[37]

Once their susceptibilities were aroused the southern unionists and their organisation were quick to respond. As soon as Asquith made his announcement in the House of Commons on 25 May, some members of both houses of parliament who had interests in the south of Ireland, 'greatly disturbed at the announcements recently made', met and passed a resolution viewing with 'apprehension the opening of the vexed question of home rule'; and threatened to campaign actively against a settlement.[38] Their hostility to a settlement in 1916 was shared by their fellow-unionists in the south of Ireland. The bishops of the Church of Ireland were forced by the southern Irish bishops to pass, in effect, a resolution critical of the attempted settlement.[39] Opponents of a settlement worked vigorously to close southern unionist ranks.[40] Feeling ran high among unionists in the south and west, especially in and around Dublin, and such pressure was put upon individuals that waverers began to find their lives unbearable.[41] Deep-thinking people who could see advantages in a settlement kept silent, and others who had not spoken un-favourably about the prospects of a settlement when confronted by Lloyd George or Asquith quickly changed their minds.[42] This was particularly true of the Irish officials upon whose testimony

37. See e.g. Wilson to Stewart, to A. Jameson, and to E. Watson, 16 June 1916, to F. Brooke, 22 June 1916, and to H. Franks, 1 July 1916, P.R.O.N.I., D 989A/8/10; Stewart to Long, 31 May 1916, B.L., D/14/1/45; R. Chalmers to M. Bonham Carter, 30 June 1916, Bodleian, Asquith papers, 37/77-8.

38. Midleton to Asquith, 26 May 1916, enclosing a resolution representing the unanimous opinion of 'the association of peers and Commons members connected with the 3 provinces outside Ulster', B.L., D/14/1/26.

39. Dr Crozier (Archbishop of Armagh and Primate of all Ireland) to Carson, 26 June 1916, Bishop of Down to Carson, 27 June 1916, P.R.O.N.I., D 1507/1/1916/37, 37A.

40. See e.g. Wilson to Hon. Claude Anson and to Franks, 16 June 1916, P.R.O.N.I., D 989A/8/10.

41. See e.g. Montgomery to Carson, 9 June 1916, P.R.O.N.I., D 627/429; Chalmers to Bonham Carter, 30 June 1916, Bodleian, Asquith papers, 37/77-8; Stewart's telegram to Lloyd George, 16 June 1916, complaining that 'my position has become intolerable', B.L., D/14/3/6.

42. F. Wrench to Lloyd George, reporting the private views of Bernard, 3 June 1916, B.L., D/14/2/9; Stewart to Lloyd George, 12, 16 June 1916, *ibid.*, D/14/2/34 and D/14/3/6.

Asquith had relied in May when giving the cabinet indications of a desire for a settlement and with whom Lloyd George was in close contact. Perhaps their heads had been so turned and their ambitions so stimulated by consultation with the Prime Minister and his 'deputy' that, answering within the framework of their chiefs' political ideas, they ignored the feelings of their fellow-unionists whom they had little opportunity to consult. And probably their heads were turned sharply back again on account of the vehement protests of the unionists amongst whom they had to live.[43] At any rate, by June, having experienced the hostility of southern unionists to the Lloyd George proposals, the Irish Attorney-General, James Campbell, for instance, had changed his mind. No longer could he see manifold advantages in a settlement; and in a rather heated memorandum (which only just avoided admitting that he had completely misjudged the political climate in Ireland), circulated to the cabinet, Campbell re-affirmed his faith in the union.[44] The more southern unionists learned about the proposed settlement, the more determined they were to defeat it. A new vigour affected the I.U.A. The central committee, hitherto discreet in the war, published strong resolutions hostile to any settlement, and in this it was backed by some of its various branches and affiliated associations in the south of Ireland and by the ladies of Dublin.[45]

Southern unionists were clever in using their resources. They had hoped that all Irish unionists could and would unite on general grounds in opposition to home rule in 1916; but having failed to stir up Ulster unionists, they tried to excite the anta-

43. Wrench to Lloyd George, 3, 22 June, 3 July 1916, B.L., D/14/2/9 and D/14/3/37, 47; Wrench to Carson, 15 June 1916, P.R.O.N.I., D 1507/1/1916/28; A. W. Samuels to Carson, 14 June 1916, *ibid.,* D 1507/1/1916/33; Chalmers to Bonham Carter, 30 June 1916, Bodleian, Asquith papers, 37/77–8; notes of Asquith's interview with J. H. Campbell, 13 May 1916, *ibid.,* 45/113–5; Asquith's report on his visit to Ireland, 19, 21 May 1916, B.U.L., AC 14/5/22, 23.

44. J. H. Campbell's memorandum, dated 19 June, but circulated 23 June 1916, B.U.L., AC 14/5/27.

45. The executive committee of the I.U.A. passed resolutions against a settlement in 1916 on 1, 9, 21 and 27 June and was supported by the City of Dublin Unionist Association, a special meeting of the City of Cork Unionist Association and members of the Cork branch of the I.U.A., the Junior Branch of the I.U.A., the Cork Junior Unionist Alliance, the committees of the Limerick and Kerry branches of the I.U.A., the South Co. Dublin Unionist Registration Association and the Dublin Women's Unionist Club. See *Notes from Ireland* (1916), pp. 35–6, and *Irish Times* for June 1916.

gonism of nationalists to the proposed terms.[46] Ever since the 1885 general election they had directed their energies towards British politics, and this they continued to do in 1916. Their aim was to stir up opposition to a settlement in Great Britain and to leave it to their allies in British politics to excite the antagonism of nationalists.

Their protests against a settlement were brought home to British politicians by vigorous propaganda in the press, by speeches in both houses of parliament, and by individuals and deputations who waited on ministers and who urged their case, through letters, conversation, in public and in private, upon members of both houses of parliament. Not only was the agitation vigorous—Lloyd George 'gathered from Bonar Law that the southern unionists are moving heaven and the other place to thwart a settlement'; but it was also very skilfully conducted. Even Lloyd George had to admit this, when he told Dillon that 'the accounts I hear as to the prospects of a settlement are not very favourable' and that the southern unionists are working 'hard and skilfully against settlement'.[47] Grasping the essentials of effective propaganda in Great Britain,[48] they avoided extremism and too much reliance upon sectional opposition to home rule, and they made themselves appear as the long-suffering guardians of the imperial interest. This appearance was made all the more effective, since they expressed a willingness to submit to a great scheme of imperial federation to be operated after the war.[49] Having established their credentials as disinterested and responsible critics of the settlement, they stressed three points calculated to appeal to British politicians, especially conservatives. Firstly, they remarked upon the treachery involved in breaking the party truce, associating the whole cabinet with the Lloyd George proposals.[50] Secondly, they criticised and disparaged the American

46. Stewart to Long, 31 May 1916, B.L., D/14/1/45; Dillon to Lloyd George, 11 June 1916, *ibid.*, D/14/2/25; Lloyd George to Dillon, 12 June 1916, *ibid.*, D/14/2/31.

47. Lloyd George to Dillon, 10, 12 June 1916, *ibid.*, D/14/2/24, 31.

48. Montgomery to Carson, 9 June 1916, P.R.O.N.I., D 627/429; Stewart to Long, 31 May 1916, B.L., D/14/1/45.

49. See e.g. the statement made by the southern unionist deputation to Asquith and Lloyd George, 27 June 1916, *Notes from Ireland* (1916), pp. 34–5; Midleton to Chamberlain, 13 June 1916, B.U.L., AC 14/5/16, 17.

50. See e.g. the resolutions passed by various unionist organisations in the south of Ireland, *Notes from Ireland* (1916), pp. 35–6.

argument, emphasising especially the humiliation involved in the subordination of the interests of the British empire to the alleged exigencies of an alien political situation.[51] Lloyd George found this an increasingly difficult argument to handle. The more protracted the negotiations, the more effective the argument was likely to become, he told Dillon:

For the moment the wiser heads here know the value of conciliating the Irish vote in America, but there are men amongst us who are already saying: Are we to be bullied by these Americans who are pocketing hundreds of millions of our gold. This temper will also grow.[52]

Thirdly, and most effectively, they went to great lengths to show that a settlement would not bring peace and contentment to Ireland, and would hinder instead of aid the war effort. This they did by showing that few people in Ireland were satisfied with the proposed settlement; that power would soon be in the hands of Sinn Fein which would be loyal to Germany and hostile to the empire; and by showing in detail the seditious nature and activities and the growth of Sinn Fein.[53] So effective was this last gambit that Lloyd George was forced to take action to prevent newspapers from publishing paragraphs 'of the most gruesome character as to disloyal demonstrations in Ireland' that southern unionists sent to London newspapers; though he could not prevent such paragraphs from being published by the *Morning Post* which, in fact, became the main medium for southern unionist press propaganda.[54]

FIVE

Having, apart from Lloyd George's manoeuvres, almost a clear field, the southern unionists' activity was effective in averting a

51. Resolution of the South Co. Dublin Unionist Registration Association, *Notes from Ireland* (1916), p. 36.
52. Lloyd George to Dillon, 10 June 1916, B.L., D/14/2/24.
53. See e.g. *Notes from Ireland* (August 1916).
54. Lloyd George to Dillon, 10 June 1916, B.L., D/14/2/24; Wilson to Beresford, 1 July 1916, P.R.O.N.I., D 989A/8/10. For examples of southern unionist letters, see *Morning Post*, 27 May (J. M. Wilson) and 3 July (Major P. Newman).

settlement in 1916. Their agitation created an atmosphere unfavourable to the passage of any home rule bill acceptable to
Irish nationalists. On the one hand, the southern unionists helped
to create at cabinet level an atmosphere unfavourable to a settlement. On the other hand, they stirred up opposition to a settlement among the rank and file of the unionist party.

They helped to prejudice the chances of agreement on a settlement at cabinet level in two ways. In the first place, they helped
to precipitate and prolong a crisis in the coalition cabinet, enerva-
ted by suspicions and prone to crisis, by bringing home to the
unionist members what Lloyd George was doing in their name
and without their consent. They were able to precipitate a crisis,
for, having made the decision that Lloyd George should meet the
Irish parties to discuss the possibilities for a settlement of the Irish
question after the war and having obviously thought that they
had shelved the Irish question, ministers turned once more to the
war, where their attention was absorbed by the naval war in the
North Sea and by Kitchener's death. The unionist ministers were
thus in ignorance of the development of the Lloyd George
negotiations.[55] Lloyd George was aiming at a quick and deft
settlement,[56] and had it not been for the southern unionists, he
might have been able to present to the cabinet a *fait accompli*. The
southern unionists forced Lloyd George to show his hand, and in
doing so precipitated a crisis of confidence and created an atmosphere of suspicion between the liberal and unionist sections of
the cabinet. It was not until the end of May that the unionists
learned of the turn that the Lloyd George negotiations had taken,
and they learned from southern unionists. The activities of
southern unionists, such as Stewart and Midleton at the end of
May, turned the attention of unionist ministers abruptly back to
the needs of the Irish situation. By visiting Lansdowne and Long
they forced these ministers to face up to their Irish responsibilities
and to discuss the situation with Lloyd George. Having been
approached by southern unionists at the end of May, the two
unionist ministers saw Lloyd George on 30 May when he

55. See e.g. Lansdowne, 'The proposed Irish settlement', 21 June 1916;
Chamberlain to Asquith, 22 and 23 June 1916, and Asquith to Chamberlain,
22 June 1916, *ibid.*, AC 15/1/4, 9, 10; Bonham Carter's account of the cabinet
crisis, June–July 1916, Bodleian, Asquith papers, 41/149—68.
56. Lloyd George to Dillon, 10 June 1916, B.L., D/14/2/24.

explained his proposals. Then, on 1 June, at a meeting of the
cabinet committee on Ireland, Lansdowne and Long emphatically
stated their objections to the scheme.[57] These protests, subsequently expressed in a flurry of letters and memoranda, started
a chain reaction in the cabinet leading to a full scale cabinet crisis.[58]

Besides beginning the process, the southern unionists aided the
chain reaction by bringing 'unwonted pressure' to bear upon the
unionist members of the cabinet.[59] After Redmond had increased
the tension within the cabinet by publicly associating the unionist
ministers with Lloyd George's proposals, the southern unionists
quickly followed up the advantage.[60] On 13 June Midleton
forwarded to unionist ministers a copy of a resolution passed on
6 June by southern unionist members of parliament;[61] and, as
soon as Law returned from Paris, he was confronted with this
strong, though thoughtful, protest.[62] The southern unionist peers
and M.P.s (sitting for British constituencies) were convinced that
'the spread of the rebellion and seditious feeling require administrative measures which it is impossible for Mr Redmond's
party to countenance' and that any weakening of the government
may result in a second grave rebellion; and they regarded the
present proposals as 'highly dangerous from the point of view of
the conduct of the war'. Moreover, the covering letter from
Midleton not only underlined their conviction but also warned
that the introduction of the Lloyd George scheme would 'shatter
the unionist party without saving Redmond', and that the warning
had 'very strong backing among your supporters wholly un-
connected with Ireland'. At once grave and threatening, it was a
protest that no party leader could afford to ignore.[63]

57. Lansdowne, 'The proposed Irish settlement', 21 June 1916; Long, 'The
Irish situation', 15 June 1916 and 'The Irish difficulty', 23 June 1916, B.U.L.,
AC/14/15/13, 14, 28.
58. See below, pp. 69–75, 77–8.
59. Lloyd George to Dillon, 10 June 1916, B.L., D/14/2/24.
60. See e.g. Long to Asquith, 12, 13 June 1916, Bodleian, Asquith papers,
16/193–4; Bonham Carter's account of the cabinet crisis, June–July 1916, *ibid.*,
41/149–168.
61. See e.g. Midleton to Chamberlain, 13 June 1916, enclosing a resolution
passed at a meeting of southern unionist members of both houses of parliament
on 6 June, B.U.L., AC 14/5/16, 17.
62. Midleton to Law, 19 June 1916, enclosing the resolution passed at the
meeting of southern unionist members of both houses of parliament on 6 June,
B.L., 53/3/3.
63. Law to Midleton, 21 June 1916, B.L., 53/6/75.

These protests from the 'cream' of southern unionists were supported by deputations and personal representations from among the less well-known southern unionists in a way that presaged the future split in southern unionist ranks.[64] In addition to the official I.U.A. deputations, that enthusiastic unionist, Wilson, organised a deputation to visit unionist cabinet ministers to tell their story. Wilson was at first a little hesitant for fear of appearing to usurp the authority of the I.U.A., but the crisis was so severe that his efforts were appreciated.[65] Wilson, therefore, got up his deputation which waited upon several unionist ministers and upon Lloyd George, who appeared very anxious to see them.[66] Apart from a copy of the judicious statement made by the deputation, there is no record of the proceedings of the Wilson interviews, but it is likely that in conversation they made no little play of the rumour that unionist ministers had approved of the Lloyd George negotiations and it is certain that they made a considerable impression upon unionist ministers.

This persistent southern unionist pressure created a crisis of confidence among unionist members of the cabinet and caused unionist ministers to re-appraise their position in the coalition. This is significant, for though at a later date some southern unionists cited the reception given to their deputations in 1916 as proof that unionist politicians were no longer interested in maintaining the union, a closer look would have shown that a carefully handled agitation, playing on the prejudices of unionist politicians, might have paid dividends. For instance, though for the sake of cabinet solidarity the unionist Secretary of State for India, Austen Chamberlain, on 21 June, deliberately left a southern unionist deputation 'with the impression that, much as I disliked home rule in any and every form, I approved what had been

64. See e.g. carbon copies of Wilson's 'out letters dealing with political matters on a high, cabinet level', P.R.O.N.I., D 989A/8/10; Wilson to Chamberlain, 15 June 1916 and Long to Chamberlain, 14 June 1916, B.U.L., AC 14/5/3; Thomas Farrington (chairman of the Cork Junior Unionist Alliance) to Law, 27 June 1916, B.L., 53/3/8.

65. See e.g. Wilson to Franks, 16 June 1916 and to Stewart, 17 June 1916, P.R.O.N.I., D 989A/8/10; Wilson to Davies, 22 June 1916, B.L., D/14/3/32.

66. Wilson to Barrymore, 19 June 1916, to Asquith and to Midleton, 22 June 1916, P.R.O.N.I., D 989A/8/10; memorandum of the southern unionist deputation's views to lay before the ministers, with a list of names of the deputation, 19, 23 June 1916, *ibid.*, D 989A/9/5; Wilson to Davies, 22 June 1916, B.L., D/14/3/32.

D

done and saw no alternative'; he nevertheless wrote to the
Prime Minister:

... before any of us were aware of the course of the negotiations, Sir
Edward Carson and the nationalist leaders were invited to summon
conferences of their respective followers to consider proposals of
which the cabinet were in total ignorance. You must permit me to
say that I think this was very unfair to your unionist colleagues. Our
position in a coalition government is in any case an extremely difficult
one. To make it at all possible we are obliged to ask, and I think we
have a right to expect, a somewhat fuller consultation than the Prime
Minister might ordinarily think necessary in an homogeneous government. As it is we have been exposed to the utmost misconception by
our friends and supporters. It will be at any time difficult, and is for
the moment impossible, for us to offer any explanation of our position;
and more serious than any of these matters (though they are not
without public importance) we are now faced with a situation which
has been gravely prejudiced by the public steps taken without our
knowledge, and we no longer have the same freedom of decision as
we should have possessed if we had been consulted at the proper time.
    The time has not yet come for me to form a final decision as to my
own conduct in this crisis . . . [67]

Unionists thus saw in the Irish negotiations a threat to their
position in the coalition and an insult to unionist members of
the cabinet. Their dismay and horror at the attempted liberal
coup found expression in hostility towards the Lloyd George
proposals, and at one stage it looked as though most of the
unionist members of the cabinet might have resigned. Of the
unionist ministers only A. J. Balfour, First Lord of the Admiralty,
supported the proposals on their merits. The cabinet was in
turmoil, and Lloyd George did not exaggerate when he wrote on
17 June that the unionist members of the cabinet were in a 'state
of mutiny' and opposed to the operation of home rule in war
time.[68] Memoranda flashed between unionist members of the

    67. Chamberlain to Asquith, 22 June 1916, B.U.L., AC 15/1/9.
    68. For a commentary on the attitude of the cabinet to the negotiations in
June 1916, see Lloyd George to Dillon, 9, 10, 12, 17, 20 June 1916, B.L.,
D/14/2/20, 24, 25, 31 and D/14/3/11, 22, and T. P. O'Connor to Redmond,
20, 21 June 1916 in D. Gwynn, *Life of John Redmond*, pp. 509–11. For Balfour's
attitude, see his memorandum on 'Ulster and the Irish crisis', 24 June 1916,
B.U.L., AC 14/5/30.

cabinet, meetings were held and deputations sent to the Prime Minister, while unionist members went through a period of agonising re-appraisal.[69] At one time Lloyd George forecast the break-up of the coalition with either the unionist or liberal ministers resigning and the formation of a coercionist government.[70] Events proved him wrong, for no liberal resigned and only one unionist, the Earl of Selborne (President of the Board of Agriculture and Fisheries, a convinced and die-hard imperialist), resigned from the cabinet.[71] The rest of the unionists remained; but, Balfour apart, were in such a frame of mind as to be of little help to Lloyd George or the success of his proposals when further difficulties arose. On the one hand, Law was extremely nervous and, along with other ministers such as Chamberlain and Lord Curzon, an Irish representative peer and Lord Privy Seal, agreed to the continuation of negotiations only reluctantly, on the ground that by the time they had learnt of the direction of negotiations it would have been disastrous to the peace of Ireland and the empire to abandon them at such a late stage.[72] On the other hand, others like Lansdowne and Long were less easily satisfied and remained in the cabinet, it would seem, to frustrate the scheme.

This was the second way in which the active opposition of the southern unionists helped to create in the cabinet a mood unfavourable to a settlement. Their continued hostility to home rule made Lansdowne and Long extremely reluctant to agree to Lloyd George's proposals. These two ministers were less ready than their cabinet colleagues to sink their objections to home rule. The reason that they were less easily satisfied seems to lie in their responsiveness to southern unionist pressure.

The point is difficult to illustrate precisely as far as Lansdowne

69. See e.g. the files of correspondence in the Austen Chamberlain papers relating to the crisis of June and July 1916, B.U.L., AC 14/5.

70. Lloyd George to Dillon, 10, 20 June 1916, B.L., D/14/2/31 and D/14/3/22.

71. Jenkins, *Asquith*, pp. 399–402; Selborne to Asquith, 16, 24 June 1916, Bodleian, Asquith papers, 16/198–201.

72. Asquith's report to H.M. of the cabinet meeting of 27 June 1916, P.R.O., Cab. 37/150/23; R. Cecil's memoranda on the Irish question, 26 June 1916 and 5 July 1916, B.U.L., AC 14/5/11, 31; Chamberlain to Lansdowne, 23 June (misdated 23 July) 1916, *ibid.*, AC 14/5/5; Law to Midleton, 21 June 1916, B.L., 53/6/75; Lloyd George to Asquith, 20 June 1916, *ibid.*, D/14/3/21; Bonham Carter's account of the cabinet crisis, June–July 1916, Bodleian, Asquith papers, 41/149–68.

is concerned, but, as a large Irish landowner and a president of
the I.U.A., he shared the southern unionists' dislike of partition
and was generally solicitous of their welfare. In 1916 he showed
this concern when criticising the government's Irish policy.[73]
He asked Midleton to keep him informed of southern unionist
views, and Midleton obliged. Summing up their views he wrote,
'I believe you will not be surprised to know that we shall fight
to the death against a concession being made during war', and
thus left Lansdowne in 'no doubt as to the position which you
and your friends mean to adopt'.[74] In the case of Long, a vice-
president of the I.U.A., the connection between southern
unionism and his attitude to home rule in 1916 can be more
clearly demonstrated. Through his mother and his wife he had
close ties with ascendancy Ireland and his spell as Chief Secretary
in 1905 had broadened these links.[75] His firm policy of law and
order, contrasting with the relaxed attitude of his predecessor
that had precipitated the devolution crisis, so endeared him to
Irish unionists that there developed a mutual admiration society.
To southern unionists, Long was the statesman that Ireland
needed, 'strong, silent, sympathetic, constitutional, a pillar steadfast in the storm'; to Long, southern unionists were 'the strength
and flower of the Irish nation', and on one occasion he asked them
'respectfully but earnestly . . . to let me become one of the Irish
unionist forces . . . to devote the rest of my political life . . . to

73. See above; Lansdowne to Asquith, 28 June 1916, B.L., D/14/9/43;
Lansdowne to Asquith, 12 July 1916, Bodleian, Asquith papers, 37/98–100;
R. Cecil to Lansdowne, 4 July 1916, quoted in Cecil's memorandum of 5 July
1916, B.U.L., AC 14/5/31; Lansdowne, 'The proposed Irish settlement', 21 June
1916.

74. Midleton to Lansdowne, 9 June 1916, and Lansdowne to Midleton,
11 June 1916, P.R.O., 30/67/31, ff. 1630–2, 1633–5.

75. 1st Viscount Long of Wraxall (1854–1924); son of R. P. Long of Wilts.
and a daughter of rt. hon. W. W. Dick of Humewood, Co. Wicklow; m. a
daughter of 4th Earl of Cork and Orrery; ed. Harrow and Oxford; conservative
M.P. for N. Wilts. (1880–5), E. Wilts. (1885–92), W. Derby division of Liverpool
(1893–1900), S. Bristol (1900–6), S. Co. Dublin (1906–10), Strand division of
Middlesex (1910–18), St George's, Westminster (1918–21); parl. sec. to Local
Government Board, 1886–9; Pres. of Board of Agriculture with seat in cabinet,
1895–1900; Pres. of Local Government Board, 1900–5; Chief Sec. for Ireland,
1905; created Union Defence League, 1907; contender for unionist leadership,
1911; President of Local Government Board, 1915–16; Sec. of State for Colonies,
1916–18; First Lord of the Admiralty, 1919–21; vt, 1921. W. Long, *Memories*
(1923) and Sir Charles Petrie, *Walter Long and his Times* (1936).

the great cause, the maintenance of the union'.[76] Having been
Chief Secretary and having sat for four years as M.P. for South
Co. Dublin, Long was considered the unionist party's leading
authority on Irish affairs. As such he was all sweetness and light
when Lloyd George's exploratory mission was decided upon,
offering to put at his disposal 'my knowledge and experience of
Ireland, now extending over more than 50 years' and influence
over friends.[77] Even when, at George Stewart's behest, Long
hurried to Lloyd George and learned of his proposals, he protested
little. It is true that he and Lansdowne stated their objections, but
at the beginning of June neither threatened to resign and both
were prepared to allow negotiations to continue for the sake of
the war.[78] By 11 June, however, Long was in a distressed state
and threatened resignation unless the scheme were dropped.[79] It
was pressure from his friends in Ireland, especially in the south,
that caused him to take up this new and threatening attitude.

When Long had agreed to the continuation of negotiations, at
a meeting of the cabinet committee on Ireland on 1 June, he had
emphasised the need to obtain the consent of the unionists of the
south and west of Ireland. In his opinion,

no settlement arrived at between Ulster and the nationalists could be
regarded as complete, but that it would be necessary, in conformity
with the decision of the government, to obtain also the assent of the
unionists of the three southern provinces, not of course to the abandonment of their opposition to home rule, but to their willingness to
accept a scheme which appeared to them to have some prospect of
successful operation.[80]

The next few days were critical, for they proved to Long that
the southern unionists were unwilling to accept any settlement
in 1916. Whether, as Lloyd George alleged, this pressure upon
Long was directed by Midleton and his friends, or, as Long
imagined, was entirely spontaneous, there can be no doubt that

76. *Dublin Daily Express,* 4 Jan. 1906.
77. Long to Lloyd George, 23 May 1916, B.L., D/14/1/9.
78. Long to Lloyd George, 30, 31 May 1916, *ibid.,* D/14/1/41, 43; Long, 'The
Irish difficulty', 23 June 1916.
79. Long to Lloyd George, 11 June 1916, B.L., D/14/2/28; Long to Asquith
11, 13 June, Bodleian, Asquith papers, 16/193–7.
80. Long, 'The Irish difficulty', 23 June 1916.

Long was bombarded with letters of protest from unionists in the south and west of Ireland; and these protests were given more direct force when he was visited by old friends from the south of Ireland, such as Wilson who stayed at his home in Wiltshire and who dined with him in London.[81] The protests were made all the more effective because not only was the southern unionist case carefully argued but the southern unionists touched Long on a very sensitive spot. Not only did they appear as reasonable men willing to help the government by discussing the problem of home rule after the war.[82] They also accused Long of betrayal, especially after Redmond's announcement of 12 June that the Lloyd George proposals had been made with the consent of the cabinet. To such a charge Long was always hypersensitive; and, coming from men with whom he had been so intimately associated, it greatly distressed him.[83] He was deeply moved by the protests and appeals of southern unionists, telling Asquith at the end of July that he received 'very painful letters from my own friends in my own quiet county of Wicklow, and broken hearted accounts from sick and wounded soldiers home on leave. Some pray to be sent back rather than listen to this sedition.'[84] As might have been expected from a man such as Long, he reacted violently and determinedly. He was statesman enough to seek confirmation of the southern unionists' reports from General Maxwell, the C.-in-C. in Ireland;[85] but before he had received Maxwell's reply, he wrote to Lloyd George and the Prime Minister on 11 June that he could no longer support the negotiations owing to the grave accounts that he had received of the condition of Ireland. He justified his new position on two grounds: that the condition of Ireland was graver than when the question was first discussed and that therefore it was not the time

81. See e.g. Lloyd George to Carson, 3 June 1916, P.R.O.N.I., D 1507/1/1916/25; Long to Asquith, 8 June 1916, Bodleian, Asquith papers, 16/185–6; Long, 'The Irish difficulty', 23 June 1916; Wilson to Lloyd George, 6 June 1916, B.L., D/14/2/15; Wilson to Brooke, 22 June 1916, P.R.O.N.I., D 989A/8/10.

82. See e.g. Long to Asquith, 8 June 1916, Bodleian, Asquith papers, 16/185–6; Stewart to Long, 31 May 1916, B.L., D/14/1/45; southern unionists' resolutions opposing a settlement, June 1916, *Notes from Ireland* (1916), pp. 35–6.

83. Long to Asquith, 13 June 1916, Bodleian, Asquith papers, 16/193–4; Long, 'The Irish difficulty', 23 June 1916.

84. Long to Asquith, 29 July 1916, Bodleian, Asquith papers, 16/221.

85. Long to General Maxwell, 9, 13 June 1916, Maxwell to Long, 11 June 1916, B.L., 53/3/2.

to embark upon a political experiment; and that he was very strongly of the opinion that the U.S.A. would not interfere with munitions and other supplies.[86] Just how much his interpretation of the Irish situation in 1916 depended upon the persistence of the southern unionists is underlined in his letter to Asquith on 11 June. Long wrote that

The unionists of the three provinces are alone in their declared opposition which is not based upon any political or religious opinion, but upon a conviction that any such change in the government of Ireland must lead to grave trouble, probably even to disaster. I cannot persuade myself that the views of the Irish unionists are not well founded.[87]

Apart from working at cabinet level, the southern unionists played on the unionist susceptibilities of members of both houses of parliament. They brought home to members the existence of an attempt to implement home rule in 1916 and stirred up opposition to that proposal in a manner that, as has been seen, roused Lloyd George's admiration.[88] Midleton was an indefatigable critic in the House of Lords of the government's Irish policy,[89] and among members of the lower house Walter Guinness, M.P. for Bury St Edmunds, was equally active, lobbying assiduously against a settlement and 'observed in all parts of the house button-holing tory members'.[90] For instance, on 22 June, there was a meeting of unionist members of the House of Commons at which Guinness spoke for half an hour, entirely on details showing the growing power of Sinn Fein and its danger.[91] Although Harmsworth wrote disparagingly of Guinness's efforts, it is likely that this southern unionist pressure was at least partly responsible for the strong feeling that developed in the unionist party against any concession in 1916. On the one hand, there was no other organised effort on behalf of the union. On the other hand, their propaganda went almost unchallenged.

86. Long to Lloyd George, 11 June 1916, *ibid., D/14/2/28.
87. Long to Asquith, 11 June 1916, Bodleian, Asquith papers, 16/195–7.
88. See e.g. Lord Salisbury's memorandum on Ireland, 13 June 1916, B.U.L., AC 14/5/15.
89. *Parl. Deb.* (*Lords*), 5 ser., xxi, cols 810, 819–24, 960–71, 1022; and xxii, cols 420–1, 503–6, 635–41, 649–50.
90. Harmsworth to Bernard, 6 July 1916, B.M., Add. MS 52782, ff. 82–4.
91. R. M'Neill to Carson, 22 June 1916, P.R.O.N.I., D 1507/1/1916/36.

The unionist leaders, absorbed in the war effort and concerned about their own attitude to Lloyd George's proposals—Law was in Paris at a crucial time—neglected their followers and failed to educate them on the need for a settlement, thus leaving a vacuum of which the southern unionists were well able to take advantage. Lloyd George's negative approach to southern unionist propaganda was insufficient; something more positive was needed. As one member complained,

until the party meeting, we have been left without any guidance whatever to form the best opinion of which we were able during the last fortnight . . . and I feel that you and your colleagues are placed in a position of unnecessary difficulty by reason of the disagreement which has been permitted to grow up through lack of proper guidance or information from such people as the whips.[92]

This vacuum and lack of leadership left many unionists dependent upon southern unionist spokesmen and propaganda in the press for information about Ireland upon which to base their attitude to a settlement.[93] This is not to say that all unionists opposed a settlement and that unionists opposed a settlement of the Irish question simply because the southern unionists opposed it; but it does mean that the southern unionists beat Lloyd George at his own game. They brought home to unionists the severity of the crisis; roused unionists' susceptibilities by emphasising the imperial aspect of the proposed settlement in a way that fitted in with their former views and general prejudices; and gave their opposition some direction.

Even when Law eventually turned his attention to his supporters, the chances are that it came too late and, in any case, his influence was offset by the hostility of some of his colleagues to home rule. On 7 July a meeting of the unionist members of the House of Commons, postponed from the 28 June, was finally convened, but it served only to show the difficulties that awaited any attempt to force a settlement through parliament. Law did his best to persuade the rank and file to accept a settlement. Lansdowne who also addressed the meeting made no secret of

92. Sir Richard Ashmole Cooper (M.P. for Walsall) to Law, 10 July 1916, B.L., 53/4/4.
93. See e.g. G. E. M'Clelland to Law, 14 July 1916, *ibid.*, 53/1/8, an interesting file of letters opposing the Lloyd George proposals.

his hostility to home rule. The meeting was obviously opposed to a settlement (believing it to be a dangerous concession in time of war, which had all the appearance of being extorted by rebellion and revolution instead of being based upon a just assessment of the merits of the case); and it had to be adjourned without coming to any conclusion.[94] The unionist rank and file thus opposed a settlement on grounds popularised by the southern unionists.

SIX

The net result of the southern unionist activity among members of the unionist party was to make a settlement impossible in 1916. In order to keep in the cabinet such important and influential unionists as Lansdowne and Long, an already reluctant cabinet made certain modifications to the Lloyd George scheme and adopted a policy which Lansdowne made sure that Redmond would find himself unable to accept.

June was a trying time for the cabinet. While the government could afford the loss of Selborne, Lansdowne and Long were too important in unionist circles to let go lightly. Thus, once most unionists after the expenditure of much time and energy had sorted out their own attitudes, the cabinet spent more time discussing ways of keeping Lansdowne and Long in the cabinet.[95] The situation was made all the more tense owing to Long's depth of feeling and the way in which he expressed his tension by helping to direct southern unionist energies. Not only did Long circulate distressed memoranda and threaten to resign from the cabinet if the scheme were implemented, but he actively worked against a settlement. The sequence of events and the early protests of the southern unionists against a settlement show that the charge that Long stirred up southern unionists was ill-founded;[96] but, it is true that, once Long felt himself under pressure from his friends in Ireland and misunderstood by them, he tried to square himself with them by helping to direct the southern unionist agitation and this increased the sense of crisis in the cabinet. It

94. Blake, *The Unknown Prime Minister*, pp. 286–7.
95. See e.g. Chamberlain to Asquith, 1 July 1916, Bodleian, Asquith papers, 37/79–80; Chamberlain to Lansdowne, 23, 30 June 1916, B.U.L., AC 14/5/5, 9.
96. O'Connor to Redmond, 20 June 1916 in D. Gwynn, *Life of John Redmond*, pp. 509–10.

was he who advised and helped Wilson to bring more pressure to bear upon the cabinet and upon the rank and file of the party in the hope that 'this would react upon the cabinet and strengthen the hands of those who are friends who are there' (*sic*).[97] Lloyd George's reluctance to believe that Long's decision had been arrived at after long and anxious consideration, and his scathing charges of disloyalty,[98] only heightened Long's tension. A man governed by his heart as much as by his head, he was caught in a painful dilemma, being torn between his duty to the empire and his loyalty towards his friends in Ireland. Whichever decision Long made, it would have been, to him, a hateful one.

Against such emotional attitudes the cabinet could make little headway. Since even the Irish unionist officials had altered their views, the supporters of a settlement could appeal only to Lansdowne's and Long's patriotism in order to avert their resignations and further opposition. When the cabinet met on 27 June to discuss Ireland, Asquith told his colleagues that resignations would be 'not only a national calamity, but a national crime' at 'this critical conjuncture' of the war. Reluctantly and somewhat sceptically Lansdowne and Long agreed to hold over their resignations to allow a committee of the cabinet to consider amendments to the Lloyd George proposals which would safeguard the war effort and the minority in Ireland.[99] The cabinet met again on 5 July and resignations were averted. 'Subject to the conditions that imperial control of matters relating to the war and public order was during the war secured', Lansdowne felt that 'it was his duty not to resign at the moment'. And Long felt 'very reluctantly compelled to associate himself with Lord Lansdowne's resolution not to resign'. Asquith thus, prematurely it transpired, regarded his trouble as over and a settlement secure.[100]

97. Wilson to Brooke, 23 June 1916, P.R.O.N.I., D 989A/8/10. That this activity did increase the cabinet's sense of crisis, see Chamberlain to Asquith, 22, 23 June 1916, B.U.L., AC 15/1/9, 10, and Salisbury's memorandum on Ireland, 13 June 1916.

98. Lloyd George to Long, 12 June 1916, B.L., D/14/2/32; Lloyd George to Dillon and Asquith, 20 June 1916, *ibid.*, D/14/3/21, 22.

99. Jenkins, *Asquith*, pp. 400–1; Asquith's report to H.M. of the cabinet meeting of 27 June 1916, P.R.O., Cab. 37/150/23; Lansdowne to Asquith, 28 June 1916, B.L., D/14/3/43.

100. Asquith's report to H.M. of the cabinet meeting of 5 July 1916, P.R.O., Cab. 37/151/8; Jenkins, *Asquith*, p. 401.

Well might Asquith have been optimistic, for these were minor, even unnecessary concessions, and might have been acceptable to the nationalists had it not been for the use Lansdowne made of them.[101] Although Lansdowne had decided not to resign, his hostility to home rule had not abated one jot, and he used his position as government spokesman in the Lords to frustrate a settlement.[102] This attitude is less surprising than might appear at first sight. On the contrary, considering the nature of their highly developed loyalty to the union as well as to the empire, any other course by Lansdowne and Long would have been more surprising. Neither Long nor Lansdowne were convinced that a settlement was necessary to aid the war effort: indeed, they thought the contrary to be the case. Moreover, they refrained from resigning not because they were eventually persuaded of the correctness of the cabinet's Irish policy and soothed by minor concessions, but because of the need to maintain the appearance of national solidarity at home during time of war. Resignations would mean the break-up of the coalition and weaken the war effort. What weighed most with Lansdowne in deciding not to resign was the domestic situation; or so he told the cabinet:

If he and others resigned, the result must be a break-up of the coalition government, with a consequent period of recrimination and political chaos, which might possibly necessitate the worst of evils—a general election.[103]

Thus, it was only natural that he should try to reconcile his loyalty to the union with his loyalty to the empire by frustrating negotiations. On 30 June he aroused nationalist suspicions by announcing in the Lords that the 'consultations' which were in progress were 'certainly authorised' by the government but did not bind it, and that the unionist section of the cabinet had not accepted the Lloyd George proposals.[104] This had a bad enough effect on nationalists, but even worse was to come. As Mr Jenkins has written, 'on 11 July, Lansdowne, a moderate on many

101. Cecil's memorandum on Ireland, 5 July 1916; D. Gwynn, *Life of John Redmond*, pp. 516–18.
102. See e.g. the tone and content of Lansdowne's letter to Asquith, 28 June 1916, B.L., D/14/3/43.
103. Asquith's report to H.M. of the cabinet meeting of 5 July 1916.
104. D. Gwynn, *Life of John Redmond*, p. 516.

issues but always a cold and determined extremist on anything touching his position as a Kerry landlord, placed a dagger firmly into the back of the agreement.'[105] Speaking for the government in the House of Lords, he stressed that the exclusion of Ulster must be permanent and that southern Ireland would, in effect, be governed by a strengthened Defence of the Realm Act with which the Dublin parliament would not have the right to interfere. The tone and temper of the speech was even more calculated to irritate nationalists than its content. Lansdowne stated that even the bill would not be ready for some time, and that it would certainly not pass through parliament without a considerable interval for discussion. Meanwhile, he expressed the most complete confidence in Maxwell's administration in Ireland (which was supported by 40,000 troops), and altogether he treated the Home Rule Act as being open to complete revision by discussion in parliament.

Redmond regarded this speech as 'a gross insult to Ireland' amounting to 'a declaration of war on the Irish people' and to 'the announcement of a policy of coercion'.[106] The practical significance of the speech was that it created a new atmosphere of suspicion among the nationalists, confirming the 'morbid suspicions' of men such as Dillon. For the speech raised the question of the whole basis of the negotiations, since nationalists had understood that the settlement was to have been a purely provisional arrangement. The southern unionists were quick to take advantage of the situation, and in a letter to *The Times* Midleton 'remarkably confirmed Redmond's interpretation of Lloyd George's proposals'. The publication of these conflicting views as to what the government really intended to do 'produced the worst possible impression in Ireland' and Redmond could ask for no more concessions from his followers to accept a permanent settlement.[107]

Lansdowne's speech crystallised opinion and put an end to the home rule negotiations. The cabinet were reluctant to try to bridge the gap that had been exposed. It was not just that, when it became clear that the nationalists regarded a settlement as

105. Jenkins, *Asquith,* p. 402.
106. *Ibid.*; D. Gwynn, *Life of John Redmond,* p. 518.
107. Midleton to *The Times,* 13 July 1916; D. Gwynn, *Life of John Redmond,* pp. 518–21.

provisional and that the Ulster unionists believed it would be permanent, the cabinet were afraid to make further concessions to Redmond. They seemed determined to do exactly the opposite, and, for example, struck out the special provision by which Irish representation remained unchanged (a vital provision which Redmond regarded as a guarantee that the proposed settlement would be provisional).[108] The reason seems to be that the cabinet were trying to escape from a settlement. Owing to tension within the cabinet and to the prospect of future tension in parliament if a bill were proceeded with, the unionist ministers in the cabinet were only too glad to drop the bill and once again to put the Irish question into cold storage. Already too much time had been spent on the Irish question that summer in trying to reconcile differences, to the detriment of departmental work and the war effort. Moreover, it was feared that even more time would be wasted, since it was reckoned that there would be fierce opposition to the bill in both houses of parliament.[109] Lord Robert Cecil, Under-Secretary for Foreign Affairs, thought that the bill would have to be forced through parliament 'after long and angry debates' and that 'no minister during the war can face such a prospect as that with equanimity'.[110] Thus, when Redmond announced his intention to oppose the bill at every stage, there was little incentive to try to win him round and the attempt at a settlement in 1916 was dropped. Attempts to introduce a bill were abandoned and the cabinet reverted to the old system of government; the Home Rule Act remained on the statute book but inoperative, and the union remained intact as in 1914.[111]

SEVEN

Indeed, the whole situation in 1916 was reminiscent of that of 1913–14. Once again the southern unionists acted as a catalyst in British politics, determining and controlling the nature and

108. *Ibid.*, pp. 520–2; Blake, *The Unknown Prime Minister*, pp. 287–8; Jenkins, *Asquith*, p. 402.
109. Asquith's report to H.M. of the cabinet meeting of 27 June 1916; Cecil's memorandum on Ireland, 17 July 1916, B.U.L., AC 14/5/37; Harmsworth to Bernard, on the prospects of any home rule bill in the Lords, 6 July 1916, B.M., Add. MS 52782, ff. 82–4.
110. Cecil's memorandum on Ireland, 17 July 1916.
111. Jenkins, *Asquith*, p. 402; D. Gwynn, *Life of John Redmond*, pp. 522–3.

extent of British reaction to developments in Ireland. In 1916 as in 1913–14, negotiations were proceeding between the Ulster unionists and the nationalists; but there was an air of unreality surrounding both sets of negotiations. For, owing to the opposition of the southern unionists and their playing on the prejudices and ideas of unionists in Great Britain, either no agreement between Ulster and nationalists was likely to be implemented, or, once their points of difference became clear, no serious and sustained effort would be made by the British parties to secure agreement between the Ulstermen and the nationalists.

Whatever effects the failure of these Irish negotiations had upon British politics, the southern unionists should be given credit or responsibility for them, since they were largely responsible for turning the 1916 negotiations into a crisis. Time and space preclude an exploration of the significance of the events of June and July for subsequent developments in British politics.[112] But the influence of the crisis on southern unionism is relevant and in some respects disappointing. Largely through their own efforts the southern unionists had once again avoided home rule; but few lessons were drawn from the episode. Various individuals continued to urge upon the cabinet the need for firm government, but there was no concerted action through the I.U.A. When the British government abandoned its plans to proceed with home rule in 1916, unionists in the south of Ireland again concentrated upon the war. If it had done anything, the crisis had convinced some southern unionists that some form of home rule was inevitable and made them think seriously about the prospects of a settlement in the future.

112. For ideas as to how the home rule crisis affected the liberal and unionist parties and leaders, see e.g. Blake, *The Unknown Prime Minister,* p. 288; Phillips, *The Revolution in Ireland,* p. 110; A. J. P. Taylor, *English History 1914–1945* (1965), pp. 57–8.

IV

Phase Four:
Reconciliation: The Southern Unionists
and the Irish Convention 1917-18

IN the shorter term the Rising had caused a reversion to negative unionism. In the longer term, however, the Rising and the subsequent crisis in British politics caused a further weakening of unionism in the south. Once the immediate crisis had passed, some southern unionists were willing to adopt a more positive attitude towards changing conditions than had been the case between the outbreak of war and the Rising. Whereas before Easter 1916, thought on the unionist position had been vague and negative, after the Rising some southern unionists began to consider plans for a settlement of the Irish question on lines other than those laid down by the 1914 act. It was this more positive attitude that led southern unionists to play a leading role in the Irish convention of 1917-18, and it was due mainly to their efforts that it did not break down by December 1917 and that eventually a majority was able to agree upon a scheme of Irish self-government.

TWO

Ever since the Rising and its aftermath there had been a gradual growth of feeling among an influential body of southern unionists that home rule was inevitable and that southern unionists should contribute to a settlement to render home rule as harmless as possible. The reasons for this changing, more positive, attitude on the part of some southern unionists were complex. A curious blend of pessimism and optimism, the new attitude was based upon a re-assessment of the British and Irish political situations, especially in the light of the Rising and the subsequent crisis. It is, of course, difficult and dangerous to generalise: some, like Bernard, moved faster than others, such as Midleton and the fifth Earl of Desart,[1] but they all believed that the old policy of

1. Hamilton John Agmondesham Cuffe, 5th earl and vt (I), 7th baron (I), 1st baron (U.K., 1909); (1848-1934); ed. Radley and Cambridge; midshipman

negative unionism was no longer a viable policy and looked for an alternative.

These southern unionists, soon to be dubbed 'Midletonites', were depressed and concerned about the likely development of Ireland after 1916 if somebody did not lead a new departure. Reflecting on the Rising and its aftermath, they saw a number of things that dismayed them. Firstly, the crisis had shown that there was little future in the British connection as it then stood: they reckoned that the union was a losing cause and unlikely to offer much protection either to southern unionist or to Irish interests. The events of 1916 had underlined the fact that there was on the statute book an unsatisfactory Home Rule Act which contained no 'safeguards for the interests of the minority either as regards representation or otherwise' and whose financial provisions were of 'the most unsatisfactory character'.[2] This was indeed the 'cardinal fact',[3] for the act would come into operation at the end of the war and could not be wished away. Admittedly, there was a temptation to argue away the act since it had been passed by methods which its opponents considered discreditable, but it was recognised that repeal was most unlikely. As one correspondent of the *Irish Times* pointed out, 'the passing of the Act of Union was assisted by methods whose morality, to put it mildly, was somewhat dubious; yet it was nearly one hundred and twenty years before it was repealed'.[4] Moreover, some southern unionists felt that they could no longer count upon considerable support in British politics, as they had done in the past. The whole perspective of British politics had been altered by the war so that only the most pressing points of the Irish question could be considered by any British government. This changing condition of British politics had to be considered, especially by those southern unionists in close touch with British politics and politicians. By 1917 it could be said that no major British party

in R.N., 1860–63; barrister, 1872; Assistant Solicitor to the Treasury, 1878; Solicitor to the Treasury, Queen's Proctor and Director of Public Prosecutions, 1894–1909; British member of the International Court of Arbitration at the Hague; P.C.; Desart Court, Co. Kilkenny.

2. Circular letter issued by the I.U.A., 15 Apr. 1918, justifying the position taken up by the southern unionist representatives at the convention (hereafter cited as I.U.A. circular, 15 Apr. 1918), P.R.O.N.I., D 989A/8/22.

3. A. F. Blood's letter in *Irish Times*, 29 Mar. 1918.

4. G. Hanlon's letter, *ibid.*, 8 Apr. 1918.

supported the old unionist cause any longer, for the unionists formed part of a coalition government which had tried to modify the union. This had struck some members of the I.U.A. deputations in 1916 when they had been 'repeatedly reminded that the Home Rule Act was on the statute book'.[5] How far the cabinet would have yielded in future to strong southern unionist pressure in favour of the union is an open question and one which did not occur to Midletonites who concluded that 'indeed, the Asquith cabinet, the coalition cabinet, and the Lloyd George cabinet are all committed to the principle of home rule, and the majority of people in Great Britain regard its establishment when possible as a foregone conclusion.'[6] This argument about the state of British politics proved a very adaptable one as time went on. A favourite variant was to dwell on the consequences of the growth of the labour movement in Great Britain: a labour government would assuredly concede to the most extreme nationalist demands and therefore a more extreme measure had to be forestalled.[7] Others took the argument further, arguing that it was better to withdraw Irish affairs from Westminster before a labour government came to power, for thereby Ireland would escape the reign of anarchy and rapine which would follow such an advent.[8] Lastly, even if the union could be sustained for a few more years, some southern unionists doubted whether it would be in Ireland's best interests: 'the best that could be hoped for would be a perpetuation of Birrellism—surely the most unalluring prospect in the world'.[9] Thus, whereas previously a large measure of support in Britain and a belief in the efficacy of the union had encouraged southern unionists to persist in and publicise their unionism, their reappraisal of the British political situation and of the value of the union after 1916 helped to convince them of the futility of negative unionism.

Secondly, the political situation in Ireland also required a reassessment on the part of some unionists. On the one hand,

5. I.U.A. circular, 15 Apr. 1918; see also Lord Desart to Bernard, 25 May 1916, B.M., Add. MS 52781, ff. 145–6.

6. Midleton to Iveagh, 20 Sept. 1918, printed copy in P.R.O.N.I., D 989A/8/20A.

7. *Ibid.*; Midleton to Bernard, 25 May 1917, B.M., Add. MS 52781, ff. 46–8.

8. See e.g. W.H.T. Gahan's letter in *Irish Times*, 15 Mar. 1918, and R. Bagwell's letter, *ibid.*, 18 Mar. 1918.

9. T. R. Garvey's letter, *ibid.*, 9 June 1917.

Ulster's decision to accept partition dismayed them, for they objected to partition on two broad grounds. It had weakened the cause of the union in British politics and removed the biggest obstacle to the implementation of the act of 1914, an obstacle which had allowed southern unionists in 1914 to regard the act as a dead letter. Moreover, partition would make home rule even less tolerable and would not bring peace to Ireland: the exclusion of the large unionist population of the north-east would weaken the loyal and constitutional element in a Dublin parliament upon whom southern loyalists would rely for protection; exclusion would mean that the new Irish parliament would not be financially viable; nationalists would resent exclusion; and the division of Ireland upon religious lines would only accentuate the separation of the north and south, while the Protestant majority's likely harsh treatment of the Catholic and nationalist minority in the north would lead to reprisals on the Protestants in the south.[10] On the other hand, the Rising had demonstrated the determination and increased the strength of extreme nationalism which was likely to dominate an Irish parliament such as that envisaged by the 1914 act. In sum, therefore, some southern unionists saw that, unless there was a new departure in Irish politics, the union would be dissolved by the operation of the highly unsatisfactory (from their point of view) act of 1914; Ireland would be partitioned; and the southern parliament would be dominated by extreme nationalists who, it was feared, would have little regard for southern unionists' views and interests.[11]

These considerations put southern unionists in an unhappy frame of mind. However, if the Rising had helped to convince some of the futility of their old policy, it had also given them hope for the future. The Irish political situation gave southern unionists not only an incentive to look for a new and positive alternative to their old policy; it also pointed to the direction in which such an alternative was to be found. Southern unionists found this alternative in co-operation with Redmond and the

10. See e.g. I.U.A. circular, 15 Apr. 1918; Bernard to Lloyd George, 3 June 1916, B.M., Add. MS 52781, ff. 1–9; Desart to Sir Hutcheson Poe, 23 Aug. 1916, *ibid.*, ff. 151–3; and Appendix D for Desart's memorandum on the Irish situation to the cabinet committee on Ireland, 22 Nov. 1919, P.R.O., Cab. 27/69/2/41.

11. See e.g. Midleton to Lord Milner, 2 June 1917, B.L., F/38/2/9, and to Law, 19 June 1917, *ibid.*, 82/1/17.

moderate nationalists: all loyal and moderate men in Ireland should co-operate in order to prevent the supremacy of extreme nationalism. In part this changed attitude towards Redmond's party was the continuation of that *rapprochement* in train since the beginning of the war: Redmond's support for the war effort had impressed some southern unionists who wanted to repay such valour and patriotism 'by joining hands with our nationalist fellow countrymen. . . who look for unionist co-operation to strengthen their hands in a *bona fide* contest with anarchy and lawlessness'.[12] But it was more than gratitude that encouraged unionists by 1917 to adopt a more positive attitude towards Redmond and his followers. Springing from the Rising there were two more motives, one a sense of duty, the other a sense of opportunity, that gave the pre-Rising *rapprochement* a more positive aspect. On the one hand, the Rising had shown the determination and violence of extreme nationalism. For some southern unionists it had been a traumatic experience for which they held themselves partly responsible. The eighth Viscount Powerscourt thought that the upper classes by holding aloof from the national movement and by holding nationalism in contempt had allowed the movement to slip into the control of the wrong people:

There has always been a distinct tendency amongst some of the upper classes in Ireland, to ridicule any outward sign of nationalist Ireland or sentimental Celtic manifestations and to term them unwarrantable, political, or even disreputable.

I contend that this patriotic sentiment *cannot and should not* be squashed. Owing to this neglect by the upper classes of seeing the necessity of catering for this, it has fallen into the hands of unprincipled organisers and is at once seized and moulded by such people, into channels, to suit their own ends, which are invariably disreputable in the extreme.

If Irish national sentiment became respectable and was organised by respectable people, who would introduce sound principles into it, it would be a great power for good in our country . . .

All that I have said does not prevent me from seeing that there is a fine leaven on the other side, of national prosperity, brought about by the possession of land and the development of agriculture, and that now is the accepted time to try and bring all the forces into harmony.[13]

12. A. F. Blood's letter in *Irish Times,* 29 Mar. 1918.
13. Memorandum by the 8th Viscount Powerscourt on 'Reasons for present rebellion', n.d., B.M., Add. MS 52782, ff. 50–51.

Not all shared this feeling of guilt, but many agreed upon the need to contain the extreme movement not by repression but by bolstering up the constitutional movement. The United Irish League had seemed bad enough, but Sinn Fein was unspeakably worse. Southern unionists stood for law and order and some felt it their duty to support Redmond against the revolutionary movement, if necessary in an Irish parliament.[14] On the other hand, the development of Sinn Fein seemed to provide an opportunity for southern unionists to take once more an active part in Irish political life. Indeed, the growth of the revolutionary movement gave southern unionists the biggest incentive not only to alter their views but also (in a sense) to change them completely and to help bring about that self-government they had spent years trying to stave off. It cut across the line of Irish political development since the 1880s. Not only did southern unionists see a need to support the constitutional movement, they also believed that that movement needed their support and thought that Redmond should and would be prepared to win that support by making substantial concessions to southern unionist opinion when the time came to draw up another scheme of Irish self-government.[15] Thus some southern unionists could foresee a new peaceful Ireland, governed by an Irish parliament which would be dominated by a centre constitutional party comprising moderate nationalists and unionists from the north and south of Ireland.

These ideas were floating around in private by 1917. Those southern unionists who undertook a re-appraisal were not at all clear on the details of a settlement which would avoid partition and maintain a close association with the British empire; but they were making suggestions and were positively prepared to accept some form of home rule in the future. It should not be thought that this change of view was lightly undertaken without regard to the difficulties which a new Irish government should face, or that the advocates of a new departure had an oversimplified view of the likely development of a new Irish state. In fact, they emphasised those difficulties, which they attributed mainly to liberal misgovernment over the last ten years or so: owing to weak and vacillating administration a spirit of lawlessness was

14. See e.g. Bernard to Lloyd George, 3 June 1916, *ibid.,* 52781, ff. 1–9.
15. See e.g. Midleton to Bernard, 22 Mar. and 12 May 1917, *ibid.,* ff. 43–4, 45; and to Milner, 2 June, B.L., F/38/2/9.

held to have grown up in Ireland which could be exorcised not by legislation but only by years of firm administration of laws dissociated in the Irish mind from English laws.[16] But these difficulties seemed an added attraction to men of big ideas such as Midleton or Bernard who reckoned that many of the unionists of the south and west were prepared to make 'great sacrifices to ensure any stable form of government under which life and property shall be secure'.[17]

The recognition of these difficulties partly explains why these southern unionists did little publicly. Some observers regarded the southern unionists as the only people who could lead a new departure on the Irish question.[18] The 'devolutionists', for example, tried to hurry them along, urging in 1916 that unionists should declare their support for Redmond and the constitutional party and for the principle of home rule;[19] but the thinking southern unionists were not to be hurried. As far as they were concerned a settlement was a matter of timing. They considered precipitate and public action inappropriate: the bitter feelings aroused by the nationalists' condemnation of Maxwell's action should be given time to settle down; no settlement should be attempted before the end of the war; no action for a settlement was advisable before then since it was impossible to foretell the line-up of opinion in Britain and Ireland by the end of the war.[20] Meantime all the energies of southern unionists should be concentrated on the war effort. Thus, when the question of home rule plus exclusion was under discussion in March 1917, the I.U.A. was non-committal, not because all its members were unalterably opposed to home rule but because they were waiting for the right opportunity to assert their own views.[21] Timing was important to them, but they recognised that some form of home

16. See e.g. Bernard to Lloyd George, 3 June 1916, B.M., Add. MS 52781, ff. 1–9.

17. *Ibid.*

18. See e.g. M. Frewen to Long, 25 Dec. 1915, and a copy of a letter from W. O'Brien, 10 Jan. 1918, N.L.I., F. S. Bourke collection, MS 10723.

19. See e.g. the correspondence relating to the Irish Constitution Committee in the Bernard papers, B.M., Add. MS 52781, ff. 89–104, 121–4, 154, and T.C.D., Bernard correspondence 1 (1893–1919), 104–7.

20. See e.g. Desart to Hutcheson Poe, 23 Aug. 1916, B.M., Add. MS 52781, ff. 151–3; Hutcheson Poe to Bernard, 25 Aug. 1916, *ibid.*, ff. 111–12.

21. Midleton to Bernard, 22 Mar. 1917, *ibid.*, ff. 43–4.

rule was inevitable and wanted 'a new departure',[22] quite different
from the 1914 act and arrived at after full consultation.

THREE

Such was the receptive state of mind of leading southern unionists
when Lloyd George approached Midleton in May 1917 about
the possibility of southern unionists entering a convention of
Irishmen to settle the Irish question. Ever since he had become
Prime Minister in December 1916, Lloyd George had been under
pressure from the Irish Parliamentary Party to settle the Irish
question, and he now used the device of a convention as a convenient way of keeping nationalists quiet for a time and of
forwarding the war effort by conciliating the large and influential
Irish population in the United States (which had recently declared
war on Germany).[23] The convention offered southern unionists
the right sort of opportunity to assert their newly evolving views.

It was not just that Lloyd George appears to have handled
Midleton with consummate skill, when urging him to persuade
the I.U.A. to take part in a conference.[24] Nor was it merely the
pressure of public opinion that compelled such a self-professed
patriotic group to accept an invitation to aid the war effort.[25] The
reason that the convention provided a suitable opportunity to
evolving southern unionists was that they were wholeheartedly
behind the war effort, and appreciated the patriotic motives
prompting a convention and the need for all parties to make
sacrifices for the common good. For instance, although Midleton
had never taken the American argument seriously,[26] as a former
Secretary of State for War he could appreciate the need for manpower in wartime and was persuaded that an Irish settlement
would bring forth more recruits from a grateful Ireland. As he
later recorded, in October 1917 he spent a fortnight

22. Midleton to Law, 15 Dec. 1916, B.L., 81/1/60.

23. He offered the various parties concerned in the Irish question the choice
between partition and a convention. They chose the latter.

24. Midleton, *Records and Reactions*, pp. 233–4; Midleton to Lloyd George,
21 June and 12 July 1917, B.L., F/38/1/2, 6.

25. For the note of self-sacrificing patriotism struck by southern unionists, see
e.g. Midleton to Lloyd George, 21 June 1917, *ibid.*, F/38/1/2; Midleton to Law,
19 June 1917, *ibid.*, 82/1/17.

26. Midleton, *Records and Reactions*, pp. 233–4.

at Sir Douglas Haig's headquarters in France, where with our forces now fully developed the highest hopes were centred. Haig sent me to the headquarters of three armies, but despite the splendid spirit of all ranks, I came away with little hope of an early solution. This made an Irish concordat specially desirable, as recruits for armies of 4,000,000 men were growing short.[27]

To some southern unionists it seemed only patriotic, and in no sense a surrender, to enter into discussions with Ulster unionists and nationalists to draw up a scheme of government for *all* Ireland which would (unlike the 1914 act) strengthen and unite the unionist party in Ireland; which would contain adequate safeguards for unionists, including those in the south; and which would enable southern unionists to play an active role in Irish politics again. Even if in the absence of Sinn Fein a convention could not result in a general settlement, it could, at least, by evolving a policy upon which the other three parties agreed, create an atmosphere which would ultimately form the basis of a solution.[28] Some found this harder to appreciate than others. They resented being at the beck and call of a British government which had often ignored their views in the past. Midleton especially, despite his changing views, found that when the time came to act upon his new ideas the decision to do so proved an irksome one which caused him some distress.[29] Nevertheless, he recognised that an opportunity existed for a new departure, seeing that 'the solution on which Ireland can be united depends on realising that new forces have arisen, that nationalists can never be set over unionists but must co-operate with all loyal men and that the act of 1914 must be scrapped'.[30]

Thus Midleton needed little persuading to agree to the idea of a convention, and after a meeting with some Irish peers at his London house on 18 May, he told Lloyd George that he opposed the proposal for partition but agreed to try and persuade the southern unionists, as represented by the I.U.A., to enter the convention.[31] This was not an easy task for Midleton to under-

27. *Ibid.*, p. 239; see also leader in *Irish Times*, 2 June 1917.
28. Campbell to Law, 26 May 1917, B.L., 80/6/19.
29. See e.g. Midleton to Law, 19 June 1917, B.L., 82/1/17; and to Lloyd George, 21, 28 June, 12 July 1917, *ibid.*, F/38/1/2, 4, 6.
30. Midleton to Milner, 2 June 1917, *ibid.*, F/38/2/9.
31. See *Irish Times*, 19 May 1917, for the text of their reply.

take, for he was not adept at handling difficult situations. Although
a man of ideas and a hard worker, he appeared at first sight to be
'a pig-headed pedant' and was not adept at handling those who
disagreed with him.[32] This defect in a leader was to be important
in 1918, when some members of the I.U.A. began to oppose
Midleton; but in the middle of 1917 it was not so important,
because even those who later opposed him were, for practical
purposes, willing to be guided by his advice.

He had little difficulty with the executive committee of the
I.U.A. which comprised some of his closest sympathisers. On 23
May that committee met to consider Lloyd George's suggestion
and agreed to summon a meeting of the general council, the
supreme governing body. A further meeting of the executive
was held on 31 May to consider details. It was then pointed out
that 'while delegates would naturally be bound to express in the
convention their belief that the maintenance of the legislative
union was the best and safest solution of the "Irish question",
they would be also bound to consider and discuss and possibly
agree to such other solution as would safeguard imperial interests
and the rights of the minority in the south and west'. This did not
amount to precise advice and the executive committee passed
two resolutions which were to commit the southern unionists to
participation in the convention in order to 'submit to the British
government and the British parliament a constitution for the
future government of Ireland within the empire'. The second
resolution appointed a sub-committee, weighted in favour of the
more substantial and less 'representative' members of the I.U.A.,
to arrange details and to select delegates. All this was, of course,
subject to the approval of the general council which met on the
following day, 1 June. It met at Molesworth Hall to consider the
resolutions of the executive committee. It was the largest and
most representative meeting of that body ever held, and nobody
denied that the question of the convention was 'fully discussed'.
Midleton found the meeting and his task of persuading southern
unionists to enter the convention a tough one; but, when the
resolutions were put to the meeting, they were passed with only
one dissentient. The argument that they could not enter a convention without either surrendering their principles or being held

32. See e.g. Sir Frederick Ponsonby, *Recollections of Three Reigns* (1951),
pp. 126–7.

responsible for the breakdown of the convention if they clung to principles, did not carry much weight. The general feeling seems to have been one of regret that the question of Irish self-government had been raised during the war, but now that it had been brought up, members of the council felt it their duty to consider it. Thus the I.U.A. expressed its readiness to 'take part in a convention of representative Irishmen'.[33] Apparently, therefore, the southern unionists had accepted the views of Midleton and his associates, and had agreed to enter the convention with an open mind, prepared to accept some form of Irish self-government.[34]

Appearances were deceptive, however. Admittedly, few questioned the wisdom of entering the convention, now that the Irish question had again been raised.[35] But not all southern unionists thought that it would result in a settlement.[36] Some of the rank and file undoubtedly hoped that a settlement would result. Wilson, a determined unionist who had no motive to exaggerate the strength of the 'compromise' section, reported to Long from Cork that

from a certain section I found more desire and hope for a settlement through the medium of the convention than I have met with elsewhere. Notably a person immersed in a big commercial concern, who, from

33. For the meetings of the I.U.A., see I.U.A. circular, 15 Apr. 1918; minute book of the executive (general) council of the I.U.A., 1889–1920, 1 June 1917; Midleton to Milner, 2 June 1917, B.L., F/38/2/9; C. B. Moffat to I.U.A., 22 May 1917, P.R.O.N.I., D 989A/8/6.

34. See e.g. the comment of the *Irish Times*, 2 June 1917.

35. Nobody ever denied this, not even Midleton's critics who later organised themselves (I.U.A. circular, 15 Apr. 1918; circular letter issued by the Southern Unionist Committee, 20 Mar. 1918, criticising the position taken up by the southern unionists in the convention and the action of the executive committee of the I.U.A. in upholding their stand, P.R.O.N.I., D 989A/8/20B. This latter circular is henceforth cited as S.U.C. circular, 20 Mar. 1918).

36. Unfortunately, no detailed record of the meetings of the executive and general council is available; only their resolutions have been recorded, the committee's in later correspondence (I.U.A. circular, 15 Apr. 1918), the council's in a minute book (P.R.O.N.I., Mic 110). However, an assessment of the attitude of the rank and file of the southern unionists at the time of the convention is made less difficult by Midleton's letters in the Lloyd George and Law papers and by two files of papers among the I.U.A. collection in the P.R.O.N.I.—one contains letters of apology for inability to attend meetings of the executive committee (D 989A/8/6), the other the draft manuscript and typescript notes relating to 'Wilson's tour' (D 989A/9/7). Such evidence shows that not all southern unionists accepted the Midletonite view of the state of the union and the prospects of the convention.

his boyhood has been a strong unionist, now hopes that the eternal feuds in Ireland may be dissolved in that way.[37]

On the other hand, others were prepared to accept the convention on tactical grounds, reckoning that no agreement would be possible. 'Mr W.' of the Cork corporation, probably Williams the coachbuilder, saw little good coming from co-operation between unionists and Redmondites, and thought that unionists had entered the convention only on account of British public opinion which demanded sacrifices in war time.[38] Unionists like this seem to have agreed to the convention, confident that 'seeing the divided state of parties here no good can come of it',[39] especially since it was lacking Sinn Fein representation.[40] This division of opinion as to the prospects of a convention was to be found not only in Cork, but also in other counties visited by Wilson, notably Sligo, Dublin, Westmeath and Kilkenny.[41]

Moreover, there was some difference of opinion as to what the delegates' functions and aims should be. Not all southern unionists regarded the union as a lost cause and wanted their delegates to work for a settlement on the basis of Irish self-government. While it had been explained at the meeting of the general council of the I.U.A. that some form of home rule might be the result of the convention, it had also been said that the delegates would express 'their belief that the maintenance of the legislative union was the best and safest solution of the "Irish question" '.[42] Much therefore, depended upon the delegates' interpretation of the situation, but it is evident that, though it was never suggested that they should consult the general council during the convention,[43] they were not given a *carte blanche*. Despite assertions later made by Midletonites that at the meeting of the general council 'the point that some form of home rule must result was made perfectly clear',[44] not all southern unionists accepted or realised this. Lloyd George's remarks on the convention had been ambiguous. He had expressly stated in the House of Commons

37. Wilson's tour, South county and city of Cork, Sept. 1917.
38. *Ibid.*
39. M. Goodbody to I.U.A., 21 May 1917, P.R.O.N.I., D 989A/8/6.
40. Wilson's tour, Westmeath, Sept. 1917.
41. *Ibid.*
42. I.U.A. circular, 15 Apr. 1918; S.U.C. circular, 20 Mar. 1918.
43. *Ibid.*
44. Midleton, *Records and Reactions*, p. 236.

that 'no-one, by the mere fact of going to the convention, can be assumed to be pledged to acceptance or rejection of any particular proposal or method for the government of Ireland'. Some took this to mean that the union was not precluded from discussion as a possible form of government for Ireland.[45] Some absent members of the executive committee, at least, thought that this should be the primary duty of unionist delegates. 'You may take me', wrote Arthur Hugo Burdett of Coolfin, King's Co., 'as considering that the only way to govern Ireland successfully is to uphold the union *firmly* . . .'[46] and Thomas Farrington, an analytical chemist and chairman of the Cork branch of the I.U.A., wrote that 'unionists should be allowed to attend without prejudice to their convictions, and it should be open to them to advocate *fair play for the union* as the best solution of the Irish difficulty'.[47] To men holding views such as these it was unthinkable that unionists should actually produce a scheme of home rule at the convention.

The views of the I.U.A. and the southern unionists were not, therefore, as clear-cut as the voting of 1 June had suggested. The Midletonite view of the need for a new departure had not been wholeheartedly endorsed. In retrospect it is obvious, as it was to certain people in close touch with southern unionist opinion at the time,[48] that a crucial phase had been reached in the development of the I.U.A. and in the evolution of southern unionist opinion. There were elements of disintegration, and much depended upon the way the delegates acted in the convention and the way in which the leaders of southern unionist opinion handled their constituents.

FOUR

Having decided to enter the convention, the I.U.A. tried to ensure that its representatives could participate under the most favourable conditions. On 2 June Midleton and Stewart saw the Irish Chief Secretary, Sir Henry Duke, and asked for two pledges: that the reference to the convention should be limited to drawing up a constitution within the empire; and that there should be no

45. S.U.C. circular, 20 Mar. 1918.
46. Burdett to I.U.A., 22 May 1917, P.R.O.N.I., D 989A/8/6.
47. Farrington to I.U.A., 22 May 1917, *ibid.*
48. See e.g. Wilson's tour, Dublin, 30 Aug. 1917.

further release of Sinn Fein prisoners. Unqualified pledges were
evidently given on both counts, but the latter was broken, much
to the disgust of southern unionists. Thinking that the release of
extremists would inhibit nationalists from coming to a compromise on the convention and unhappy about its size, Midleton,
in particular, showed signs of second thoughts. Missives and
deputations of protest were sent to ministers, but, realising the
opportunity that existed for a settlement, southern unionists duly
accepted Lloyd George's formal invitation to attend the
convention.[49]

Its total membership was ninety-five, consisting of the chairmen of county councils; the lord mayors and mayors of the six
county boroughs; eight representatives of urban councils; five
representatives from each of the main political parties, the Irish
Parliamentary Party, the Ulster Parliamentary Party and the
I.U.A.; four representatives of the Roman Catholic hierarchy; the
two archbishops of the Church of Ireland; the Moderator of the
General Assembly; the chairmen of the chambers of commerce of
Belfast, Cork and Dublin; two Irish representative peers; various
representatives of labour; and fifteen other persons nominated by
the government.[50] The convention was thus largely nationalist.

It held its first meeting on 25 July at Trinity College, Dublin.
The fact that this should have been chosen as the venue was,
perhaps, symbolic for southern unionism. On the one hand, it
was a happy choice, because it was fitting that the monument
to the Anglo-Irish tradition should be the scene of what became
an Anglo-Irish attempt to lead a new departure in Irish politics.
On the other hand, there was a less happy sign, for Trinity College
also epitomised the decay of Anglo-Irish power and influence.
Just as southern unionism had to be refurbished for the convention, so did Trinity College. Only at the last moment had Trinity
been chosen as the venue for the convention, and it was a decision

49. For these efforts, see Midleton's letters to Lloyd George and Law in June
and July, B.L., F/38/1/2, 4, 6, 7 and 82/1/17; and Midleton's memoranda and
letters, P.R.O., 30/67/33, ff. 1692–1715.

50. *Report of the proceedings of the Irish convention* (1918), Cd 9019, p. 9 and
appendix II. Sinn Fein, the All-for-Ireland party and the trades councils of Dublin
and Cork refused to send representatives, and one chairman of a county council
also refused to accept Lloyd George's invitation. During the course of the proceedings the convention lost three members by death (Sir Henry Blake, Sir
Alexander McDowell and John Redmond) and two (Edward McLysaght and
George Russell) through resignations.

which gave the Board of Public Works in Dublin some anxious moments as it hurried to prepare the College for the opening session. For it needed no little attention before it could be considered fit to receive the convention: the Board of Works had only eight days in which to clear out, clean from top to bottom, paint, and furnish the equivalent of about 'four fair sized dwelling-houses, apart altogether from the preparation of the convention hall'—Regent House—'a room of about 60′ by 50′ and about 30′ high'. One official wrote:

You can have no idea of the neglected condition of the premises: I doubt whether they had been touched for thirty years.

Our staff worked with the greatest energy and though they were hampered by the fact that one process could not be begun till another had been finished they never lost a minute, so that by Monday the 23rd, I was able to show the Chief Secretary the premises with a certainty that they would be all right for the opening day, with uniformed attendants, special stationery, books of reference, even down to brandy for any old gentleman who might collapse on the long staircase, and on the next day His Excellency the Lord Lieutenant inspected the completed works.

Of course, it had always been known that the acoustics were bad, but otherwise the opening day was a great success. But I was asked whether anything could be done to improve the acoustics, and by working all night our people effected a very great improvement which for instance quite satisfied the Archbishop of Dublin.[51]

The southern unionists, their resentments overcome by the sense of occasion and opportunity, entered the convention in an optimistic mood and with a high idea of their own role. Stewart, that 'great land agent', accepted Lloyd George's invitation 'in the earnest hope that the deliberations and result there of [sic] may conduce to the welfare of my country';[52] and Midleton was not alone in thinking that the success of the convention lay largely with the southern unionists and with the realisation by moderate nationalists of their importance and value in any settlement of the Irish question.[53] This optimism was not altogether misplaced. The southern unionists played a leading role in the convention

51. G. A. Stevenson to W. G. A. Adams, 1 Aug. 1917, B.L., F/66/1/48.
52. Stewart to Lloyd George, 19 July 1917, *ibid.*, F/37/5/154.
53. Midleton to Milner, 2 June 1917; Milner to Lloyd George, 5 June 1917, *ibid.*, F/38/2/9.

socially and politically, Midleton and Bernard, in particular, making significant contributions to the proceedings.[54]

They were able to become influential for a number of reasons. Firstly, though few, they were a powerful and experienced group in the convention. The group comprised: the five representatives allotted to the I.U.A.—Sir Henry Arthur Blake, a former cadet of the Irish constabulary and a retired colonial civil servant who had recently ended his official career as Governor of Ceylon, Andrew Jameson, Midleton, John Blake Powell, and George Stewart; Bernard, attending as the Protestant Archbishop of Dublin; Lords Mayo and Oranmore and Browne, representing the Irish peers; Edward Henry Andrews, a wine, spirits and tea merchant, representing the Dublin chamber of commerce; and Lord Desart and Sir William Goulding, government nominees.[55] Although they spoke individually and were each free to offer suggestions and to express individual views, these southern unionists tended to act as a recognisable team, meeting on occasion at Lord Iveagh's house for dinner, or, more often, at the offices of the I.U.A. in Grafton Street.[56] Despite representing a comparatively small section of the community, 'they had the self-confidence bred by generations of governing'.[57] As Midleton said, numerically weak as were the southern unionists,

they were hardly negligible, as the event proved. They consisted of Dr Bernard, Archbishop of Dublin, probably the most distinguished

54. Until recently the best published account of the convention was that contained in *John Redmond's Last Years* (1919), written by one of the most active nationalists in the convention, Stephen Lucius Gwynn, the Oxford-educated and Protestant home rule M.P. for Galway city, 1906–18. Containing lengthy summaries of important speeches, it is especially helpful on the role of the southern unionists on whom Gwynn pinned his hopes of an agreement, while its essential accuracy is borne out by other evidence such as *The Irish Convention: Confidential Report to H.M. the King by the Chairman.* This report consisted of a series of letters written by Sir Horace Plunkett while the convention was sitting, summarising many speeches, often with quotations. It was printed though not published, and there are copies in the library of T.C.D. and in the Midleton papers in the P.R.O. Gwynn's account has now been superseded by Dr McDowell's book, *The Irish Convention*.

55. 'The southern unionists' note', *Report of the Proceedings of the Irish Convention,* p. 48. Sir Maurice Dockrell, chairman of an important Dublin firm of builders' suppliers and M.P. for Rathmines (1918–22), was to have been one of the I.U.A.'s representatives but withdrew for personal reasons.

56. See below, pp. 103–4, 108–9; and S. Gwynn, *John Redmond's Last Years,* p. 264

57. McDowell, *Irish Convention,* p. 127.

Irishman of the day; four peers, Desart, Mayo, Oranmore and myself, two of whom had held high office; Powell, a Roman Catholic king's counsel, shortly to become a notable judge; Sir Henry Blake, an ex-governor, with Andrew Jameson, Sir William Goulding and George Stewart, all business men of high calibre.[58]

Moreover, they were encouraged to exert their influence and powers by the atmosphere they found in the convention and the respect accorded to them.[59]

Secondly, unlike other groups in the convention, the southern unionists paid little attention to opinion outside the convention. They did consult the executive committee of the I.U.A. on four occasions and talked over fiscal problems with the Guinnesses,[60] but, unlike the Ulster unionists, they made no serious effort to keep in close touch with the rank and file of their party. In part this was the fault of the general council for not insisting upon some channel of communication and consultation in respect of the convention; but it had always been the policy of the I.U.A. to allow the more substantial members, with broader knowledge, to direct the affairs of the association within the limits laid down in the constitution, and in the past the executive committee and officers had not given any reason for the rank and file to distrust them; perhaps they had been slack at times, but they had always been on the right lines.[61] Such irresponsibility, accentuated by the

58. Midleton, *Records and Reactions*, p. 236.

59. *Confidential Report*, para. 29. See also Oranmore's comment in the debate on the 1920 government of Ireland bill in the Lords. 'About six weeks after the convention had been sitting I happened to make a speech in which I put forward—temperately, I hope, but very resolutely—the claims of the southern unionists, and, when I had finished, a member of the convention, whom I had never met before, came to me and said, "Me lord, Oi have often read about ye, but Oi have never met ye and Oi have never hurrd you before; and, to till ye the truth, now Oi have met ye and now Oi have hurrd ye, Oi loike ye a great deal better than Oi expected". Well, my lords, that feeling was entirely reciprocated by the union[ists]. We liked the nationalists a great deal better than we expected; we found that they were ready to concede to us any safeguards that we deemed necessary. They were not only ready but were anxious that we should have full representation in both houses of parliament, because they recognised that without our help and co-operation it would be impossible successfully to start an Irish parliament.' [*Parl. Deb.* (Lords), 5 ser., xlii, 23 Nov. 1920, cols 470–1.]

60. I.U.A. circular, 15 Apr. 1918; Desart to Bernard, 1 Dec. 1917, B.M., Add. MS 52781, ff. 166–9.

61. Nobody criticised the *Irish Times*'s assertion of 2 June 1917 that Midleton 'has been a wise and broad-minded counsellor of the Alliance, whose interests at this critical time could not be in more capable hands'.

atmosphere of conference, which had affected skilled negotiators at different times, undoubtedly increased the usefulness of the southern unionists in the convention, but, as will be seen, they did mishandle a potentially explosive situation. Midleton did recognise that southern unionists were 'very sensitive' and inclined to think that any concessions meant desertion of principle.[62] Considering, therefore, the momentous issues at stake, he and his colleagues might have taken their constituents more closely into their confidence, in order to mobilise enthusiastic southern unionist support for a new departure and to allay and to combat the discontent and suspicions of a man such as Wilson, who reported to Long that a person 'very closely associated with the Ulster cause' had given him

a very interesting account of the very thorough manner in which Ulster is carrying on her proceedings at [the] convention and outside of it, viz., by advisory committees (3) in Belfast, and an office in Dublin, and the fullest and freest discussion of all details. On these committees are men representative of all interests—workingmen, and leaders of all trades and commerce in the north, no section is omitted or ignored, a true democracy. How different from the procedure of the southern section which is enveloped in mystery![63]

Thus insulated from the views of their constituents and oblivious to most undercurrents of feeling, the southern unionists' representatives could put all their energies into bringing the convention to agreement,[64] though they were to do so at the cost of southern unionist unity.

Thirdly, they were judiciously conciliatory. On the one hand, they expressed their willingness to listen to and to consider schemes of self-government. Charges that at a very early stage they proposed a home rule scheme were misleading. Much to their disgust, Ulster unionists thought that one of the southern unionists, Powell, had drafted a home rule measure to be submitted anonymously to the convention, and that Midleton was privy to the transaction. They later repeated this charge[65] which was misleading. According to Midleton, the truth of the matter

62. Midleton to Bernard, 23 May 1917, B.M., Add. MS 52781, ff. 46–8.
63. Wilson's tour, 'Notes on the convention', Dublin, 30 Aug. 1917.
64. See below, p. 114.
65. McDowell, *Irish Convention*, pp. 114–15; *The Times*, 5 Nov. 1919.

was this.[66] Powell, an accomplished draftsman, had some time between 1914 and 1917 sketched a modification of the Home Rule Act of 1914 in order to meet some of the main unionist objections. The chairman of the convention, Plunkett, who was seeking suggestions from every quarter during an adjournment of the convention, specifically invited Powell to put in his clauses (which proposed two parliaments for Ireland). Midleton had not even seen a copy of these proposals, nor had they ever been submitted to the southern unionist group; and, in reply to a telegram, Midleton made it clear that anything Powell submitted must be purely personal. On hearing that his leader disagreed with it, Powell thereupon appears to have withdrawn his paper promptly. In a convention dominated by nationalists, the southern unionists did not have to initiate discussion on home rule: nevertheless, they did not make a sustained attempt to advocate the union as a satisfactory form of government. It is true that they frequently stated that 'we have not changed our view that the preservation of the union of Great Britain and Ireland under the imperial parliament is still the best policy for both countries';[67] but since they considered their main task was 'to consider what concession could be made to nationalist opinion in regard to a constitution',[68] they could scarcely press the old case for the union. On the contrary, they tried to discourage such talk, and, while unwilling to propose a scheme of home rule, at an early stage they made it clear that they were willing to assist in the settlement of the Irish question, provided that settlement contained provision for fair finance and adequate safeguards for minorities and the maintenance of imperial supremacy. At the beginning of August Powell made this clear to nationalist leaders behind the scenes,[69] and their views were put officially by Lord Oranmore and Browne, who revealed for the first time 'the real mind of the southern unionists'. As Plunkett wrote in his report:

It was not felt that the real mind of the southern unionists had been

66. Letter in *The Times*, 6 Nov. 1919.

67. Memorandum by southern unionists on fiscal autonomy, *Report of the Proceedings of the Irish Convention*, appendix VII. For other instances, earlier in the convention, see Mahaffy's diary of the proceedings of the convention, T.C.D., Irish convention papers, MS 2987.

68. *Ibid.*

69. S. Gwynn to Redmond, 3 Aug. 1917, N.L.I., MS 15192.

E

revealed until Lord Oranmore, whose speeches in the House of Lords somewhat uncompromisingly supported that party, had spoken. He began by repeating that his party was satisfied with the present position —an admission which seemed a little inconsistent with his natural complaint that southern unionists were completely excluded from any share in local government. Nevertheless, the convention had already shown that a better spirit prevailed, and his party were prepared to co-operate in the search for an agreed settlement. They had been promised guarantees and these must be precisely defined. What they claimed was, first, adequate representation in the lower house; secondly, an upper house sufficiently strong to guarantee religious liberty; thirdly, freedom from oppressive and differential taxation. These guarantees must be made constitutional and not rest as mere assurances of contemporary politicians. Further, the final supremacy of the imperial parliament must be made real and effective, not merely the theoretical supremacy embodied in colonial constitutions. Also, any settlement arrived at must be final—that is, must not be open to attacks by agitators—and this security might be effected, he thought, by a provision requiring a three-fourths majority for any change in the constitution. The southern unionists agreed with the northern unionists that the war debt was a debt of honour in which Ireland must bear her share.[70]

Moreover, not only was their attitude conciliatory, they also added many a happy touch to the proceedings, taking the edge off tension that arose on occasions.[71]

On the one hand, then, the southern unionists clearly stated their readiness to consider home rule and their reservations. On the other hand, they were conciliatory in the way they acted. They did not isolate themselves but tried to work with other groups. They co-operated with moderate home rulers, such as Lord Dunraven, who attended some of their meetings;[72] but more significantly they tried to avoid extremes and to maintain friendly contact with nationalists and Ulster unionists and to coax them along to a settlement. This balancing act became increasingly

70. *Confidential Report,* para. 29.
71. See e.g. *ibid.,* para. 130; and the comments on Oranmore in S. Gwynn, *John Redmond's Last Years,* p. 313, and in S. Bullock to Adams, 3 Jan. 1918, B.L., F/63/2/2.
72. Midleton, *Records and Reactions,* p. 235; Dunraven, *Past Times and Pastimes,* ii. 59.

difficult to maintain, and since it led to close co-operation with the nationalists it eventually brought down Ulster's wrath on the southern unionist delegates. Perhaps this drawing together of nationalists and southern unionists was inevitable, since both had much to lose by the maintenance of the *status quo* or the implementation of partition. Nevertheless, the southern unionists made considerable efforts to maintain workable relationships with all groups.

It might have been expected that the two unionist groups would have co-operated especially closely in the convention, but mutual suspicion prevented them from forming a solid alliance, even at the beginning of the convention, when Midleton recorded an example of the preremptory and unfriendly attitude of the Ulster delegation.[73] Since the Ulster unionists' acceptance of the principle of partition in 1916, many southern unionists (who had been concerned about Ulster's treatment of them during the crisis over the third home rule bill) had become even more suspicious of the reliability and willingness of Ulstermen to protect southern unionist interests; and Ulster unionists, who had hoped that southern unionists would have shown more sympathy with the mode of their protest against the third home rule bill, were equally doubtful of the soundness of some southern unionists.[74] This gap widened during the convention, especially as a result of the 'Powell incident', which enhanced the suspicions of Ulster unionists.[75] Nevertheless, the southern unionists did make great efforts to maintain workable relations with Ulster unionists. They were conciliatory. They tried to smooth over the Powell affair. Midleton, Desart and Jameson met the Ulster leaders and expressed regret that the scheme had been put forward; and, having listened to a firm talking to by Hugh Thom Barrie, the leader of the Ulster group, who told them that an official expression of regret should be conveyed to the Ulster group and that their own group should be properly organised, they sent a very polite letter, stating that they wished to co-operate with the Ulster group as much as possible and would not put

73. Midleton, *Records and Reactions*, pp. 235–7.

74. Stewart to Montgomery, 11 May 1917, P.R.O.N.I., D 627/431; Midleton to Montgomery, 12 May 1917, *ibid.*; D. Pack Beresford to Montgomery, 10 Sept. 1917, *ibid.*, D 627/430.

75. McDowell, *Irish Convention*, pp. 114–15.

forward any scheme without consulting it in advance.[76] They also tried to discuss individual matters, such as the customs, with them.[77] On the other hand, they were willing to put pressure upon the Ulster unionists in open session: as, for instance, at Belfast on 25 September, when Jameson appealed to the Ulster group to come to the convention's assistance and depart from their attitude of silence.[78] As the convention went on, southern unionists found themselves increasingly out of sympathy with Ulster's attitude of silence and became more and more concerned to force them to agree to a settlement, but this was only after considerable effort had been made to arrive at an amicable agreement. On 25 September, Midleton discussed the situation with Barrie who thought that 'no time so favourable for settlement would ever recur as the present' and who said that Ulster unionists would only accept a scheme of self-government if given a disproportionately large share of representation, emphasising that control of the customs by the imperial parliament and Irish representation at Westminster was a *sine qua non*.[79] Midleton in particular was anxious to avoid any breakdown between Ulster and southern unionists in the convention. He was only too ready to explain his views to them,[80] and until a very late stage hoped for co-operation between the two unionist groups. For instance, as late as February 1918 he was in touch with Barrie, advocating united action to throw responsibility for any breakdown of the convention upon the extreme nationalists.[81]

Southern unionists also tried to maintain a workable relationship with the nationalists. In discussion they showed a high idea of the rights of an Irish parliament and a desire for an effective parliament with real power in Ireland, and behind the scenes they sought to discuss Irish problems with nationalist leaders. In early August, Powell had a long talk with Gwynn and told him that southern unionists were 'moving towards us', that Midleton especially had moved quickly, and that they deprecated general

76. *Ibid.*

77. Midleton's memorandum of a conversation with Barrie, 25 Sept. 1917, P.R.O., 30/67/33, f. 1730.

78. S. Gwynn, *John Redmond's Last Years,* pp. 298-9.

79. P.R.O., 30/67/33, f. 1730.

80. Midleton to Barrie, 27 Oct. 1917, and Barrie to Midleton, 3 Nov. 1917, *Ibid.*, ff. 1744, 1748.

81. Midleton to Barrie, 22 Feb. 1918, *ibid.*, f. 2062.

discussion, since they would therefore be obliged to make a case for maintaining the *status quo*.[82] And early in October Midleton and Bernard met Devlin privately at 12 Fitzwilliam Square to discuss the growth of Sinn Fein and the restoration of law and order.[83] No agreement was reached but the episode was indicative of the changing attitude of southern unionists and of their desire to co-operate with men of all constitutional political parties in Ireland.

This is not to say that they had suddenly become Redmondites, subordinating their views to those of Irish nationalists and accepting all nationalist platitudes. As might have been expected of a group in transition, their views were not always clearly thought out, and they were still distinctive. As Oranmore's speech showed, they not only made it clear that they would accept a parliament for all Ireland, they also stated the limitations that had to accompany any settlement, emphasising that they had to be satisfied on three crucial issues—imperial security, finance and security for minorities. Their contributions to a scheme of self-government were perhaps characteristic of an imperially-minded ascendancy group. Although moving away from the old unionist position, they were moving only gradually. How far they were from accepting the values of democratic and narrow nationalism may be judged from their attitude towards the customs and the question of minority representation. They wanted one-tenth of the representation of the lower house (and additional representation for Ulster), rejecting proportional representation as an inadequate safeguard, since the wealthier section of the population, contributing most taxation, was so scattered that it would be unrepresented; and they asked for a high property qualification for the Senate. These demands were made not only on narrow class grounds but also on the wider grounds that

At present and not improbably for some years to come, the whole weight of the unionist party will be required to enable the nationalists to hold their own with the revolutionaries. So long as unionist strength is frittered away by voting in driblets in different constituencies, we

---

82. Gwynn to Redmond, 3 Aug. 1917, N.L.I., MS 15192.
83. Memorandum of interview, B.M., Add. MS 52782, ff. 175-7.

shall be powerless to affect the issue. A majority vote for an Irish republic may consequently be cast in the first Irish parliament.[84]

Their suggestions, however, were constructive, and they placed before the convention alternative methods of giving representation to their class, the methods varying from the device of two electoral registers—one Catholic and the other Protestant—to a terminal nomination in the lower house.[85]

They also showed scant understanding of or sympathy with nationalist sentiment and often appeared poised uneasily between Ireland and the empire. This was particularly apparent when the question of the fiscal relations between Ireland and Great Britain was raised. To men accustomed to thinking in imperial terms, it was quite natural to envisage a flexible system of finance weighted in favour of imperial control. But it must have been irksome for nationalists to have been constantly reminded that Ireland should have power to secure her own economy only if 'its attainment could be secured without endangering other, and, in our opinion, even more important interests'; that 'to ignore imperial security in framing a constitution . . . is to prejudice Irish as well as imperial interests'; and that 'if Ireland is still to remain an integral part of the British empire, she must be prepared to make some sacrifice commensurate to that which Great Britain is making'.[86] Nevertheless, the expression of such distinctive views probably increased the influence of the southern unionist group in the convention by demonstrating their sincerity and willingness to compromise.

For these three reasons—natural ability and confidence, concentration upon the convention, and the judiciously conciliatory way they acted—the southern unionists came to exert a decisive influence upon the convention. Obviously, such a small group could not immediately exert any decisive influence upon a convention of almost one hundred men, and early on they were defeated over the selection of a chairman and the procedure to be adopted by the convention.[87] But, experienced men of

84. Midleton's memorandum on minority representation, 18 Aug. 1917, T.C.D., Irish convention papers, MS 2987.

85. *Ibid.*; and *Confidential Report,* para. 72.

86. See especially the southern unionist memoranda on fiscal autonomy and the customs, 26 Nov. 1917 and Jan. 1918 (*Report of the Proceedings of the Irish Convention,* appendix VII, and B.L., F/63/2/7).

87. Midleton, *Records and Reactions,* pp. 237–8. After the preliminaries, the election of a chairman (Sir Horace Plunkett) and a secretary (Sir Francis Hopwood,

affairs, they bided their time and waited for an opportunity to assert their views and influence effectively. And they had to wait a long time, for there were many obstacles to expeditious discussion, not the least being the character of the sincere but woolly-minded chairman and the procedure he had adopted. But by November their chance came to bring the convention to agreement on a scheme of self-government for the whole of Ireland, which would not only safeguard the interests of unionists in Ireland, but which would also enable unionists to play once more a leading role in Irish public life.

FIVE

By the early autumn the convention really got down to work. It had reconstructed the grand committee representing all groups and charged it with preparing for submission to the convention a scheme which would meet the views and difficulties expressed by different speeches during the course of the opening sessions. To expedite business this committee resolved itself into a series of sub-committees, one to deal with the question of electoral reform and the composition of the Irish parliament, a second with land purchase, a third with a possible territorial force and police; but the 'marrow of the business' rested with a sub-committee of nine.[88]

On this last sub-committee were three Ulster unionists, three parliamentary nationalists, two independent home rulers and one southern unionist, Midleton, who delighted Redmond by 'showing an Irish spirit which I never expected' and standing up for the claims of an Irish parliament if there was to be one.[89] Charged with drawing up a scheme of self-government, the sub-committee worked in difficult circumstances. It met against a background of wrangling between nationalists and Ulstermen in

later Lord Southborough), the adoption of standing orders, the consideration of the general course of procedure to be followed, the appointment of a grand committee of twenty members to advise the chairman, Plunkett insisted on a presentation stage, when various schemes of self-government were discussed by the whole convention at meetings held in Dublin, Belfast and Cork. These proceedings lasted until the end of September.

88. For a convenient summary, see the chairman's report in *Report of the Proceedings of the Irish Convention*, pp. 11–18.

89. S. Gwynn, *John Redmond's Last Years*, pp. 304, 308.

parliament over the franchise bill and over the policy of the government in Ireland. Moreover, there was little real leadership in the two dominant sections. Redmond had virtually abdicated his functions as leader of the home rulers, and the most accommodating Ulsterman, Sir Alexander McDowell, became ill and was replaced as Ulster's spokesman by Hugh McDowell Pollock, whose temperament unsuited him for the critical work of bringing men's minds together.[90] Thus, despite eleven meetings and a large measure of agreement on the protection of minorities (over which the nationalists were prepared to make large concessions), the sub-committee of nine reached deadlock over finance. The nationalists demanded immediate and full fiscal control without which, they held, no nation could keep itself or its self-respect: the Ulster unionists stood out for the fiscal unity of the United Kingdom in order to protect the interests of the commercial and industrial classes of Ulster.[91] It looked, therefore, as though the convention would meet again in December without having a scheme to consider. A breakdown seemed inevitable.

This was the sort of situation which gave a minority group such as the southern unionists their opportunity. Unlike the Ulster unionists and nationalists who were considering interests outside the convention, the southern unionist group had their minds fixed solely on the convention and were determined to 'go to the extremest limit in their power' to see 'what could be removed from the present system without disturbing the essence of the union'.[92] Therefore, when discussions in the grand committee between 22 and 25 November produced no compromise, Midleton announced that, to save the convention, he and his group would put before it certain proposals as a *via media*.[93] Henceforth, the southern unionist contribution to the convention can almost be described as Midleton's contribution. He came to play a very prominent role as leader and spokesman of the southern unionist group. An experienced politician, he provided the detailed leadership of the group, guiding tactics and formula-

90. *Ibid.*, pp. 304–8, 310–11.
91. *Ibid.*; *Report of the Proceedings of the Irish Convention*, pp. 11–18.
92. S. Gwynn, *John Redmond's Last Years*, pp. 310–11, 314; Midleton, *Records and Reactions*, p. 240.
93. *Confidential Report*, para. 108.

ting and defending their views (for instance, Desart reckoned that Midleton's memorandum on the customs had put the case in a way not previously considered and expressed his willingness to be guided by Midleton's advice).[94] Yet in doing so he was not dictating policy to the group, merely acting on the general lines laid down by his colleagues. He could not have achieved his position in the convention or submitted a scheme without their encouragement and support. He relied on the advice and support of Bernard and Desart to sustain him, particularly in his interviews with British politicians; the willingness of these and men such as Powell, Jameson and Stewart to compromise, and their desire to bring the convention to a successful conclusion, encouraged Midleton to make the first real attempt to secure agreement and then to make concessions over excise;[95] and their speeches in the convention and activity behind the scenes helped to win support for what became known as the Midleton scheme. How dependent Midleton was on such support can be illustrated by Bernard's activity. At the beginning of November Midleton proposed to Bernard that they should have an interview with Redmond and Bishop O'Donnell of Raphoe to put pressure upon nationalists to concede Irish representation at Westminster and imperial control of customs; but Bernard refused on the ground that it would lead to no useful result. However, three weeks later Bernard 'intervened energetically and effectively' in the grand committee, insisting that a mere *non possumus* by Ulster would not do, and thus creating an atmosphere favourable to the presentation of compromise proposals.[96]

The proposal which the southern unionists laid before the grand committee was a wide measure of self-government, with substantial safeguards for minority interests. The salient features of this proposal were the reservation to the imperial parliament of

94. Desart to Midleton, 3 Nov. 1917, P.R.O., 30/67/33, ff. 1745–7. See also the tributes of Powell (to Midleton, 1 Dec. 1917) and Jameson (to Midleton, 13 Feb. 1918), *ibid.*, 30/67/33, ff. 1772–4 and /36, ff. 2059–60.

95. See e.g. Midleton to Bernard, 22, 23 May, 8 Dec. 1917, B.M., Add. MS 52781, ff. 45–8, 59–60; Desart to Bernard, 1, 5 Dec. 1917, *ibid.*, ff. 166–70; the notes relating to southern unionist interviews with cabinet ministers, 5 Dec. 1917, 6, 13 Feb. 1918, *ibid.*, ff. 19–21, 26–8, 29–31; Powell to Bernard, 25 Nov. 1917, *ibid.*, 52782, ff. 183–4; Powell to Midleton, 28 Nov., 1 Dec. 1917, P.R.O., 30/67/33, ff. 1766–9; Midleton to Jameson, 17 Nov. 1922, *ibid.*, /52, ff. 3101–4.

96. McDowell, *Irish Convention*, p. 129.

the right to impose and collect customs duties, and the payment out of the receipts from such duties of an imperial contribution (to be fixed after detailed enquiry by a joint commission representing both Great Britain and Ireland). Having made this demand on behalf of the unionists, it conceded to the nationalists full control of all purely Irish affairs, including internal taxation.[97] This was the first concrete scheme to be proposed and its significance for the convention and for the development of southern unionism can scarcely be overstated. For the first time an influential body of Irish unionists had agreed, not as individuals but as representatives, to accept home rule in a wider measure than had been provided for in the bills of 1886 and 1893 and the act of 1914: many of the limitations of these previous schemes were struck out by the southern unionists.

To the southern unionists this scheme represented a fair compromise between unionism and nationalism. It split the difference over the question of fiscal autonomy, and conceded to the Irish parliament all that the nationalists claimed, including a large measure of fiscal autonomy, save that the customs were reserved. In fact, the nationalists were offered a parliament for the whole of Ireland, with full and complete control over every purely Irish affair, both legislative and administrative. 'On these lines', southern unionists believed, 'all legitimate national aspirations will be satisfied.'[98] On the other hand, although the nationalists were not asked to give up anything that had been conceded to them by previous home rule proposals, Irish unionists were offered better safeguards than previously. Midleton's proposals kept the power of the Crown over all imperial services undiminished; the reservation of the customs prevented even the possibility of a trade war (harmful to Ulster industry) between Britain and Ireland; Irish representation at Westminster was retained as a corollary to leaving the imperial parliament powers of Irish taxation; and the scheme, by suggesting generous representation in both houses to minorities (on lines agreed in the sub-committee of nine), offered sufficient guarantees of fair legislation. Moreover, the scheme would allow Irish unionists to

97. *Confidential Report*, para. 108.
98. Memorandum on fiscal autonomy, 26 Nov. 1917, *Report of the Proceedings of the Irish Convention*, appendix VII.

play once more a full part in Irish political life. Certainly the southern unionists considered themselves sufficiently safeguarded by such a scheme; and to Ulster Midleton said:

We share every danger threatening you—we have many dangers you need not fear. Yet, we have no similar anticipations. Are you still determined to stand out?[99]

In sum, therefore, the Midleton scheme offered what its supporters considered to be a satisfactory answer to the problem of the pacification and unity of Ireland. A nationalist leader would be able to lead a combination of 'all sane elements in the landowning and land-cultivating classes'.[100] No Irish leader had ever before been able to present such an appeal to unionist opinion as would come from the man who represented the convention party.

The scheme was defended energetically in a series of memoranda and in private meetings and conversations. At the end of November Powell talked over the situation with Bishop Kelly of Ross and on 12 December Midleton and Bernard met Redmond at Lord Iveagh's house; and on 27 November the Ulster unionist delegates and members of the advisory committee had 'a very interesting pow-wow with the southern unionist lot'. The difficulty was, however, that though the scheme represented a new ideal for some southern unionists, it could still be criticised from both a nationalist and Ulster viewpoint, the former demanding control of customs, the latter opposing any powers of taxation being given to an Irish parliament. Such criticism prevented the grand committee from agreeing to recommend the scheme to the convention due to meet in December. Nevertheless, the southern unionists still regarded their scheme as a workable compromise, and were determined to submit it to the full convention.[101]

The crucial issue was, of course, the customs. Plunkett advised Midleton to try to reach some agreement with the nationalists, but Midleton was not prepared to compromise further and was determined to waste no time and to resolve the fiscal issue.[102]

99. S. Gwynn, *John Redmond's Last Years*, pp. 314–15.
100. *Ibid.*, p. 315.
101. McDowell, *Irish Convention*, pp. 129–33.
102. *Ibid.*, pp. 132–3.

He and his colleagues, therefore, sought the aid of the British government to break down opposition to their scheme. Desart was a little dubious of this tactic,[103] but three considerations encouraged southern unionists to seek government intervention. In the first place, their decision had not been an easy one and it was felt that the support of the unionist members of the cabinet would help the Midletonites to carry their friends outside the convention in support of their great advance.[104] Secondly, arguing that 'it is time that Ulster ceased to dominate imperial policy', they thought that their record of loyal support for the empire and for law and order in Ireland would oblige the government to listen to their views and to support their attitude.[105] Thirdly, their attempts to secure agreement had the support of Plunkett and officials of the convention and the cabinet, such as Southborough and Professor W. G. S. Adams, who saw in the Midleton scheme a chance of saving the convention and of bringing it to a successful conclusion. They did not regard the scheme as perfect, nor did they accept all the southern unionist reasoning—they were especially doubtful of the degree of pressure that could be put upon the Ulstermen; but they recognised that the southern unionists had made a great advance, and deserved support, having 'rendered a very great service to the convention at a critical moment'.[106] Therefore, in December and January the officials actively canvassed the Midleton scheme among members of the convention;[107] urged the southern unionists to put their views firmly to the government;[108] and pressed upon the government the importance of these views, the necessity for government intervention on the lines suggested, and the need to handle southern unionists carefully in order to

103. Desart to Bernard, 1 Dec. 1917, B.M., Add. MS 52781, ff. 166–9.

104. Midleton to Adams, 22 Dec. 1917, B.L., F/66/1/56; Adams to Lloyd George, 5 Dec. 1917, *ibid.*, F/63/1/43.

105. Bernard to Harmsworth, 19 Jan. 1918, B.L., F/66/2/6. See also Bernard to Lloyd George, 3 June 1916, B.M., Add. MS 52781, ff. 1–9, and Midleton to Law, 11 June 1917, B.L., 82/1/17.

106. Adams to Lloyd George, 5 Dec. 1917, *ibid.*, F/63/1/44.

107. See e.g. Adams's report of an interview with Redmond, dated 6 Dec. 1917 but marked not submitted, and his report of an interview with Lord Londonderry, 10 Dec. 1917, B.L., F/63/1/45, 47.

108. See e.g. Adams to Bernard, 3 Dec. 1917, *ibid.*, F/66/1/54 (also in B.M., Add. MS 52781, f. 118).

prevent them from withdrawing from the convention if their views were not accepted in their entirety.[109]

Thus encouraged, the southern unionists tried, through letter and deputation, to persuade ministers to support their scheme and to put pressure upon nationalists and Ulster unionists to agree to it. They were particularly concerned about Ulster, which, they thought, had contributed little to the idea of a settlement. They thought, rightly, that if Ulster agreed to their scheme, the majority of nationalists would fall into line. They believed that though nationalists preferred fiscal autonomy, many would be prepared to accept the Midleton scheme, but only if Ulster was prepared to meet them on that ground; otherwise they would demand full fiscal autonomy. If, then, there was to be any chance of substantial agreement and the convention was to avoid failure and an early break-up, it was necessary to persuade Ulster to accept some such compromise as was proposed. During the early part of 1918 this southern unionist resentment at Ulster's unhelpful attitude became almost a phobia and the Midletonites were partly responsible for a press campaign against Ulster. But in November and December 1917 they wanted the Prime Minister to tell Ulstermen that partition was dead and that Ulster could no longer rely upon past pledges and the protection of the British government and the majority of the British public, arguing that the safeguards contained in their scheme could be regarded as a 'fair vindication of past pledges to Ulster'.[110] On 28 November Bernard asked the Archbishop of Canterbury to bring the southern unionists' view to the government, telling him 'the only way out that I can see is that the government should bring pressure to bear on *both* parties', but especially upon Ulster unionists who were sheltering behind past pledges. Davidson passed the letter on to Curzon who read it to the cabinet, and on 5 December 1917 the southern unionists were invited to meet Lloyd George and other members of the cabinet. They put their position to the ministers and the whole interview centred round the extent to which Lloyd George would tell Ulster of the danger she ran by clinging to her old policy, and the

109. Adams's reviews of the progress of the convention, 3, 4, Dec. 1917, Adams to Lloyd George, 5, 10, Dec. 1917, B.L., F/63/1/41, 42, 43, 44, 46; Adams to Lloyd George, 4 Jan. 1918, *ibid.*, F/63/2/7.

110. Midleton to Adams, 22 Dec. 1917, B.L., F/66/1/56.

question of how far southern unionists could guarantee that the convention would accept the Midleton scheme.[111]

Having prepared the ground behind the scenes, the southern unionists outlined their new position when the convention reassembled on 18 December. Midleton paved the way by giving notice of a motion (which explicitly reserved the levying of customs duties) for 2 January, explaining his proposals 'in a speech of great power and dignity'.[112] The southern unionists, he said, felt that a mistake had been made in attempting to come to an agreement not on the basis of principle, but with a view to conciliating outside opinion. His party still believed in the union, but they came into the convention to make a settlement. The deadlock showed that the time had arrived for definite proposals. His proposals were not made with a view to bargaining. The essential points of their scheme, as embodied in his resolution, were the supremacy of the United Kingdom parliament, representation at Westminster, and contribution by Ireland to imperial expenditure. These conditions were absolute and could not be reduced. The nationalist members, he admitted, had dealt with them generously in the matter of representation, and he appealed to Ulster to treat his proposals with corresponding generosity and not to remain the one outstanding party. They had all got to choose between compromise and chaos.

SIX

This insistence upon imperial control of the customs needs some explanation.[113] Had the southern unionists been willing to

111. Murray, *Archbishop Bernard*, pp. 319–21; Bernard's notes on the meeting at 10 Downing St., 5 Dec. 1917, B.M., Add. MS 52781, ff. 19–21. For other examples of southern unionist pressure, see Midleton to Adams, 22, 28 Dec. 1917, B.L., F/66/1/56–8; and Colvin, *Life of Lord Carson*, iii. 304–5.

112. *Confidential Report*, para. 111. The motion was 'That, in the event of the establishment of an Irish parliament, there shall be reserved to the parliament of the United Kingdom full authority for all imperial services, including the levying of customs duties, but subject to the above limitations the Irish parliament shall control all purely Irish services, including judicature and police with internal taxation and administration.'

113. This section is based, unless otherwise stated, on the memoranda circulated in the convention by the southern unionists (*Report of the Proceedings of the Irish Convention*, Appendix VII, and B.L., F/63/2/1) and on a private memorandum circulated at the end of October 1917 by Midleton among his southern unionist colleagues (T.C.D., Irish convention papers, MS 2987).

concede to an Irish parliament control of customs, they would have received the enthusiastic support of all nationalists in the convention. They accepted as a matter of course that any Irish parliament should have sufficient funds to pay the expenses of government, and in general were quite willing to concede large powers to the proposed parliament. They were willing to allow the Irish parliament control over internal taxation and over excise. Though usually coupled with the customs, the surrender of the excise could be justified in terms of the need to protect the Irish distilling and brewing industries from crushing impositions from a temperance parliament; but they would not allow an Irish parliament to impose customs duties. Some nationalists, particularly Bishop O'Donnell, argued that the Irish parliament should be given complete control over all branches of taxation, including customs and excise. The control of customs was particularly necessary, these nationalists held, for 'efficiency, economy and self-reliance', for sufficient revenue, to achieve justice in direct taxation, and to secure the wellbeing and development of the Irish economy.[114]

While agreeing with the desirability of these objects, southern unionists disagreed that fiscal autonomy involving control of the customs was necessary to secure them. They had four broad grounds of objection to Irish control of the customs: economic, class, imperial and tactical.

The economic arguments were twofold. In the first place, southern unionists had a very restricted view of the role of government. Their idea was that government expenditure should be kept to the minimum, and that control of customs was not necessary to secure sufficient revenue to meet legitimate expenditure. Bishop O'Donnell, basing his calculation on the Treasury estimate for 1917–18 and on current expenditure on Irish services, argued that without customs the Irish government would show a deficit of at least £398,000. He further calculated that with increased expenditure on land purchase, education, public works and territorial forces the deficit would grow. Southern unionists objected to this pessimistic view. On the one hand, they reckoned that the original calculation seriously underestimated the amount of revenue likely to accrue to an Irish parliament in peace time

114. For the nationalists' views on finances, see *Report of the Proceedings of the Irish Convention*, pp. 36–45 and Appendix IV.

from excise, income and super tax, death duties, etc., and from the post office, etc. They thought that with the end of the war and the lifting of restrictions on the output of beer and spirits, revenue from excise was likely to be double the estimate made by O'Donnell. On the other hand, southern unionists thought that O'Donnell overestimated the likely expenditure of an Irish government. Not only did they reckon that any increased expenditure on land purchase would either be repaid to the Irish parliament or be regarded as a payment *pro tanto* by Ireland to whatever contribution she was to make towards imperial expenditure, but they also doubted whether the time was suitable for ambitious schemes of reconstruction and development on the part of any country in the world, suggesting that 'Ireland . . . cannot reasonably expect to be placed in an exceptional position in this respect'. Secondly, southern unionists failed to see how control of the customs would stimulate Irish economic development. Granted free trade with Great Britain, they argued that only a small proportion of Ireland's import trade could be affected by the adoption of a protective policy, since the bulk of her imports of manufactured goods and raw materials came from Great Britain. Moreover, they maintained that, with the likely dislocation of trade and shipping in the post-war world, Ireland would benefit from a free trade policy: the shortage of shipping would ensure a high market for Irish agricultural produce, and Irish labour would be in demand to replace losses in manpower in Great Britain and on the continent. Furthermore, they also refused to believe that the customs policy of the imperial parliament would necessarily hinder the Irish economy. Not only was the British fiscal system unlikely to be changed, it was also extremely unlikely that any customs duties imposed by the imperial parliament upon articles of general consumption would endanger Irish interests; for, it was held, it would be equally to the interest of those who represented the British workman and those who represented the Irish farmer and labourer, to make the necessaries of life available as cheaply as possible, and Irish representation in the imperial parliament would ensure that this consideration would be kept in mind. Anyway, special precautions would be taken before any changes were made to consider special Irish interests.

A second ground of objection to conceding the customs was

more narrowly class based. It was never explicitly stated by
southern unionists in the convention, but it was suggested by
others and is well worth noting. Granard, one of the government
nominees, told Asquith that

people like Lord Iveagh have got at him [Midleton] and say, what is
to become of us at the end of fifteen years unless the imperial government controls the customs. It is an agricultural country and it is
naturally in the interests of the people to get their tea and sugar cheap;
surely the first thing they would do would be to increase the income
tax out of all knowledge and tax us out of existence.[115]

The third broad objection was more vital and was based upon
imperial grounds. Accustomed to thinking as much in imperial
as in Irish terms, they held that all legitimate Irish national
aspirations could be satisfied without control of the customs.
According to southern unionists, the question of fiscal autonomy
'must be considered from a wider standpoint, and that to ignore
imperial security in framing a constitution for a country, which
it is admitted by all sections of practical politicians must remain an
integral part of the British empire, is to prejudice Irish as well as
imperial interests'. On the one hand, to concede control of the
customs (and as a consequence the right to enter into independent
fiscal relations with other countries and to make commercial
treaties) to such a small country at the heart of the empire would
be to endanger the security and well-being of the empire and to
create friction between Great Britain and Ireland. For customs
duties affected not only fiscal relations between Great Britain and
Ireland but also between the United Kingdom, the Dominions
and foreign countries. On the other hand, the retention of the
customs by the imperial parliament could be taken as Ireland's
contribution to imperial expenditure: southern unionists did not
think that the estimated amount was excessive, while it had the
added advantage of removing the question of such a contribution
from the sphere of controversy. This, the imperial argument,
was a most compelling one for southern unionists, as can be seen
by the manner in which they wrote of it: they considered the
leaving of all taxation which is the subject of treaty in the hands

115. Lord Granard to Asquith, 17 Jan. 1918, quoted in McDowell, *Irish
Convention*, p. 152.

of the British parliament 'to be vital in the interests of the empire'. Moreover, they regarded a willingness to leave the customs to the imperial parliament as an indication of nationalist recognition of the supremacy of the imperial parliament, insisting that for the privilege of remaining an integral part of the empire Ireland 'must be prepared to make some sacrifice commensurate to that which Great Britain is making.'

Lastly, the southern unionists refused to concede the customs on what may be called tactical grounds. On the one hand, and this argument has not received sufficient attention, they wanted a settlement to apply to all Ireland, and knew that without imperial control of customs Ulster unionists would never agree to a settlement. As has been seen, Barrie had made this perfectly clear to Midleton, and this argument against concession weighed heavily with Midleton and, therefore, his colleagues whom he guided. In his private memorandum on customs, he wrote 'I believe that if we are to hope for a settlement by Ulster we must put matters on a satisfactory basis with regard to the members at Westminster and the customs.'[116] On the other hand, southern unionists regarded the leaving of the customs to the imperial parliament not only as a recognition by nationalists of imperial supremacy, but also as a token of nationalist good faith and a recognition of the advances made by southern unionists. While they were willing to make considerable concessions in order to reach a settlement, they did not think that concessions should be made by one side alone, and they pointed out to nationalists the advances that had been made over the 1914 act, particularly in respect of finance. They considered that they had 'made sacrifice of principles very dear to us in the hope that by mutual agreement as Irishmen we may heal long-standing differences', and looked for a similar sacrifice on the part of nationalists.

The southern unionists were very proud of their memoranda on finance, but two comments (at least) may be made on their stand over the question of fiscal autonomy. Firstly, the manner of their concessions over finance was unfortunate in some respects and did not help to convince staunch advocates of fiscal autonomy of the worth of southern unionists' fiscal views. For instance, soon

116. See also Desart's comment on Midleton's private memorandum on customs, to Midleton, 3 Nov. 1917, P.R.O., 30/67/33, ff. 1745-7.

after Powell had told the convention that the Midleton scheme represented their last word on the subject of self-government, an amendment to that scheme was circulated on behalf of southern unionists.[117] Secondly, the southern unionist stand was not well thought out. They had not really explored the difficulties involved in the separation of customs from excise; they had not worked out plans to administer the financial system they envisaged; and some of their calculations were very woolly. For instance, having argued that the 1917–18 figures for income and super tax under-estimated the amount of revenue that an Irish parliament would receive, they went on to say 'However, if we are wrong in thinking that the above estimate of Irish revenue for 1917–18 is short of the true revenue, probably by £1,000,000 or more, we consider that any deficit on the existing Irish expenditure . . . should be made good by the transfer of an appropriate sum from the exchequer of Great Britain in each year during the war'. Moreover, some of their arguments, particularly those sub-ordinating Ireland's interests to the 'more important interests' of the British empire and those restricting Ireland's expenditure on education and public works, must have been irksome to nationalists.

However, the real point of the southern unionist stand on the customs was not that it did or did not reveal them as financial experts. The point is that their stand reflected the size of the step that the southern unionists' representatives had taken in putting forward a compromise proposal. To them imperial control of the customs was a symbol not only of the imperial connection but also of nationalist good intentions, and they regarded it as a necessary bridge between their old and new positions.

SEVEN

Partly because of this insistence on imperial control of customs, the southern unionist initiative was not entirely successful. Nevertheless, it had considerable effect upon the convention. It drew it away from deadlock and re-vitalised it. After a desultory and disappointing November and early December, there ensued

117. See e.g. O'Donnell to Redmond, 22 Dec. 1917, in D. Gwynn, *Life of John Redmond*, pp. 575–7. Though the amendment did not affect the principle of imperial control, it should be noted.

in December and January a period of hopeful activity, involving optimistic interviews, much correspondence between southern unionists, nationalists and convention officials, and useful discussion in the convention. By the beginning of January 1918 it even looked as though the southern unionists would achieve their end and that their scheme would be accepted by the convention.[118] But the propitious moment was lost, with the result that extremists on either side had time to organise and frustrate a settlement. Nevertheless, the southern unionist scheme and activity laid the basis for eventual agreement between southern unionists and a majority of nationalists in the convention, and ensured by the end of 1917 that a majority of the members would agree on a scheme of home rule.

Their activity contributed to this happy result in two respects. In the first place, the southern unionists encouraged the government to take a more positive attitude to the proceedings of the convention and to put some pressure upon the dissenting parties in order to prevent a break-down. Although the government would not, and felt that it could not, give Ulster an ultimatum, as southern unionists had hoped,[119] and although the government did not accept their scheme in its entirety (when it made certain proposals to the convention in February 1918),[120] Lloyd George was grateful for the southern unionist intervention and received southern unionists in a very flattering manner.[121] In December 1917 the government and Lloyd George in particular was in a difficult position *vis-à-vis* Ireland and the convention. Lloyd George was under pressure from Redmond to cajole Ulster into agreement; yet while he appreciated the value of a settlement, Lloyd George was immersed in the details of the war and could spare little time to consider Ireland, especially as the continued existence of the old forces against home rule within and without the cabinet would render perilous any intervention.[122] In this

118. For this optimistic activity, see McDowell, *Irish Convention*, pp. 133 ff.
119. See e.g. Bernard's notes on the meeting at 10 Downing Street, 5 Dec. 1917, B.M., Add. MS 52781, ff. 19–21; Harmsworth to Bernard, 21, 22 Jan. 1918, *ibid.*, ff. 22–5.
120. See below, pp. 126–7.
121. Bernard's notes on the meeting at 10 Downing Street, 5 Dec. 1917, B.M., Add. MS 52781, ff. 19–21.
122. See e.g. the exchange of letters in Nov. 1917 between Redmond and Lloyd George quoted in D. Gwynn, *Life of John Redmond*, pp. 569–72; Curzon to Archbishop of Canterbury, 17 Oct. 1917, B.M., Add. MS 52782, f. 180.

situation the new departure of the southern unionists' representatives became an essential element in the government's calculations and in two ways encouraged and enabled the government to take a more positive line towards the convention.

On the one hand, the southern unionist decision to accept a modification of the union altered the balance of forces within the cabinet. It was afterwards said that the southern unionist action in the convention had weakened the hands of the unionist members of the cabinet,[123] and Carson's resignation shows that there is some truth in this.[124] The opposition of the southern unionists to home rule had been one of the essential ingredients in the unionist party's opposition to home rule, and it is understandable that the southern unionist action made ministers like Curzon, who was in indirect touch with Bernard, less opposed to intervention in the convention and weakened the case of those opposing a settlement and government pressure on Ulster unionists.[125] But it would be more accurate to say that the southern unionist decision strengthened the hands of the home rule ministers in their dealings with their unionist colleagues, enabling Lloyd George to write on 12 January, 1918, to Ulster's champion, Law:

I take a very serious view of the Irish situation. If the southern unionists and the nationalists agree, as they are likely to, the position of *any* government that refuses to carry out that compact will be an impossible one. I simply could not face it. For if the government refuse to act under these circumstances, everyone in Great Britain and throughout the world—notably in America—would say that we were sacrificing the interests of the war to that of a small political section. In fact, they would say we were doing it merely because Carson was in the government.

I know what there is to be said on the other side, but it will be said in vain. The Irish in America would be more rampageous than ever, and Wilson's position, embarrassing enough as it is now with Germans

123. Carson, *Irish Times*, 4 Dec. 1918.
124. Colvin, *Life of Lord Carson*, iii. 305–6, 308–11.
125. Canterbury to Bernard, 15, 18 Oct. 1917, B.M., Add. MS 52782, ff. 178–80; Bernard to Canterbury, 28 Nov. 1917; Canterbury to Curzon, 30 Nov. 1917, *ibid.*, ff. 186–9; D. Gwynn, *Life of John Redmond*, pp. 578–9. For instance, at the end of December Midleton had gone to London to discuss the convention's prospects with Lloyd George, and on 1 January he returned to Dublin with a document, dated 31 Dec. 1917, that was in Curzon's handwriting, was initialled by Lloyd George, and pledged the Prime Minister to energetic action on the southern unionist scheme, under certain conditions (see below).

and Irishmen on his flank, would become untenable. The Irish are now paralysing the war activities of America. You must remember it would come out that the President, through House, made a special appeal to us, and that representations were made to us by Spring Rice and F.E. and others. This is the opportunity for Ulster to show that it places the empire above everything, and if the little Protestant communities of the south, isolated in a turbulent sea of Sinn Feinism and popery, can trust their lives and their property to Midleton's scheme, surely the powerful communities of the north might take that risk for the sake of the empire in danger. If America goes wrong we are lost. I wish Ulster would fully realise what that means. I am afraid they don't.

Beg Barrie, who is from all I have seen of him a sensible and broadminded fellow who is above the mere bigotries of any sect, to lift his province to the high level of this opportunity. If Ulster declines then if the government do not deal with the situation, the only alternative is for Carson to take the responsibility for running the war; form his own cabinet; run Ireland on Ulster principles, and take the risks with America. I certainly cannot accept the responsibilities in the present critical situation of directing the war with a great row in Ireland over the refusal of the British government to accept a scheme proposed by the Protestant unionists of the three Irish provinces.[126]

On the other hand, and perhaps this is more important where a man of Lloyd George's temperament is concerned, the southern unionist scheme gave the government a line of approach in dealing with the dissenting parties. Since November Lloyd George had been under pressure from Redmond to intervene and to force Ulster to abate the demand for fiscal unity, and Lloyd George had been able to give only very evasive answers. Perhaps it is going too far to say that the Midleton scheme prevented Lloyd George from taking any action that would have precipitated the breakdown of the convention; but it did seem to provide the ideal solution to Lloyd George's dilemma. There is a world of difference between his letters to Redmond on 26 November and the 15 December by which date Lloyd George was fully acquainted with the Midleton scheme. The former letter gave Redmond no encouragement whatsoever, the latter was able to hold out the hope that 'the best hope of a settlement lies along the lines of the southern unionist proposals, and I shall put

126. Lloyd George to Law, 12 Jan. 1918, B.L., 82/8/4.

this view before my colleagues in the cabinet . . . You may rest
assured that I am most anxious to do what is in my power to
secure without delay a settlement of the question'.[127] And, once
having determined and been able to intervene effectively in the
convention, Lloyd George was able to coax the convention along
in 1918.

The second respect in which the southern unionists' activity
renewed the vigour of the convention and laid the basis for a
majority agreement was by its effect upon nationalists. The
Midletonites' willingness to compromise and their pressure on
the government encouraged many nationalists to believe that a
settlement was possible. They gave Redmond and his followers
courage to continue to work for and vote for proposals acceptable
to southern unionists. They did so in two ways. First, the
Midleton scheme was regarded by many nationalists as a great
advance by southern unionists, and many saw that it offered a
real chance of a settlement which had to be taken. They discounted
the objections put forward by their more extreme colleagues and
thought that the generous advance by those who 'have put behind
them all bitter memories' deserved an equally generous response
from nationalists.[128] Several reasons led Redmond and his
followers to consider seriously Midleton's scheme. There was an
intuitive response to the advance made by those whom Midleton
represented. Gwynn recorded,

The southern unionists were the old landowning and professional
class, friendly in all ways of intercourse, but politically severed and
sundered from the mass of the population. Now, they came forward
with an offer to help in attaining our desire—quite frankly, against
their own declared conviction that the union was the best plan, but
with an equally frank recognition that the majority was the majority
and was honest in its intent.[129]

The very phrases in which Gwynn and Redmond described the
southern unionists' magnanimity are significant of their gratitude
to the scattered few, 'who had suffered most and who might

127. D. Gwynn, *Life of John Redmond*, pp. 569–73.
128. See e.g. S. Gwynn, *John Redmond's Last Years*, p. 320, for a summary of
Redmond's speech to the convention on 4 Jan. 1918.
129. *Ibid.*, p. 313.

naturally have entertained most bitterness', and who 'had had the hardest battle to fight in the struggle over home rule'.[130] These emotional responses were reinforced by more practical considerations. The continued growth of Sinn Fein meant that constitutional nationalists had to emerge from the convention with allies and with a workable scheme of self-government, if the constitutional movement were to survive in Ireland.[131] Moreover, agreement would mean the completion of land purchase on favourable terms (on the basis of a sub-committee report) and Ireland would escape further war taxation.[132]

Admittedly there were drawbacks to an agreement with the southern unionists, and not all nationalists were willing to pay such a high price. There was the customs. Some, like Bishop O'Donnell, criticised Midleton's attitude to the customs as ill-thought out, and insisted upon Irish control of the customs.[133] However, others were not prepared to judge the southern unionists as financial experts and to allow the customs to be an obstacle to agreement. After pressure from moderates, such as Gwynn, the southern unionists decided to concede the collection of customs to the proposed Irish parliament,[134] and this concession was sufficient to decide Redmond and many of his followers to come to terms with the southern unionists. Imperial control of the customs seemed a small price to pay for agreement with their former opponents. Redmond recognised that southern unionists would not compromise further on a point important to them more as a symbol of close union between the two kingdoms than by reason of the economic advantages attributed to it. He considered that nationalists would be 'political fools' not to cement an alliance with the southern unionists on account of not having immediate control of customs 'which we all declare we would not

130. *Ibid.*, p. 320.
131. See e.g. the notes of Redmond's speech to the convention, 4 Jan. 1918, given in D. Gwynn, *Life of John Redmond*, pp. 580–2; Redmond to T. P. O'Connor, 2 Dec. 1917, and O'Connor to Redmond, 29 Dec. 1917, *ibid.*, pp. 577–8.
132. See e.g. Redmond to Michael Governey, 14 Feb. 1918, *ibid.*, pp. 592–3.
133. D. Gwynn, *Life of John Redmond*, pp. 574–6, 578, 583–5.
134. S. Gwynn, *John Redmond's Last Years*, pp. 316–7; Desart to Bernard, 16 Dec. 1917, B.M., Add. MS 52781, ff. 171–12; Bernard's notes on interview with Redmond, 12 Dec. 1917, *ibid.*, 52782, ff. 190–3; Gwynn to Bernard, 28 Dec. 1917, *ibid.*, f. 197; Gwynn to Redmond, 21 Dec. 1917, N.L.I., Redmond papers, MS 15192.

and could not put into force against England'.[135] Another obstacle
to agreement with the southern unionists was the question of the
consent of Ulster. Before committing themselves on the southern
unionist scheme some nationalists wanted to be assured of
Ulster's attitude. They feared the consequences if they and the
southern unionists reached an agreement which Ulster rejected.
They feared that if Ulster stood out, there would not be 'substantial agreement' and that the basis on which southern unionists
and nationalists had united would be treated not as a final
settlement, but as a bargaining offer, to be whittled down by the
government in conformity with Ulster's demands and to the
complete discredit of moderate nationalism.[136] But to Redmond
and many of his followers the question of Ulster's consent was
not an insuperable difficulty. This was the second way in which
southern unionists brought nationalists to agreement. Their
pressure on Lloyd George had enabled him to encourage
Redmond to persevere in the convention and then had also
elicited from the Prime Minister the written pledge that

if the southern unionist scheme is carried by the convention with
substantial agreement—i.e., with the opposition of Ulster alone—the
P.M. will use his personal influence with his colleagues . . . to accept
the report and to give it legislative effect.[137]

Nationalists would have preferred a more concrete commitment
on the part of the government as a whole, but many felt that
they could have all the more confidence in the above and later
pledges because of the conversion of the southern unionists. This,
they hoped, would mean a profound change in the attitude of the
House of Lords to the Irish question and in 'all those social
influences whose power we had felt so painfully'. Therefore,
Gwynn believed, the government could undoubtedly carry a
measure giving effect to a compact between southern unionists
and nationalists.[138]

135. S. Gwynn, *John Redmond's Last Years*, p. 320; Redmond to Governey,
14 Feb. 1918, quoted in D. Gwynn, *Life of John Redmond*, pp. 592–3. See also
e.g. the views of Sir Bertram Windle, to Lloyd George, 26 Jan. 1918, B.L.,
F/66/2/8.

136. See e.g. O'Donnell to Redmond, 14 Jan. 1918, quoted in D. Gwynn,
Life of John Redmond, pp. 584–5.

137. *Ibid.*, p. 579.

138. S. Gwynn, *John Redmond's Last Years*, pp. 313, 333–4.

EIGHT

The southern unionist activity and initiative thus moved the convention away from deadlock and laid the basis for agreement with nationalists. As has been said, their achievement might have been greater. When at the beginning of 1918 Midleton laid his slightly revised scheme before the convention, Redmond advised acceptance. The outlook seemed fair, but, largely owing to Plunkett's obsession with land purchase, further consideration was postponed for a few days. In the event no vote was taken on the scheme, since the extremists on either side had had time to organise and the propitious moment was allowed to pass. Thereupon the government intervened to try to reduce the differences: deputations from the convention, including one from the southern unionists, were interviewed in London; pressure was put upon the Ulster unionists to accept a settlement; and on 25 February, in a letter to the chairman of the convention, Lloyd George not only pledged the government to action on receipt of the convention's report, but also indicated the lines upon which a report should be made, lines which reserved to the imperial parliament more powers than had the Midleton scheme. Thereupon, by common consent, the Midleton scheme was dropped for a series of resolutions tabled by Lord MacDonnell which were in substance an acceptance of the government's suggestions.

Henceforth, the conference was concerned largely with voting. Though still active and prominent in debate, the southern unionists now played a less distinctive role, co-operating in the main with moderate nationalists to reach a settlement and to vote down the extremists of both sides. The Ulster unionists revived their demand for exclusion which the southern unionists helped to defeat by 52 votes to 19; but the biggest source of tension was the fact that the Lloyd George proposals reserved the customs to the imperial parliament. Eventually, however, a compromise was proposed by Macdonnell (to the effect that customs and excise should be under the control of the imperial parliament during the war, and thereafter until the question had been considered and a decision arrived at by the imperial parliament, the decision to be taken not later than seven years after the conclusion of peace); and it was carried only by a majority of 4, a combination of 34 nationalists and Ulster unionists being defeated by 38 southern unionists and Redmondites. This was the crucial vote and once it was out of the way a majority of the convention, 66 in all, including 10 southern unionists and 45 nationalists, agreed upon a scheme of self-government for all Ireland on 5 April 1918.[139]

For this majority the southern unionists were largely responsible. On the surface the majority was due to the willingness of some nationalists to give up the customs and to the active intervention of the government in the affairs of the convention, but behind both these factors was the southern unionists' scheme and activity. Their willingness to agree to Irish self-government and their energy in working for it did not suit everybody, but their self-sacrifice saved the convention from breaking down in 1917 and paved the way for agreement. On the one hand, they encouraged and enabled the government, and especially the Prime Minister, to intervene in the convention; and, on the other hand, they encouraged Redmond and many of his followers to continue working for a settlement at the end of 1917. Had Redmond been in better health and spirits and shown energetic leadership, a vote might have been taken in January on the Midleton scheme. It was not, but Redmond's advice to nationalists to co-operate with the southern unionists had its effect after his death. As

139. On the progress of the convention from January, see McDowell, *Irish Convention*, pp. 142 ff.

The scheme upon which a majority agreed recommended the immediate establishment of self-government by an Irish ministry responsible to a parliament consisting of two houses, composed on highly artificial lines. For fifteen years southern unionists were to be represented by nominated members, and Ulster was to have extra members elected by special constituencies representing commercial and agricultural interests. The Irish parliament was to have a general power to make laws for Ireland and to have full control of internal administration and direct taxation. There were, however, limitations to the power of the proposed Irish parliament, in addition to the general reservation of the supreme power and authority of the imperial parliament over all persons and causes in Ireland. On the one hand, certain restrictions were to be imposed on its power in matters within its competence, mainly directed to safeguarding the liberties of the Protestant minority and the interests of existing Irish officers. On the other hand, certain imperial matters, right of peace or war, army and navy, treaties and foreign relations, were specifically excluded from its competence, and the question of customs and excise was postponed in accordance with the terms of Macdonnell's motion. Representation at Westminster was to continue, forty-two members being elected by panels formed in each of the four provinces by members of the Irish House of Commons in that province, and a fifth composed of members nominated by the House of Commons.

Gwynn has recorded, and his own letters bear out the truth of what he wrote in 1919:

That advice was not to refuse the hand of friendship which offered itself from men who by alliance with us could take away from the home rule demand all sectarian character: who could bring for the first time a great and representative body of Irish landlord opinion and Irish Protestant opinion into line with the opinion of Irish tenants and Irish Catholics. In order to act upon this advice men needed to face a powerful combination of forces and much threatened unpopularity: they had to encounter the hostility of an able and vindictively conducted newspaper; they had to separate themselves politically from the united voice of their own hierarchy; they had to break away from the politician who for many years now had equalled Redmond in his influence in Ireland and surpassed him in popularity. All of them were representative of constituents, all were living among those whom they represented; not a man of them but knew he would worsen his personal and political position by what he did. Yet, for that is the true way to state it, they stood to their own dead leader's policy.[140]

Not all nationalists accepted this view and followed their dead leader's advice, but many did support a settlement acceptable to southern unionists in order to achieve a majority report for self-government for all Ireland.

This was the southern unionists' decisive contribution to the convention. Once again the southern unionists had proved themselves a significant factor in the Irish question. By making the first concrete proposal for home rule and by canvassing it vigorously, they ensured that a majority of the convention would agree upon a scheme of Irish self-government. Apart from illustrating the importance of the southern unionists, the convention marks a significant stage in the decline of a distinctive Anglo-Irish political standpoint. On the one hand, it led to a split in southern unionist ranks; on the other hand, it confirmed some southern unionists in the view that an agreed settlement of the Irish question was not only possible but also desirable.

140. S. Gwynn, *John Redmond's Last Years*, pp. 329–30; see also the note of the less moderate nationalists in *Report of the Proceedings of the Irish Convention*, p. 41, and Sir Bertram Windle's comments in Monica Taylor, *Sir Bertram Windle. A Memoir* (1932), p. 269.

V

Phase Five: Disagreement, 1918

THE southern unionist stand in the convention marked a significant stage in the decline of a distinctive, united Anglo-Irish
political movement in two respects. Not only did it represent a
real attempt to come to terms with the home rule movement and
an abandonment of the negative unionism that had existed since
1885, it also led to the first serious rift in southern unionist ranks,
as the Midletonites failed to convert the I.U.A. to their views
and eventually split the organisation. In fact, the convention
ushered in the fifth phase in the decline of southern unionism
(1918–19), a phase characterised by disagreement and division as
to the future development of the unionist movement in the south.

TWO

That there was substantial division of opinion over the convention became clear on 1 January 1918 when that latent hostility
to a settlement came to the surface at a meeting of the executive
committee of the I.U.A. The executive committee was a large
body, with some 140 members entitled to attend.[1] These were
the presidents and vice-presidents—*ex-officio* representatives
elected by each of the county branches, 20 members elected by
the general council, and not more than 46 members co-opted by
the foregoing. In view of the large *ex-officio* element, thirty-eight
presidents and vice-presidents, mainly Irish peers, and the fact
that the last elections had been held in 1913, the executive committee was not by 1918 necessarily representative of or in close
touch with southern unionist opinion. Nevertheless, it was the
body summoned to hear an important statement by Midleton.[2]

1. I.U.A., *Annual Report 1912–13.*
2. This account is based upon: I.U.A. circular, 15 Apr. 1918; S.U.C. circular,
20 Mar. 1918; John E. Walsh's letters in *Irish Times,* 11, 14 Mar., 3 Apr. 1918;
Denis R. Pack Beresford, letter *ibid.,* 12 Mar. 1918; Midleton, *Records and
Reactions,* p. 242.

It will be recalled that this was a crucial time at the convention, especially for the southern unionists who had put forward the Midleton scheme to prevent deadlock and a break-up. Midleton had anticipated difficulties even from his own supporters in the south and the object of this meeting of the executive committee was evidently to strengthen his position by obtaining the explicit approval of the I.U.A. Thus the Midletonites seem to have taken great care to ensure a sufficiently large though sufficiently favourable attendance. Although the summons to the meeting was marked 'most urgent', no indication was given of the momentous nature of his proposed statement and only a few people appeared to know that the committee was to be asked to consent to the modification of the Act of Union. The attendance was large enough for the meeting to be moved from the offices of the I.U.A. to the Shelbourne Hotel, but the forty-five members attending hardly constituted a mass meeting, as Midleton later suggested. Moreover, they represented barely one-third of those eligible to attend meetings of the executive committee and had more people known of the nature of the meeting the attendance might have been greater.[3] Nevertheless, there were more than sufficient to constitute a quorum and the meeting proceeded.

Midleton was determined to carry the meeting in favour of the delegates. Having made his statement of what the delegates proposed to do, he asked the meeting if they wanted to hear the views of a very distinguished member of the convention, Archbishop Bernard. Though a strong unionist, Bernard was not a member of the I.U.A. and undoubtedly 'the introduction of a stranger to, and the pressure of outside influence at' a meeting of the executive committee was irregular.[4] It was, however, scarcely improper, or such as to invalidate the meeting, and no one ever disputed that, having been given the opportunity to hear the archbishop, the committee 'unanimously requested' Midleton to invite him 'to give them his counsel'. No text of Bernard's speech appears to have been available, but he did urge the advantages of the settlement he had been helping Midleton to bring about.[5] Then the executive committee was invited to approve the action of the delegates.

3. Major O'Connor, letter in *Dublin Daily Express,* 16 Mar. 1918.
4. S.U.C. circular, 20 Mar. 1918.
5. I.U.A. circular, 15 Apr. 1918.

Their action was not unanimously approved. As yet there seems to have been no personal animosity towards the delegates, but a few members of the committee were determined to maintain the union. Richard Bagwell, the historian, was seconded by Major John Robert Bramston Pretyman Newman[6] in moving a resolution thanking 'the unionist delegates for the trouble they have taken at the Irish convention' and recording 'our unabated attachment to the legislative union, for the maintenance of which the Alliance was framed [*sic*], and still exists.' This resolution must have put the executive in a delicate position: to have approved it would have seemed a rebuff to Midleton and the delegates; to have rejected it would have been tantamount to dissolving the I.U.A. After debate, therefore, this resolution was withdrawn and another expressing confidence in the delegates was put to the meeting. This resolution, that 'we heartily thank our representatives for the work they have done in the Irish convention, and feel that the interests of the southern unionists should be left in their hands', was carried by 41 votes to 4. This virtual approval of the delegates' intentions did not go unchallenged. Still hoping to retrieve the situation, their critics asked 'that the further consideration of Lord Midleton's statement be adjourned, and that immediate steps be taken to arrange a conference between this committee and the Ulster Unionist Council.'[7]

The opponents of a settlement contradicted all the arguments put forward to justify the delegates' action.[8] Also interpreting their interests in relation to the British and Irish situations, they still believed that their interests could and would be best served by maintaining the union. On the one hand, they firmly rejected the Midletonites' pessimistic view of the British political situation. On the other hand, they could find no cause for optimism in the Irish situation.

6. (1871–1947); ed. Charterhouse and Cambridge; capt. 5th Royal Munster Fusiliers and major in 17th Batt. (Footballers) Middlesex Regt; M.P., Enfield division of Middlesex (1910–18), Finchley (1918–23); D.L., J.P., H.S, (1898), Co. Cork; Newberry Manor and Milshannig House, Co. Cork.

7. S.U.C. circular, 20 Mar. 1918.

8. No detailed record of the executive committee's discussion appears to be available, and some objections to the delegates' action crystallised only as the dispute with the Midletonites developed, particularly arguments relating to the feasibility of maintaining the union. With this reservation, however, it is possible to get some idea of the motives of those who opposed the delegates from the subsequent press controversy, verified and expanded by earlier correspondence.

They saw hope in the British situation. The union was not a lost cause. The act of 1914 could be disregarded, even repealed, for it had been placed on the statute book by 'one of the greatest acts of political fraud that history has recorded' and by methods which were a 'fraud upon the constitution':[9] the liberal government had had no mandate for it, and it had been put on the statute book in defiance of all pledges that the subject would not be re-opened during the war and that it would be accompanied by an amending bill dealing with Ulster. 'It is not thus that ancient constitutions are overthrown in a democratic country, or that any binding sanctions can be claimed for the acts of those who were guilty of such machinations.' Thus Midleton's opponents felt able to conclude 'the union is not dead. It cannot be killed by means such as these'.[10] Having disposed of, perhaps, the main strut of the Midletonite case for a settlement, they dismissed most of the others almost out of hand. They admitted that the union had been shown up in a bad light of recent years, but this, they held, was not the fault of the system of government under the union, but of the liberal government which had failed to operate it:

What Ireland wants is men, not measures. The most perfect system which the wit of man could devise becomes a mockery in the hands of weak and incompetent statesmen . . . The machinery of government is there. What is needed are men who will use it.[11]

Changes in the Irish government in May 1918 strengthened them in this view that what Ireland needed was strong men. With the appointment of Lord French as Lord Lieutenant it seemed that southern unionists had at last found a friend in effective power in Dublin Castle. The appointment of a man of such military prowess, who had broken 'the first onrush of the German hordes at the zenith of their strength and preparedness with his "contemptible little army"', was hailed with relief by Irish loyalists who generally believed that he had been appointed with a free hand to take such steps as he deemed necessary for the

9. J. M. Wilson, letter in *Irish Times,* 30 Mar. 1918; Walsh, letter *ibid.,* 8 Apr. 1918.

10. Walsh, *ibid.*

11. 'Call to unionists', 4 Mar. 1918, P.R.O.N.I., D 989A/1/10.

maintenance of order and the restoration of trade and business in the country.[12] Even though this was not wholly true, and some southern unionists were disappointed to learn that French believed that the establishment of an Irish parliament was inevitable, many were still able to find comfort in his presence and administration. Himself an Irishman, he involved himself in Irish life in a way that impressed many southern unionists. His residence and property at Drumdoe on the shores of Loch Key in Co. Roscommon were at least a comforting testimony to his faith in the Irish future, for he started buildings and extensions 'which must have cost a mint of money, with a full intention of settling down and making it his home'.[13] And, unlike his immediate predecessors, he showed a great concern for the southern unionist class, especially the ladies among them. He so delighted Margaret ffolliott by visiting her that she wrote, 'he appears to take a genuine interest in his new job, and to be bent on carrying it out with more firmness and discretion than we have been accustomed to of late years'.[14] Moreover, with French's arrival in Ireland, there was a marked improvement so that by 1919 Ireland was comparatively peaceful. Discerning and unbiassed observers might have attributed this to the policy adopted by Sinn Fein of seeking international recognition of the Irish republic; but the critics of the new departure preferred not to see it this way. Having long argued that what was wrong with Ireland was not the Act of Union but the men who operated it, they willingly attributed any improvement to French's administration, and were encouraged to hope for firm administration in the future.[15]

As far as these determined unionists were concerned, the Midletonite case was easy to demolish. The argument that British politicians no longer supported the union was regarded as no argument at all, for it was up to Irish unionists to make them care

12. Sir Henry Augustus Robinson, *Memories: Wise and Otherwise* (1923, reprinted 1924), pp. 261–3. Robinson, 1st bt (1857–1927); abandoned a business career in favour of the civil service; inspector for Local Government Board, 1879–91; a commissioner, 1891–8; vice-president, 1898–1922, responsible for implementing the 1898 local government reform; K.C.B. and P.C., 1902; bt, 1920; Foxrock, Co. Dublin.

13. *Ibid.*, p. 262.

14. Margaret ffolliott to Montgomery, 17 Aug. 1918, P.R.O.N.I., D 627/436.

15. See e.g. the tenor of the memorandum laid by a deputation from the I.U.A. before the Chief Secretary for Ireland, c. Mar. 1919, *ibid.*, D 989A/8/23.

F

for the union. They considered that the Irish unionist case had gone by default in the past—an attitude in which they were confirmed when they learnt that the delegates had made little effort to secure the union at the convention.

The liberals had had no mandate for home rule and thus the issue should be submitted 'honestly' to the electors. What was now needed was not compromise but a vigorous effort on behalf of the union in British politics: to the objection that southern unionists were 'voiceless and powerless in the House of Commons', they retorted 'they are determined to remain so no longer'.[16] The changing condition of British politics was also lightly regarded. Not even the prospect of a 'democratic or socialist government' deflected the delegates' opponents. With a touching faith in democracy, in Great Britain that is, they predicted that

The democracy of England would see clearly enough that government of Ireland by the King's enemies would not promote content and prosperity in that country, or safeguard the interests of the United Kingdom.[17]

This rosy view of the prospects of the union in British politics was in part the result of their pessimistic view of the Irish situation: they preferred the devils they did not know to the devils they believed they knew. The optimistic attitude of the delegates towards the future of Ireland was almost diametrically opposed to the view held by their opponents. Whereas the former had been dismayed by Ulster unionists' acceptance of partition in 1916, their opponents regarded it as irrelevant—it had been actuated 'by a patriotic desire to do their utmost to secure the success of our aims', and conditions had since altered so that Ulster still remained the biggest obstacle to home rule.[18] The basis of the delegates' opponents' pessimistic view of the Irish situation lay not in the increasing exclusiveness of Ulster unionism but in their continued suspicion of Irish nationalism and Irish nationalists.

Admittedly some nationalists had assisted in the war effort, but

16. Walsh, letter in *Irish Times*, 23 Mar. 1918.
17. Walsh, letter *ibid.*, 16 Mar. 1918. See also R. Bagwell, *ibid.*, 18 Mar. 1918.
18. Walsh, letter *ibid.*, 3 Apr. 1918.

that did not signify any change of heart among nationalists, for
many nationalist leaders had not assisted in the war effort. Dillon,
for instance, boasted of never standing on a recruiting platform;
and Wilson asked of one correspondent, 'Does he remember that
at least seventy out of the eighty nationalist members have done
nothing during these terrible years of war to further its cause?'[19]
If anything, nationalism had seemed to become more intransigent,
more extreme, during the war as the older party was being
overshadowed by and being gradually absorbed into the developing Sinn Fein party, a party which made a profession of anarchy
and sedition.[20] It was not just the pro-German activities of Sinn
Fein that dismayed some southern unionists and intensifed old
objections to home rule; for the determined nature of Sinn Fein
made a deep and fearful impression upon them. One correspondent wrote thus to Wilson, and his letters are worth quoting at
length:

The active Sinn Feiners are all young and intelligent men, generally
teetotallers. Unlike the ordinary political fellows, they do not patronise
public houses and talk there over matters. They are silent and know
how to keep their mouths closed, but they think and plot the more . . .
the fact is they are—a great many of them—'brainy' in well-to-do
positions; they speak little in public, and as in all secret political
gatherings—suffering as they think under great wrongs—there is a
danger of an outburst. Of course you know in Cork we always talk
and do not act—that may be the case, but this silence on a matter
which is deep in the hearts of thousands of young fellows in the city
is to say the least very ugly and portends something more than usual
happening unless they [are] pulled up in time . . .[21]
. . . The next rebellion will commence at a pre-arranged minute at
night, and isolated residents in the country will be held up as hostages
if not 'done down' without any warning. What is to prevent 20 German
submarines landing 100 German and American-Irish officers each
with cargoes of arms all round the coast? What is to precipitate this
second revolution will be the immediate fear of compulsory service
and the salutary lesson the Irish harvesters are now receiving in
England . . .
What the military authorities cannot grasp is that it is of paramount
necessity that the British garrison should show itself in every parish in

19. Wilson, letter *ibid.*, 30 Mar. 1918.
20. *Ibid.*; Walsh, letters *ibid.*, 30 Mar., 2, 6 Apr. 1918.
21. M. H. Franks to Wilson, 5 Mar. 1917, P.R.O.N.I., D 989A/8/7.

Ireland before the long summer nights turn into dark winter nights. Now is the time to exercise the troops—cavalry and infantry and guns—by route marches and staff rides.[22]

Whether or not Sinn Fein actually planned to take hostages is an important question but just as important was the impression created among southern unionists by Sinn Feiners and rumours about Sinn Fein. Others had noticed its determination and efficiency in by-elections in 1917. After its activities at North Roscommon, which Sinn Fein won in February, one unionist reflected: 'I can only conceive that the type of person working the Sinn Fein cause was exactly similar in appearance and manner with those who must have carried through the French revolution.' Southern unionists could expect short shrift from such men under any system but the union.[23] And it was, perhaps, singularly unfortunate for the success of the Midletonite attempt to lead a new departure that at the beginning of 1918 there was a series of incidents of land grabbing which touched the very basis of southern unionist existence in Ireland.

In many respects these were cogent arguments against modifying the union, but as counter-arguments they did not move the committee, and the proposal to adjourn was lost by 8 votes to 34.[24] Apparently, therefore, the southern unionists had approved the action of Midleton and the delegates. The executive committee of the I.U.A. had endorsed their action by a substantial majority and no one had suggested at the meeting that the committee was out of touch with southern unionist opinion: there had been some dissentients, more, in fact, than in 1917, but their views had not weighed with the committee. Yet what was striking, apart from the number of people who did not attend the meeting and the factor of surprise, was the persistence of the minority in moving two resolutions.

THREE

Indeed, it might have been instructive for Midleton to have enquired more deeply into the reasons for this persistence. How

22. Franks to Wilson, undated but probably summer 1917, *ibid.*
23. Quoted in Wilson's report on the North Roscommon by-election, *ibid.*, D 989A/9/7/.
24. S.U.C. circular, 20 Mar. 1918.

could a minority interpret the facts of the case so differently from the rest of the committee? It may have been a question of personal differences. Walter Long later suggested that the differences between the I.U.A. and the Anti-Partition League were based upon 'a great deal of personal feeling',[25] and some of the delegates' opponents certainly felt bitter at their 'betrayal';[26] but these personal animosities were in the main the result of the delegates' action, not a reason to oppose them. Partly it was a matter of age. A man like Richard Bagwell, born in December 1840 and to die in December 1918, confessed that he was too old to change his views.[27] Partly, too, it was a matter of training and temperament. Though not a member of the I.U.A., Bernard was, perhaps, a good representative of the attitude of the delegates. Though of conservative temperament, he was a man of affairs with an acute brain, quicker than most men to see the potentialities of a given situation and anxious that he or the institutions he served should play a leading role in modern life. For instance, despite the obvious prejudices and wishes of laymen in Ireland, he had tried to broaden the Church of Ireland; and he adopted the same approach to the union in 1917–18 in attempting to broaden the basis of unionism in the south of Ireland.[28] His attitude to social and political questions was almost in complete contrast to that of Henry Macnamara who remained to the end a staunch opponent of Irish self-government. Although a flamboyant personality and character who produced an even more flamboyant son, Francis, on questions of social and political order he was a staunch conservative, almost revelling in the *status quo,* forbidding, for instance, his son to mix too freely with the peasantry. Francis Macnamara's daughter has recorded:

To go back to my earliest memory of the owl and pampas grass. The place was my grandfather's house, Ennistymon House, County Clare. This was an elegant white Georgian house like so many other country houses in Ireland. Standing on a hill where once the Macnamaras had built a castle against the pirates sailing up the river from the sea at

---

25. Report by Long on his visit to Ireland, Jan. 1920, B.L., F/34/1/6.
26. See below, pp. 154, 163-4, 172, 177, 179, 181-2.
27. Montgomery to H. T. Barrie, 21 Jan. 1918, P.R.O.N.I., D 627/433. Bagwell and Bernard clashed over the issue at a meeting of the standing committee of the synod of the Church of Ireland.
28. Murray, *Archbishop Bernard, passim.*

Lahinch, or against rival chiefs on land, it dominated the river and the scoop of a valley . . . The river gave us joy in the summer with an innocent flow of clear water, yet it held many of the country girls' tragedies. In a swirly backwater below the house the corpses of newborn babies conceived out of wedlock were found drowned together with unwanted kittens and puppies. . . .

My grandfather . . . was high sheriff of County Clare and he owned most of the land in the county and the market town of Ennistymon. He was a fine figure of a man, stocked with the old traditions, a die-hard of the old régime, and to quote the Irish phrase for blustering high spirits, 'If he took off your head to-day he would put two on you tomorrow'.

For the rook shoot the top half of my grandfather was dressed like Sherlock Holmes with a deerstalker hat and a splendid check tweed cape. His lower half sported leather gaiters and tweed knicker-bockers. . . .

When I was fifteen I painted this scene of the rook shoot from memory with Henry Vee in his cape aiming his gun up at the dark basket nests while the parent rooks flapped in the sky.

In a sense this painting is a memorial to Henry Vee, to the best in his life. He was a famous shot, the landlord of the manor, a man of authority in the county. At the end of his life he was stripped of all these assets.[29]

But, in the main, the root of disagreement lay in the nature of southern unionism, the fine gradations of Anglo-Ireland. Generalisations are dangerous, but by 1918 southern unionism was resolving itself into its three component parts now that the clear cut struggle of the 1880s had been outmoded. Those with large British interests, or with interests and traditions in Ireland that transcended likely political issues in an independent Ireland, could, when compelled to face the issue of self-government squarely, bring themselves to accept home rule, partly in the hope of forestalling greater dangers, partly in the knowledge that their position and experience would enable them to become active and influential in a new Irish state. Bernard, in attempting to broaden the basis of unionism in the south of Ireland, not only saw that the union was a losing cause; he also reckoned that the decline of Redmond's party gave men such as he an opportunity to play a leading role in a new Irish state.[30] Perhaps the fact that

29. Devas, *Two Flamboyant Fathers*, pp. 17–20.
30. Murray, *Archbishop Bernard*, pp. 316, 327.

some of those he acted with were made senators in the Irish Free State showed how right these calculations were. For instance, Andrew Jameson, the head of a large distilling industry, a governor of the Bank of Ireland, a man of almost unequalled commercial experience, could see himself as indispensable to the success and right working of any new Irish government: he was made a senator and played an active role in the state that was eventually established.[31] However, other southern unionists felt that they could not afford to take such a cool and detached view of life and of the Irish situation. The delegates' opponents were mainly smaller men, living scattered around Ireland and occupying much coveted land. The focus of interest of men like Wilson was Ireland. Their lives revolved around their estates and were based upon a traditional view of Irish society, in which the landed gentry played a leading and crucial role, not only in their own interests but in the interests of the peasantry and of Ireland as a whole. The man who wrote 'no greater disaster could overtake a country such as Ireland than the total elimination of its resident gentry'[32] was the eldest son of a fourth son; and though his circle of acquaintances in British politics included Walter Long, his sphere of activity was limited, and he came to rely upon the struggle over the union for a vigorous interest in life.[33] It is, therefore, instructive to bear in mind the comparison between his background and that of the Earl of Mayo[34] in trying to explain the difference between static and advancing southern unionists, between natural and progressive conservatives among the Anglo-Irish.

Even with professional men, a similar line of division is noticeable. Among the most active of the delegates' opponents was John Walsh (1875–1941), of 1 Burlington Road, Dublin, the honorary secretary of the Southern Unionist Committee. His grandfather had been Master of the Rolls in Ireland; his father was archdeacon of Dublin; and Walsh himself can be represented as a moderately successful barrister whose life and interests centred narrowly upon Dublin.[35] His prospects under a Catholic

31. See below, pp. 297–8.
32. See above, p. xv.
33. See e.g. the comment of his wife, Alice, to Walsh, 6 July 1918, P.R.O.N.I., D 989A/8/17A.
34. See above, pp. xv–xvi.
35. *Burke's Landed Gentry of Ireland* (1958), p. 738.

dominated Irish government must have seemed very slight compared with those of Powell, a successful Roman Catholic lawyer, one of the most active of the southern unionist delegates and later Solicitor-General for Ireland and then a judge.[36] Men such as Macnamara, Wilson and Walsh could see little virtue in a policy that recommended, in effect, the repeal of the union and the establishment of an Irish parliament. They could see little hope of representation in an Irish nationalist parliament; and, if they did not always imagine that only terror awaited them should the union be dissolved, they certainly thought that their lives would be uncomfortably circumscribed. And events in 1918 only served to underline their apprehension about life under home rule, as some of their class were subjected to landgrabbing.

For instance, the land of one staunch unionist family at Holly-brook, 'a lonely locality' in County Roscommon, the ffolliotts, was invaded by members of the local Sinn Fein association.[37] The land was owned and farmed by two sisters, Margaret and Maria, and it appears to have been the major source of their income, their late father Colonel John ffolliott having vowed to spend his last penny in defence of the union.[38] As far as Margaret ffolliott was concerned, the farm was managed efficiently with due regard to national welfare. A considerable amount of arable was tilled in rotation 'by a particularly capable and hard-working land steward'; in the past couple of years, in view of the national need, the amount of tillage had been increased and lea broken in the best old pasture; and despite adverse weather conditions 'fine crops were secured' of grain, hay and roots. In addition milch cows were kept, a large number of pigs (6 litters in 1917), calves and lambs were bred and reared; some stall feeding was done (14 head in 1917, 20 in 1918); and the usual dealing in store cattle carried on. Nor had the interests of labourers and tenants been neglected. Although aware of the economic disadvantages of conacre, the Misses ffolliott had let a considerable amount of land in conacre for potatoes for labourers and tenants with small holdings, as well as grazing for their milch cows; in the last year

36. See above, p. xix n. 13
37. The following is based upon: Margaret ffolliott to Montgomery, 3 Mar. 1918, enclosing copies of letters to the Chief Secretary, Duke, 23, 25, Feb. 1918, P.R.O.N.I., D 627/432.
38. Col. J. ffolliott to Montgomery, 10 May 189?, *ibid.*, D 627/428/96

more conacre had been asked for and given, and they were prepared to give more in 1918. But Sinn Fein activity ruined this rhythm in 1918 and threatened to jeopardise good farming. On 11 February 1918, the Misses ffolliott received a letter from the Sinn Fein club in the nearby village 'demanding' an unspecified amount of land from them for two year conacre at £2, below the usual rate. Sensibly, they replied that in view of 'all we were already doing for the neighbours we thought this an unreasonable demand, but were nevertheless prepared to meet it as far as might be possible, if applicants sent in their names and requirements'. This reply was ignored, and two days later a crowd of two hundred with three bands was said to have marched to a recently laid down pasture field of nineteen statute acres which the leaders proceeded to divide 'in the name of the Irish republic' among about thirty of their number—several of them alleged to have been sons of well-to-do farmers on the estate. This *coup* was followed up, and the field, containing a rich harvest of hay and a number of young cattle, was turned up in patches all over with nine ploughs and pairs of horses.

Not unnaturally, the Misses ffolliott objected to these developments. Not only would they entail financial loss (since the field taken over was one on which the ffolliotts were chiefly depending for pasturing fifty ewes with lambs that season, and either these or forty or fifty head of young cattle would have to be disposed of at 'considerable loss'); but, more importantly, these happenings would be a deterrent to future farming enterprise, and to allow such conduct to continue unchecked would make it 'impossible for any good, economic farming to be carried on in this country'. According to Margaret ffolliott, the field in question was only recovering from the effects of previous conacre tillage and would, if made to produce a crop of potatoes in 1918 and one of corn the following season, under the usual conditions of conacre (inadequate manuring etc.), be rendered useless for at least ten years to come. Thus she felt obliged to write to the Chief Secretary to

ask earnestly for protection in carrying on my farming operations. I request that you will give adequate police help to clear the land occupied by the Sinn Feiners, and to enable me to retake possession of the land. Also I request protection for my house which is occupied only by my sister and myself without servants; and it would be

vitally necessary also to have protection for my steward and his family
and for my other labourers.[39]

Whatever the merits of the invaders' case, such incidents,
rendering necessary an appeal to the executive, must not only
have showed the likely content of life under home rule, but also
have indicated the inadequacy of the Irish for the responsibilities
of home rule, thus confirming the delegates' opponents in their
unionism. This was certainly the case with Margaret ffolliott
who told an Ulster unionist:

Personally, I have never been able to imagine—even in my most
utopian moments—any possible compromise between the many-
aliassed party of disorder and their opponents in Ireland, as to a separate
Irish parliament. Everything I hear advocates of 'compromise' and
'concession' say on the subject appears to me to beg the whole question
absolutely.[40]

Men and women, such as Wilson and Margaret ffolliott, may
be easily laughed at, or dismissed as mere die-hards; but it is
important to appreciate the basis of their continued stand on the
union. Their lives were based so firmly upon Ireland and upon
an unyielding faith in a traditional social structure that they did
not appreciate the changes that were taking place in British
politics and which were helping to alter the basis of southern
unionism as it had existed since the 1880s. It was not that they
took no notice of British politics: it was just that they were so
concerned with events in Ireland that when they looked for, and
found, support in Britain, they assessed the strength and reliability
of that support on the evidence of the past and of their limited
contacts, such as Wilson's friendship with Walter Long. Their
continued campaign in British politics from 1918 onwards and
the collapse in 1922 show how a belief in support from Britain
was a necessary basis of southern unionism. The trouble was that
the die-hards assumed a static situation in Great Britain, and too
often interpreted their interests primarily in the light of events in
Ireland. The result was that when they looked to British politics
for support, the wish was often the father of the thought. Thus

39. Margaret ffolliott to Duke, 23 Feb. 1918 (copy), *ibid.*, D 627/432.
40. Margaret ffolliott to Montgomery, 3 Mar. 1918, *ibid.*

the plea, that the likely advent to power of a labour government rendered some form of home rule desirable, was dismissed with the words 'we have no real reason to believe that a strong labour party in England would be anarchical or socialistic. . . . Moreover, the Irish working classes would be no less dangerous than the people of the larger island'.[41]

This refusal to face up to facts is evident in their continued denial of the validity of Irish nationalism and national movements. Their vision may have been limited but Midleton's critics were not stupid or insensitive. Not liking to feel themselves at odds with the true feelings and wishes of the mass of their fellow countrymen, they tried to explain away nationalism as if it did not exist. Even after the return of seventy-three Sinn Fein candidates in the December 1918 general election, they persisted in believing that Irishmen did not really want self-government, refusing to accept the result as a vote in favour of Sinn Fein. Totally divorced from the inward looking nationalism of Sinn Fein, they explained away the 1918 election results in terms of Irish discontent with high taxation and state control during the war, and they dismissed the so-called national agitation by developing their conspiracy theory. According to the private reflections of J. M. Wilson,[42] the election gave no indication of the strength of Sinn Fein support in Ireland, for it had been held at a time when the government was unpopular not only in Ireland but also in Great Britain. High taxes and state control, especially the threat of conscription, had, Wilson argued, made a large number of subjects anxious to express their discontent by voting for whosoever gave the government the greatest annoyance. Thus, the post-war discontent (which had caused riots in Glasgow, Liverpool and London, and led to great unrest in labour circles) had taken the form in Ireland of a vague revolutionary republican movement, which attracted 'everyone who was discontented, from government officials whose posts were on the verge of abolition through economy, to unemployed labourers bewildered by economic conditions'.[43] Having dealt with the 1918 elections and popular support for Sinn Fein, southern unionists were faced with the fact of an organisation dedicated to breaking the British

41. Bagwell, letter in *Irish Times*, 18 Mar. 1918.
42. A piece entitled 'Self-determination' [1921?], P.R.O.N.I., D 989A/8/10.
43. *Ibid.*

connection. But they dealt with it easily. As befitted an ascendancy group on the defensive, they continued to use a conspiracy theory to discredit Irish nationalism, and as befitted a largely landed group, they again argued that the nationalist movement was in reality an agrarian movement supported only by the greedy, 'farmers who sought their landlords' land, labourers who sought the farmers' land, and placehunters who sought for places at the expense of both'.[44]

This agrarian theory was the traditional southern unionist line, but, though the contempt or hostility of some southern unionists for the nationalist movement had not abated since the 1880s, they did, in a sense, move with the times, and by 1920 the agrarian theory had grown into a more elaborate conspiracy theory of a three-prong attack upon the British empire. Admittedly the prime aim of this new development was to discredit Irish nationalists in British eyes, but it was not entirely a propaganda piece without relevance to the southern unionist situation. The new argument was that to concede to the demand for self-government would be disastrous to Ireland and therefore to the United Kingdom and the empire, for there were in Ireland not one but three revolutionary movements. There was the political, the Sinn Fein movement: animated by the most bitter hatred of England and the empire, and guided by the I.R.B., 'a treasonable and seditious organisation, bound by secret oaths, to work for and secure the absolute independence of Ireland'. Then there was the Irish labour movement, powerfully organised into the Transport Workers' Union, which was working for a 'workers' republic' on 'soviet principles'. Finally, there was the agrarian movement. Although, they continued, these three movements were actuated by one immediate common purpose, the establishment of Irish independence, so varied were they in their ultimate aims that, once independence was established, the ultimate divergence would lead to a disruption of society, 'something like civil war', the consequences of which would be as bad for the empire as for Ireland.[45] It would be tempting to regard this as an

44. *Ibid.*
45. For examples of this approach, see a circular appeal issued by the I.U.A. to British unionists, marked 'Personal and urgent', 5 May 1920, and the statement by a deputation from the I.U.A. to the annual conference of the National Unionist Association at Liverpool, 17–20 Nov. 1921, copies in P.R.O.N.I., D 989A/9/29 and D 989A/8/23.

explanation for the civil war that did later develop, but there is no evidence to suggest that pro- and anti-treatyites can be so conveniently divided upon these lines. However, the theory is an interesting one in showing the intellectual devices resorted to by such an essentially conservative group as the 'die-hard' southern unionists in an attempt to justify their own almost untenable position.

They were too committed to the social and political system in which they had grown up to be able to appreciate the scale of the obstacles facing the maintenance of the union. It is understandable that, to them, 'the question of the union is not susceptible to compromise: the choice is between defence and surrender'.[46] Perhaps, events justified their pessimistic view of a home rule Ireland. (Though it is just possible that the die-hards' attitude brought trouble on their own heads, the facts remain that, whereas Jameson at least was an active member of the Irish Senate, Macnamara narrowly escaped assassination in 1919 and died eventually in a flat in Kensington High Street, Wilson's mansion was burned out and he ended his days in exile in London, and Margaret ffolliott found it desirable to retire to Great Britain.) At any rate, however justifiable or not their views, men and women of this calibre would certainly not be silent after 'finding their cause abandoned by their leaders'.[47]

46. Bagwell, letter in *Irish Times*, 18 Mar. 1918.
47. Walsh, letter *ibid.*, 11 Mar. 1918.

Phase Five: Division and Disunity,
February 1918–January 1919

SUCH opinions and such determination were obstacles to Midleton's attempt to convert southern unionists to his new departure. Yet they were not insurmountable, nor need they have led to an open rift in southern unionism. The likelihood was that Midleton could convert the majority of the I.U.A. to his new policy, thus isolating his critics. Moreover, if one section or other had to secede from the I.U.A., the past history indicated that the odds were in favour of the Midletonites remaining in control.

Probabilities were belied by events. Partly because of the way Midletonites mishandled the situation, and partly because of the intervention of Ulster unionists in the affairs of the I.U.A., Midleton's opponents ended up in control of a reformed I.U.A. committed to a staunch unionist policy. This split and *bouleverse-ment* developed through four stages. Firstly, between February and May 1918 Midleton's opponents organised themselves to keep the I.U.A. on the straight and narrow unionist path and if necessary to reform the organisation. Though energetic, these critics were full of misgivings, and some tactful handling by the Midletonites might have prevented the new movement from gaining momentum. Secondly, in June and July Midletonites and their critics struggled for control of the executive committee of the I.U.A., and by August southern unionism seemed irretrievably split. Thirdly, in the early autumn there was a *détente*, largely because of the conciliatory attitude at last adopted by the Midletonites, and it looked as though differences could be settled within the framework of the I.U.A. Finally, in January 1919 there came the split, following a long wrangle throughout December over the relations between Ulster and southern unionists. The Midletonites seceded from the I.U.A. and formed a new association, the Unionist Anti-Partition League. For the first time there was an open and irreparable breach in southern unionist ranks. An outline of the dispute has been given by Professor Phillips in his book on the *Revolution in Ireland*[1] and by Dr McDowell in his *Irish Convention*.[2] But since the split was significant for the future influence of southern unionists, and since the process by which it occurred is intrinsically interesting (especially in showing how active and energetic southern unionists could be in defence of their interests and what a determined minority could achieve within a party organisation neglected by its leaders), the development of southern unionism in 1918 deserves more detailed treatment.

TWO

Finding their leaders unresponsive, the dissidents began to organise. Midleton thought that the Ulster unionists were the guiding spirits behind the new movement, but this is misleading. Shortly after the delegates' action at the convention was known, there were protests not only at the meeting of the executive committee, but also by branches of the I.U.A. in Cork.[3] Admittedly, the Cork unionists looked to Carson for help, but they received little encouragement from the U.U.C. Owing to the fact that a good deal of the evidence relating to the Midletonites' opponents is derived from largely northern sources, it is difficult to see who initiated the re-organisation of opinion in the south. Hugh de Fellenberg Montgomery of Blessingbourne House, Co. Tyrone, and some of his friends in the north thought that the southern unionist delegates had weakened Ulster's case against home rule and were therefore anxious to rally southern unionist opinion for the union:[4] his papers could give the impression that he was behind the move to organise the opponents of the delegates, but, in fact, he acted only slowly and indecisively.[5] The real initiative seems to have come from a hot-headed southern

1. Pp. 144-6.
2. Pp. 194-5.
3. T. Farrington to I.U.A., 6 Feb. 1918; M'Neil to Pretyman Newman, 8 Feb. 1918, forwarding resolutions of the senior and junior branches of the I.U.A., P.R.O.N.I., D 1507/1/1918/1.
4. Montgomery to J. R. Fisher, 31 Jan., 4 Feb. 1918, *ibid.*, D 627/433. Montgomery (1844-1924); ed. Oxford; capt. Fermanagh militia; P.C.; senator, Northern Ireland.
5. Montgomery to Stronge, 9 Feb. 1918, *ibid.*, D 627/432.

unionist, Colonel Charles Davis Guinness of Clermont Park, Dundalk, who tried to organise among his friends on the executive committee of the I.U.A. a demonstration against Midleton and his friends.[6] His activity started a limited chain reaction. It encouraged other opponents of the delegates, such as the aged and tired Bagwell, that resistance to Midleton was still possible; and it galvanised into action others who hoped to restrain Guinness, in whose judgement they had little confidence, and to ensure that the case against the delegates was properly presented.[7] The result of various small conclaves and letters was a meeting in the Shelbourne Hotel on 20 February.

It was a small meeting consisting of the four dissidents and a few friends with the revered Bagwell in the chair. One thing those attending were sure of was that the union should be maintained, and a strong resolution to this effect was unanimously accepted. How this could be achieved was a different matter. Obviously immediate action was necessary. Those present resolved themselves into a committee, subsequently known as the Southern Unionist Committee, with John E. Walsh as honorary secretary, and circulated their resolution to certain people in the hope of building up a firm nucleus of opinion to organise in defence of the union. But their ultimate success depended upon getting a wide body of support throughout the southern provinces, and a sub-committee was appointed to prepare for publication in the press a statement against any form of home rule. One difficulty was the recent action of the executive committee, and therefore a second sub-committee was asked to submit a report upon it to the committee.[8]

These sub-committees reported the following week to an enlarged meeting. Though the attendance only amounted to twenty-two, the reception given to their previous resolution

6. Stronge to Montgomery, 8 Feb. 1918; Guinness to Montgomery, 16 Feb. 1918, *ibid.* Guinness (1860–1939); ed. Eton; brevet-col. in Royal Artillery, served in South African war; a spirited unionist and country gentleman who did his own harvesting during labourers' strikes; H.S., Co. Louth, 1918.

7. Montgomery to Bagwell, 8 Feb. 1918, P.R.O.N.I., D 627/433; Montgomery to Maude, 9 Feb. 1918, to Stronge, 9 Feb. 1918; Bagwell to Montgomery, 9 Feb. 1918, *ibid.*, D 627/432. Bagwell was regarded as a necessary figure-head, a respectable man of weight among 'hot-heads'.

8. S.U.C. minute book, 20 Feb. 1918 P.R.O.N.I., D 989A/1/10; Stronge to Montgomery, 20 Feb. 1918, *ibid.*, D 627/433.

gave the S.U.C. heart. That support came from Ulster was particularly encouraging. Sir Edward Carson had written that he 'noted the names of those present at the meeting, and was much gratified at the conclusion at which they had arrived'; and Colonel Robert Gordon Sharman-Crawford, the M.P. for East Belfast who attended the meeting as a visitor, 'extended sympathy to the project from Ulster'. Offices were authorised to be procured, but there was no talk of forming a separate organisation to rival the I.U.A. The report by the sub-committee reconciled the S.U.C.'s stand with the majority decision of the executive committee in January: it discovered rather belatedly that the executive committee could be held not to represent southern unionist opinion. Thus encouraged, all that the S.U.C. wanted was to ensure that, if the majority of southern unionists did not endorse the executive committee's action, the southern unionist case against home rule and for the union would not go by default, as they considered had happened in the recent past. On the one hand, they issued a general and public appeal to all unionists. On the other hand, they tried to galvanise the local organs of the I.U.A. into action to ensure that southern unionist opinion would find expression.[9]

The general appeal appeared in the press of the United Kingdom on 4 March with the title 'Call to unionists'; it was also sent to politicians in Great Britain. 'The circumstances of the present time', read the 'Call',

imperatively demand that all true Irish unionists, especially those outside Ulster, should reiterate, with no uncertain voice, their conviction that in the maintenance of the legislative union between Great Britain and Ireland, and in the firm, just, and impartial administration of the law, lies the only hope for the future of our country and the security of His Majesty's dominions.

This propaganda not only tried to appeal to British politicians by emphasising the 'exhibitions of disloyalty and treason in Ireland during the present terrible war'; it also tried to broaden the basis of support for the union in the south of Ireland. In particular, it tried to win over farmers, especially those who had purchased their farms, by stressing that 'increased taxation . . . would be the inevitable result' of home rule and that the

9. S.U.C. minute book, 28 Feb. 1918.

present revolutionary movement is fostered and supported by the younger and more irresponsible members of the community . . . whose ideas and methods are exemplified by the forcible appropriation of the private property of their neighbours, and defiance of all law.

The 'Call' ended with an 'appeal to all, outside Ulster, who are in agreement with the above, to communicate the fact, without delay, to John E. Walsh, at 36, Molesworth Street, Dublin'.[10] This general appeal was to be supplemented by attempts to get the whole machinery of the I.U.A. working again in favour of the union.[11]

It was an ambitious scheme, amounting almost to an attempt to take over the I.U.A., but for the moment the S.U.C. shrank from such decisive action. The reason for this hesitation was the fact that the initial response to the 'Call' was poor. In the first few days only 175 replies were received,[12] and Lord Barrymore, one of the most respected unionist leaders, dismissed it out of hand, venturing to

express the opinion that, instead of sending their names to this new body, it would be far wiser for all southern Irish unionists to continue to support the Alliance, which . . . may be trusted to represent their interests at the present crisis, as in the past.[13]

Moreover, the influential press in Great Britain and Ireland gave the 'Call' no support. It was banned by the Harmsworth press[14] and received no encouragement from the *Irish Times,* which made much of the fact that the 'Call' had only twenty-two signatories.[15] What support the 'Call' did receive came from the less influential elements of British and Irish politics: the *Morning Post, Britannia,* the organ of the Women's party in Great Britain, the Dublin Unionist Registration Association, the Dublin central council of the Women's Unionist Associations, the *Dublin Daily Express* and the *Cork Constitution.* Local secretaries of the I.U.A.

10. 'Call to unionists', P.R.O.N.I., D 989A/1/10.
11. S.U.C. minute book, 28 Feb. 1918.
12. *Ibid.,* 7 Mar. 1918.
13. Letter in *Irish Times,* 9 Mar. 1918.
14. S.U.C. minute book, 7 Mar. 1918.
15. *Irish Times,* 4 Mar. 1918. The signatories included 2 peers, a baronet, a general, 2 historians, 5 country gentlemen, 2 K.C.s, 3 other barristers, a Cork businessman, and Major Pretyman Newman, M.P.

seemed hostile[16] and such enthusiastic unionists as Margaret ffolliott found the largest landowners in her county weak on the union.[17] Although, as time went by, there were increasing signs that the executive committee might really have been rushed into a decision on 1 January, and that some members would have attended had they known what was to have been discussed,[18] the S.U.C. was aware that the weight of opinion was against the 'Call'. If there was not widespread support for the Midletonites, there was certainly a feeling among southern unionists that the 'Call' was premature. Many felt that the delegates were the best men chosen by the I.U.A. and should be given a fair chance to reach a settlement: when that settlement was reached and announced would be the time to judge.[19] In fact, the 'Callers' were in danger of being dismissed as a bunch of hotheads.

Clearly the S.U.C. felt on the defensive, and the signs are that the movement could have been halted, given careful handling by the Midletonites. But they seemed incapable of concession or tact. Midleton aloofly urged southern unionists to reserve their judgement until the convention reported, submitting that until then 'the unionist cause will be best served by silence'.[20] His supporters outside the convention gave the S.U.C. and the 'Call' short shrift. Denis Pack Beresford, an honorary secretary of the I.U.A., wrote disparagingly of the S.U.C.'s belated claims that the general council of 1 June 1917 had not agreed to modify the union and that the executive committee of 1 January 1918 had been unrepresentative and rushed into a decision on the new departure.[21] Another Midletonite, Thomas Stephen Francis Battersby, an ambitious barrister and an accomplished swimmer and diver, impugned the S.U.C.'s motives. He accused it of 'taking advantage of the enforced silence of the delegates to create an atmosphere of prejudice against them . . . [in] . . . an unworthy attempt to create disunion in the ranks of southern unionists'.[22] The S.U.C. was always sensitive to such charges of

16. S.U.C. minute book, 7 Mar. 1918.
17. Margaret ffolliott to Montgomery, 14 Mar. 1918, P.R.O.N.I., D 627/432.
18. Major O'Connor's letter in *Dublin Daily Express*, 16 Mar. 1918.
19. Margaret ffolliott to Montgomery, 18 Mar. 1918, P.R.O.N.I., D 627/432.
20. Letter in *Irish Times*, 16 Mar. 1918.
21. Letter *ibid.*, 13 Mar. 1918.
22. Letter *ibid.*, 2 Apr. 1918; see also 22 Mar. 1918.

dishonourable conduct,[23] but Midleton did not follow up his advantage by taking into his confidence the general body of southern unionists. The most that was done was to consult the executive committee again on 23 March.[24] At this meeting Midleton again stated the issues involved at the convention, outlining the proposed settlement about to be voted upon. The 'Callers' were fully heard, but again their views did not sway the committee against the delegates. If anything their criticisms did the very opposite. A resolution, recording 'unbounded confidence in the delegates sent to the convention by the Irish Unionist Alliance', thanking them 'for their efforts on its behalf', and hoping 'they will continue those exertions', was passed by 43 votes to 17.

The Midletonites again failed to follow up their advantage. They did not give sufficient time and thought to winning over opinion. This aloofness was in part due to the poor opinion they had of their opponents. Bernard, for instance, had long held the lesser Irish gentry in contempt,[25] and it was true that the S.U.C. had a poor public image. Even their most sympathetic supporters recognised that some of the leading 'Callers' were 'hardly an impressive type of man' and had reputations as 'wild men'.[26] Therefore, the Midletonites did not regard the 'Call' as so serious a threat as a lofty word of discouragement would not stem. When this proved insufficient, they were content to outmanoeuvre their opponents rather than to convert the mass of southern unionists to their views. Their attitude to the first meeting of the general council of the I.U.A. since the previous June underlines this negligence.

The report of the convention was finally published on 13 April, and a meeting of the general council to discuss it was arranged for 3 May. The S.U.C. prepared for this meeting with enthusiasm. Immediately the report was issued, the S.U.C., glad that the issue was now in the open, and strengthened in its views

23. Montgomery to Barrie, 26 Mar. 1918, P.R.O.N.I., D 627/433; Walsh and Wilson, letters in *Irish Times,* 3 Apr. 1918.
24. I.U.A. circular, 15 Apr. 1918; Montgomery to Fisher, 26 Mar. 1918, P.R.O.N.I., D 627/432.
25. Murray, *Archbishop Bernard,* pp. 80–1.
26. Stronge to Montgomery, 22 Feb. 1918; Montgomery to Bagwell, 8 Feb. 1918, P.R.O.N.I., D 627/433.

by the conscription crisis,[27] published its criticisms.[28] The old arguments against home rule were strengthened by new ones at a time 'when the fate of the empire is in the balance in these hours of desperate struggle in the plains of France'; and the proposed Irish constitution with its distinctive minority safeguards was condemned as a 'travesty of democracy' which would not be tolerated even for the temporary period proposed. It was a vigorously written document, urging southern unionists not to relinquish 'all that they have ever fought for, and all that unionism stands for today—loyalty to king and empire—the bulwark against pro-Germanism, anarchy, and sedition'. Steps were taken to ensure an adequate attendance sympathetic to the 'Call', to see that the general council did not endorse the delegates' action.[29] With financial aid from the Dublin Unionist Registration Association, the S.U.C. contacted the local branches of the I.U.A. and members of the general council. Few details of this activity are available, but the committee did, for instance, get in touch with the Dublin and South County members of the general council who were in sympathy to ensure their attendance, and prepared a shorter version of its comments on the convention report specially aimed at unionists in Ireland.[30]

This work was not without its problems, not the least being the question of the Ulster branches and members. Owing to an informal agreement between Ulster unionists and the I.U.A., the former were undecided whether to attend, for it was felt that they might prejudice the S.U.C.'s case, giving the appearance of dictation from Ulster.[31] The committee felt, however, that the support of the Ulster members of the I.U.A. could be useful. It would have preferred to win without the Ulstermen, but would rather win with them than lose without them: 'we ought to use every means in our power to get as many votes as we could.'[32] The committee got little encouragement from the U.U.C.[33] and

27. See below, pp. 164-5.
28. *The Convention Report and Home Rule,* copies in P.R.O.N.I., D 989A/8/17.
29. See e.g. S.U.C. minute book, 24 Apr. 1918; Margaret ffolliott to Montgomery, 18 Apr. 1918, P.R.O.N.I., D 627/432.
30. Copy in P.R.O.N.I., D 989A/8/17.
31. W. Jellett to Stronge, 3 Apr. 1918; Montgomery to Jellett, 5, 10 Apr. 1918; Stronge to Montgomery, 10, 29 Apr. 1918; Montgomery to Stronge, 29 Apr. 1918, *ibid.,* D 627/432.
32. S.U.C. minute book, 24 Apr. 1918.
33. Jellett to Montgomery, 7 Apr. 1918, P.R.O.N.I., D 627/432.

therefore wrote to Carson asking for his advice,[34] and to the Ulster members drawing attention to their rights.[35] In the end Carson, who supported the S.U.C.'s stand, advised attendance,[36] and several Ulstermen did attend the meeting.[37] Lastly, the committee took steps to arrange for speakers at the meeting and for the reporting of the proceedings, cleverly allowing the terms of their resolution 'to be known as late as possible'.[38]

As thorough as these preparations were, they could easily have been countered by some positive leadership on the part of the Midletonites. The delegates had the sympathy of the majority of the I.U.A. Even the S.U.C. recognised that it had still to move carefully. Some of its members felt contempt for Midleton and his attempt to set up a middle party, yet in order to win over the main body of southern unionists they had to sink these personal feelings.[39] Any attempt to criticise the delegates unduly would have been ill-received. Sir Maurice Dockrell, who for personal reasons could not be one of the delegates, as originally intended, pleaded for unity in view of the 'vastly important issues' confronting Ireland and southern unionists. 'Is "divide and conquer" to be our epitaph?' he asked. For the delegates he argued, 'Surely many stalwarts would have succumbed to an atmosphere of such "sweet reasonableness" and "mutual accommodation"'. On the other hand, those who issued the 'Call' 'have . . . acted as a brake upon the wheel that is driving forward panic legislation'.[40] This appeal made an impression upon Walsh who replied insisting that the S.U.C. sought only 'to consolidate the forces of unionism'.[41] The committee had other evidence too of the need to tread warily. At one of its meetings it was reported that 'a very strong feeling prevailed in the county (Limerick) against any personal attack' on the delegates' action; for, though the delegates 'had gone wrong and ought to be repudiated', it was recognised they had 'worked hard'.[42] Therefore, the S.U.C. decided that its

34. S.U.C. minute book, 24 Apr. 1918.
35. S.U.C. circular to Ulster members, 25 Apr. 1918, copy in P.R.O.N.I., D 627/432.
36. S.U.C. minute book, 2 May 1918.
37. See e.g. Montgomery to Stronge, 29 Apr. 1918, P.R.O.N.I., D 627/432.
38. S.U.C. minute book, 24 Apr., 2 May 1918.
39. *Ibid.,* 24 Apr. 1918.
40. Sir Maurice Dockrell, letter in *Irish Times,* 27 Apr. 1918.
41. Walsh, letter *ibid.,* 29 Apr. 1918.
42. S.U.C. minute book, 24 Apr. 1918.

resolution at the general council should be confined to dissociating the council from the convention report and affirming the I.U.A.'s faith in the union, avoiding personal attacks.[43]

Even with these precautions to keep discussion at a high level, the S.U.C. was still not sure of winning its point. On the day before the meeting of the general council, the 'Callers' spent much time wondering what to do if they were defeated, eventually deciding that they would leave the hall as a body in protest. In an attempt to avoid such a proceeding, they resolved to communicate with the executive of the I.U.A. to tell them that they would be moving a resolution, that it was 'a very dangerous thing to have disunity', and making it clear that 'we are meeting the delegates and Lord Midleton in brotherly love'. All that the 'Callers' asked was that the delegates should admit their mistake, then the danger of a split would be averted. Admittedly, it was a peculiar sort of brotherly love, for the S.U.C. also affirmed that 'our position is stone wall' and 'it's for him to move, not us'.[44] But such blustering only reflected the S.U.C.'s uncertainty.

Unfortunately for the future of southern unionism, the Midletonites took advantage neither of their own position as controllers of the I.U.A. and as southern unionism's late representatives at the convention nor of the weakness of the S.U.C. Even in private and to their most sympathetic supporters, the delegates gave contradictory explanations of their attitude and never bothered to explain inconsistencies.[45] Though they tried to mobilise support among Irish peers,[46] their relations with the main body of southern unionists were obviously more remote. For instance, their defence of their action at the convention was not circulated to members of the I.U.A. until 22 April[47]—after the S.U.C.'s attack on the convention report—and was scarcely a rallying cry. After attacking the 'Call', the delegates went on to defend and justify their settlement. The 'Call' was dismissed as

43. *Ibid.*

44. *Ibid.*, 2 May 1918.

45. See e.g. R. G. Cosby to Bernard, 24 May 1918, T.C.D., Bernard correspondence 1 (1893–1919), 151.

46. Circular signed by Midleton, Mayo, Desart and Oranmore, 16 Apr. 1918, P.R.O., 30/67/38, f. 2271.

47. I.U.A. circular, 15 Apr. 1918. Despite the date it does not appear to have been actually received by members until about 22 April (Montgomery to Stronge, 22 Apr. 1918, P.R.O.N.I., D 627/432).

superfluous, for all its practical suggestions 'have been anticipated by the delegates' (i.e. the firm administration of law, the development of the resources of Ireland, and the federation of the empire). More to the point though, the delegates claimed to have secured 'a drastic change in the inequitable provisions of the act of 1914' which ensured that 'if home rule is established, the government of Ireland, in which the southern unionists have had no participation for over thirty years, will be controlled not by one section of Irishmen as under the act of 1914, but by leading Irishmen of all classes'; and they justified their consent by reference to the majorities of the executive committee. The delegates thus openly joined battle with the authors of the 'Call', alleging that many signatures had been obtained from persons unaware of the immense changes secured. Yet they did so with very little real effort or enthusiasm, still treating the issue with a certain aloofness. A grandiloquent final paragraph hoped of members of the general council, shortly to meet,

that in the interests of the empire, which can only be secured at this unparalleled crisis by a majority in whatever parliament exists, capable of overawing republican and separatist doctrines, you will suspend your judgement till you have the full details which will demonstrate the wisdom and patriotism of the course adopted by your delegates.

Midleton did not attend the meeting of the general council on 3 May, but, despite his absence and their inadequate preparations, the Midletonites neatly outmanoeuvred the S.U.C.[48] After a preliminary skirmish about the presence of Ulster members, the vice-chairman, George F. Stewart, made a full statement of the position taken up by the delegates in the convention. William Morgan Jellett K.C., soon to be M.P. for Dublin University,[49] then moved, on behalf of the S.U.C., a resolution that the general council,

48. This account of the meeting is based upon: I.U.A., minute book of the executive (general) council, 1889–1920, 3 May 1918; Montgomery to Bates, 4 May 1918 and Stronge to Montgomery, 7 May 1918, P.R.O.N.I., D 627/432. The terms of the resolutions are to be found in the minute book.

49. (1858–1936); ed. Royal School, Armagh, and Trinity College, Dublin; barrister practising on N.E. circuit; secretary to Lord Ashbourne as Chancellor of Ireland; defeated for Dublin University in 1918, but M.P., 1919–22; appeared in most of the important cases in the Free State, dying 'father' of Irish bar; 36 Fitzwilliam Square, Dublin.

while fully recognising the time and trouble our delegates have devoted to the work of the convention, profoundly dissent from the conclusions set forth in the majority report, and do hereby re-affirm our unalterable adherence to the fundamental principle of the Alliance —the maintenance of the legislative union between Great Britain and Ireland—and pledge ourselves to do all in our power to maintain that legislative union.

This clear attempt to bring the I.U.A. into line with the S.U.C.'s programme, and to repudiate the basis of the delegates' action, was not successful. Lord Wicklow, a friend of Midleton, seconded by Major O'Connor (who had not been present at the meeting of 1 January), moved a resolution, leaving the matter in mid-air, as it were. This second resolution thanked the delegates for their services, but did not disapprove of them, holding that the actions of the leaders of the nationalist party in uniting with the Sinn Fein organisation in opposition to the proposals of the government and their propaganda in the country have

profoundly affected the considerations which led the delegates to accept the proposals embodied in the report of the convention and the executive committee to approve of the action of the delegates.

The issue was neatly shelved, for this resolution, refraining from passing any motion 'which might cause division in unionist ranks', was followed up by another proposing the adjournment of the meeting. Clever speeches were made, urging unity and that the nationalists should be allowed to reject the forthcoming home rule bill. Finally, the resolution for adjournment was hurriedly carried on a quick show of hands by 82 votes to 51.

Neither side had, therefore, been defeated. The Dublin correspondent of *The Times* could write with a semblance of truth that the general council had approved of the policy of their delegates at the convention.[50] The S.U.C. was quick to deny this,[51] but was in no position to claim victory for itself. Indeed, not having bargained for an adjournment, the 'Callers' were rather non-plussed. Though the S.U.C. tried to convince itself that 'the result of the meeting could in no view be construed as a

---

50. *The Times,* 4 May 1918.
51. Walsh, letter *ibid.,* 7 May 1918; see also his letter in *Irish Times,* 9 May 1918.

defeat of the supporters of our movement',[52] the proceedings could scarcely be called a vindication of the 'Call'. The only clear point that had emerged was that most members of the general council wanted to avoid disunity.

THREE

Instead of providing a strong motive for agreement, this virtual stalemate produced a heated battle for control of the I.U.A. Some desultory conferences were held between members of the S.U.C. and Midleton, Stewart and Jameson, to try and frame a resolution on which all could agree, but these proved abortive.[53] The Midletonites would agree only to conditional support of the union. And they remained in control of the I.U.A.

The S.U.C. now determined to challenge this control. The 'Callers' were driven to take further steps, partly by their own momentum,[54] and partly by the need to win the support of Ulster unionists for a joint campaign in British politics against home rule. What worried the 'Callers' was the fact that in the early summer of 1918 another home rule bill was expected, based upon the convention report. Steps had to be taken to mould British opinion against it. Major Pretyman Newman, M.P., one of the original 'Callers', made arrangements to form a small committee of M.P.s to put down amendments to the impending bill on behalf of the S.U.C.;[55] and another manifesto dealing with 'The crisis in Ireland' was sent to politicians in Great Britain, emphasising the changing circumstances which had outmoded the convention report, and 'most important of all . . . THE IMPERIAL CONSIDERATION'.[56] The trouble was that such

52. S.U.C. minute book, 3 May 1918.
53. *Ibid.*, 15 May 1918.
54. Although Walsh had a habit of exaggerating for effect the number of subscribers to the 'Call', claiming by June some 13,000–14,000 adherents, the 'Call' does seem to have gradually gained adherents. Exact numbers are impossible to determine, but many members of the S.U.C. thought that the potential support was much greater: the fact that many unionists were engaged in war work, 'lack of organisation, disgust at the absence of any sort of government during recent years, the prevailing terrorism . . . prevented many from supporting this movement through fear of the consequences to themselves and their property. . . .'
55. S.U.C. minute book, 3 May 1918.
56. Issued 31 May 1918, copies in P.R.O.N.I., D 989A/1/10.

propaganda work was expensive. Yet the S.U.C. had only £25 in hand[57]—with a home rule bill in the offing.

In these circumstances, the idea of a joint committee for propaganda purposes, so successful between 1908 and 1914, was revived, and the secretary of the S.U.C. consulted with Barrie, a leading Ulster unionist.[58] The S.U.C. received no official or direct encouragement from the U.U.C., for the activities of southern unionists during the war and especially in the convention had made Ulster unionists very suspicious of their reliability and usefulness.[59] The official policy of the U.U.C. was to keep aloof from the southern unionists' squabble. Identification with one side or the other might have given the impression that unionism was divided and weakening in the north as well as in the south, and the general view was that the union and Ulster were best served by Ulster 'remaining a separate entity' and fighting home rule in her own way.[60] Nevertheless, Ulster unionists had an obvious interest in seeking the re-establishment of a sound unionist association in the south of Ireland, and, therefore, individual Ulster unionists were encouraged to stiffen southern unionist attitudes on the union. Admittedly, the managers of the U.U.C. never denied the possibility of reviving the joint committee and said that there could be no question of co-operation with the southern unionists as then organised; but at no time does it seem that they instructed the S.U.C.'s northern sympathisers to promise a revival of the joint committee. However, Ulstermen such as Montgomery and Sir James Stronge of Tynan Abbey, Co. Armagh, for a long time Grand Master of the Orange Lodge of Ireland, misled the S.U.C. Such landed gentlemen had as much in common with unionists in the south as they did with those in Ulster, and had long been associated with the former on questions relating to land, home rule and the Church of Ireland. It seems likely that they were much affected by an impression prevailing in the south that Ulster had deserted southern unionists by accepting partition in 1916 and insisting

57. S.U.C. minute book, 15 May 1918.

58. *Ibid.*; Jellett to Montgomery, 8 May 1918, P.R.O.N.I., D 627/432.

59. R. D. Bates (secretary of the U.U.C.) to Montgomery, 2, 8, 29 May 1918, Montgomery to Bates, 21 May 1918, *ibid.*; Barrie to Montgomery, 27 Apr., 18 May 1918, C. C. Craig to Montgomery, 13 May 1918, Fisher to Montgomery, 13 May 1918, Stronge to Montgomery, 10 May 1918, *ibid.*, D 627/434.

60. Bates to Montgomery, 8, 11 May 1918, *ibid.*, D 627/432.

upon it in the convention, and thus, exceeding their brief, tried to counteract Ulster's adverse image by holding out the prospect of a revival of the joint committee if the I.U.A. were reformed.[61] Whatever the motives, Sharman Crawford advised the S.U.C. that 'nothing should be done until the Alliance is put on a proper representative basis', and the committee accepted this view.[62]

Such pressure and prospects drove the S.U.C. on. Since the I.U.A. as then constituted could not be persuaded to declare unequivocally for the union, it had to be transformed and put on a properly representative basis.[63] Some 'Callers' wanted to drive Midleton and his friends out of the I.U.A., but after discussion the S.U.C. decided to avoid personalities and to move circumspectly, taking one step at a time. The first step was to secure the election of a new executive committee for the I.U.A. No attempt would be made to amend the constitution until the S.U.C. had obtained a working majority on the executive committee. Accordingly, a requisition signed by 'Callers' was sent to the I.U.A., which fixed a meeting of the general council to elect twenty members to serve on the executive committee. The S.U.C. did not intend to be outmanoeuvred at this meeting: the 'Callers' were not going to move any resolution, save an amendment to any motion that might be put upholding the action of the delegates at the convention. It was hoped to confine the proceedings to the election of twenty members to the executive committee.

Circumspection did not alter determination. The linchpin of the S.U.C. was Walsh who, surrounded by a group of devoted women helpers, carried out the committee's instructions with resource and enthusiasm.[64] A list was drawn up of twenty candidates for election by the general council to the executive committee, and the S.U.C. asked its supporters to plump for sixteen.[65] Steps were taken to ensure the election of the nominees. Attempts were made to get into working order the machinery

61. See e.g. G. de L. Willis to Montgomery, 13, 21 May 1918, and Montgomery to Willis, 20, 24 May 1918, *ibid.,* D 627/432 and 434; Stronge to Montgomery, 8 May 1918, *ibid.,* D 627/432.
62. S.U.C. minute book, 15 May 1918.
63. *Ibid.,* 15 May, 6 June 1918.
64. J. P. Newman to Walsh, 13 June 1918, Alice Wilson to Walsh, 23 May 1918, Eileen Murray to Walsh, 20 July 1918, P.R.O.N.I., D 989A/8/17A.
65. S.U.C. minute book, 15 May 1918.

for electing members to the general council: this meant reviving
county branches and affiliated associations after their lapse in the
war and persuading them to send delegates favourable to the
'Call'. The Dublin Unionist Registration Association needed no
canvassing and immediately offered to affiliate to the S.U.C. to
assist financing the good work. This led to the formation of new
committees in Co. Cavan, Queen's County and Co. Fermanagh.
As on the previous occasion the S.U.C. sought the attendance of
Ulster members and Montgomery worked particularly hard to
galvanise them into action. For instance, there was some difficulty
with the Fermanagh branch of the I.U.A. Many supposed members were either dead or abroad, the secretary was ageing and
seriously ill, and the representative on the general council had
resigned. Undeterred, Montgomery persuaded the former
representative to agree to re-election, and supervised, in the
ailing secretary's home, a meeting of the Fermanagh branch
(comprising the secretary and another Fermanagh unionist)
which returned Montgomery's nominee as representative of the
Fermanagh county branch on the general council of the I.U.A.[66]

These careful preparations paid off, especially since the
managers of the I.U.A. appear to have made no attempt to
counter them. When the general council met on 7 June, the
'Callers' acted with great restraint. Midleton's justification of the
delegates' action, hingeing upon the fact that the act of 1914 had
been passed, was 'heard with great respect by the audience' and
was 'greeted with some applause, and often with tokens of dis-
approval, as regards which the latter seemed to be predominant'.
A vote of confidence in the delegates was avoided, and the
S.U.C.'s nominees were elected by an overwhelming majority.[67]

Delighted by this success, the S.U.C. went forward with the
next step. On 5 July the executive committee was to meet to
co-opt other members, and the S.U.C. continued its energetic
and now optimistic activity to secure the co-option of its own
nominees. Branches of the I.U.A. not represented at the last
meeting of the general council were persuaded to send representatives to the executive committee, and old supporters were

66. Montgomery to Walsh, 24, 27 May 1918, to E. M. Archdale, 18, 22 May
1918, to Col. R. H. P. Doran, 22 May 1918; Archdale to Montgomery, 20 May
1918; Walsh to Montgomery, 29 May 1918, P.R.O.N.I., D 627/432.
   67. *Dublin Daily Express,* 8 June 1918.

exhorted to outvote the *ex-officio* members of the committee
who were Midleton's supporters and who gave him effective
control of the Alliance.[68] This optimism was shortlived. The
S.U.C.'s success on 7 June had finally awoken Midleton and his
friends to the strength and importance of the 'Call'. Although
Midleton wrongly attributed the S.U.C.'s victory to the presence
of Ulster representatives,[69] he could no longer treat the S.U.C.
with as much indifference as he had done in the past.[70] The trouble
was that his opponents' activity was now undermining his
position in British politics. The *Dublin Daily Express,* in a report
notable for its restraint and moderation, declared that the election
of the sixteen nominees of the 'Call' was a 'remarkable endorse-
ment of [the] "Call to unionists" ', holding that

especial importance was attached to the proceedings, as upon the result
of the election depended the question whether the home rule proposals
of the Irish convention were to be adopted or repudiated by a majority
of the council of the I.U.A.[71]

This view evidently prevailed in Great Britain: Lord Curzon,
then Lord President of the Council, speaking in the House of
Lords on the government's Irish proposals, stated that 'the
southern unionists . . . dissociated themselves from and threw
over' Lord Midleton who had 'fought so good a battle in what
he rightly conceived to be the interests of his country'.[72] Realising
that the dispute with the S.U.C. was weakening his authority in
Britain,[73] Midleton sought to retrieve the situation.

68. Walsh to Montgomery, 10 June 1918, P.R.O.N.I., D 627/432. Antrim,
Kerry, Kilkenny, King's county, Limerick and East Wicklow had not sent
representatives to the 7 June meeting, but since then East Wicklow and Limerick
had organised and Kerry was believed to have taken active steps. For indications
of the S.U.C.'s activity, see e.g. Montgomery to Webb, 12 June 1918, to Margaret
ffolliott, 15 June 1918; Stronge to Montgomery, 12 June, 3 July 1918; ffolliott
to Montgomery, 20 June 1918; Walsh to Montgomery, 21, 29 June 1918; Knox
to Montgomery, 26 June 1918, *ibid.*
   69. Midleton, letter in *The Times,* 22 June 1918. About thirty Ulstermen had
attended the meeting, but about fifteen came from one of the 'southerly' counties.
Besides, the majority for the 'Call's' nominees was so large that the votes of the
Ulster representatives had little effect on the results of the elections.
   70. For indications of Midleton's reaction, see e.g. H. McCalmont to Walsh,
29 June 1918, H. L. Tivy to Walsh, 9 July 1918, P.R.O.N.I., D 989A/8/17A.
   71. *Dublin Daily Express,* 8 June 1918.
   72. *Parl. Deb. (Lords),* 5 ser., xxx, 20 June 1918, col. 329.
   73. Midleton, letter in *The Times,* 22 June 1918.

An attempt was made to bludgeon the 'Callers' into submission. For the first time the managers of the I.U.A. showed some energy, not only in defending the delegates' attitude at the convention, but also in whipping up support, especially among the *ex-officio* members of the executive committee, for the forthcoming co-option meeting.[74] These efforts were partly successful. The *ex-officio* members attended in great strength and thus Midleton's supporters easily outnumbered those of the S.U.C. who provided the majority of the elective element on the committee. The result was that Midleton's nominees were adopted; the smallest number of votes cast for them being 36, the highest for the S.U.C.'s nominees being 33.[75]

But Midleton's efforts were not wholly successful, for he did not crush the S.U.C. Once more Midletonites had mishandled the situation and driven the S.U.C. into an extremely antagonistic attitude.[76] Although earlier in the year the 'Callers' had drawn up an elaborate programme of reform of the I.U.A., all the indications were that they would not press forward this programme, if they were reasonably treated by the I.U.A. The Midletonites, however, appear never to have tried to understand the position of the 'Callers'. It is difficult to see why Midleton had not tried to secure the co-option of at least some of the S.U.C.'s nominees. As it was, this latest in a series of tactical errors on the part of the southern unionist leadership looked like precipitating a breach in the I.U.A. Incensed at the way their previous efforts to secure increased representation on the executive had been nullified by the outvoting of the elective element by the un-elected element on the committee, the 'Callers' decided without further reference to Midleton to press on with their programme. It was decided to ask for a meeting of the general council in the autumn to amend the constitution of the I.U.A. and to put the organisation back on the right path. Meantime, the S.U.C. re-affirmed its faith in the union, and carried out its intention to

74. Midleton to Stewart, 12 June 1918, P.R.O., 30/67/39, ff. 2316–8; see also Walsh to Montgomery, 29 June, 1 July 1918; Stronge to Montgomery, 1 July 1918, P.R.O.N.I., D 627/432.
75. S.U.C. minute book, 5 July 1918.
76. *Ibid.*; Walsh to Montgomery, 26 July 1918, P.R.O.N.I., D 627/432. The S.U.C. rejected Midleton's suggestion for a meeting on the ground 'that nothing further of value would be gained by the holding of a further conference as suggested by him'.

work independently and to persuade the next meeting of the executive committee of the I.U.A. to affirm its absolute faith in the union.[77]

FOUR

Though Midleton and his associates were largely responsible for this parlous state of affairs, some things may be said in mitigation. The excuse that the confidential nature of the proceedings of the convention precluded consultation with the general council[78] does not really hold water, in view of the fact that Ulster unionists had established a series of advisory committees and that the southern unionist delegates had consulted the executive committee of the I.U.A. Nevertheless, some other excuses can be made to explain why the Midletonites mishandled their opponents and neglected the main body of southern unionists. Not only did they have little time or energy to concern themselves with public relations. They also had by the end of April little inclination to discuss and defend the convention report.

Events had virtually invalidated the work they had put into the convention. In the spring of 1918 the British government, faced with constantly rising pressure on manpower resources, passed a new Military Conscription Act which not only raised the age of exemption but empowered the government to extend the operation of the act to Ireland by order in council. All nationalist Ireland at once united in protest against this threat to introduce conscription there. A conference called by the Lord Mayor of Dublin asserted that the proposal was a 'declaration of war on the Irish nation'; the Irish Parliamentary Party, now led by Dillon, withdrew from the House of Commons; the Roman Catholic bishops issued a statement condemning the new policy and affirming that 'the Irish have a right to resist by every means that are consonant with the law of God'; and a one-day strike, effective everywhere except in the north-east, was a clear indication of national solidarity.[79]

77. See e.g. *ibid.*; Guinness to Montgomery, 28 July, 16 Aug. 1918; Stronge to Montgomery, 21 Sept. 1918, P.R.O.N.I., D 627/432. ffolliott to Montgomery, 17 Aug. 1918; Ricardo to Montgomery, 1 Sept. 1918, *ibid.*, D 627/436. Montgomery to Guinness, 30 July 1918, to Fisher, 16 Aug. 1918, and to secretary of I.U.A. and Stronge, 24 Aug. 1918, *ibid.*, D 627/432, 434, 436.

78. Midleton, letter in *Irish Times*, 16 Mar. 1918.

79. J. C. Beckett, *The Making of Modern Ireland* (1966), pp. 444-5.

This conscription crisis hit at the very basis of the new departure. Midletonites began to doubt the wisdom of introducing home rule at such a time. A time when people were idling, tillage was suffering, nationalists were parading on working days, and Protestants were allegedly threatened into signing anti-conscription pledges,[80] was scarcely a propitious moment to implement home rule. Moreover, the Irish Parliamentary Party's alignment with the extreme nationalists in opposition to conscription underlined the difficulty, if not impossibility, of establishing a centre party of unionists and moderate nationalists. So much for the Midletonite view that:

It is not too late to hope that, if a 'Call' were made by a blended nationalist and unionist brotherhood on those Irishmen of fighting age who are still, alas, standing aloof, to serve their country in the war, the response would be such as to silence the daily taunts of the English press—so humiliating to endure, so impossible to answer.[81]

Midletonites were almost inclined to agree with Carson's view that it would be foolhardy to act upon the convention report and 'in the midst of the gravest crisis of the fate of European civilisation, hurriedly to impose some new solution which will place Ireland under the joint rule of *Sinn Fein,* nationalists, and the Roman Catholic hierarchy'.[82] What Ireland needed was firm government and the restoration of law and order.

Midletonites were confused and disillusioned. Midleton, for instance, did not know where his duty lay. The government was intending to act upon the convention report; yet the condition of Ireland and Dillon's attitude to conscription made home rule virtually impossible at the moment. Then there was the question of conscription. Opposition to conscription was mounting and the measure could be enforced only with considerable bloodshed; yet 'the men who write to me from Flanders have not had their boots off for a fortnight, and the Divisions which come out of action can no longer be made up to strength'.[83] Desart was deeply depressed by the situation and retreated to England:

80. See e.g. J. J. Joly of King's County to Canon Jesson, 1 May 1918, copy in B.L., 83/3/7.
81. A. F. Blood, letter in *Irish Times,* 29 Mar. 1918.
82. Letter, *ibid.,* 2 May 1918.
83. Midleton to Bernard, 20 Apr. 1918, B.M., Add. MS 52781, ff. 72–3; Midleton, *Records and Reactions,* pp. 247–52.

G

To us here—we personally find little or no difference so far in the
civility of our men about the place—except a sort of indefinite feeling
that our lots are separate, but our English servants are feeling the
difficulty much and are having a bad time. The Irish servants and
people about the place keep aloof from them—old servants who have
been on terms of close friendship with them, including a girl who has
been with us for years in London and here. They say to them they have
been told in chapel to fight for Ireland, that Germany will help them,
and that when[?] the Germans come all things to Ireland will follow. . . .
This is probably only talk . . . but the salient fact is that the threat to
deprive them [?] of their comfortable existence protected by the
British navy, making large profit by the inflated prices paid in Great
Britain, owning their farms and homesteads by the credit of the
United Kingdom, lying soft and growing fat in ease, has united them
all, and made England the common enemy.[84]

Not all could leave Ireland so easily, but those delegates remaining
found they could not justify views which they now recognised as
outmoded by events, for in April 1918 Ireland would not be
pacified by home rule. According to one of their sympathisers,
'owing to the anti-conscription revolt of the nationalists and the
attitude of the hierarchy and priests', southern unionists, including
Bernard, Jameson, Powell and Stewart, 'are now unanimously of
opinion that no scheme of home rule such as their delegates
supported at the convention could be safely introduced.'[85]
   Disillusionment was then one excuse for the Midletonites'
inept handling of the 'Call'. A second excuse was that their
attention was fully absorbed elsewhere at crucial times. This was
particularly true of Midleton. The 'Call' had been published at a
critical time in the convention. The beginning of March had been
a tense period for the convention which was discussing the
government proposals, especially the reservation of the customs,
and Midleton's energy and will for political controversy were
sapped as he waited despondently in London for nationalists to
make up their minds on the customs.[86]
   Even after the convention Midleton's labours were not at an
end. The reason that he missed the meeting of the general council

84. Desart to Bernard, 23 Apr. 1918, B.M., Add. MS 52781, ff. 175–9.
   85. Memorandum by A. W. Samuels (Irish Attorney-General) on the Irish
situation, 10 May 1918, B.L., F/44/9/3.
   86. Midleton to Bernard, 9 Mar. 1918, B.M., Add. MS 52781, ff. 67–8.

on 3 May was his continued absorption in high politics. Owing to the part he had played in the convention, the government decided to offer him the Lord Lieutenancy of Ireland, and at the end of April and the beginning of May, Midleton was involved in discussions with the Prime Minister and other ministers on the best means of dealing with the new developments in Ireland.[87] The episode is particularly interesting in showing how differently British ministers and southern unionists viewed the Irish situation and the sort of measures necessary to contain it. The government was willing to give way on some points, and agreed that Midleton should go to Ireland as one of three Lords Justice; but on other points Midleton and the government could not agree. Owing to the parliamentary situation and the need for recruits, the government wanted to press forward immediately with their dual policy of home rule and conscription, Lloyd George in particular being in a bloodthirsty mood.[88] On the whole, southern unionists opposed this dual policy and wanted both measures dropped, advocating instead a firm policy to restore law and order. Midletonites shared this concern about the state of Ireland, especially the consequences of the conscription issue and the attitude of the Roman Catholic priesthood. The reflective Bernard took the opportunity to probe the motives and political attitude of the Roman Catholic hierarchy and concluded that they had been forced to come out against conscription in order to keep control over their people and to prevent bloodshed.[89] Other southern unionists were more concerned with the practical effect of the church's stand.[90] They did not see how conscription could

87. The essential accuracy of Midleton's account of this episode in *Records and Reactions*, pp. 247–52, is confirmed by the following correspondence: Midleton to Bernard, 20, 24 Apr., 1, 4 May 1918, B.M., Add. MS 52781, ff. 72–8; Stamfordham to Lloyd George, 25 Apr. 1918, B.L., F/29/2/23; Midleton to Lloyd George, 25, 30 Apr. 1918, *ibid.,* F/38/1/11, 12; Long to Law, 1 May 1918, Midleton to Law, 2 May 1918, *ibid.,* 83/3/1, 4; Law to Midleton, 27 June 1918, *ibid.,* 84/7/43; and various memoranda by Midleton, P.R.O., 30/67/38, ff. 2282–2311.

88. Midleton reported that Lloyd George said 'Ireland might run in blood, it was nothing to what was going on in France etc. and he thought that after all the bloodshed they would take home rule like lambs generally.' (Midleton to Bernard, 4 May 1918, B.M., Add. MS 52781, ff. 77–8).

89. Bernard to Archbishop of Canterbury, 30 Apr. 1918, printed in Murray, *Archbishop Bernard*, pp. 323–6.

90. See e.g. A. W. Samuels's memoranda on Ireland, 2, 10 May 1918, and Campbell's memorandum to Law, 4 May 1918, B.L., F/44/9/3 and 83/3/7, 15.

be carried out. With the priesthood condemning conscription, it was doubtful if the Royal Irish Constabulary could be relied upon to enforce the measure. In any case, such were the feelings aroused by the conscription issue that it could be carried out only in face of fierce resistance and considerable bloodshed and by the use of exceptional measures which, it was doubted, the government would persist in. It was not that southern unionists were particularly squeamish or cowardly; in fact, during April they showed singular courage in protesting against home rule, even though Sinn Fein was making a house-to-house canvass for signatures to the anti-conscription pledge and warning all those who refused to sign that they 'will be marked out for future vengeance'. It was not panic that determined the southern unionist attitude to conscription, but a realistic and informed appreciation of the Irish situation and temperament: they had a 'lively recollection of the rebellion' and knew that 'the rebels were a handful then to a host now, with the priesthood at their back'.[91] Indeed, it was possible for southern unionists to believe that Ireland was on the verge of civil war. Midleton shared these views. He thought that the dual policy would be difficult to carry out, since it would alienate loyalists and the R.I.C. and at the same time drive all nationalists together. Moreover, Midleton was very sceptical of the government's determination to carry out any policy in Ireland firmly, and particularly wary of the support he would receive from the government and the House of Commons. Nevertheless, because he could not see clearly where his duty lay in view of 'the *great and immediate* need for recruits on the western front', he agreed to go to Ireland on certain conditions.[92] Apart from making detailed policy suggestions, he demanded a free hand in advising on policy, particularly as to whether or not and when home rule should be attempted.[93] He was, in effect, asking for power without responsibility for any unpopular measures

91. Campbell to Law, 4 May 1918, B.L., 83/3/15.
92. Midleton, *Records and Reactions*, pp. 247–52; Midleton to Lloyd George, 30 Apr. 1918, B.L., F/38/1/12.
93. Midleton demanded that he be given a completely free hand in Ireland; that the Lords Justice should have the status of cabinet ministers and be consulted on all questions of policy relating to Ireland; that if the home rule bill passed through parliament, the time of putting it into force would be subject to their views as to the condition of Ireland; adequate cabinet support for immediate action; that conscription be passed and implemented immediately; the immediate

that might be enacted, and the government found his conditions too stringent:

I cannot go to Ireland unless it is made public that the Lords Justice will advise on all questions of policy, so that it may be clear that I am not bound by the 'stand or fall' declarations of the ministry on home rule and conscription.[94]

The government would not concede to these demands. Discussions broke down and Lord French was appointed Lord Lieutenant instead; though by June the dual policy had to be dropped.[95]

'Nerve-racking'[96] negotiations and changing conditions meant that Midletonites had little time or inclination to consider popularity and their relations with the 'Callers'. In March the 'Call' had seemed a trifling distraction to men engaged on the great work of settling the Irish question. In May the dispute was distasteful as well: as Desart wrote to Bernard, 'I am not proud of my country just now and it will only take a good quarrel between unionists to complete the story.'[97] By June and July, when the convention policy had collapsed completely and the government had abandoned its twin policies of home rule and conscription, it is not surprising that the Midletonites had angrily tried to crush the S.U.C. which continued to demand a public confession of error.

FIVE

Not until the summer of 1918 did the Midletonites realise their mistake. Only then, seeing that the S.U.C. needed delicate

---

arrest of leading Sinn Feiners; the prohibition of anti-conscription meetings; the suppression of anti-conscription newspapers; a recognised procedure for dealing with conscientious objectors; sufficient labour to carry on transport services; in the last resort an arrangement with Ulster unionists in regard to the timing and nature of home rule as would prevent Ulster joining the south in resistance to conscription.

94. Midleton to Law, 2 May 1918, B.L., 83/3/4.
95. Law to Midleton, 27 June 1918, *ibid.*, 83/7/43; Midleton, *Records and Reactions*, p. 252; Colvin, *Life of Lord Carson*, iii. 356–9.
96. Midleton, *Records and Reactions*, p. 249; Midleton to Bernard, 24 Apr. 1918, B.M., Add. MS 52781, f. 74.
97. Desart to Bernard, 23 Apr. 1918, *ibid.*, ff. 175–9.

handling, did they begin to make serious efforts to maintain unity among southern unionists. Partly they had been driven to seek conciliation, because the sheer assertion of their leaders' views had proved insufficient to maintain the authority of the I.U.A. over the usually amenable southern unionists. Partly their reasons were more complex, as much the outcome of chronology and psychology as of expediency. Changing circumstances had made it possible and necessary to seek, albeit gradually, a reconciliation with the S.U.C. In the first place, released from the claustrophobic atmosphere and British orientation of high politics during the summer recess and in closer touch with their constituents, Midletonites were in a better position to appreciate the feelings of their constituents and the strength and depth of feeling among subscribers to the 'Call'. Secondly, with the passage of time the dispute over the convention report had become irrelevant. Since the circumstances necessitating the convention had passed, and since the conscription crisis and the weakness of the Irish government had invalidated the report, Midletonites could come to terms with the S.U.C. without loss of face. Lastly, they were genuinely anxious to serve the best interests of southern unionism as they saw them. The government was still committed to some form of home rule, so that, while not altering their views that a settlement might have to come, the Midletonites thought it prudent to prepare for all eventualities. They were anxious to avoid a split in the I.U.A.: united, southern unionists might defeat home rule, or at least obtain better terms; divided, their opinion would be disregarded.[98]

For immediate and practical purposes, then, there was little difference between Midletonites and 'Callers'. Anxious to maintain the authority of southern unionism, Midleton and his friends tried to come to terms with the S.U.C. For the first time since the

---

98. Midleton to Stewart, 19 Aug. 1918, P.R.O., 30/67/39, f. 2327; Iveagh to Midleton, 17 Sept. 1918, and Midleton to Iveagh, 20 Sept. 1918, printed copies in P.R.O.N.I., D 989A/8/20A; Midleton to Bernard, 31 Aug. 1918, T.C.D., Bernard correspondence 1 (1893–1919), 161. In his letter to Bernard, after discussing the alternatives open to the government in respect of Ireland (of going back on its pledges and saving the six counties or of putting aside the whole question as 'so often done before'), Midleton concludes 'it is difficult to see which, and I have no idea whether our people will be wise enough to keep their powder dry and keep the Alliance together. Anyhow I shall do my best for this while I am in Ireland.'

dispute began the Midletonites put forward their views and handled opposition not only forcefully but also tactfully and skilfully. In July Midleton had approached the S.U.C., and the I.U.A. passed a resolution against home rule. Piqued by their defeat over co-option, the S.U.C. had disregarded Midleton's approach and had chosen to regard the resolution as equivocal.[99] Nevertheless, Midleton and his friends had certain factors in their favour: with time, especially during the traditional summer holiday in British politics, the S.U.C.'s pique might lessen, and there was the latter's fear of appearing to split southern unionism. The Midletonites took full advantage of these factors. It was not until 10 September that the S.U.C. sent out its requisition for a meeting of the general council to reform the I.U.A., and Midleton used the request and the interval to advantage. Most notably a cleverly contrived correspondence between him and Iveagh stressing the need for unity was circulated to members of the council and then published.[100] It evidently embarrassed the S.U.C.,[101] which is not surprising, for Iveagh wrote appealingly:

Let us close our ranks for the final struggle. If we win, we shall have done well indeed. If we are beaten, let us make the best terms possible for ourselves and our successors in the heritage of freedom in the south.

Midleton now tried to work harmoniously with his opponents. His tactics were a nice combination of attack and concession[102] which succeeded in disarming the S.U.C. When the executive committee next met, on 1 October, Midleton was again elected chairman, but concessions were made to extreme unionism.[103] The date for the general council was fixed for 1 November, and a sub-committee, which included several members of the S.U.C., was appointed to consider draft amendments to the constitution.

99. S.U.C. minute book, 5 July 1918.

100. Iveagh to Midleton, 17 Sept. 1918 and Midleton to Iveagh, 20 Sept. 1918, P.R.O.N.I., D 989A/8/20A.

101. See e.g. Walsh's reply to Midleton's letter (undated), printed copy, *ibid.*; Guinness to Montgomery, 22 Sept. 1918 and Jellett to Guinness, 22 Sept. 1918, *ibid.*, D 627/439.

102. Midleton to Donoughmore, 31 Aug. 1918, P.R.O., 30/67/39, ff. 2328–31.

103. Reports of the meeting in *Dublin Daily Express* and *Irish Times*, 2 Oct. 1918.

Then a resolution, deploring the government's intention of re-opening the Irish question as disastrous to Great Britain and Ireland, was endorsed by the committee. At last the 'Callers' had got what they wanted; even the *Irish Times* tactfully admitted that Midletonites had seceded from the attitude they took up at the convention.[104] Nobody would have disputed the S.U.C.'s self-congratulation that 'the proceedings that day . . . were a virtual triumph for the "Call to unionists" movement'.[105] An outright split in the southern unionist movement seemed, there-fore, to have been avoided, for the S.U.C. resolved to take no further action 'which would support any difference of opinion among unionists'.[106]

The reconciliation was not absolutely complete, but it seemed to provide the basis for a working compromise. There was continued disagreement between the two sections of the I.U.A., this time over what amendments should be made to the con-stitution. The difficulty as far as the S.U.C. was concerned was that, although it was represented on the sub-committee to draw up amendments, the Midletonites still had control of the executive committee and could, therefore, decide which amendments to recommend officially to the general council. The main disagree-ment lay over whether or not the Ulster members of the I.U.A. should be permitted to take part in the discussion of issues con-cerning partition.[107] The less temperate and more suspicious of the 'Callers' took exception to any amendment excluding Ulstermen, seeing in it a revival of the attitude taken up by the Midletonites at the convention.[108] Nevertheless other 'Callers', including after reflection their Ulster sympathisers,[109] were less perturbed over what they regarded as an inessential point. Though willing to prolong the existence of the S.U.C. as a pressure group,[110] they were more concerned to keep the I.U.A. united. Some may even have sympathised with the Midletonite distrust

104. *Irish Times*, 2 Oct. 1918.
105. S.U.C. minute book, 1 Oct. 1918.
106. *Ibid.*
107. Walsh to Montgomery, 24 Oct. 1918, P.R.O.N.I., D 627/434.
108. Walsh to Montgomery, 4, 25 Oct. 1918, *ibid.*
109. Montgomery to Guinness, 17 Oct. 1918, to Fane Vernon, 18 Oct. 1918, to Walsh, 20 Oct. 1918; Vernon to Montgomery, 17 Oct. 1918; Stronge to Montgomery, 19, 28 Oct. 1918; Archdale to Montgomery, 26 Oct. 1918, *ibid.*
110. Guinness to Walsh, 9 Oct. 1918, *ibid.*

of Ulster,[111] but, in the main, the less intemperate members of the S.U.C. felt that they had gained the substance of what they set out to achieve, viz., the summoning of a general council to consider amendments to the constitution of the I.U.A., and a re-affirmation of its fundamental principle as the maintenance of the union. Moreover, with another battle for the union likely in the near future, they were anxious to avoid even the impression that unionism was divided or weakening in the south and were reluctant to deprive themselves of the financial resources of such eminent men as Iveagh and the political influence of the Irish representative peers and an ex-cabinet minister like Midleton.[112]

Otherwise the situation would be grotesque, because we should then possibly have in the future a home rule bill, being discussed and debated in the House of Lords by so-called 'professing' unionists, who themselves were not considered in Ireland to be sufficiently staunch to the union to be admitted to the membership of the executive committee of the I.U.A., an association established and continued for the sole purpose of maintaining the union.

So, personally, I think it would be folly to attempt to throw an ex-cabinet minister like Lord Midleton, and other prominent Irish peers, like Lords Barrymore, Iveagh, Donoughmore and Mayo, into the arms of those, like Lord Macdonald [*sic*], who are openly hostile to the union.[113]

Since, therefore, the less moderate 'Callers' were unlikely to act alone and seem also to have been wary of too close an identification with Ulster,[114] and since the indications were that, with one or two exceptions, the Midletonites wished to settle outstanding matters amicably,[115] the prospects were that when the general council met on 1 November, the unity of southern unionism would be maintained.

111. Newman to Guinness, 14 Oct. 1918, *ibid.*

112. *Ibid.*; and Newman to Guinness, 11 Oct. 1918; Guinness to Walsh, 9 Oct. 1918; Guinness to Montgomery, 17 Oct. 1918; Montgomery to Barrie, 2 Oct. 1918, P.R.O.N.I., D 627/434.

113. Guinness to Walsh, 9 Oct. 1918, *ibid.* This letter was written before the dispute over the amendment had gathered momentum, but Guinness's letter to Montgomery on 17 Oct. 1918 shows the former's attitude was unchanged.

114. Montgomery to Barrie, 2, 7 Oct. 1918, *ibid.*

115. Midleton to Stewart, 15 Oct. 1918, to Bagwell, 25 Oct. 1918, P.R.O., 30/67/39, ff. 2333-7, 2341-4.

SIX

Unhappily for the future of southern unionism, events now worked against unity. First of all an influenza epidemic caused the meeting of the general council to be postponed,[116] and then the general election delayed it yet again.[117] The general council did not actually meet until 24 January 1919. This delay proved fatal to the chances of unity, for in the meantime events, centring around Ulster, occurred which stiffened the attitudes of Midletonites and of the entire S.U.C., making both sides reluctant to compromise, especially over the exclusion of Ulstermen from the deliberations of the I.U.A.

The main cause of the trouble was the election in Great Britain and Ulster which underlined the fears of Midletonites that in any home rule settlement southern unionists would be deprived of the protection of the Ulster interest. The election meant that Lloyd George had to square himself on his attitude towards Ulster, if the coalition was to be maintained. He, therefore, in a letter to Law, who had always supported the Ulster cause, virtually committed the government to the partition of Ireland; and Ulster unionists once more accepted the idea. Consequently, Midletonites held,

so-called 'unionist' candidates have almost universally confined themselves, if they have spoken about home rule at all, to advocating the exclusion of the six counties of north-east Ulster, and seem to think they are satisfying all unionist requirements by this course. The remainder of the House of Commons are, apart from the Ulster M.P.s, to a man, pronounced home rulers.[118]

Such an attitude in Great Britain meant that the southern unionist activity in the convention had been wasted. This knowledge was made harder, indeed bitter, to swallow by another consequence of the election. The Ulster unionist delegates and leaders had to

116. Stronge to Montgomery, 28 Oct. 1918, P.R.O.N.I., D 627/434.
117. Jellett to Stewart, 6 Nov. 1918; Walsh to Montgomery, 7 Nov. 1918, *ibid.*, D 627/436. The suspicions of these, the less moderate members of the S.U.C., were further enhanced by this move.
118. 'Memorandum as to partition', n.d., but issued apparently in Jan. 1919, by the Midletonite section of the executive committee of the I.U.A., copy in P.R.O.N.I., D 989A/9/12.

make many speeches, and they seem to have tried to deflect attention from their own participation in the convention by concentrating on the congenial task of criticising the action of the southern unionist delegates. For instance, Carson was reported as telling a meeting in Belfast in support of the official unionist and coalition candidate for the Ormeau division:

He might say that the Irish convention gave him more trouble than anything with which he had to do in connection with the whole home rule question, and it drove him out of the cabinet in the middle of the war. Never was Ulster in a more dangerous position than when the convention was drawing to a close, and for this reason: the southern unionists lost their courage. They gave the case away, proceeded Sir Edward. 'I do not believe that they represented anybody but themselves. They said that we were traitors, whereas, as a matter of fact, it was they, under the leadership of Lord Midleton, who were prepared to say: "If we go down, Ulster must come down too." Not likely . . . (applause). . . .'[119]

Not unnaturally, Midleton and his friends reacted vehemently to such declarations. An intemperate correspondence flashed between Carson and Midleton, to be followed by a press controversy among their respective adherents;[120] and it only put Midletonites in an intransigent mood. They argued that southerners had always been excluded from the deliberations of the Ulstermen in the past, and that Ulstermen had tried to get the best terms they could for themselves in the event of home rule being forced upon them. Therefore, southern unionists were entitled to consider their own interests without hindrance from the north, especially when a selfish north could be present at deliberations of the general council of the I.U.A. in the shape of some 107 delegates.[121] Thus, when the executive committee met on 6 January 1919 to consider which of the sub-committee's recommendations should be put to the general council later in the month, the Midletonites not only intended to propose that members representing the six counties be excluded from the

119. *Irish Times*, 4 Dec. 1918.
120. See e.g. the correspondence between Midleton and Carson, printed in *Irish Times*, 31 Dec. 1918. Carson's letter and copies of Midleton's are in P.R.O., 30/67/39, ff. 2349-50, 2355, 2356-8.
121. 'Memorandum as to partition'.

I.U.A.'s deliberations, but now made it a matter of principle. Should the general council not agree to this amendment, the Midletonites threatened to resign from the Alliance and to form a separate organisation;[122] even though they knew that such a division would weaken the southern unionist case.[123]

In the circumstances of January 1919 this attitude was certain to split the I.U.A. The S.U.C. did not share the Midletonite intense distrust of Ulster unionism, and had worked closely with Ulster unionists over the past year. It had never liked the proposal to exclude the Ulster members for it continued to believe that co-operation with Ulster unionists was essential for the maintenance of the union. Not only did the 'Callers' hope, with the support of Ulster unionists, to put the I.U.A. on a more representative basis;[124] in a wider sense, they saw co-operation between unionists in the north and south as the best means of maintaining the legislative union intact. Believing that partition was unacceptable to most shades of nationalist opinion they thought that the only way to defeat home rule was through pressing the Ulster objection.[125] Midleton's amendment would endanger such co-operation and, therefore, in the executive committee on 6 January, the 'Callers' tried to dissuade the executive committee from adopting such an amendment. The committee, with its built-in Midletonite majority, was not impressed by their arguments and decided to recommend to the general council that resolution which would lead to the exclusion of Ulster members from many of the key discussions of the I.U.A.[126]

122. Stronge to Montgomery, 6 Jan. 1919, P.R.O.N.I., D 627/437; S.U.C. circular letter, 6 Jan. 1919, urging attendance at the meeting of the general council, *ibid.*, D 989A/11/6.

123. See e.g. Midleton to Bernard, 14 Dec. 1918, B.M., Add. MS 52781, ff. 80–2.

124. See e.g. Stronge to Montgomery, 6 Jan. 1919, P.R.O.N.I., D 627/437.

125. See e.g. S.U.C. circular, 6 Jan. 1919; circular issued by the reformed I.U.A., Feb. 1919, explaining the split, copy *ibid.*, D 989A/8/23; Jellett to Montgomery, 6 Jan. 1919; Montgomery to Walsh, 3 Feb. 1919; Walsh to Montgomery, 5 Feb. 1919, *ibid.*, D 637/434.

126. 'Should any proposal for the future government of Ireland, involving the possible exclusion of any part of Ireland, come up for consideration at any meeting of the Irish Unionist Alliance or the council or executive committee thereof hereinafter mentioned, the members representing the parts of Ireland outside the areas to be excluded, shall be the only persons competent to discuss or resolve upon the action to be taken by the Alliance. Presidents or vice-presidents who reside or own property in a province or county shall, for the purposes of this rule, be deemed to be members representing such province or county.'

This decision put the S.U.C. in a quandary.[127] Anxious to avoid appearing intransigent and the accusation of splitting the I.U.A., it hoped at first to reach a compromise. It was decided immediately after the meeting of the executive committee to move at the general council a carefully worded amendment to Midleton's proposal that would not give him an excuse to resign.[128] This moderation was soon modified, however, by two, perhaps three, factors. In the first place, the renewal of the controversy between Midletonites and Ulster unionists over the convention and the relative merits of the Ulster and Midletonite stands, accompanied as it was by a prolonged debate in the press by all interested parties, revived and strengthened the S.U.C.'s suspicions of Midletonite reliability on the union.[129] In the second place, the S.U.C. was led to believe by those Ulster unionists with whom they were in close touch that future co-operation between Ulster and southern unionists now depended not only upon reform but also upon Midleton and Stewart being deprived of the leadership of the I.U.A. In May and October such Ulster sympathisers as Montgomery and Stronge had been on the side of moderation. On those occasions, because of long-standing friendship with Midleton, fear that disunity in the south would weaken the entire

127. S.U.C. circular, 6 Jan. 1919; Stronge to Montgomery, 6 Jan. 1919, and Montgomery to Barrie, 9 Jan. 1919, P.R.O.N.I., D 627/437. The defeat of William Jellett in the previous December in a four-cornered contest for the Dublin University seats probably helped to make the S.U.C. cautious. Jellett had been more sympathetic than his opponents to Ulster, explaining publicly that, while opposed to home rule for any part of Ireland, he quite recognised that should home rule become inevitable, Ulster had an absolute right to insist that 'she should not be dragged into the waste and ruin entailed by any such scheme'.

128. Their 'colourless' counter-resolution ran: 'Should any matter or question affecting a particular county or counties only, or on which it may appear desirable to obtain the opinion of any particular county or counties, come up for consideration at any meeting of the general council or executive committee and a resolution be submitted and carried at such meeting by a majority of two-thirds of those present that the members or representatives of the branches of other counties be excluded from the deliberation thereon, such members or representatives shall not be competent to take part at that meeting in the deliberations on such matter or question or to vote on any resolution relating thereto provided that no such resolution passed at a meeting of the executive committee shall be operative unless and until it has been confirmed at a meeting of the general council by a majority of two-thirds of those present at such meeting. Provided further that no resolution so passed shall be binding on the members or representatives so excluded from such deliberations.'

129. I.U.A. circular, Feb. 1919; Walsh to Montgomery, 16 Jan. 1919, P.R.O.N.I., D 627/437.

case against home rule, and respect for the history and traditions of the I.U.A. with which they had long been associated, they had used their influence against those hotheads on the S.U.C. who had wanted to depose Midleton and Stewart. By January 1919, however, their attitude had changed. Midleton's controversy with Carson seems finally to have convinced these Ulstermen that Midleton was thoroughly untrustworthy and likely to compromise Ulster's position. His proposed amendment would make it impossible for Ulster representatives to be present if a home rule bill in accordance with the Lloyd George compromise was being discussed. Midletonians would accept the bill on condition that there was no partition and would pack a meeting of the I.U.A. executive to carry their proposal and would put Ulster in as big a hole over the matter as they could.[130]

Therefore, Montgomery and Stronge with increasing insistence urged upon the S.U.C. (and perhaps other unionists in the south and west through the press controversy) not only the necessity of defeating Midleton's resolution but also the desirability of forcing him to resign.[131] Montgomery especially put over his view cleverly. On the one hand, he played upon the 'Callers'' suspicion of their delegates' behaviour at the convention by emphasising the weakening effect that it had upon the position not only of Ulster but also of Carson and the unionist members of the cabinet. On the other hand, he argued the advantages of Ulster's position not only to unionists in the north but also to those in the south. Even if partition, so objectionable to nationalists, did not prove an insurmountable obstacle to home rule, the exclusion of the Protestant north-east from the jurisdiction of a Dublin parliament would give nationalists an incentive to behave fairly towards the southern minority in the hope of persuading Ulster unionists to enter an all-Ireland parliament. The available documentary evidence does not permit it to be firmly stated that the S.U.C.'s Ulster contacts actually threatened that, unless Midleton resigned,

130. Stronge to Montgomery, 17 Jan. 1919, *ibid.*; see also, Montgomery to Stronge, 5 Dec. 1918, to Walsh, 9, 16 Dec., *ibid.*, D 627/434; and to Farnham, 6 Jan. 1919, to Barrie, 9 Jan. 1919, and Stronge to Montgomery, 6, 14 Jan. 1919, *ibid.*, D 627/437.
131. See e.g. Montgomery to Walsh, 16 Dec. 1918, *ibid.*, D 627/434; to Farnham, 6 Jan. 1919, to Walsh, 13 Jan. 1919, and Stronge to Montgomery, 6 Jan. 1919, *ibid.*, D 627/437.

they would withdraw from the I.U.A., or promised that Ulster would co-operate with southern unionists once Midleton and Stewart were overthrown. The evidence does indicate, however, that Montgomery and Stronge believed and implied just this; and, more importantly, the S.U.C. understood from their Ulster contacts that future co-operation between southern and northern unionists depended on Midleton's defeat. Disunity seemed a small price to pay for resumed co-operation between north and south.[132]

These two factors—revived suspicions and pressure from Ulstermen—had much effect upon the S.U.C. Their proposed amendment now seemed too mild: by giving Midleton the substance of what he wanted, it might give the impression that the S.U.C. was also suspicious of Ulster unionism and at least sympathised with Midleton's views. Therefore, in order to prove its good faith and sincerity to supporters in the south and north, the S.U.C. unanimously agreed to change its policy.[133] On 16 January it decided not to compromise but resolutely to oppose Midleton's resolution and to discount 'the risk to the cause of Lord Midleton and his supporters resigning', for

we have ascertained that there will be a grave danger of alienating the sympathy of many of our warm supporters in the south and west, unless we take up a firm attitude.[134]

Having made up their minds to oppose Midleton and his friends, the 'Callers' now made vigorous preparations to ensure a large and well-informed attendance of their supporters, particularly from the north,[135] and seriously looked around for a suitable successor in the event of Midleton resigning. Their task was made easier by the discontent of unionists in Monaghan, Cavan and Donegal at Carson's re-adoption of the principle of six-counties

132. See the exchange of letters between Montgomery, Stronge, members of the S.U.C., and Barrie in Dec. 1918 and Jan. 1919, *ibid.*

133. Montgomery to Walsh, 13 Jan. 1919 and Walsh to Montgomery, 16 Jan. 1919, *ibid., D 627/437.*

134. Walsh to Montgomery, 16 Jan. 1919, *ibid.*

135. Compare e.g. the way in which the S.U.C. circulated their amendments in a clearly tabulated and concise form, with the reasoned though dreary statement in which Midleton urged the general council to support his amendment. (See I.U.A., minute book of the executive (general) council 1889–1920, 25 Jan. 1919; and the 'Memorandum as to partition'.) For efforts to whip up support in Ulster, see e.g. Stronge to Montgomery, 6 Jan. 1919; L. Cunningham to Montgomery, 13 Jan. 1919; Montgomery to Walsh, 13 Jan. 1919, P.R.O.N.I., D 627/437.

exclusion in 1918. Perhaps this is a third reason why the S.U.C. decided to oppose Midleton directly, or rather felt able to oppose him, by 1919. The 'Callers' had always been aware of their unimportance as compared to the Midletonites, and they may have gained confidence from the fact that they could now draw upon the comparatively eminent unionists of the three northern counties. At any rate, after many messages and with the aid of Montgomery, the S.U.C. persuaded Lord Farnham[136] of Co. Cavan, a firm but respected opponent of home rule and of partition, 'to accept the honourable and extremely responsible post of chairman' in the event of a change of officers of the I.U.A.[137]

The general council met in special session on the morning of 24 January to consider amendments to the constitution. Both sides had apparently prepared the ground well for there was a 'record attendance of members';[138] but the S.U.C. seemed to have prepared their ground more advantageously. The 'Callers' had always directed their efforts to numbers rather than to quality, and constantly kept the rank and file of southern unionism provided with detailed information of their views and policy. It is true that on occasion Midleton had shown some energy in rounding up support, but his efforts were always directed to the more elevated southern unionists and showed if not an impatience with the rank and file, certainly condescension; and there is no evidence that Midleton and his friends had canvassed their amendments either widely or energetically.[139] The

136. Arthur Kenlis Maxwell, 11th Baron Farnham (1879–1957); lt in 10th Hussars, serving in South African war; served in 1914–18 war as lt-col. in North Irish Horse, taken prisoner by the Germans, May 1918; Irish representative peer, 1908–1957; Farnham, Co. Cavan. The only possible southern candidate, Bagwell, had died in December 1918. For the reasons and negotiations leading to Farnham's selection, see Montgomery to Farnham, 6 Jan. 1919; Farnham to Montgomery, 9 Jan. 1919; Montgomery to Walsh, 13 Jan. 1919; Stronge to Montgomery, 14 Jan. 1919; Walsh to Montgomery, 16 Jan. 1919, P.R.O.N.I., D 627/437.

137. Farnham to Montgomery, 20 Jan. 1919, *ibid.*

138. The sources for this meeting are the minute book of the executive (general) council 1889–1920; *Irish Times*, which supported Midleton, and *Dublin Daily Express*, which supported the S.U.C., 25 Jan. 1919. More intimate detail and comment is provided in Montgomery's letter to Fisher, 27 Jan. 1919 (P.R.O.N.I., D 627/437), and a memorandum on the I.U.A. by Fane Vernon, 31 Jan. 1919 (*ibid.*, D 989A/9/16A) which evidently formed the basis of the I.U.A. circular, Feb. 1919. The split received considerable coverage in the British press, national and local.

139. See above, p. 179 n. 135.

result was that most of the 'Callers'' amendments were approved by the meeting, and the I.U.A. was put on a more representative basis.

In future the executive committee would represent a wider section of southern unionists more directly than ever before. In October, the S.U.C. might have been content with this victory, but in January it was not. Nor was Midleton prepared to accept defeat readily. He spoke effectively on the crucial motion to exclude Ulster members from certain of the southern unionists' deliberations, making two telling points:[140] that by accepting office under the then present government, certain Ulster unionists (Londonderry, Craig and Barrie)[141] had accepted its home rule programme which involved exclusion; and that so-called unionist candidates in Great Britain at the last general election had seemed content with exclusion. Then he and his friends seem to have tried to protract the debate with the object of getting the question talked out.[142] Jellett almost assisted Midleton. He spoke forcibly against the motion on the grounds that it in effect recognised partition and anticipated what might never become practical politics; that it was calculated to arouse resentment among northern members 'at a time when it is of paramount importance to keep in close touch with Ulster'; and, further, that it was opposed to the fundamental conception of the I.U.A. But he was so offensive that he created sympathy for Midleton.[143] In these circumstances it was well that the 'Callers' had prepared their ground thoroughly, 'for it would have been impolitic for us to take up time meeting all the Midletonian points'.[144] A division was forced and Midleton's proposal, which received only 62 votes, was defeated 'by a large majority'.[145]

The crisis had finally arisen. The meeting was adjourned and

140. Montgomery to Fisher, 29 Jan. 1919.

141. Barrie had become on 15 January 1919 Vice-President of the Department of Agriculture and Technical Instruction; Craig private secretary to the Minister of Pensions on 10 January; and Londonderry had a minor office, representing the Air Ministry in the Lords.

142. Montgomery to Fisher, 27 Jan. 1919.

143. See e.g. Powerscourt to Midleton, 30 Jan. 1919, P.R.O., 30/67/40, f. 2368.

144. Montgomery to Fisher, 27 Jan. 1919.

145. *Irish Times*, 25 Jan. 1919. Ironically enough, of the 400 odd members of the general council present, only 46 came from the six north-east county branches, so that the votes from the northern members in no way affected the result.

a compromise was suggested on the basis of a separate southern unionist committee within the I.U.A. for matters affecting only southern unionist interests. Midleton declined this offer, and the 'Callers' refused to concede further.[146] They would have preferred to have avoided a split, but by January 1919 the consequences of a split seemed to be less serious than the exclusion of the Ulster representatives, the necessary corollary of Midleton's remaining in the I.U.A. That would have made it impossible even to discuss with Ulster unionists the best methods to defeat home rule in any shape or form and seemed a reversion to a course adopted at the convention 'with fateful results'. Midleton's insistence thus 'only served to revive feelings of mistrust which had formerly arisen'.[147] To the S.U.C. at any rate, Midleton and his friends were obstacles to the successful fight against home rule and in the circumstances the I.U.A. would be in a stronger position without them.

When in the afternoon the general council met to elect officers, Midleton made another considered statement as to his attitude and position and declared that in view of the rejection of his amendment to the constitution, he could not remain president of the I.U.A. A number of appeals were addressed to him by several speakers to withdraw his resignation, but he was adamant. Thereupon, he and sixty of his friends refused to participate further in the meeting; declined to allow their names to go forward for honorary positions; and finally resigned from the I.U.A.

The general council continued its proceedings without the Midletonites, in diminished but not drastically reduced numbers. Farnham took over the chair and the council, now in ordinary session, elected its officials, giving very few votes to those who sympathised with Midleton. Just how far Midleton had misjudged the council's mood, and how far the views of the S.U.C. prevailed, can be seen in the resolution passed unanimously by the council in the afternoon:

That this meeting of the general council of the Irish Unionist Alliance, consisting of representatives from every county branch in Ireland, hereby reaffirms its unalterable opposition to home rule for the whole

146. Fane Vernon's memorandum, 31 Jan. 1919.
147. I.U.A. circular, Feb. 1919.

or any part of Ireland, recognising that the real object of all home rule movements is, as it has always been, total separation. We emphatically state that it is the duty of all unionists to stand and work together against any form of home rule. We pledge ourselves to do all in our power to maintain intact the legislative union between Great Britain and Ireland, which is the only road to progress, and to defeat a policy which it is now clear would result in the handing over of the whole or any part of Ireland to those who during the war have actually sought to procure the defeat of our armies and the disruption of the empire.

While the general council was straightening out its ideas, Midleton and his friends were forming their own organisation. They justified their secession partly in terms of the 'violent and deliberately provocative attitude'[148] of their critics and partly in terms of principle. Arguing that the I.U.A. was being re-organised in the interests of Ulster unionists, they felt that to remain in it 'with full knowledge that the interests of southern unionists would be sacrificed to the interests of Ulster in the event of legislation on partition lines being introduced by parliament', would be to betray 'the great body of unionists living outside the six Ulster counties whose exclusion had been guaranteed by both the great English parties and accepted by Sir Edward Carson'.[149] The new organisation, the Unionist Anti-Partition League, was announced on 25 January 1919, with a mere twenty-five members. Its object was 'vigorously to combat partition and to enlighten British and colonial opinion on the danger of a Sinn Fein state and the injustice to southern unionists'.[150] It implied some future acceptance of home rule and was a confession by Midletonites of their failure to turn the I.U.A. away from extreme unionism.

SEVEN

The formation of the A.P.L. also represented the first serious rift in southern unionism and the failure of the I.U.A. to maintain

148. Unpublished memorandum explaining the reasons for the split in the I.U.A. and formation of the A.P.L. (n.d., but *c.* end Jan. 1919, probably the basis of an official statement issued to the press at the beginning of March), P.R.O., 30/67/40, ff. 2372–3.

149. *Ibid.*

150. *Irish Times*, 25 Jan. 1919. Of the 25, 15 were peers or sons of peers, 1 was a baronet, the remainder substantial businessmen or landed gentry (Jameson, Stewart, Henry Bruen of Co. Carlow, etc.).

its position as the comprehensive organisation for unionist
opinion in the south of Ireland. In retrospect, the split has an air
of inevitability about it. Two sections interpreted the same
evidence in the light of their different circumstances. But neither
the split nor the form it took were inevitable. It was not at all
certain that the Midletonites would secede from the I.U.A. and
form their own organisation. In the early stages of the dispute
the S.U.C. was much on the defensive, aware that there was a
large body of opinion whose susceptibilities must not be offended.
But the Midletonites contented themselves with delivering stern
rebukes to the 'Callers' through the press, making no attempt to
take the general council into their confidence. The result was that
the initiative fell to the 'Callers' who even got their criticism of
the convention report out before the delegates published a defence
of their action. Nor is there evidence that the delegates and their
supporters tried to whip up support among the mass of members
of the general council prior to its meeting in May. Only after
the S.U.C.'s nominees had been elected to the executive committee did Midleton really begin to take the 'Callers' seriously.
After that setback he appreciated that the S.U.C. needed careful
handling, and the resolution of the executive committee on 1
October was extremely clever, and based on the assumption that
the S.U.C. had a large body of support among southern unionists.

These concessions of 1 October make all the more surprising
the subsequent attempt of the Midletonites to exclude Ulster
members. In fact, this was the resurrection of an old antagonism
between a minority of the I.U.A., particularly in and around
Dublin and Cork, and the Ulstermen. The aggressiveness of the
Ulster unionists had long been repugnant to men like Midleton,
yet it had not precluded co-operation previously. There had also
been attempts to exclude Ulster members from some I.U.A.
meetings on previous occasions, but these had not been made
essential conditions of Midleton's remaining with the I.U.A.
The Prime Minister's acceptance of partition in his letter to Bonar
Law was significant, yet in 1916 the I.U.A. had been faced with
partition. The only really new factor in the situation at the end of
1918 was the bitter attack made by Ulster unionist leaders upon
the southern unionist delegates. Such criticism warped the judgement of Midleton and his friends, perhaps understandably. They
had put much energy into the convention, only to see the Ulster

unionists obstruct their efforts: and as far as Midleton was concerned, it was work undertaken at a considerable risk to his
hitherto successful political career and in spite of his previous
declarations on a question to which he owed his rise to political
prominence. But pique is an unsatisfactory political counsellor,
and in this instance it forced the Midletonites into trying to bring
to an end that policy of co-operation between unionists of the
north and south which had always been the policy of the I.U.A.,
and into making it a crucial issue. Admittedly, under pressure
from their Ulster advisers, the 'Callers' were becoming increasingly intransigent; but up to the last minute they were anxious to
avoid a split. (Indeed, the secession of Midleton and his friends
nullified their patient efforts to modify the constitution of the
Alliance.) The S.U.C. was prepared to go a long way to give
Midleton the substance of what he asked for, if only he made
some reassuring concession to their viewpoint; but Midleton's
mind was closed to compromise and he refused to make what he
must have regarded as a concession to his Ulster unionist critics.
It was the Ulster question that precipitated the actual breach in
the I.U.A. and determined its nature; but if responsibility for
the split had to be pinned upon one man, that man would be
Midleton, who never took criticism lightly.

The irony is that neither Midleton nor the S.U.C. actually
wanted a breach, for they saw it could only weaken the southern
unionist case. And they were right. Perhaps the 'Callers' deserve
some sympathy. It did not matter that they found themselves in
control of the I.U.A. Nor did it matter that it was now firmly
committed to the union and could with justice claim to have a
broader basis of support in the south of Ireland than the A.P.L.
The facts that an influential body of southern unionist opinion
was prepared to accept home rule, and that southern unionism
was divided, were sufficient not only to destroy almost entirely
the force of the southern unionists' case against home rule, but
also to limit severely their influence on any settlement of the
Irish question.

VII

Phase Six: Marking Time, 1919

THE weakening effect of a split on southern unionism had been feared, but in the early part of 1919 no attempt was made to heal the breach. On the contrary, it was deepened by another press controversy,[1] and there was considerable bitterness between the two southern unionist associations. The new controllers of the I.U.A. felt that the A.P.L. represented 'nobody but some ninety noblemen and country gentlemen', of whose motives they were highly suspicious. While allowing that in some conversion to the new departure was sincere and genuine, they were sceptical of 'death-bed repentances' and felt that they had been deserted by the more eminent unionists for largely selfish reasons:

Some members of this group have residences in Ireland, but reside elsewhere, while others have business interests at stake. Their advocacy of home rule against their convictions is largely dictated by motives of self-interest (and a desire to protect their residences and businesses).[2]

On the other hand, the controllers of the A.P.L. had a low opinion of the I.U.A., which they held to be 'really a negligible quantity', consisting of nonentities, puppets of Ulster unionists, and without funds.[3]

Nevertheless, in the circumstances of 1919, it was not clear whether the split would continue, for the two organisations had much in common. Some unionists maintained contact with both sides, mainly at a local level, according to the *Annual Report* of the I.U.A. for 1919–20 and the list of members of the A.P.L. published in the press.[4] For instance, Lords Mayo and Oranmore were members of the London committee of the A.P.L., but

1. See e.g. *Irish Times*, 31 Jan., 13 Feb. 1919; *Dublin Daily Express*, 29 Jan., 2, 4 Feb., 3 Mar. 1919; Walsh's letter in *Morning Post*, 3 Feb. 1919.
2. Memorandum on the 'Position of southern unionists', P.R.O.N.I., D 989A/11/9.
3. Report by Long on his visit to Ireland, Jan. 1920, B.L., F/34/1/6.
4. I.U.A., *Annual Report 1919–20*, appendices; *Irish Times*, 25, 27 Jan., 12 Feb. 1919.

Mayo appears also as a vice-president of the I.U.A. and Oranmore as president of the Mayo county branch; while Richard Edmund Longfield of Longueville, Mallow, Co. Cork, was a subscriber to the funds of the I.U.A. as well as being an early adherent of the A.P.L. Moreover, southern unionism was marking time in 1919 when home rule was shelved temporarily. It was not a foregone conclusion that southern unionism would once again try to come to terms with the new Ireland, this time going further in the direction of full self-government. The potential of both organisations varied enormously, but in practical terms their aims differed little in 1919. Both favoured a programme of Irish reconstruction; and both emphasised the desirability of maintaining the union. It was possible that the two organisations would co-operate in opposing any new home rule bill, and, if this proved impossible, it was not clear which organisation would become the effective representative of southern unionism in any settlement of the Irish question.

TWO

The A.P.L. hoped to unite all unionists in the south of Ireland into a single powerful organisation, and steps were taken to consolidate its position. In terms of organisation, it was similar to the I.U.A. Offices were taken at 102 Grafton Street; meetings were organised; and an organisational structure and programme were worked out. Two committees were established, a London committee consisting of the Irish peers, Sir Robert Woods (M.P. for Trinity College), Walter Guinness and Colonel Wyndham Quin, and a Dublin committee.[5] The aims of the A.P.L. were threefold: to maintain the legislative union between Great Britain and Ireland; to secure Ireland against partition; and to safeguard the liberties and interests of Irish unionists, especially those of the southern provinces, and to promote the material prosperity of Ireland.[6]

The views of the Leaguers on reconstruction, discussed below, were sensitive and straightforward, but their attitude towards the maintenance of the union was ambiguous, as their programme suggests. In 1919 they had reverted to the position taken up after the Rising, and their attitude depended largely upon events in

5. *Irish Times*, 12 Feb. 1919.
6. Constitution of A.P.L., copy in P.R.O., 30/67/40, ff. 2370-1.

Great Britain and Ireland. On the one hand, they wanted to uphold the union. The attitude taken up at the convention had been rendered anachronistic by the development of Sinn Fein, and the A.P.L. intended to take measures 'to enlighten public opinion in Great Britain on the danger of establishing any government in Ireland in which the Sinn Fein party would have a preponderance, and of handing over the southern loyalists to an exclusively Sinn Fein parliament'.[7] Moreover, it had the resources to launch a campaign against any home rule bill. Well represented in the Lords (who could hold up any bill for two years), and with money to finance propaganda in the constituencies—because Lord Iveagh was backing it, there was no doubt of the A.P.L.'s being able to carry on an active campaign.[8]

On the other hand, the Leaguers recognised the difficulties of resisting home rule. The arguments, about the 1914 act and Ulster, that had led some unionists to consider compromise at the time of the convention still held good, and the Leaguers recognised that some form of home rule would be inevitable. Thus, while willing to fight home rule as long as it was possible to do so effectively, they believed that, in the event of opposition to home rule becoming futile, 'it is the duty of all unionists outside the excluded counties to join together in an organisation powerful enough to force the government to provide them with adequate representation and safeguards',[9] whatever constitution might be imposed on the southern provinces, to protect the 350,000 loyalists of the south against being swamped by ten times the number of separatists. Their decision and their attitude, whether to oppose or improve any home rule bill, had to wait upon events.[10]

THREE

The I.U.A. was not so ambiguous. Firmly committed to the union, it re-organised in 1919. Having ousted the Midletonites, the 'Callers', now in control of the I.U.A., tried to develop co-operation with Ulster unionists and were pathetically anxious to respond to the stringent conditions their potential allies were

7. A.P.L.'s official statement, *Irish Times,* 1 Mar. 1919.
8. Long's memorandum on his visit to Ireland, Jan. 1920.
9. A.P.L.'s official statement, *Irish Times,* 1 Mar. 1919.
10. See also Lord Arran to Midleton, 25 Apr. 1919, P.R.O., 30/67/40, ff.2374-5.

laying down.[11] Activity was the order of the day: the executive committee of the I.U.A. was to meet regularly, an appeal for funds was made, branches which had lapsed were re-established, and, as if to epitomise renewed vigour and determination, a branch of the I.U.A. was formed for the first time in years in Monaghan by the affiliation of the Monaghan Unionist Association to the I.U.A.[12] How active these branches were is difficult to tell: the fact that they existed at all was sufficient for the purposes of the I.U.A., for the main work continued to be in British politics. A poor response to its appeals for funds was to hinder this work in the future,[13] but the I.U.A. remained optimistic.

To suit the condition of post-war British politics, a two-fold policy was now adopted: union and reconstruction. It was realised that no object would be served by merely protesting against home rule, for the 'English people are far too busy endeavouring to put their own "house in order" to think much of Irish politics'. The I.U.A. decided to develop ideas expressed in the 'Call' and fell back on the Balfourian policy of economic and social development in Ireland. On the one hand, it supported the reconstruction policy of the then Chief Secretary, Ian Macpherson; on the other, it continued propaganda on behalf of the union.[14]

To facilitate this dual policy a branch of the I.U.A. was re-established in London, at 25 Victoria Street, Westminster, and a committee set up there. This London committee of the I.U.A. consisted of interested southern unionists resident in London and certain extreme conservatives, like Gershom Stewart, the former Hong Kong merchant and M.P. for the Wirral, who opposed home rule as an ignominious surrender.[15] Its main object was to

11. See the exchange of letters between Montgomery and Stronge and 'Callers' in Jan. and Feb. 1919, P.R.O.N.I., D 627/437.

12. I.U.A., *Annual Report 1919–20*; Walsh to Montgomery, 7 Feb. 1919, and Fane Vernon to Montgomery, 6 Mar. 1919, P.R.O.N.I., D 627/437; and I.U.A.'s appeal for funds, copies *ibid.*, D 989C/1/28.

13. Long's comments on the I.U.A.'s funds in his report on his visit to Ireland, Jan. 1920.

14. I.U.A., minute book of the London committee, 5 Mar. 1919; *Annual Report 1919–20*.

15. *Ibid.* Among the original members of the revived London committee were the following members of both houses of parliament: Earls of Leitrim and Ancaster; Lords Bellew, Beresford, Dunalley and Farnham; Col. C. R. Burn Sir John G. Butcher; Sir Edward Carson; L. Lyons; Gen. Sir Hugh MacCalmont; Major Pretyman Newman; Col. W. G. Nicholson; G. Stewart.

supervise the work of the I.U.A. in Great Britain. Since in 1919 there was no immediate prospect of home rule, the I.U.A. decided to concentrate upon a policy of social reconstruction in Ireland and set up a parliamentary committee, from members of parliament belonging to the London committee, to look after the interests of southern unionists during the passage through parliament of reconstruction measures and to co-operate with Ulster unionists on these measures.[16]

On behalf of southern unionists the London and parliamentary committees interested themselves in a wide range of measures: a health bill, a transport bill, land purchase, education, agricultural development and the organisation of industries.[17] The I.U.A. in Dublin kept in close touch with the committees and often the views of the Dublin office prevailed.[18] Nevertheless, the London committee appears to have been very thorough in its work, setting up a number of sub-committees to prepare material for general debates and for certain bills, such as the Ministry of Health bill, and sometimes working through the Irish Unionist Party.[19] How influential the I.U.A.'s views were is hard to estimate, but it is likely to have been slight. The main trouble was that it had no significant group behind it in the House of Commons, and despite pressure from the London committee, the Dublin committee would hear of no working compromise with the more influential Midletonites.[20] Too often the I.U.A. was too dependent upon the Irish Unionist Party, which, consisting mainly of Ulstermen, seems to have had little time for suggestions put forward by the parliamentary committee, for instance over the Ministry of Health bill.[21] But it is doubtful whether even with the enthusiastic support of the I.U.P., the I.U.A. could have achieved much, when the outstanding example of Irish unionist frustration was the education bill, so vigorously championed by Carson.

Perhaps it was only just that the I.U.A.'s views had little influence, owing to the nature of these views on reconstruction. Although it was held to be a reversion to the pre-Asquithian

16. I.U.A., minute book of the London committee, 5, 13 Mar. 1919.
17. See e.g. *ibid.*, 13 Mar. 1919.
18. See e.g. *ibid.*, 13, 20, 27 Mar. 1919.
19. See e.g. *ibid.*, 13 Mar. 1919.
20. *Ibid.*, 27 Mar. 1919.
21. *Ibid.*, 20 Mar. 1919.

unionist policy of co-operation with Irish nationalists in economic
and non-political matters, it was adopted at a time when there
were few Irish nationalists in parliament and it was in no sense
a movement to regenerate Ireland. The I.U.A.'s views were
scarcely original and their programme was largely eclectic: the
most interesting view they put forward, that demanding an
integrated transport system for Ireland with a 'well-organised
system of light motor transport operated in connection with the
existing lines of railways', can be regarded as an adaptation of a
scheme suggested before the war by Iveagh.[22] In fact, the I.U.A.'s
reconstruction was natural conservatism at its best, a soundly
practical and recognisable defence of the interests of southern
unionists in relation to the Irish situation. The significance of
their insistence upon the early completion of land purchase is
obvious enough,[23] but this view may also be gathered from a
resolution passed by the standing committee of the I.U.A.,
arguing the necessity for effective safeguards in the housing bill

to restrict the power of local authorities with disloyal majorities to
drive loyal subjects of His Majesty out of the country by destroying
the amenities of their houses and the value of their lands, by com-
pulsorily acquiring building sites without regard to the convenience
and interests of the owner.[24]

This attitude was in marked contrast to that taken up by the
progressive conservatives of the A.P.L. who also adopted an
Irish reconstruction policy in 1919. On many points of detail the
two organisations agreed: for example, on the desirability of
proportional representation in local government elections,
private bill legislation and an Irish Ministry of Health;[25] but their
whole approach to the problem of reconstruction was different.

22. *Vice-Regal Commission on Irish Railways, Including Light Railways, 5th and
Final Report*, Cd 5247 (1910), p. 9. For the I.U.A.'s view, see memorandum laid
by a deputation from the I.U.A. before the Chief Secretary for Ireland, *c.* Mar.
1919, P.R.O.N.I., D 989A/8/23.
23. I.U.A., minute book of the London committee, 10 Apr. 1919.
24. Walsh to Montgomery, 26 June 1919, P.R.O.N.I., D 627/437.
25. Compare e.g. the programme of the I.U.A. in the minute book of the
London committee with the views expressed by A.P.L. unionists in March 1919
(*Irish Times*, 15 Mar. 1919). See also the debates on the local government
(Ireland) bill, *Parl. Deb. (Commons)*, 5 ser., cxiv, 24 Mar. 1919, cols 101–3,
121–6, 126–7, 139, 176–8.

Whereas the I.U.A. was narrowly defensive, the views of the
A.P.L. were expansive and, at times, romantic. Unlike the I.U.A.
which was governed by visions of a bitter past and by apprehensions about the future, the members of the A.P.L. were inspired
by a vision of a united and prosperous Ireland. Whereas the
I.U.A. hoped to revert to the old unionist policy, the A.P.L.
believed that it was putting forward a new policy. Midleton
thought that too many reforms of the previous generation had
been 'offshoots of some department in London'; and he and
Walter Guinness thought that a great opportunity for Irish
reconstruction would be lost, unless the first step were taken
towards true reform by the transfer of initiative from those
London departments to the Irish government.[26] Only then would
there be truly Irish policies, inspired in Ireland, organised in
Ireland, and steered to success by Irish enterprise and Irish brains.
The quality of the A.P.L.'s approach to Ireland after the first
world war may be judged from the way in which Guinness urged
the local government bill on the House of Commons in 1919.
He recognised the distinctiveness of Ireland, telling the House that

Ireland differs from England in race, temperament and social organisation, and that difference must be reflected in the legislation suitable
for that country;

and he looked forward to a happier Ireland after proportional
representation had encouraged and strengthened moderate
opinion there, had broken down 'the prejudice of centuries' and
had allowed 'Irishmen of all sorts and conditions to work together
for the benefit of Irish administration'.[27]

This emphasis on Ireland and Irish was not a new thing. The
hope of the *Irish Times* (which endorsed the A.P.L.'s approach)
that the result of truly Irish reconstruction would be an 'increase
in public self-respect'[28] was very reminiscent of Plunkett's
Ireland in the New Century. But what was new was the enthusiasm
and apparent sincerity with which a southern unionist organisation took up and acted upon these ideas in contrast to former
southern unionist attitudes and to the current attitude of the

26. *Irish Times,* 15 Mar. 1919.
27. *Parl. Deb. (Commons),* 5 ser., cxiv, 24 Mar. 1919, cols 121–5.
28. *Irish Times,* 15 Mar. 1919.

I.U.A. And it was only fair that if any Irish group influenced the government's reconstruction policy in Ireland it was the A.P.L., not the I.U.A.[29]

The second part of the I.U.A.'s policy was to try to strengthen and maintain the union. Pressure was put upon the government. Through deputations and parliamentary activity, the I.U.A. urged upon the government changes in the spirit and character of the administration in Ireland, including not only the 'urgent necessity which now and always exists for the fearless, firm and impartial administration of the law in the country', but also loyalty to subordinates and the introduction of a paid and trained magistracy.[30]

The I.U.A. also hoped to create, perhaps re-create, in Great Britain and the colonies a climate of opinion favourable to the union. What perturbed it most were the facts that 'active and insidious propaganda against the union, often powerfully inspired, has been carried on in certain sections of the English press', and that owing to the convention there existed in England a widespread impression that 'no serious opposition to home rule exists in Ireland outside Ulster'.[31] However, the I.U.A. was confident that it could counter that propaganda and impression, mainly by enlightening opinion in Great Britain and the colonies as to the true state of Ireland, and believed that such enlightenment could and would come from a revival of the old Irish unionist propaganda methods—from a wide distribution of literature, by press work, by the provision of canvassers and speakers, and by active participation in parliamentary elections.[32] The conduct of a campaign like that of 1908–14 was by 1919 out of the question: apart from lack of funds, the condition of British politics and parties was unfavourable. But the size of these obstacles was not fully appreciated in 1919, when for most of the year home rule

29. The introduction of proportional representation was generally attributed to the influence of Walter Guinness. See e.g. Devlin's speech, *Parl. Deb. (Commons),* 5 ser., cxiv, 24 Mar. 1919, cols 152–4.

30. I.U.A., *Annual Report 1919–1920*; memorandum laid by a deputation from the I.U.A. before the Chief Secretary, *c.* Mar. 1919. Sometimes their efforts were unavailing: see e.g. Law to I.U.A., 28 May 1919, 'the extreme pressure of my engagements makes it impossible for me to receive any additional deputation this week', P.R.O.N.I., D 989A/8/24.

31. I.U.A., appeal for funds, Mar. 1919, *ibid.,* D 989C/1/28.

32. *Ibid.*

as a practical issue was dead. Thus the I.U.A. could be content with a minimum of propaganda, pointing out in various newspapers the danger of granting independence to Ireland.[33] It could while away time discussing and elaborating propaganda schemes,[34] confident that, when the home rule issue was again raised, British politicians and the British public would again be prepared to take an interest in Ireland and be receptive to Irish unionist propaganda. The I.U.A. was sure that when the crisis came southern unionists would be able to meet it effectively.[35]

33. See e.g. the letter from the I.U.A. published in the *Glasgow Herald*, 15 Nov. 1919.

34. See e.g. a memorandum on a press campaign by Gilbert Weston, 'a political and parliamentary journalist of no inconsiderable experience', mid 1919, P.R.O.N.I., D 989A/8/23; and the comments of Fisher, the U.U.C. agent, to Montgomery, 3 May 1919. 'The I.U.A. people are talking of making a fresh move on this side but so far there is no *action*', ibid., D 627/437.

35. See e.g. the optimistic tone of the appeal for funds in Mar. 1919. 'A small donation to its funds will provide the weapons by which the battle must eventually be won.'

VIII

Phase Seven: Decline, Demoralisation and Dominion Home Rule, 1920-21

How southern unionism developed after 1919 depended on events, and events in 1920 and 1921 determined that it should enter a new phase. Changes in British and Ulster politics and the passing of the 1920 Government of Ireland Act emphasised the futility of trying to maintain the union, while the Anglo-Irish war underlined the growing uselessness of the union as a means of fostering and protecting southern unionist or Irish interests. Moreover, there was a gradual realisation that rule by Sinn Fein promised more peace and stability than continued British rule. In face of such developments southern unionism ceased to mark time, and the years 1920-21 saw the penultimate stage in the story of a distinctive Anglo-Irish political movement in the south of Ireland. By the middle of 1920 southern unionists were once more trying to come to terms with the new Ireland, as many abandoned their unionism and in some cases tried to find a settlement acceptable to the mass of the Irish nation and on broader lines than that envisaged at the convention. Inevitably, unionist organisation was affected by this weakening of unionist sentiment. The split was confirmed. The right wing activists of the I.U.A. became demoralised and confused, while their organisation sank into impotence. The initiative passed to a weakened and almost divided A.P.L. which decided to try to improve the 1920 government of Ireland bill and which came to be regarded in British politics as the effective representative of southern unionist opinion.

TWO

In 1919 it may have been possible to believe that the union could be maintained, but by 1920 the futility was obvious. The I.U.A. had been optimistic, but this optimism soon dissolved when its anticipated support failed to materialise. Most importantly, the expected renewal of close ties between north and south did not occur. The split had left Ulster unionists suspicious of the reliability of southern unionists and subsequent events not only confirmed these suspicions but also raised grave doubts in the minds of Ulstermen most sympathetic to the I.U.A. It could be argued that Ulster unionists were concerned only with their own interests whatever southern unionists thought; but there was a considerable body of opinion in the U.U.C. that thought that Ulstermen had a duty to protect unionists in the south. However, events and issues ensured that that opinion would diminish and would be ignored.

The question of proportional representation in local elections was a bone of serious contention. Proportional representation was introduced into Irish local elections in 1919 in order to prevent Sinn Fein from sweeping the board and to allow minority representation on the basis of the Sligo experience. Although the I.U.A. did not want to press an issue which would hinder co-operation between north and south, many southern unionists, followers of both Midleton and the I.U.A., believed that the introduction of proportional representation would at least give them an opportunity to play a role in local politics again.[1] Their expectations were not high. They realised that the Sinn Fein party would continue to hold a majority on the local councils; but they thought that proportional representation would give 'the man of ordinary weight in local affairs, the man whom everybody trusts, his chance of taking an interest in local affairs',[2] and that the presence of even a handful of such moderates would be able to bring about reform by gaining inside knowledge of local administration and by criticism and publicity.[3] These modest expectations led M.P.s with connections in the south of Ireland to support the measure, and this action by supporters of the I.U.A. was much resented by Ulster unionists who thought that proportional representation would threaten their majorities in Ulster without conferring much benefit on unionists in the south and west. There were sharp altercations between Pretyman

---

1. See e.g. Farnham to Montgomery, *c.* 28 Mar. 1919, P.R.O.N.I., D 627/437; and the debate on the local government (Ireland) bill, *Parl. Deb. (Commons)*, 5 ser., cxiv, 24 Mar. 1919, cols 101–3, 121–6, 126–7, 139, 166–9, 176–8.
2. Pretyman Newman (I.U.A.), *ibid.*, col. 168.
3. Walter Guinness (A.P.L.), *ibid.*, col. 125.

Newman and Ulster unionists in the House of Commons,[4] and the question drove a further wedge between unionists in the north and the south. Even the usually sympathetic Montgomery, fearing that unionist control over Tyrone county council would be jeopardised by proportional representation, felt that while the southern unionist desire for minority representation

is a good many degrees less foolish than the Midletonite acceptance of Bishop O'Donnell's so-called 'safeguards', the feeling at the bottom of your action in favouring P.R. at the expense of the solidity of unionist Ulster, is not entirely without resemblance to their action in jumping at provisions which would enable them, as they thought, for a few years to play a part in a Dublin parliament.[5]

The result was that this episode gave Ulster unionists a good reason to refuse to revive the joint committee. Although they would be prepared on occasion to consult with the southern unionists, they refused to have any formal and permanent committee on the ground that 'although we realise that our aims are the same as those of the Irish Unionist Alliance, we feel that there are occasions on which the attainment of those aims will be sought along different lines'.[6]

The I.U.A. was naturally disappointed, but made the best of its reduced circumstances to carry on a limited propaganda in British politics. Much more serious was the attitude of Ulster unionists to the 1920 government of Ireland bill. By this bill, introduced in February 1920, the British government proposed to establish two single-chamber Irish parliaments, one for the state of Northern Ireland consisting of six of the nine counties of the historic province of Ulster, and another for the state of Southern Ireland comprising the remaining twenty-six counties.[7]

4. *Ibid.,* cols 117, 118, 119, 170.
5. Montgomery to Farnham, 25 Mar. 1919, P.R.O.N.I., D 627/437.
6. C. C. Craig (M.P. for South Antrim and brother of James) to Farnham, 12 May 1919, *ibid.,* D 989A/8/23.
7. These two parliaments, to be chosen by proportional representation, were each to be empowered to legislate for its own area in all matters, except the crown, defence, foreign affairs, external trade, lighthouses, cables, currency and land purchase, while certain services—police, postal services, the registry of deeds and the public record office—were provisionally reserved for imperial control. Their financial powers were to be limited and Ireland was to make a substantial contribution to the imperial exchequer. Irish representation at Westminster was

H

On 10 March 1920 the U.U.C. decided not to oppose this new bill, much to the dismay of the I.U.A. Belief that the opposition of Ulstermen to any form of home rule would kill any home rule bill had been an important basis of the I.U.A.'s hopes of maintaining the union. Now this belief was belied, and what made matters worse was the way that some Ulster unionists appeared to welcome the opportunity to have a parliament of their own. The reaction of the I.U.A. was complicated by the resentment of those members who came from the three Ulster counties included in Southern Ireland, resentment at what they regarded as their betrayal by the U.U.C. These unionists, from Cavan, Donegal and Monaghan, still clung to the belief that the exclusion of the nine counties of Ulster would wreck home rule, and in the late spring of 1920 Farnham tried in vain to cajole the U.U.C. into reversing the six-counties decision. The more sympathetic six-counties unionists tried to pacify the angry three-counties men with the complicated argument that the surest way to kill home rule was to set up an impregnable position for Ulster:[8] but men like Farnham would not be persuaded that 'Carson and his political satellites were out to kill home rule either by flank, direct or other attack'.[9] Thus embittered and angered, many three-counties unionists resigned from the U.U.C. in high dudgeon. The other members of the I.U.A. were not so much bitter as disappointed and bewildered by the U.U.C.'s decision. In a way they recognised that Ulster unionists had a right to look after their own interests, but they thought that Ulstermen would at least have put up a fight on their behalf. This southern unionist confusion is well seen in a rather subdued letter from Walsh, asking Montgomery to attend a meeting of the executive com-

---

to be retained though reduced. The bill was and is often referred to as the partition bill, but its framers hoped that it would eventually lead to Irish unity. The two Irish parliaments were to be enabled to send representatives to an all-Ireland council which was to be entrusted with certain functions in relation to private bills and with legislative and administrative powers in respect of railways and the contagious diseases of animals. The two parliaments were, by agreement, to be able to transfer functions to the council. Moreover, to encourage unity, the imperial parliament would be able, under specified conditions, to transfer certain of the reserved powers to the council and, at any time after the date of Irish union, might transfer the control of customs and excise to the Irish parliament.

8. See Buckland, *Irish Unionism,* ch. X, for the U.U.C.'s decision to accept six-counties partition and the three-counties' reaction.

9. Farnham to Montgomery, 13 Apr. 1920, P.R.O.N.I., D 627/435.

mittee of the I.U.A. and give his views on the Ulster situation which

is puzzling us not a little . . . we feel a little puzzled about Ulster's attitude. We gather that Ulster would only establish her parliament in the event of the southern parliament being established, but the speeches of some northern members lead one to believe that Ulster is inclined to jump at the idea of a parliament. If Ulster merely accepts her parliament in the event of the southern parliament being established, or demands to be omitted from the bill altogether, the road to the union would remain open. Once, however, the Ulster parliament is established, the road back to the union would be closed.[10]

The U.U.C.'s decision not only upset the members of the I.U.A. but also adversely affected the attitude of their British supporters. Although the state of British politics (the lack of interest in the Irish question, the declining unionism of the 'unionist' party) bothered them, the members of the London committee of the I.U.A. had been willing to oppose the government of Ireland bill and arrangements were under way to finance a campaign against it.[11] But the U.U.C.'s decision not to oppose the bill put them in a quandary and they were divided over whether or not to oppose the bill.[12] In the circumstances they consulted Midleton.

Now it so happened that Ulster's attitude to the new bill had been one of the factors that would determine the attitude of the A.P.L., and now Midleton urged that the London committee should co-operate with the recently re-formed committee of southern Irish peers in meeting the bill. It was agreed that the bill was impossible and Midleton's advice appears to have been decisive in determining the London committee upon a course of action which in principle and tactics was opposed to that which the Dublin committee wanted to adopt. The latter wanted the bill opposed outright, believing that there was no half-way

10. Walsh to Montgomery, 15 Apr. 1920, *ibid.*
11. I.U.A., minute book of the London committee, 4 Mar. 1920; Richard Dawson (I.U.A.'s agent in London) to I.U.A., 8 Mar. 1920, P.R.O.N.I., D 989A/9/20.
12. The following account is based upon accounts of a meeting of the London committee of the I.U.A., 11 Mar. 1920, contained in I.U.A., minute book of the London committee, 11 Mar. 1920; and Dawson to I.U.A., 12, 15 Mar. 1920. See Dawson to I.U.A., 8 Mar. 1920, for the importance of the Ulster decision, P.R.O.N.I., D 989A/9/20.

house between union and a republic; but the London committee, advised by Midleton, thought that there was no hope of defeating the bill outright and decided to oppose the bill only on the second reading and to stress the necessity for uniting on certain amendments in order that the Lords might insist upon safeguards for southern unionists. The Dublin committee wanted to convene a meeting of unionist members of parliament to concert opposition to the bill, but the London committee decided that this would serve only to accentuate differences.

As befitted people immersed in politics, the London committee's reasoning was complex and calculating. It objected to a meeting of M.P.s on the grounds that as there were several coalitionists who were unionists in name only, a meeting called to get common action on the second reading 'might cause disputation which would tend to make the party less disposed to combine on amendments such as those mentioned above'.[13] On the other hand, the committee found comfort in the facts that Midleton and Bernard would address a meeting of unionists—albeit from an A.P.L. viewpoint; and that Colonel Sir John Gretton, a member of the London committee and M.P. for the Burton division of Staffordshire, was chairman of the unionist reconstruction committee in the House of Commons, of which an Irish sub-committee had been formed to oppose the bill, and which 'can exercise good influence in quarters which we could hardly reach, for it will not be supposed to be biassed by self-interest as Irish unionists might be'. The reasons for not opposing the bill were equally tortuous. It could not be defeated; the 1914 act was a 'kind of strait waist-coat' which made rejection of the bill practically impossible; and the U.U.C.'s decision had weakened opposition. Moreover, any attempt to defeat the bill by supporting labour or radical amendments would, if successful, bring the 1914 act into operation, and might bring into power a government which would pass an infinitely worse measure. How widely the views of the London committee differed from those of the I.U.A. in Dublin, and the demoralising effect of the former's decision upon members of the I.U.A., may be judged from the formal letter that the London secretary was instructed to write on behalf of the London committee to the Dublin office:

13. Dawson to I.U.A., 12 Mar. 1920, *ibid.*

they were heart and soul with you and adopt the line they take as tactically in the best interests of southern unionists . . . Their hatred of the bill and anxiety to do their best is beyond doubt. But the conditions are such that they are like men walking in fetters.

After this the London committee of the I.U.A. seems to have ceased to function, and there was no serious attempt to have the bill rejected.

THREE

Not only did southern unionists of all complexions come to realise the difficulties facing any attempt to maintain the union, they also began to wonder whether it was even worth trying. With the onset of the Anglo-Irish war, the union was becoming obviously valueless, even to them. The British government was finding it increasingly difficult to maintain order. By 1920 a systematic campaign of murder and intimidation affected the whole country as the Republic, as re-affirmed by the Dail Eireann in January 1919, tried to make good its claim to be the legitimate government of Ireland. Those serving the usurping foreign government were guilty of treason and had to be punished.[14] Thus throughout 1920 and 1921 there was a succession of executions of policemen, English officials, magistrates and private persons suspected of being informers; and in the circumstances many private scores and quarrels were settled. The development of the terror may be gauged from the increased number of murders of Crown officials: from 1 January to 31 December 1919, 17 policemen had been killed; but from 1 January to 31 December 1920, 165 policemen were killed and 251 wounded. Its extent can be judged from the following figures: between 1 January 1919 and 1 January 1921, 182 policemen were killed and 265 wounded; 50 military killed, 122 wounded; 39 civilians killed and 108 wounded; and from 1 January 1919 until 19 February 1921, 70 courthouses and 536 police barracks were destroyed; 212 police barracks were

14. Phillips, *Revolution in Ireland,* pp. 166–246. Written from an Anglo-Irish viewpoint, this work is a particularly interesting source for the period, but for a less coloured account of the Anglo-Irish war, see E. Holt, *Protest in Arms* (1960).

damaged; and there were 3,052 raids for arms.[15] Moreover, the Anglo-Irish, by reason of their past, their politics, their religion, and their larger stake in the country, had most to fear from the growth of lawlessness, and they suffered their fair share of outrage.

The story is so familiar that it need not be repeated in great detail here: suffice it to say that the diurnal of *Notes from Ireland* from 1920 and 1921 makes distressing reading, listing as it does some of the outrages perpetrated in Ireland against loyalists, including several members and former members of the I.U.A. There are assassinations, attempted assassinations, house burnings (sometimes to prevent its use by the military), housebreakings for arms;[16] there is land-grabbing and cattle driving.[17] Of course, some southern unionists and their friends made attempts to understand the reasons behind these outrages. Land-grabbing and cattle-driving needed little or no explanation, nor did threats by unsold tenants of strikes against rent; but that did not lessen the

15. See the various returns of outrages in Ireland between 1919 and 1921, especially Cmd. 709 (1920) and Cmd. 1165 (1921).

16. An exhaustive list would be too long, even if it could be drawn up, but the following examples are fairly representative. Towards the end of 1919 there were a number of incidents affecting members or former members of the I.U.A. For instance, on 18 November there was a raid on the residence of Mrs Carden of Fishmoyne, Co. Tipperary; on 24 November Lt-col. F. St L. Tottenham of Mount Callan, Co. Clare, was severely injured by masked and armed raiders who made off with guns, rifles, revolvers and a quantity of ammunition; on 5 December there was a murderous attack on H. V. Macnamara's shooting party in Co. Clare; and on 13 December, the residence of J. Pike of Co. Cork was raided. In the first part of 1920 there were many raids for arms, including those on Fraser Meadows of Thornville, Co. Wexford; C. Graham of Bimnenadden, Co. Sligo; R. C. Langford, the High Sheriff of Co. Limerick; and J. F. Williamson of Mallow, Co. Cork. By May, burnings had got under way: Southport House and Roundmount House, Co. Roscommon, went up on 7 May; Sandersgrove, Co. Wicklow, on 13th; Lord Ashtown's shooting lodge, Glenahiry, Co. Galway, on 21st; and Annesgrove House, Co. Tipperary, on 31 May.

17. There were attempts at cattle driving on N. J. Walpole's land in Co. Roscommon on 20 Dec. 1919 and 22 Jan. 1920, but it was not until April 1920 that the movement seems to have got under way. On 7 April crowds assembled on the lands of a Mr Levin and smashed the windows and doors of his residence because he refused to divide up the land among them. On 12 April there was a big cattle drive on the property of Col. J. D. Fetherstonhaugh, of Rockview, Co. Westmeath. On 23 April a deputation called on H. L. King of Ballyline, King's county, and presented him with a document to give up a quantity of land for his signature; and there was a determined effort to redistribute the land on Lord Ashtown's estate in Co. Galway—several cattle drives took place and graziers were warned to remove their stock or abide by the consequences.

danger to unsold parts of estates.[18] The violence was easily explained by the fact that

the stoppage of emigration since 1914 has shut up in Ireland about 200,000 of the ablest and most enterprising of our youths. They can find no answer of employment here but owing to the profits made by their fathers in the war they can afford to live in idleness and have thrown themselves heart and soul into the work of conspiracy and crime. For the first time in Irish history they have got out of hand so far as their church is concerned and their bishops are afraid to openly defy them lest they may be courting defeat.[19]

There is some truth in this analysis of the Irish situation in 1920–21, but true understanding did not alter the fact that normal social life came to an end in some areas. For instance, owing to the unsettled state of the county the last meet of the West Corby hounds had been held as early as 17 March 1919, and for Miss Somerville life did not return to normal until 1924.[20] Boredom was as much a problem as insecurity, if we are to believe Miss Farrell. Parts of motors were taken away, thereby limiting social intercourse; and relations with the military became strained,[21] the same military upon whom the Anglo-Irish had largely relied to enliven their lives. At this time, Lynch-Robinson lived in dread of knocks on his front door at night and found that the only welcome callers at his home in Collon were the cadets who were 'always cheerful and amusing company', but who 'very seldom called . . . and even then they did not stay long, as they thought that to do so might endanger our lives by getting us the reputation of being too friendly with them'.[22] In other parts, where there were attempts to carry on life as normal, interruption came suddenly, if not altogether unexpectedly; as on 16 January 1920 when a ball party was held up in County Galway and motor cars damaged,[23] or on 25 May 1921, when the burning of the Customs House in Dublin interrupted the finals of the Local Government Board's annual golf tournament.[24]

18. See e.g. Montgomery to Carson, 1 July 1921, B.L., F/6/3/25.
19. Campbell to Law, 8 Jan. 1921, *ibid.*, 100/1/13.
20. Cummins, *Dr. E. Œ. Somerville*, p. 50.
21. See below, pp. 210–11.
22. Lynch-Robinson, *Last of the Irish R.M.s*, pp. 162–3.
23. *Notes from Ireland* (1920), p. 8.
24. Robinson, *Memories Wise and Otherwise*, pp. 310–11.

Sometimes the end was tragic, and it is difficult to decide whether men and women, like Miss Winifred Barrington, the twenty-four year old daughter of Sir Charles Barrington of Glenstal, Co. Limerick, killed on returning from a fishing party in a martial law area,[25] were extremely brave or extremely foolish in trying to carry on life as usual.

Admittedly, the situation varied from district to district. By January 1921 eight counties and two cities were under martial law,[26] and elsewhere the incidence of terror was not uniform. For instance, some parts of Sligo suffered while others escaped;[27] and while some, like Mrs Charlotte Perceval of Ballymote, Co. Sligo, experienced particularly brutal raids,[28] most raids for arms were carried out with the minimum of discomfort to the raided. It was also true that the terror of 1920–21 differed from that of the Land League days in that landlords were no longer the first object of class contempt and attack.[29] But what was general throughout the south and west was a sense of insecurity of life and property. Since the worst days of the Land League the large country houses had lived with their neighbours in comparative security of life and property; but with the Anglo-Irish war none could consider themselves safe. Lennox Robinson relates the pathetic though symbolic instance of that country house in the south west of Ireland whose front door was shut only in winter and even when closed could be opened from the outside by merely turning the handle; there had been a key to the door but it had been mislaid years before and the master of the house

25. She had been accompanied by Major Henry Biggs, district inspector of the auxiliary division of the R.I.C., and died during an I.R.A. ambush on the major. The Sinn Fein paper, the *Irish Bulletin* (19 May 1921), blamed the officers for this and similar episodes, because of the state of the country and the unusually severe war waged by the 'army of occupation' using 'methods of barbarous violence and terrorism which place it outside the pale of civilisation. British officers engaged in this war have no right to go about accompanied by ladies' and 'they are directly responsible for any harm that may unhappily befall them in the event of an attack. This is the rule in all wars.'

26. Cork city and county, Clare, Kerry, Kilkenny, Limerick city and county, Tipperary, Waterford and Wexford (Phillips, *Revolution in Ireland*, p. 191).

27. Lennox Robinson, *Bryan Cooper*, pp. 132–3.

28. *Irish Times*, 8 Mar. 1920.

29. See e.g. D. Corkery, *The Hounds of Banba* (1920). The story 'Unfinished symphony' underlines the point that the ascendancy as such was not resented in the Anglo-Irish war.

never troubled to get a new one made; but with the Anglo-Irish war the doors had to be locked and the windows barred.[30]

Admittedly, County Clare was particularly badly hit, but a report on the condition of the west of Ireland by R. F. Hibbert, a resident in that county and a member of the general council of the I.U.A., seems typical of what any member of the southern unionist class might have to experience at any time:

> The condition of affairs in my neighbourhood in Co. Clare is beyond description; there is no protection whatever for life and property.
>
> Recently an attempt was made by some forty masked men, armed with rifles, revolvers, and axes, to raid my house. They got in by rushing the back premises of the house. They reduced the servants to a state of terror by threatening to shoot them, seized the steward's gun, and tried to gag him with a rifle butt. I immediately armed myself with a repeating rifle, and fired on the raiders from the lobby, forcing them to retire, one of their number being wounded. I have since been warned repeatedly that my life is in danger.
>
> The houses of most of the respectable people in the neighbourhood have been raided, but such is the terrorism that exists, that many who have suffered in this way are afraid to report what has occurred to the authorities, lest worse should befall them.
>
> I reported the raid on my house to the authorities, who sent down a small detachment of infantry, but recalled them after about three weeks. The police were then withdrawn from Scariff, and the barracks closed, leaving no police at all for a distance of over fifteen miles.
>
> Two nights after the closing of the barracks the petty sessions court, opposite the barracks, was broken into, and everything in it destroyed. A week afterwards about two hundred men pulled down the barracks with pickaxes and crowbars.
>
> As far as personal property goes, last week my boathouse, and other outhouses, were raided, while timber is constantly stolen, fences and walls thrown down, etc. As there are no police and no petty sessions, there is no redress.
>
> I hear their next move is to smash up all the post offices and post office equipment, and should they wish to do so, there is absolutely nothing to prevent them.
>
> About a month ago one of my herds tried to join the Royal Irish Constabulary. Fifteen masked and armed men surrounded his house one night, and searched for him, but luckily did not find him, as he

---

30. Lennox Robinson, *Bryan Cooper,* p. 130.

was hiding under the bed in a back room. Had they found him he would undoubtedly have been shot, as has happened in the case of other young men who expressed their intention of joining the police.

Every night gangs of armed men assemble in different houses, and walk the countryside, terrorising the respectable inhabitants. It is because they are so well armed, and so reckless in the use of their arms, that this terrorism exists. They collect subscriptions in this way, as everyone is afraid to refuse to subscribe. From dark to dawn law-abiding people scarcely dare to sleep.

Owing to the withdrawal of police all regulations are disregarded, and the public houses remain open night and day, consequently, as may be imagined, the state of drunkenness and robbery is appalling. Even the farmer's crops are stolen out of the ground to buy drink.

Our tenants, having previously refused to purchase their holdings, decided to do so just before the war. So far as I can see, they will now adopt the attitude that if they wait a little longer, they will get their lands free.

The state of the country is such that I and my family have to leave and shut up the house. I have little doubt that when we are gone, and there is a caretaker in charge of the house, it will be broken into and destroyed. Others in the same position as myself agree with me that we will find great difficulty in procuring caretakers who will undertake to look after houses which have had to be abandoned in this way.

Personally I believe that the raids on houses were field days, and preparations for something bigger for the Republican Army, and also the attacks on barracks.

I am making arrangements to remove my furniture, etc., as it is impossible to insure in Ireland against damages caused by civil disturbances.[31]

Life was as uncertain in the east as it was in the west. Lady Howard tried to carry on her normal routine in County Wicklow, continuing her visits to funerals and friends in Dublin, giving retainers notice and engaging new maids, attending the nurses' committee, and paying attention to pig prices, but all this went on against a backcloth of suspense. Her diary, recording the growth of violence in Dublin and Wicklow, the reduction of her neighbours' stakes in Ireland, and the kidnapping of her relative, Lord Bandon, frequently laments that 'Everything is dreadful' 'This is all too dreadful'.[32]

31. Copy in P.R.O.N.I., D 989A/8/23.
32. Diary for 1921, 30 Mar., 25 June 1921, N.L.I., MS 3624.

As Hibbert indicated, all this went on with little protection from the central government. Southern unionists' high hopes of French as the head of the Irish administration did not materialise, and frequently reiterated cries for decisive administration[33] went almost unheeded. The trouble was that the British government hardly had a defined policy for Ireland. Preoccupied with what they considered to be greater affairs, but faced with a deteriorating Irish situation, ministers aimed not so much at settling the Irish question, but at keeping the situation 'ticking over' until they felt they had sufficient time and energy to deal properly with it. Meantime they tried to keep the question at arms length by the use of temporary expedients, seemingly hastily conceived and equally hastily abandoned in face of strong opposition. The time for decisive action did not come until the middle of 1921. Until then British policy was aimed not at an immediate settlement of the Irish question, nor at the protection of loyalist interests in Ireland, and thus southern unionists found little comfort in either government attempts at conciliation or repression.

The government's conciliatory measures dismayed those who still clung to the union without satisfying those unionists in favour of a settlement. On the one hand, unionists of the old school were dismayed at changes in the Irish administration, when Sir Hamar Greenwood succeeded Macpherson as Chief Secretary in April 1920. These changes meant that southern unionists, even those as eminent as Bernard,[34] no longer had easy access to the men at the top. In May 1920 the permanent head of the English civil service, Sir Warren Fisher, roundly condemned the Irish administration (with the exception of General Sir Nevil Macready, the C.-in-C. in Ireland) as 'almost woodenly stupid and quite devoid of imagination', listening solely to the ascendancy party which reminded him of

some people in England—mainly to be found in clubs and amongst

33. See e.g. speeches made at the a.g.m. of the I.U.A. in 1920, *Dublin Daily Express,* 20 May 1920; and *Notes from Ireland* (1920), pp. 14, 15, 18, for the activity of the executive committee.

34. Bernard to Lord Stamfordham, 18 Oct. 1920, B.M., Add. MS 52783, f. 70. He wrote: 'I am not communicating with Sir Hamar Greenwood [about Maynooth's apparent support of assassination, which, according to Bernard, ought to be brought to the attention of the Vatican] as I hardly know him. I have never seen him since he was sworn in as Chief Secretary, but I don't think that he knows very much about the undercurrents of opinion in this country.'

retired warriors and dowager ladies—who spend their time in denunciation of the working classes as 'socialists' without ever condescending (or indeed being able) to analyse what they mean.[35]

It was obviously to break down this isolated system of administration that in 1920 the long-serving Sir John James Taylor resigned as Assistant Under-Secretary and made way for Sir John Anderson, who became Joint Under-Secretary, and other of the 'brightest ornaments' in the English civil service. Quite rightly unionists regarded these changes as the beginning of the end, as evidence that the government had concluded that the struggle had come to an end and had sent over the new men to placate Sinn Fein and prepare the way for home rule.[36]

On the other hand, those southern unionists hoping for a compromise settlement were equally dissatisfied with the government's supposedly conciliatory policy. The 1920 government of Ireland bill, conferring so few powers on the Irish parliaments, was not a genuine attempt to settle the Irish question, but was introduced solely for the convenience of the British government and to prevent the automatic coming into force of the 1914 act.[37] Southern unionists were less concerned with the feelings of the government than with the Irish situation, so that the bill was criticised not only by no-compromise unionists[38] but also by those unionists who wanted peace and thought the bill too narrow to provide the basis for a settlement.[39] These latter unionists therefore pressed the government to broaden the bill, but in vain. The government's attitude was that since a genuine settlement was possible at some later date, 'the fewer concessions we make now the better for whatever we give at present would not be looked upon as final but would be regarded as a jumping off ground for further concessions'.[40]

Nor did the government's efforts to maintain law and order

35. Fisher's supplementary report on the Irish civil service, 15 May 1920, B.U.L., AC 25/4/16.

36. Robinson, *Memories Wise and Otherwise*, pp. 292-5.

37. Law to Balfour, 19 Oct. 1919, B.L., 101/3/159: 'Something has to be done because the home rule bill comes automatically into force on the ratification of the last treaty'.

38. Report of the a.g.m. of the I.U.A., *Dublin Daily Express*, 20 May 1920.

39. See below, pp. 224-5.

40. Law to Long, 30 Sept. 1920, B.L., 103/5/9.

always please southern unionists, whom they seldom protected. The government was reluctant to adopt firm measures against the Irish rebels, and the measures it did adopt were either ill-conceived or not persevered with, and were designed not to protect loyalists but to wage war on the I.R.A. Admittedly, some southern unionists condemned the Black and Tans, the Auxiliaries and reprisals as immoral and ineffective,[41] but this view was by no means unanimous. Others thought that the auxiliary forces could have put down Sinn Fein if men such as General Tudor, the Chief of Police in Ireland, had been given a free hand,[42] and unionists of all complexions were ready to defend reprisals as a desperate necessity. Even Bernard, who complained of the drunken behaviour of the Tans in Dublin streets, was prepared to defend reprisals on theological grounds, for, as he explained to one critic, 'it is a law of God that sin should issue in pain and that crime should, from the highest Christian standpoint, be punished with severity if need be'.[43] Yet reprisals were a double-edged weapon, for they led to further retaliation and increased that sense of insecurity experienced after the withdrawal of police from certain areas.[44] The police, the most obvious targets for the rebels, were withdrawn from outlying stations and concentrated in larger barracks, leaving those areas to be policed by patrols of police and soldiers in motor cars. These patrols provided little comfort to southern unionists who believed that the smaller barracks should have been strengthened, not vacated, and who thought that there was only the remotest chance of the patrols being in the right place at the right time.[45]

This was indeed the case. On 14 June 1920, the largest house in Co. Limerick, Mount Shannon, was burnt out.[46] It appears that it was generally recognised that the Hermitage, formerly belong-

---

41. See e.g. Lennox Robinson, *Bryan Cooper,* p. 132; Desart to Bernard, 13 Sept. 1920, B.M., Add. MS 52781, ff. 180–2.

42. See e.g. Lord Ashtown to Law, 14 Nov. 1921, B.L., 107/1/66; Robinson, *Memories Wise and Otherwise,* pp. 288, 295–6.

43. Bernard to A. Martin (Moderator of the General Assemblies of the United Free Churches of Scotland), 14 Mar. 1921, in reply to the latter's letter of 10 Mar. advocating joint representation on the part of churches in favour of a conciliatory Irish policy, B.M., Add. MS 52783, ff. 79–80, 81–2.

44. Lynch-Robinson, *Last of the Irish R.M.s,* p. 162.

45. R. E. Longfield to Montgomery, 16 Mar. 1920, P.R.O.N.I., D 627/435.

46. *Notes from Ireland* (1920), p. 24; *Irish Times,* 16 June 1920. Mount Shannon had belonged to Lord Clare but had recently been sold to an American.

ing to Lord Massy, would be next. The police had been withdrawn from nearby Castle Connell two weeks earlier so that the
only source of possible help was the military.[47] However, at this
time southern unionists could expect little help from this quarter.
Considering the number of soldiers in Ireland at the time, this
may appear strange, and it did puzzle southern unionists that the
military should be cooped up in large barracks for most of the
time doing nothing, instead of patrolling the streets and country
in 'parties of not less than fifty'.[48] But the military did not believe
in such flexibility of troop movements, they preferred to think in
terms of large-scale military manoeuvres rather than policing
operations to protect loyalists. Some appreciated the difficulties in
which southern unionists were placed in 1920–21, but most local
commanders felt almost contempt for southern unionists. Not
only were loyalists unable or unwilling to assist the suppression
of rebellion even by way of giving information: they were also
a nuisance, obstacles to and distractions from efficient military
activities. In *Mad Puppetstown* there is much truth in the description of Major Holt's attitude after his friend and brother officer
had been ambushed and killed while driving out with Aunt
Brenda: not only did he condemn 'that blasted, blasted woman.
If he hadn't come out here to see her, if only he hadn't been half
off his head about her. And he knew he was for it'; he also
extended his condemnation to all loyalists, saying with sudden
nervous anger, 'If there were no loyalists in Ireland . . . there'd
be a great deal less trouble for us in the country'.[49]

The essential truth of such an episode is borne out in reports
that Macready received from officers commanding martial law
areas in 1921.[50] These reports show that few commanding officers
had any high regard for southern unionists and the help that they
would give to the military. One officer reported of the loyalists

47. The account of the burning of the Hermitage is based upon some typescript
copies and extracts of correspondence to Col. Charles Guinness's wife, Lucy, from
her sister, Mrs M. I. Vansittart, whose father was the late 6th Lord Massy. The
Hermitage had been the family home. The extracts are contained in an appeal
by Guinness for protection of country houses and a description of the state of the
country, and are dated 16, 17 June 1920, P.R.O.N.I., D 989A/8/23.

48. Campbell to Law, 20 Nov. 1920, B.L., 99/7/2.

49. Farrell, *Mad Puppetstown*, pp. 163–4, 166.

50. Enclosures with Macready to Miss Stevenson, 20 June 1921, B.L.,
F/36/2/19. Macready had asked for appreciations of the general situation in their
districts from general and brigade commanders of martial law areas.

in the area that 'there seems to be an anxiety for a settlement and a real desire for something to be done, always provided no action is called for from them as individuals'. Another wrote:

Personally I have no very high opinion of the politic[al] value of the loyalist. He is too ceaseless in his complaints against the government, and is too full of the 'if only' spirit in the past tense. He is too fond of saying 'if only the government had done so and so in the past' forgetful of the fact that he himself had advised the government not to do it at that time;

and another, more charitable, thought that 'it may be they could give us "news", but if they did they would be shot by the I.R.A., their farm servants giving them away'. In many senses the military's attitude was unfair, but it was understandable in a war situation. The result was that southern unionists in general should have expected little help from the military, for they received little. In the particular case of the Hermitage, there is no record of the military's attitude to appeals for help: there are only the facts that no military protection was forthcoming and that the Hermitage was burnt down on 16 June.

Not only were large estates and family mansions liable to attack, less prominent Protestants and old retainers were also terrorised and likely to be victimised. Some, it is true, did not take threats seriously, and the Reverend H. T. Hutchings of Ballymascanlan Rectory, Co. Louth, sent back

my 'notice of death' (prepare for death with a coffin and the most obscure remarks) to the Sinn Fein organising secretary, and told him that three weeks to prepare for death was far too short (!) and that I felt sure they had made a mistake in sending it to me; that I was sure the letter was not authoritative, and would they be so good as to enquire into the matter and punish the offender as they thought fit by putting him in a bog . . .[51]

In the main, however, for as many who could laugh at such threats, there were those who were terrified of their lives, particularly since there was little redress for any crime, as in some areas the British courts were not functioning, part of a general collapse of British administration at that time.

51. Extracts from a letter from Hutchings to Guinness, n.d., P.R.O.N.I., D 989A/8/23.

FOUR

Disturbing as this situation was, southern unionists were able to see a glimmer of hope in the Irish situation, which enabled them to abandon the British connection with more confidence. Some constructive elements in Sinn Fein led them to believe that self-government could restore peace to Ireland and thus help to protect their interests. By the middle of 1921 this feeling became stronger, as the Sinn Fein leadership sought southern unionist aid, but even before then there was a growing tendency to look more favourably upon that advanced Irish nationalism so roundly condemned in 1918. By the middle of 1920 Midleton was distinguishing between 'men with an academic hatred of British rule who are not directly associated with outrages of a murderous character', and those 'men who have undoubtedly banded themselves together to commit the most terrible crimes'.[52] Southern unionists began to find to their surprise that they had views in common with Sinn Fein, particularly a desire for peace and order. The Republican 'government' did attempt to administer justice and prevent adventurers and criminals from taking advantage of the guerilla warfare for their own ends, establishing a police force which as far as possible carried out the decisions of the Republican law courts set up in the middle of 1920.[53]

Southern unionists were much impressed by these exercises in government, which superseded the British administration in places. Desart reported that the outrageous behaviour of the British auxiliary forces in Kilkenny was turning orderly and quiet men and 'real old loyalists' into Sinn Feiners, since the Sinn Fein leaders had been preventing as far as they could serious outrages;[54] and Long was told that everybody accepted the supplanting of the British government by Sinn Fein in Co. Limerick. According to Long's informant, Sinn Fein ruled the county and ruled it admirably, controlling traffic at the local races, dispensing justice and recovering property so efficiently that

everybody is going over to Sinn Fein, not because they believe in it, but because it is the only authority in the county; and they realise

52. *Parl. Deb. (Lords)*, 5 ser., xl., 6 May 1920, cols 202–3.
53. Macardle, *The Irish Republic*, pp. 321–4, 345–6.
54. Desart to Bernard, 13 Sept. 1920, B.M., Add. MS 52781, ff. 180–2.

that if their lives and property are to be secured, they must act with Sinn Fein.[55]

In fact, the situation which had emerged in the 1880s had been completely reversed. Now a weakened but still active Anglo-Ireland, interpreting its interests and ideals in the light of the British and Irish situations, found the former wanting and less favourable than the latter. Now the Anglo-Irish were more suspicious of the British government and the union than of Irish nationalism and nationalists. As Bryan Cooper put it:

... Slowly realisation is coming, and side by side with the realisation that the government is either unable or unwilling to protect them is coming the yet more startling discovery that on the whole Sinn Fein is trying to prevent anarchy and maintain order ... Thieves have been apprehended, welshers punished, persons endeavouring to use intimidation for their own private ends dealt with as bringing 'discredit on the Irish Republic', and this had made a considerable impression on the unionist mind.[56]

FIVE

These developments in British and Irish politics seriously weakened unionism in the south of Ireland. Its very basis was sapped, as many Anglo-Irish families left Ireland. Anglo-Ireland had been enfeebled by the first world war which had taken its toll of the young men so that 'behind the high stone walls, at the end of the avenue, in that Georgian house or sham-Gothic castle, there remained now only an old father and mother and a couple of ageing daughters'.[57] The terror and counter-terror of the Anglo-Irish war continued to undermine Anglo-Ireland's strength. Hibbert was quick to leave Clare.[58] Cork was another badly affected area. Murders of Protestants in the West Cork area were frequent and regular occurrences between 1919 and 1921; elsewhere in Cork Protestant families from the Earl of Bandon downwards had their homes burnt out. Not surprisingly many

55. Note, 30 June 1920, which Long was circulating to the Irish affairs committee of the cabinet. The note described a conversation with an Irish friend 'resident in the country, and who has been closely identified with Irish people all his life, and is not given to making inaccurate statements'. B.L., 102/5/30.

56. Lennox Robinson, *Bryan Cooper*, p. 126.

57. *Ibid.,* p. 89.

58. See above, p. 206.

fled in terror of their lives. Among the papers of the I.U.A. are some 'Letters from a Cork farmer'; they are in typescript, perhaps intended for propaganda purposes, but they ring true.[59] On 15 March 1921 the farmer apologised for not attending a meeting, because 'it is too dangerous now for me to go any distance from home', and enclosed a list of twenty of 'my own dear friends— all Protestants—who were shot or had to leave or were preparing to leave'. It was a severe wrench to leave Ireland, financially as well as emotionally, for nobody would buy farms put up for sale. Three weeks later the farmer wrote again, this time from London. He had had to flee from Cork owing to intimidation. An armed band had entered his house, threatening his wife and daughter with whom they fought for an hour in an attempt to get at the farmer who had barricaded himself in his bedroom. In the end, a large sum of money was extorted from his daughter and orders were given that if the farmer left the house for two days or gave any information, he would be shot and the house burned. On the second day, the farmer ventured out, only to find the gang lying in wait. They made a dash for him, but he got into the house again and later managed to steal away to London. There he was stranded 'without a home, without enough to keep me for long, and no chance of being able to sell my farm. It has all come about because I was always true to the empire'. How many left is difficult to say, but even allowing for exaggeration, it is clear that many loyalists left Ireland at this time, if not always under the compulsion of a very immediate threat such as that which drove out the farmer from Cork. Lt-Colonel William Cooke Collis, of Castle Cooke, Fermoy, was a kind and tactful man with a distinguished army career, having served in the Afghan war (1879–80), in the Sudan, and in the South African war (as a.d.c. to the King). In 1921 his tenants refused to pay rent; his residence and belongings had been destroyed by rebels; and he had not received the compensation money that had been awarded to him. The result was that by November:

I have to leave the country forthwith. Until I get some of the £26,716 awarded me I have nothing to live on. There is no sale for timber.

59. Letters dated 15 Mar., 5 Apr. 1921, P.R.O.N.I., D 989A/8/23. This file of letters, etc. contains a convenient commentary on the position of Protestants and loyalists in Co. Cork.

Merely because I am and ever have been loyal is the only cause of my appalling state.[60]

Not all fled Ireland. Many of the Anglo-Irish felt it their duty to remain, like Lord Bandon[61] and Lord Ashtown who reckoned that only the auxiliary police enabled a few loyalists like himself to 'stick it' in Connaught when 'an awful lot have thrown up the sponge'.[62] Yet those who remained in Ireland had no heart to persist in the old unionist policy. It was not panic but a resigned and realistic acceptance of facts that led them to abandon reliance upon Great Britain and the union. Whichever way and with whatever courage southern unionists looked at the situation, they were impotent. Self-defence was not encouraged by the government forces: so distinguished a loyalist as Lord Dunsany, Irish landlord and man of letters, was fined £25 at a British court martial for having arms and ammunition 'not under proper control', in spite of a spirited defence in which he declared: 'I have fought against Sinn Fein, the Boers and the Germans.'[63] In any case, steel shutters and a couple of revolvers or rifles were no protection against a determined bunch of marauders, as the fate of Sir Arthur Vicars underlined;[64] while to call attention to attacks, such as those made on Protestants in Cork, might only have encouraged a religious war.[65] Even where an intrepid individual tried to intervene, he was likely to find, like Penrose

60. Cooke Collis to Barrymore, 25 Nov. 1921, P.R.O., 30/67/48, f. 2811 (forwarded to Midleton with a covering letter, 28 Nov., *ibid.*, ff. 2809–10).
61. Bandon to Midleton, 13 Feb. 1921, *ibid.*, 30/67/44, ff. 2555–7. After expressing concern about the number of Protestant farmers being forced out of West Cork for refusing to subscribe to the I.R.A., Bandon (who was later kidnapped by the rebels) continued: 'It is so horrible to feel how powerless one is to help all these poor people except by remaining in the country and doing anything that can be done, but we are all at the mercy of the "S.F.s".' The letter was sent by a friend, since it 'is not wise to say much in letters going through the post'.
62. Ashtown to Law, 14 Nov. 1921, B.L., 107/1/66.
63. R. Bennett, *The Black and Tans* (Four Square ed., 1961), p. 140.
64. Sir Arthur, of Kilmorna, Co. Kerry, was killed trying to escape from armed raiders who had removed the steel-lined shutters from the windows and occupied his house. They took valuables and burned the house, leaving nothing but the blackened walls of the house and the strong room. The latter was afterwards blown up by the military to save the plate which had been stored in it. See *Irish Times*, 20 Apr. 1921, for the land steward's account of the raid.
65. Bernard to C. F. D'Arcy, Primate of Ireland, 20 Apr. 1921, B.M., Add. MS 52783, ff. 92–3.

Fitzgerald, his unsuccessful attempt to prevent reprisals by the local military rewarded by being driven from the town where he had lived for forty-four years.[66]

Many southern unionists were reduced to despair or angry impotence, like Lord Massy's daughter, Mrs Vansittart, who was

mad with the military. They knew it [the Hermitage] was likely to be burnt and could have stopped it, if only they had put soldiers in yesterday . . . Oh that I had the power to call down a blighting curse on those devils . . . Not a soul will suffer for it! If a few had got shot it would be a relief to one's feelings. I feel too mad, so had better stop.[67]

This was no isolated example of disillusionment, for, according to one brigade commander:

Practically no such thing as a unionist remains. I can see no sign of any effort to actively help the government, but in the present state of affairs it is impossible to blame individuals. The country gentry remain as a class loyal, hospitable, and genial, but they have no authority, and the demoralising life which they are leading must lead in the end to loss of self-respect and indolence.[68]

There were resignations from the magistracy, and many unionists accepted *de facto* rule by Sinn Fein, feeling that they had no alternative but to pay the taxes demanded of them, yet often finding by way of compensation that Sinn Fein courts could enforce the payment of rents and settle agrarian disputes.[69] Cooper summed up their feelings quite nicely when he wrote in 1920:

66. Midleton, *Records and Reactions*, pp. 256–7. Fitzgerald, his 'intrepid agent', refused at first to leave Cork despite outrages. After a murder in Midleton the town authorities asked him, as the culprits did not belong to the town, to interview the general in Cork and persuade him not to take reprisals, which would have fallen on innocent persons. Fitzgerald obliged and got a favourable reply, but that night certain houses in a village five or six miles away were pulled down in consequence of another outrage. The sufferers thereupon rushed to Midleton, firing on the agent's house and forcing him to leave within a few hours the town 'where he had won the respect of everyone for forty-four years. . . .'

67. Mrs Vansittart to Mrs Guinness, 17 June 1920, P.R.O.N.I., D 989A/8/23.

68. Macready to Miss Stevenson, 20 June 1920, B.L., F/36/2/19.

69. Macardle, *The Irish Republic*, pp. 321–4, 335, 345–6; Desart to Midleton, 30 Sept. 1921, P.R.O., 30/67/46, ff. 2727–9, and Oranmore to Midleton, 3 Dec. 1921, *ibid.*, 30/67/48, f. 2818.

. . . there is a growing tendency among those whose main desire is a quiet life to say, 'The government can't protect us or govern the country. Sinn Fein is doing the latter and seems disposed to do the former. Won't it suit my book to make friends with Sinn Fein?'[70]

Not all were indolent, passively waiting upon events. Some southern unionists took positive steps to make friends with Sinn Fein, for if the changing situation had reduced some to despair, it produced in others a definite movement in favour of a wide measure of self-government. As might have been expected, the Midletonites of the A.P.L. took up where they had left off at the convention. They were now all prepared to go beyond that settlement and agree to fiscal autonomy, giving up the customs so hotly disputed in 1918. This advanced view was charmingly expressed in the House of Lords by Oranmore:

My lords, I sigh when I recall how very nearly we succeeded in affecting a settlement [at the convention]. After all, at the end, the great difference between unionists and even the most extreme nationalists was whether or not England should retain the customs. I for one am prepared to yield that point now, and I think there are a great many southern unionists who are prepared to do the same.[71]

They were only slightly embarrassed by this change of heart. Midleton argued that the sacrifice was justified in the interests of peace, in view of the 'passionate earnestness' of many nationalists on the fiscal issue and because he now realised that a customs barrier between England and Ireland could be easily and economically administered.[72]

It was mainly disgust at British attitudes to Ireland that confirmed Midletonites in their new departure. It was not just that the immediate policy of repression was ineffective—no important arrests and martial law effective only within ten miles of a strongly entrenched headquarters.[73] It was rather that they saw the government's inept handling of terrorism as yet another proof and result of the incompetence and bad faith that successive

70. Lennox Robinson, *Bryan Cooper*, p. 126.
71. *Parl. Deb.* (Lords), 5 ser., xlii, 23 Nov. 1920, col. 471.
72. McDowell, *Irish Convention*, p. 209.
73. Midleton, *Records and Reactions*, p. 256, summarising complaints he made in the House of Lords [*Parl. Deb.* (Lords), 5 ser., xl, 6 May 1920, cols 201–6].

British governments had shown in their dealings with Ireland
and southern unionists ever since 1906 and particularly since the
Rising. As early as the latter part of 1919, Cooper reckoned that

. . . There are many Irishmen who stand today in the position of
Robert E. Lee at the beginning of the American civil war, torn by a
divided loyalty. They wish to believe that the imperial government
is doing its best to be fair to Ireland; but if once that belief is shattered
their doubts will be resolved, and they are dangerous enemies.

There are strong incentives to settlement, but there is one serious
obstacle. That is the fact that no one in Ireland places the slightest
confidence in the word of any English statesman—the Prime Minister
least of all. The old Irish proverb: 'Beware the teeth of a wolf, the
heels of a horse, and the word of an Englishman' seems to have
acquired a new lease of life, and with some justification. Again and
again, over the convention, over conscription, over the reconstruction
programme, the deeds of the ministry have been inconsistent with
their words, so that all faith in them has vanished. It is not Sinn Fein
that should be asked for guarantees (since no Sinn Feiner has ever
broken his parole). It is for Mr Lloyd George to convince the people
of Ireland that he is in earnest.[74]

This belief that British rule in Ireland had failed morally as well
as administratively led Midletonites to demand that Ireland should
be given sufficient latitude to govern herself, particularly in
respect of finance. As Midleton bluntly told ministers, his
associates, 'almost all the most influential businessmen and the
largest landowners in the south, including Lord Iveagh, whose
firm . . . alone pays something like four millions to the revenue',
were now 'willing to concede their financial interest to an Irish
parliament rather than face the continuance of the chaos of the
last fifteen years. . . .'[75]

By 1920–21, Midletonites were not the only unionists to come
out in favour of a wide measure of Irish self-government.
Dominion home rule was so widely canvassed as a solution to
Ireland's troubles that it even found favour with a Dublin Castle
lawyer, William Evelyn Wylie, 'a Protestant unionist prosecuting

74. This extract is taken from 'Ireland under Sinn Fein', an unpublished work
written in late 1919 and quoted in Lennox Robinson, *Bryan Cooper*, pp. 127–8.
75. Midleton to cabinet ministers, 11 June 1921, P.R.O., 30/67/45, ff. 2629–30.

lawyer of the Carson type'.[76] Support for such a broad settlement was widespread, most obviously in badly disaffected areas. It was in Cork, where unionists 'daren't motor seven miles to the inland golf course', that a journalist was told that all parties had moved one step to the left and that unionists wanted peace under a liberalised form of self-government.[77] Even that staunchest of Cork unionists, Sir John Harley Scott, the High Sheriff, who in mid-1920 had disparaged dominion home rulers as browbeaten by their wives into the 'mistaken idea that this "will o'the wisp" would be adopted at once and that the outrages would at once cease in Ireland',[78] had by December 1920 come round in favour of a negotiated settlement.[79] But it was not only in the worst affected areas that southern unionists abandoned their unionism. Dominion home rule found favour with the J.P.s and D.L.s of Queen's County, among whom were at least two members of the I.U.A. Though not immediately threatened by violence and 'gladly recognising that the good relations which have always existed between all classes of the community have, happily, been little affected by the prevailing unrest and agitation', these gentlemen viewed

with grave concern the alarming spread of organised crime and violence throughout the greater part of the country, and, what is still more serious, the apparent inability of the government to effect the re-establishment of law and order.

They, therefore, suggested the fullest measure of dominion home rule compatible with the integrity of the United Kingdom and accompanied by generous financial treatment as affording 'the basis for that full and lasting settlement which is so essential to the interests both of the United Kingdom and the empire'.[80]

Finally, other unionists were as much influenced by the passage of the 1920 Government of Ireland Act as by the terror and

76. Lloyd George to Law, 6 May 1920, B.L., F/31/1/27; Wylie to Sir J. Anderson, 2 Aug. 1920, *ibid.*, F/19/2/17.

77. W. Ewart, *A Journey in Ireland 1921* (1922), pp. 47–9.

78. J. H. Scott to Carson, 7 Aug. 1920, B.L., F/6/3/25.

79. Scott to Lloyd George, 7 Dec. 1920, *ibid.*, F/95/2/58.

80. Petition from twenty-seven Deputy Lieutenants and magistrates of Queen's county to the Chief Secretary, c. 13 Aug. 1920, *ibid.*, F/19/2/19.

disorder. Southern unionism had always been a constitutional movement and thus some argued that since self-government was the law of the land, southern unionists in general and the I.U.A. in particular should help to work the act; and form the nucleus of a moderate constitutional party in the new Irish state.[81]

SIX

The corollary to this diminishing unionist sentiment was a weakening of unionist organisation in the south of Ireland. The split was confirmed, since events prevented any co-operation between the A.P.L. and the I.U.A. in opposition to the 1920 bill; and both organisations were shaken by events.

The A.P.L. went through a period of near crisis in the years 1920–21. First of all, there were serious differences of opinion as to how far the A.P.L. should go in the direction of dominion home rule, which threatened to nullify its influence. Then subscriptions, which had been ample in 1919, fell off drastically after 1920. However, the A.P.L. was able to surmount these difficulties: a compromise was agreed over the question of dominion home rule,[82] and the Guinness family intervened to keep the organisation solvent.[83] The A.P.L. thus remained an effective force, able, owing to the general shift of opinion away from unionism, to become the acknowledged and effective representative of southern unionist opinion in the final settlement of the Irish question.

The I.U.A. was not so fortunate. Events had virtually isolated it in Ireland. It quickly became confused and unable to take any sort of initiative. Ulster's decision, together with that of the London committee, had started the process which continued

81. See e.g. letter from the executive committee of the I.U.A. to members of the general council, 2 Feb. 1921, P.R.O.N.I., D 989A/8/23; and Dawson to I.U.A., Jan. 1921, *ibid.,* D 989A/9/20. Dawson suggested that the I.U.A. should adopt 'such a title as "Southern Irish Constitutional Association"', which 'would not arouse any disruptive memories, and would be sufficiently broad to cover the general principle which the organisation would be formed to uphold'.

82. See below, pp. 227–8.

83. R. N. Thompson to Midleton, 6 June 1921, W. Guinness to Midleton, 13 June 1921, P.R.O., 30/67/45, ff. 2624–5, 2627.

throughout 1920 and 1921. The executive committee refused to accept the suggestion that the I.U.A. should change its functions and accept the 1920 act. This decision it backed up by principle and expediency, arguing that there was no half-way house between union and complete separation, and that no purpose would be served by surrendering a principle and accepting the act, since that act was unacceptable to Sinn Fein and unlikely to operate in the south.[84] Indeed, with a naïve faith in the steadfastness of the unionist party, the committee thought that 'the unionist party in Great Britain have in the recent act gone as far as they can go in the direction of separation, and if, as is extremely possible, Southern Ireland refuses to work the act, the restoration of the legislative union can only be a matter of time'.[85]

Exactly how the I.U.A. was going to assist this process was not at all clear. In 1919 it had adopted a dual policy, but the negative side, owing to the decision of the Ulstermen, had never been put fully into operation, and it was reduced to asking the British government and parliament to choose between the union or complete independence.[86] By 1921, with a new act on the statute book and the increasing absorption of the British public in labour politics and problems, it was even more difficult to campaign for the union.[87] The I.U.A. tried to make the best of adverse circumstances, relying on letters and deputations to unionist leaders and meetings in Great Britain and Northern Ireland in order to explain the plight of loyalists in the south of Ireland and underline the danger to the empire of making concessions to Anglophobe Sinn Feiners.[88] Exactly what these and a few publications were to achieve was another matter; but members of the committee hoped that if they did not make the government adhere to the union, they would at least make ministers aware of how their measures affected southern unionists and, perhaps, encourage them to seek in their negotiations with

84. *Notes from Ireland* (1921), pp. 35–6.
85. I.U.A., letter to members of the general council, 2 Feb. 1921, P.R.O.N.I., D 989A/8/23.
86. See the various resolutions passed in 1920 by the general council and executive committee, *Notes from Ireland* (1920).
87. Dawson to I.U.A., 8 Apr. 1921, P.R.O.N.I., D 989A/9/20.
88. *Ibid., passim; Notes from Ireland* (1921), *passim*; Walsh to Craig, 20 July 1921, P.R.O.N.I., D 989A/8/15.

Sinn Fein adequate safeguards for loyalist interests.[89] However illogical and inconsistent this policy may have been, it was understandable. Men felt that they could not just sit still while matters affecting their future were being decided. The sad thing is that their efforts were so futile. They had no influential allies left. Sir James Craig was too concerned with the new state of Northern Ireland to be able to bother much about the southern unionists—even had he wanted to; and the split in the southern unionists' ranks deprived the I.U.A. of whatever influence it might otherwise have had in British politics.

89. Their confusion is well illustrated in a memorandum on matters vitally affecting the interests of southern unionists, copy in P.R.O.N.I., D 989A/8/23. 'Faced with the prospect of being deprived of their birthright of citizenship in the United Kingdom', they submitted that it was only just that they should be heard on certain matters requiring safeguards. These were: finance; customs; the rights of the existing civil service; imposition of the Irish language; retention of imperial forces and British control of the police; the composition of any new standing army for home defence; the oath of allegiance; and 'the provision of adequate means to guarantee them against acts of executive tyranny'. These were held to be 'not merely academic points; but points which touch the life of all southern unionists, of which they had experience.'

IX

Phase Seven: The A.P.L. and the Irish
Settlement, 1920–22

DESPITE these changes, southern unionism remained a significant factor in the Irish question. Southern unionists contributed to its settlement in two ways. Their willingness to accept home rule enabled fruitful negotiations to take place between the British government and Sinn Fein. Their opposition had always in the past inhibited the unionist party from seriously considering an Irish settlement on the basis of home rule, and now their changed attitude enabled the coalition government and parliament to tackle the Irish question almost with an open mind and without fear of significant opposition. The I.U.A. still persisted in its unionism, but any influence it may have had in obstructing a settlement was nullified by the activities of the Midletonites and the A.P.L. In a more positive manner, southern unionists helped Sinn Fein, for their new attitude enabled De Valera to agree to discussions as leader of the Irish nation. Moreover, the southern unionists took care of the preliminaries which had to be completed before the two sides actually met.

Southern unionists also helped to shape the settlement, thanks to the A.P.L. and the Midletonites. Dedicated to a settlement of the troubles and to securing safeguards for the southern minority, they played a significant role in the shaping of the 1920 Government of Ireland Act; in the treaty negotiations in the autumn of 1921; and in the Free State constitution discussions in the following year. The height of their influence was reached in the Government of Ireland Act: though they failed to prevent partition and to broaden the financial provisions, they did insert most of the safeguards proposed at the convention. Unfortunately, this act was superseded in the south by the Anglo-Irish treaty. Had they been more assertive in 1921 and 1922, and had the British government been more accommodating, Midletonites might have managed to have more of these safeguards included in the final settlement.

As it was, the treaty of 6 December 1921 and the constitution of the Free State contained few of the safeguards of the 1920 act. Nevertheless, the Midletonites did not fail entirely. They did get some paper safeguards in the final settlement and, more importantly, they secured the good will of the more moderate section of Sinn Fein.[1]

TWO

Having decided that the union was again a losing cause, the unionists of the A.P.L. worked hard to achieve a settlement of the Irish question. Using all the means in their power, they advocated a generous measure of self-government which at the same time included substantial safeguards for the southern minority, on lines laid down at the convention. They began with the government of Ireland bill of 1920, which they reckoned could not bring peace to Ireland, and which according to the *Irish Times* had 'not a single friend in either hemisphere, outside Downing Street'.[2]

In particular, Midletonites had three main objections to the bill.[3] In the first place, the financial provisions were inadequate and unfair to Ireland. The Joint Exchequer Board, set up to deal with financial matters arising from the act, had in effect a permanent English majority. The financial powers conferred on the sub-parliaments were derisory: they were not allowed to impose, levy, or collect customs duties, excise duties, excess profits duty, any taxes on profits, or income or super tax (though they could vary the rate of income tax). Finally, the imperial contribution of £18m. a year was too high, especially as Ireland would have no share in the consolidated fund of the United Kingdom, while the U.K. retained power to charge things to the funds of the subordinate parliaments. Such proposals, which deprived the Irish parliaments of control over some 93 per cent of Irish revenue, were condemned by southern unionists as imposed not

---

1. The following account, based largely upon contemporary memoranda and letters, substantiates that contained in D. O'Sullivan, *The Irish Free State and its Senate. A Study in Contemporary Politics* (1940), which was based mainly on the later evidence of the Dail debates on the constitution.

2. *Irish Times,* 18 Feb. 1920.

3. See e.g. the speeches of southern Irish peers on the second reading of the bill in the Lords, 23–25 Nov. 1920, *Parl. Deb. (Lords),* 5 ser., xlii, cols 467–76, 565–72, 592–608, 645–55 especially. On the question of partition, see Appendix D.

in the interests of Ireland but solely in the interests of the British Treasury. The second southern unionist objection was that the bill would establish the permanent partition of Ireland, which was acceptable neither to them nor to nationalist opinion. The establishment of two parliaments would create vested interests which would be difficult to abolish, while the council of Ireland, which the government hoped would lead to one parliament for Ireland, had no executive or administrative powers. Thirdly, the bill contained few safeguards for the minority in the south and west, despite promises made since 1916 and especially at the time of the convention. The government had been careful to reserve matters concerning the completion of land purchase and the working of the Land Acts, and had made provisions for proportional representation and safeguarding against administrative injustice and legislation based on religious prejudice; but such safeguards, where acknowledged at all, were considered inadequate by southern unionists. There were serious omissions and also some unfortunate clauses positively harmful to minority interests. There was no provision for the establishment of second chambers; southern unionists wanted a largely nominated senate with considerable powers on the lines of that accepted by the majority of the Irish convention, together with senate representation on the council of Ireland. They also wanted safeguards against the confiscation of property and excessive taxation: in particular, they wanted the original clause 23 modified. This clause, which allowed the Irish parliaments to impose income tax over and above that imposed by Westminster, was considered to amount 'to a positive invitation to a vindictive majority to persecute a minority'.[4]

The Midletonites were determined to broaden the offer made by the government to make it acceptable to the mass of the Irish people, themselves included, and to include the safeguards that had been obtained at the convention. They were optimistic of their ability to achieve this end: Desart told Bernard that 'if peace is to be attended by a wider measure, we shall probably be the section that will be able to do most to shape it and get it through'.[5]

There were difficulties, however. First of all there was the split

4. *Ibid.*, 23 Nov. 1920, col. 476.
5. Desart to Bernard, 13 Sept. 1920, B.M., Add. MS 52781, ff. 180–2.

in southern unionist ranks. It affected the confidence of the A.P.L. and its leader, Midleton, who thought that southern unionists were in danger of being dismissed as a divided minority. Moreover, it created tactical difficulties, for the I.U.A.'s supporters might move a resolution opposing the bill, which other unionists might feel obliged to support with disastrous effects.[6] This difficulty was overcome, however. In part this was due to the drift of opinion in Ireland which isolated the I.U.A., in part to Midleton's efforts. It was he who persuaded the London committee of the I.U.A. not to oppose the bill but to try to secure amendments. Then, by cautious and persistent activity he asserted his authority as a leading spokesman on the Irish question. Aware of the complications of British politics, he moved cautiously. On the one hand, he, together with Desart and Bernard, canvassed the views of the A.P.L. among the rank and file of the unionist party, among party leaders, and especially among cabinet ministers, in private and in the cabinet committee which Midleton occasionally was invited to attend.[7] On the other hand, he was extremely tactful, being unwilling to adopt tactics that might jeopardise the possibility of a satisfactory settlement: he was reluctant to embarrass the government or to criticise the Irish administration, and wanted to avoid any criticism of the current bill which would result in its rejection by parliament and in the operation of the 1914 act.[8] The result of these tactics was that he asserted the position and authority of himself and the A.P.L. at the expense of that of the I.U.A. During a debate on the government of Ireland bill in the Lords, during which nearly all the Irish peers, except Farnham, spoke of the need for a settlement,

6. Midleton to Bernard, 3 Mar. 1920 (enclosing a memorandum of a conversation with Carson and Desart, 29 Feb. 1920), *ibid.*, ff. 87–9.

7. Apart from the parliamentary debates, see e.g. *The Times*, 15, 25 Mar. 1920; Midleton to Bernard, 3 Mar., 26 July, 24 Aug. 1920, B.M., Add. MS 52781, ff. 87–9, 91, 92–5. Midleton to Law, 17 Mar. 1920, B.L., 98/8/10. Memorandum of interview with Lord Birkenhead, Mar. 1920; memorandum of meeting with Law and members of the unionist reconstruction committee, Mar. 1920; Midleton to Kerr, 19 Mar. 1920; Law to Midleton, 1 Apr. 1920; P.R.O., 30/67/42, ff. 2417, 2418–19B, 2420–1, 2442–3. Memorandum of meetings with the Irish subcommittee of the cabinet, 22 July, 5 Aug. 1920; Midleton to Long, 24 July 1920; Midleton to Austen Chamberlain, 25 Sept. 1920, P.R.O., 30/67/43, ff. 2470–2, 2473, 2492–4.

8. Midleton to Bernard, 12 Feb., 3 Mar. 1920, B.M., Add. MS 52781, ff. 83, 87–9; Midleton to Law, 17 Mar. 1920, B.L., 98/8/10.

the coalition leader there and foreign secretary, Curzon, was able to dismiss the chairman of the I.U.A. almost out of hand:

I admit that every one is not converted. Nothing will convert my noble friend Lord Willoughby de Broke. He still remains a magnificent relic of the old guard, but the backwoods in which my noble friend ranged at the head of a formidable band some years ago are now relatively deserted, and his picturesque figure is seen stalking, consoled only by Lord Farnham, amid the scenes that were once those of his adventures and triumphs.[9]

A second difficulty facing the A.P.L. was internal. There developed a dispute over tactics which threatened to split it.[10] Men such as Jameson, the vice-president, were more concerned with the state of Ireland than with the condition of British politics. They reckoned that the situation was urgent, that coercion would only heighten confusion and further endanger the position of loyalists; and demanded that Midleton be more active in promoting a quick and generous settlement on the basis of dominion home rule, which, they said, was acceptable to the Roman Catholic hierarchy and therefore to Sinn Fein. This discontent came to a head at the beginning of August, when on 3 and 4 August a deputation from the Dublin committee came over to London.[11] Midleton resented this criticism and advice, which he regarded as undermining his authority at a time when he was attending meetings of the Irish committee of the cabinet and expressing himself freely. He was not willing to be rushed into adopting tactics that would jeopardise the possibility of a satisfactory settlement.[12] In particular, he refused to put forward dominion home rule proposals, since, he held, they would be unacceptable to the government, being tantamount to separation.

However, an open rift was avoided. Midleton agreed that Jameson should put the views of the Dublin committee to Lloyd George; and the A.P.L. came out publicly on 13 August in

9. *Parl. Deb.* (*Lords*), 5 ser., xlii, 25 Nov. 1920, col. 667.

10. Sir R. Woods to Bernard, 1 Aug. 1920, B.M., Add. MS 52783, ff. 62–3; Desart to Bernard, 13 Sept. 1920, *ibid.*, 52781, ff. 180–2.

11. Midleton's memorandum of a meeting with the Dublin deputation from the A.P.L., 3 and 4 Aug. 1920, P.R.O., 30/67/43, ff. 2475–7.

12. *Ibid.*; Midleton to Bernard, 24 Aug. 1920, B.M., Add. MS 52781, ff. 92–5.

favour of a masked form of dominion home rule.[13] Midleton also made greater efforts to secure a broader and immediate settlement, and did so in an optimistic spirit. He eagerly took up the idea of co-operation with the hierarchy (suggested by the Dublin committee) in the expectation of being able to force Lloyd George into broadening the bill. Hoping to take advantage of events at the end of August, and especially of the tense situation created by Terence MacSwiney's hunger strike, Midleton asked Bernard what he thought of the following:

Would the hierarchy—if they bargain at all—drive an arrangement with A. J. Balfour; E. Talbot; you and me? With such a team we could force L[loyd] G[eorge]'s hand.[14]

Midleton intended to propose a board of customs; an Irish contribution to the imperial exchequer of £10 million a year for ten years, after which time Ireland would be free to arrange the sum payable; and that Ulster be allowed to contract out but to vote again on partition in ten years time—or earlier if Ulstermen so desired.[15]

There was some excuse for Midleton's optimism. The settlement he was recommending amounted practically to 'repeal of the union and the re-establishment of Ireland as a separate kingdom, under the same king as Great Britain, with its two houses of parliament';[16] and Bernard could not 'but think that even the most extreme Sinn Fein leaders . . . will see that such a measure . . . would give Ireland all she needs for a free life'.[17] Moreover, Midleton had access to the cabinet sub-committee on Ireland, to which he could put his views squarely and forcibly;[18] and he could contact the Roman Catholic hierarchy through Powell and

---

13. *Ibid.*; *Irish Times*, 14 Aug. 1920; and letter sent by A.P.L. to Lords Lieutenant of the counties, 18 Aug. 1920, P.R.O., 30/67/43, f. 2486. The A.P.L. asked the Lords Lieutenant, in accordance with a unanimous resolution passed on 13 Aug., to summon meetings of magistrates and others in the counties to approve a dominion home rule resolution to show the Prime Minister what moderate opinion in Ireland wanted; though the term dominion home rule was not used, since it involved control of naval and military forces.

14. Midleton to Bernard, 24 Aug. 1920, B.M., Add. MS 52781, ff. 92–5.

15. *Ibid.*

16. Bernard to Ross, 7 Oct. 1920, *ibid.*, 52783, f. 65.

17. *Ibid.*

18. See above, p. 226.

Bernard.[19] But the scheme hardly got off the ground in face of two further obstacles to his plans. The hierarchy was immovable. Bernard's contact, Dr Kelly, Bishop of Ross, saw no hope of a settlement in 1920, despite eloquent appeals from Bernard as to the great sacrifices that loyalists and Protestants were prepared to make 'regretfully but sincerely' in the interests of peace.[20] Ross reckoned that the government was not prepared for compromise and also argued against a settlement in 1920 on the novel ground that the country was not sufficiently chaotic to make any peace move successful:

Meanwhile the economic and social structure of Ireland is falling to pieces before our eyes. In my prevision the process will increase in geometrical progression. But even intelligent business men will not see, as long as they are making money. The coming winter is likely to open their eyes. When business is falling away, cattle markets impeded, schools and colleges less full, lines and ships in less demand; we will begin to have the conditions for a settlement.[21]

Midleton was no more successful with Law. He urged the unionist leader to appoint Balfour as plenipotentiary to negotiate with all parties in Ireland with a view to a settlement; but the government was not prepared to make any real attempt at compromise with Sinn Fein until the latter realised that they could not get all they demanded.[22]

Thus rebuffed, and when both these methods of public declaration and private pressure had failed, Midletonites turned to parliament, leaving tactics in their leader's hands.[23] They tried to amend the bill in parliament, to broaden the powers of the Irish parliaments and to introduce safeguards for minorities. Walter Guinness made repeated efforts to amend the bill to conform to the southern unionist viewpoint, but these were largely unsuccessful in face of the huge government majority in the Commons.[24]

19. See e.g. Powell to Midleton, 9 Oct., 13 Nov. 1920, P.R.O., 30/67/43, ff. 2499, 2513; and below, p. 233.
20. Bernard to Ross, 7 Oct. 1920, B.M., Add. MS 52783, f. 65.
21. Ross to Bernard, 11 Oct. 1920, *ibid.*, ff. 67–8.
22. Law to Lloyd George, 7 Oct. 1920, B.L., 103/4/8, and above, p. 208.
23. Powell to Midleton, 13 Nov. 1920, P.R.O., 30/67/43, f. 2513.
24. McDowell, *Irish Convention*, pp. 205–9. Two of his successful amendments gave slightly increased powers to the council of Ireland by providing it with the control of fisheries, and increased Irish representation at Westminster from 42 to 46 by providing for continued Irish university representation.

I

Therefore, the southern unionists had to rely upon Midleton and their influence in the House of Lords to achieve an agreeable settlement. Though not as powerful as in the pre-war years, owing to changing political conditions and to Ulster's decision to accept partition, the influence of the southern Irish peers was still considerable. The committee of Irish peers had been reorganised at the beginning of the year and Midleton was marshalling his forces there in a threatening manner.[25] His influence was fully recognised by the government: Curzon, who asked Midleton to suggest safeguards in committee, said, 'Commanding, as he does, very wide support from many quarters of this House no doubt he will be able to make an exceedingly effective case to us'.[26]

At first Midleton tried unsuccessfully to use his influence to obtain an adjournment so as to enable the government to negotiate a settlement, but after the Lords had agreed with the government that it was futile to attempt negotiations under present conditions,[27] he and his friends set about amending the bill.[28] Their influence could not induce the Lords to agree to all their demands, particularly those designed to deprive the six counties of their parliament and to extend the financial powers of the Irish parliaments;[29] but it did enable them to carry a number of amendments to the bill safeguarding the southern minority, sometimes in face of government opposition, as over the all-important question of the establishment of a Senate on convention lines, which was carried by 120 votes to 36.[30] Dunraven says that the bill passed in substantially the same form as it had been

25. I.U.A., minute book of the London committee, 11 Mar. 1920; Midleton to Kerr, 18 Mar. 1920, P.R.O., 30/67/42, ff. 2420–21; Midleton to Curzon, 4 Nov. 1920, *ibid.,* 30/67/43, f. 2508; and various letters from Irish peers in Dec. 1920 to Midleton, *ibid.,* 2531–2, 2534–40, 2542–6. For a list of peers with Irish interests in 1920, see Appendix B.

26. *Parl. Deb. (Lords),* 5 ser., xlii, 25 Nov. 1920, col. 680.

27. *Ibid.,* cols 645–55. His motion was defeated by 91 votes to 177.

28. For the process of amendment, see *ibid.,* xlii, cols 783–906 (1 Dec.), 915–1021 (2 Dec.), 1024–1137 (6 Dec.); xliii, cols 28–90 (13 Dec.), 118–19(14 Dec.), 393–439 (17 Dec.), 587–606 (20 Dec. 1920).

29. *Ibid.,* xlii, cols 788–816, 980–1012. For the more important ministerial discussions of these points, see the minutes of the meetings of the cabinet and of conferences of ministers in the P.R.O.: for Ulster, 11 Nov., 2, 3, 10, 15, 19 Dec. 1919 (Cab. 23/18), 24 Feb. 1920 (Cab. 23/20); for finance, 11 Nov., 3, 22 Dec. 1919 (Cab. 23/18), 13, 17 Oct. 1920 (Cab. 23/23).

30. *Parl. Deb. (Lords),* 5 ser., xlii, 1 Dec. 1920, cols 817–40.

introduced,[31] but this view underrates the influence of the southern Irish peers in the Lords. Admittedly, they could make little headway against the government's refusal to accept amendments which could be seen by Sinn Fein as surrender and could not undermine the Ulster unionists' position, but they were able to win concessions from the government. Some ministers were more willing than others to make concessions: they did so almost gratefully since they were able to redeem pledges to southern unionists and yet avoid, for instance, the responsibility for establishing second chambers for the Irish parliaments, chambers which Ulster unionists thought superfluous;[32] others did so reluctantly in order not to jeopardise the passage of the bill.[33] Whatever the reasons, the government did bow to pressure from the Lords and did accept many of the safeguards suggested by or on behalf of southern unionists.[34] As Lord Birkenhead, the Lord Chancellor, said, 'great modifications' had been accepted, despite some of their being 'among the more important matters of controversy'.[35] Thus in addition to the original safeguards contained in the bill, the final act provided considerable safeguards for southern unionists: a strong Senate with considerable powers over legislation; the abolition of the provision conferring on Irish parliaments the power to impose additional income tax or surtax; the finality of the judicial committee of the House of Lords in dealing with Irish matters; protection of private property against confiscation without compensation; Senate representation on the council of Ireland which was to have increased powers,

31. Dunraven, *Past Times and Pastimes*, ii. 69. Dunraven acted with the A.P.L unionists, though he did not agree with all their views. They opposed partition on principle, but he, while disapproving of the religious basis of partition, recognised that an all-Ireland parliament was impossible in the circumstances of 1920 (pp. 63–5).

32. Some ministers, like Long, were genuinely anxious to provide adequate safeguards for the southern unionists (Long to Bernard, 27 Sept. 1919, B.M., Add. MS 52783, ff. 59–60; Long to Law, 9 Nov. 1920, B.L., 103/5/14, 15).

33. See e.g. Birkenhead's distasteful tone in the debates on the bill, and his explanation on 17 Dec. 1920 on complaints that he had 'indulged in sarcasm in relation to the proposed constitution of these assemblies' (the Irish Senates, as proposed by the Lords) (*Parl. Deb. (Lords)*, 5 ser., xliii, col. 394).

34. Minutes of the cabinet, 16, 17 (6 p.m.) Dec. 1920 and of a conference of ministers, 15 Dec. 1920, P.R.O., Cab. 23/23. These minutes provide very little evidence as to the attitude of members of the government to southern unionist claims.

35. *Parl. Deb. (Lords)*, 5 ser., xliii, 17 Dec. 1920, col. 394.

notably the administration of fisheries and the Diseases of Animals Act. In fact, the safeguards contained in the bill were almost identical with those suggested at the convention, the only significant omission being minority representation in the lower house; and supporters of the A.P.L. were very pleased with the result, which they largely attributed to Midleton.[36]

It was unfortunate that the act was never implemented in the south, but the efforts of the southern Irish peers were not entirely wasted. They had showed their influence in the Lords and Midleton had confirmed his position as the leading and most influential Irish politician working for a compromise settlement. Birkenhead recognised him as leader of a compromise school demanding a wide settlement and safeguards;[37] Curzon's remarks on his influence have already been noted; and it is worth noting that his importance and services to Ireland were acknowledged on the other side of the House. The Marquess of Crewe, liberal leader in the Lords from 1908 to 1916, recognised

the part which my noble friend who has just spoken has played through all these discussions. Dating from the time of the convention and through all these debates in your lordships' House the noble earl has impressed everybody not merely by the deep sincerity and conviction with which he has spoken, but by his most evident desire to help in moulding this measure into a form that would be best for Ireland.[38]

THREE

However pleased southern unionists may have been with the safeguards that had been eventually inserted, they could not be satisfied with the new act. The reception given to it in the south and the continuance of violence only confirmed the A.P.L. in its view that only a more generous settlement could bring peace to Ireland. This need provided a *raison d'être* for the continued existence of the A.P.L. Old style nationalists, notably Gwynn and Major-General Robert Wanless O'Gowan, wanted to co-operate with the Midletonites to form a new centre party,

36. See the tributes paid in December 1920 to Midleton by various peers, Stewart and Jameson, and the Dublin chamber of commerce, P.R.O., 30/67/43, ff. 2531–46.

37. *Parl. Deb.* (*Lords*), 5 ser., xlii, 23 Nov. 1920, col. 440.

38. *Ibid.*, xliii, 20 Dec. 1920, col. 596.

which would put forward candidates at the first general election fixed for May; but Midleton thought that the time was not ripe for such a new party, nor for the A.P.L. to change its name.[39] In 1921 the Midletonite policy was to try to persuade the government to postpone the elections and to achieve a broader settlement. The state of British politics, notably the government's concentration on the coal strike, inhibited Midleton from bothering ministers too frequently;[40] but throughout 1921 as individuals and as groups many southern unionists, prompted by the A.P.L., urged upon the government the necessity for postponing elections and for compromise talks with Sinn Fein with a view to broadening the 1920 act, especially its financial provisions.

Some like Campbell were hasty and over-optimistic,[41] but others, notably Midleton, were more stable and statesmanlike. He urged the establishment of an Irish cabinet to meet daily so that it 'would not miss the moment for compromise if one arose',[42] and, when opportunity arose, he put his views squarely to the cabinet.[43] The group activity of the A.P.L. was highly inventive, as Midletonites combined or tried to combine with others interested in peace to urge their views on the government and to underline the urgency of the Irish situation. To persuade the government to act, they recognised that some representative and responsible Irishman or body of Irishmen had to be willing to accept a settlement short of a republic. With government encouragement, efforts were made through Powell, and a deputation of southern unionists headed by Sir William Goulding, to persuade the bishops to enter into negotiations, but the bishops remained immobile.[44] Nevertheless, the Midletonites had other irons in the fire. On 7 March Midleton, writing on behalf of 'a large body of men of all classes and creeds who are genuinely

39. Résumé of a meeting at 103 Grafton St, Dublin, 5 Mar. 1921, between Midleton, Oranmore, General O'Gowan and Captain Gwynn, P.R.O., 30/67/44, ff. 2561–2.
40. Midleton to A. Chamberlain, 7, 26 Mar. 1921, B.U.L., AC 30/1/7, 8.
41. Campbell to Law, 8 Jan. 1921, and Law to Campbell, 11 Jan. 1921, B.L., 100/1/13, 101/5/7. Law replied that he was sick of peace negotiations, because none of the negotiators had any power to speak for anybody.
42. Midleton to A. Chamberlain, 26 Mar. 1921, B.U.L., AC 30/1/8.
43. Midleton to Bernard, 9 Mar. 1921, B.M., Add. MS 52781, f. 98; cabinet minutes, 8 Mar. 1921, P.R.O., Cab. 23/24.
44. Midleton to Powell, 9, 30 Mar. 1921; Powell to Midleton, 14, 31 Mar., 3, 12 Apr., P.R.O., 30/67/44, ff. 2563, 2580, 2564–5, 2581–2, 2592–6, 2604.

anxious that if home rule be established in the south it should be done in such a manner as to enable it to be successfully worked', criticised the holding of elections in the south which would defeat the bill and aggravate existing disorders;[45] and on 29 April he and seven other Irish peers urged the government to reconsider the decision to hold elections.[46] The businessmen of the A.P.L., with the encouragement of the peers,[47] made their own contribution. Perhaps in fulfilment of Ross's prevision, Jameson and Goulding got together with a number of other large businessmen, nationalists and Roman Catholics, to consider what steps could be taken 'to terminate the present deplorable state of things in Ireland'. The result, following a speech by Midleton to some 300–400 businessmen at the Rotary Club, Dublin, on the commercial aspect of home rule, was the formation on 7 March of the Irish Business Men's Conciliation Committee. The new committee wished 'to avoid putting forward any plan', but, 'believing that peace can best be secured by a discussion between the British cabinet on the one side and the elected representatives of the Irish people on the other', was 'anxious to bring about, if possible, a joint conference of representatives of both bodies'.[48] It got in touch with both sides, and offered its services as mediator, inviting each side 'to accept our good offices and to nominate a representative, or representatives, with power to act on your behalf either in direct conference, or in negotiations conducted through us, whichever way seems most desirable to you'.[49]

45. Midleton to Lloyd George, 7 Mar. 1921 (on A.P.L. notepaper), B.L., F/38/1/13.

46. Midleton to Lloyd George, 29 Apr. 1921, *ibid.*, F/38/1/14; Dunraven, *Past Times and Pastimes*, ii. 71.

47. Midleton to Bernard, 9 Mar. 1921, B.M., Add. MS 52781, f. 98.

48. I.B.M.C.C. to Lloyd George, 31 Mar. 1921, B.L., F/19/3/13. Apart from Jameson and Goulding and one other unspecified, Charles McGloughlin (managing director of Messrs J. and C. McGloughlin, Art Metal Workers, Dublin), the other three signatories were described by Greenwood as nationalists, two being Roman Catholics. They were Sir Stanley Harrington (chairman of the Cork, Blackrock and Passage Railway, and a director of the Munster and Leinster Bank); Martin McDonagh (chairman of the Galway Harbour Commissioners); and Sir Walter Nugent (deputy chairman of the Midland Great Western Railway and a director of the Bank of Ireland). Two unionists, Bryan Cooper and Robert N. Thompson (also secretary of the A.P.L.), were honorary secretaries.

49. *Ibid.* For the activities of the I.B.M.C.C., see Greenwood to Lloyd George, 14 Apr. 1921, and to Jameson, n.d.; Jameson to Greenwood, 23 Apr. 1921, and to Lloyd George, 23 Apr., 12, 28 May 1921; Lloyd George to Jameson, 10 May 1921; B.L., F/19/3/13, 3, 18, and F/96/1/23, 34, 39, 33.

Though these representations had no immediate effect upon government policy, they did help to mark out for the Midleton-ites a peculiar and strong position in British and Irish politics in the eyes of Irish nationalists and of British ministers. That position had been outlined in the convention, when the landlord class had co-operated with moderate nationalists in a scheme of self-government, and the compromise activities of the A.P.L. in 1920 and 1921 confirmed and strengthened this position, not only in the eyes of the British government but also in the eyes of Sinn Fein. The government, having created Midleton an earl, continued to pay polite attention in private and in cabinet committee to his advice about Ireland and appointed Jameson and Stewart privy councillors, and the Irish Business Men's Conciliation Committee had been in close touch with the Prime Minister; while this committee also brought Midletonites into contact with Dail Eireann and with Sinn Feiners. For instance, in mid-June Midleton was busy arranging clandestine discussions with peaceful Sinn Feiners, and, on 16 June, met the Deputy Lord Mayor of Cork, Barry Egan, at his London house, 34 Portland Square. The meeting took place in melodramatic circumstances, for Egan feared for his life if such a meeting were discovered; but he expressed his desire for an end to violence and for negotiations between the government and Eamon De Valera, the President of the Republic, who, he thought, was reliable.[50] And Lord Donoughmore was told by two Sinn Fein sympathisers that De Valera would have no more dealings with unofficial nego-tiators, such as Lord Derby, who in April had gone to Ireland under an assumed name to interview the President.[51]

Paradoxically, the Midletonites' failure to have the operation of the 1920 act postponed strengthened their independent position. The elections for the lower house took place in May, and though the result was a sweeping victory for Sinn Fein, it reacted upon the attitude of unionists of the A.P.L., making them not only more determined, more defiant, but also more authoritative. At about the same time the election of senators for both the northern and southern parliaments occurred. Under the 1920 act, the members of the southern Senate were to be elected by

50. M. Whitehead to Midleton, 14 June 1921; memorandum of meeting with Egan, 16 June 1921, P.R.O., 30/67/45, ff. 2631, 2635.
    51. *Ibid.*

archbishops and bishops of the Roman Catholic church and
Church of Ireland, by peers and privy councillors who were
taxpayers or ratepayers in respect of property in the south or
who had residences there, and by members of county councils
voting together as provinces. The last-named took no part in the
election; but a Senate was formed, consisting mainly of members
of the A.P.L., supported by other erstwhile unionists and very
moderate nationalists. From this newly won position of authority,
Midletonites and other senators addressed a memorial to the
government, urging that the 'earliest possible steps should be
taken to recast the act', and stating firmly that 'we are not
prepared to exercise functions in connection with any body
nominated by the Lord Lieutenant to replace an elected lower
house';[52] and the Irish peers continued to press this policy on the
government in the House of Lords.[53]

This pressure and this proclamation were not responsible for
everything that was to follow, but certainly most of what followed
could not have taken place without the aid of the Midletonites.
On 24 June Lloyd George invited De Valera to 'attend a conference here in London in company with Sir James Craig to
explore to the utmost the possibility of a settlement',[54] and thus
began a series of conversations which led to a truce and to
negotiations resulting in the treaty of December 1921, the
establishment of the Irish Free State, the withdrawal of the
British from the south of Ireland and the end of unionism in the
south. Though it would be inaccurate to say that the A.P.L.'s
pressure had forced the government to negotiate, Midletonites
did play a vital role in the negotiations.

FOUR

From their peculiar position in British and Irish politics, Midleton-
ites were able to assist negotiations to end the union in three ways.
In the first place, their willingness to extend the 1920 act enabled
Sinn Fein to enter into negotiations with the British government.
The support of unionist groups in Ireland was important, even
essential, to Sinn Fein for moral and tactical reasons if Sinn Fein

52. Dunraven, *Past Times and Pastimes*, ii. 71–3. There were 19 signatories of
whom 11 were associated with the A.P.L.

53. *Ibid.*, ii. 74.

54. F. Gallagher, *The Anglo-Irish Treaty*, ed. T. P. O'Neill (1965), p. 41.

were to be able to enter into negotiations with the government from a position of strength, i.e. arguing from the idea of Ireland a nation and demanding a republic. On the one hand, the republicans and the republican leader were dominated by an idea of Irish nationality that traditionally embraced all her people, Catholics, Protestants and Dissenters: to sustain their claim, not only to satisfy others but also to satisfy their own minds, the support of the Protestant minority was necessary. On the other hand, the support of that minority was also necessary to put Sinn Fein in a strong tactical position, for the situation was very complex. In a sense the Irish position was a strong one: the creation of the Irish Republic as a partly functioning state, the establishment of Dail Eireann as its parliament and the setting up of a government responsible to the Dail, gave a certain strength. But it also limited the power of manoeuvre on the Irish side and gave strength only as long as unity among different elements in the parliament and government was maintained. The British tactics would be to destroy that unity and use the resultant confusion to their advantage, just as it had to be the Irish objective to face British probes with 'uncreviced solidarity', for which the support of the minority was desirable, if not essential.[55]

These issues had been raised in Lloyd George's letter of invitation. It suggested his line of attack, for he addressed De Valera as 'the chosen leader of the great majority in southern Ireland'. De Valera was determined to appear as the leader of the Irish nation and his retort was indirect, but, as a countermove, effective. He replied that he was consulting such 'principal representatives of our nation' as were available and also members of the national minority before he could answer Lloyd George's letter fully.[56] He then issued an invitation to a conference to the leaders of unionist and Protestant groups in Ireland, including Craig, for 'the reply which I, as spokesman for the Irish nation, shall make to Mr Lloyd George will affect the lives and fortunes of the political minority in this island, no less than those of the majority'.[57] Since Craig, safely ensconced in Northern Ireland, refused to confer with De Valera, the support of the southern unionists was all the more important.

'The spokesman for the Irish nation' knew how to choose his

55. *Ibid.*, pp. 42–3.   56. *Ibid.*   57. *Ibid.*, p. 43.

men. Representatives of the I.U.A. were not invited to confer. Invitations were sent only to Midletonite unionists (Midleton, Jameson, Sir Maurice Dockrell, unionist member for South Dublin, and Sir Robert Woods, unionist member for Dublin University) who were much surprised by them.[58] Despite the obloquy heaped upon them by the I.U.A., which repudiated them as representatives of southern unionism,[59] their difficulties should not be underrated, for it took a considerable deal of courage to decide to accept De Valera's invitation. There were strong arguments against meeting him. There was fear for their reputations, which must have been real after the fiasco of the convention. As Midleton put it,

I was most unwilling to go, as I felt pretty certain that, whatever the course of events, we should be saddled with responsibility for any concessions made, and I should not be able to control what was actually decided.[60]

Then there was the possibility that by meeting Sinn Fein they would endanger their lives, and this fear reinforced and was reinforced by a reluctance to confer with men they regarded as responsible for outrage and murder. For instance, Midleton had relatives who had suffered in outrages—a nephew murdered in the west, and a seventy-year-old cousin, Lord Bandon, kidnapped while his castle was burned.[61] But such personal considerations were countered by larger considerations, a desire to serve Ireland and the empire—a desire and duty underlined and encouraged by Lloyd George who persuaded Midleton that he should accept De Valera's invitation.[62] Therefore, Midleton and company agreed to meet him with a high and grave view of their function, while Bernard, in a sermon preached at Westminster Abbey, appealed for special prayers for those who were taking not merely their lives but also their reputations in their hands in what appeared to be such a forlorn hope.[63]

In this strained atmosphere, the meeting could easily have

58. Midleton, *Records and Reactions*, p. 258; Phillips, *Revolution in Ireland*, p. 214.
59. See e.g. Capt Foxcroft's letter in *Morning Post*, 9 July 1921.
60. Midleton, *Records and Reactions*, pp. 258–9.
61. *Ibid.*, p. 259.
62. *Ibid.*, pp. 258–9; Midleton to Lloyd George, 24 June 1921, B.L., F/38/1/16.
63. Midleton, *Records and Reactions*, p. 259.

misfired, but the initial confrontation was carefully and skilfully handled by De Valera. The unionists had agreed that, as they deeply resented the conduct of the insurgents, the proceedings should be conducted on purely business lines and 'those unmeaning civilities to which Irishmen are prone as a means of *rapprochement*' avoided. As it was doubtful at which hour they were to meet next morning, the unionists called at Mansion House and were seen by the 'Lord Mayor's secretary', 'a tall spare man with spectacles' who 'in a very friendly way arranged the hour, shaking hands with us warmly at parting and thanking us for coming over'. It is not difficult to imagine the beneficial effect on the atmosphere when the unionists went into the council chamber the following day to find two men 'of whom one was Mr Griffith, and the other claimed that he needed no introduction, as he had met us the day before. We were quite unaware that we had been talking to Mr De Valera!' Another factor facilitating discussion was the attitude of the people of Dublin who turned out to cheer the southern unionists.[64]

These happy incidents enabled discussions to proceed frankly and optimistically.[65] The conference lasted for four days, 4–8 July 1921. De Valera, complaining of 'how little by Great Britain the high purpose and self-sacrifice of the men who were fighting for the Irish cause was appreciated', and deprecating 'their being spoken of as murderers', struck the unionists as an 'uncompromising fanatic';[66] but they were favourably impressed by Griffith, and after some severe questioning of De Valera a mutually advantageous understanding was reached. Anxious to make good his claim to be the leader of all Irish people, De Valera began by asking the unionists to act as intermediaries between himself and Craig with a view to the latter's coming to Dublin to discuss Lloyd George's proposal.[67] However, he was soon convinced by

64. *Ibid.*, pp. 259–60. Arthur Griffith was the Vice-President of the Republic.
65. The essence of this account is taken from Midleton, *Records and Reactions*, pp. 260–3, and is expanded and confirmed by his rather formal memorandum on the conference on 4 and 8 July (P.R.O., 30/67/45, ff. 2646–54), his freer record of the meeting on 4 July (B.L., F/181/2/3), his letters and telegrams to Lloyd George, 4, 7, 9 July 1921 (B.L., F/38/1/18, 19, 21), and Lloyd George to Midleton, 7 July 1921 (*ibid.*, F/38/1/20).
66. Midleton's record of the Dublin conference, 4 July 1921, B.L., F/181/2/3.
67. Craig had secretly visited De Valera in Dublin on 5 May, but a long conversation on the possibility of an agreement founded on the council of Ireland clause of the 1920 act produced no result.

the unionists of the impossibility of bringing Craig to Dublin, and eventually allowed himself to be persuaded into agreeing to enter negotiations upon two conditions, which the southern unionists were to demand of the government: that there should be direct negotiations with the British government and that a truce should precede and accompany the opening of discussions. The first condition was obviously congenial to De Valera and Midletonites, because it aimed at undermining the special position of Ulster; and the question of a truce was to their mutual advantage. Despite the fact that the Irish leader took much persuading, a truce had obvious advantages to Sinn Fein at that time: light nights provided inconvenient conditions for guerilla warfare and Sinn Fein needed a breathing space. For their part southern unionists set great store by a truce. Respite from disorder was welcome for whatever reasons, and they were convinced that a truce was a necessary preliminary to successful negotiations: whereas a continuation of outrages would harden opinion all round, their cessation would create in Ireland and Great Britain an atmosphere favourable to compromise. Moreover, the general sentiment of Irishmen would ensure that 'if Mr De Valera enters on negotiations with a truce he will put a rope round his neck as far as the resumption of disorder is concerned'.[68]

In view of subsequent disappointments, it can be said that these preliminaries were mishandled by the unionists. Interested in starting negotiations, and wary of the Sinn Fein leaders, they made no attempt to get assurances from Sinn Fein as to safeguards for southern unionists in the new Ireland and thus in the negotiations that followed relied almost entirely on the good offices of the British government, or rather lack of them. On the other hand, there was good reason for Midleton to be proud of the Mansion House conference. The unionists did not rush blindly into a truce, but first by close questioning convinced themselves of De Valera's sincerity and ability to control the armed forces of the Republic; and they did achieve their immediate objectives —a truce and the opening of negotiations. In a sense this was due largely to De Valera's anxiety to establish his claim as leader of the Irish nation by gaining the support of Irish unionists and by establishing a workable relationship with Midleton and his

68. Midleton's record of the Dublin conference, 4 July 1921, B.L., F/181/2/3.

colleagues; but the unionists ought to be given credit for their courage in negotiating with men they had every reason to hate and for their willingness to lay down the basis of a workable relationship with Sinn Fein. For, after all, it was the southern unionists' support that enabled De Valera, as leader of the Irish nation, to reply accepting Lloyd George's invitation in these terms:

The desire you express on the part of the British government to end the centuries of conflict between the peoples of these two islands, and to establish relations of friendly harmony, is the genuine desire of the people of Ireland. I have consulted with my colleagues and secured the views of the representatives of the minority of our nation in regard to the invitation you have sent me. In reply, I desire to say that I am ready to meet and discuss with you on what bases such a conference as that proposed can reasonably hope to achieve the object desired.[69]

The second way in which the southern unionists assisted the treaty negotiations was in their role as intermediaries. They acted as a convenient and necessary bridge between the British government and Sinn Fein, playing a vital role in settling those preliminaries which are essential to the success of any conference, and which in the Irish case were barely susceptible to treatment in letters—if any useful result was to emerge. Midleton was sent as emissary from the Mansion House conference to persuade the British government to accept its two conditions.[70] It is difficult to see who else could have performed that invaluable function, if negotiations were to be carried on at a high and fruitful level instead of at the ineffectual penny-thriller, street corner, con-spiracy level of 1920. Considering the atmosphere of mutual suspicion at that time, it needed somebody on whose fairness, impartiality, good-will and good standing both sides could rely. The government had long used Midleton for Irish purposes and knew they could rely upon him; and the fact that Midletonites had been pressing for self-government and had attended the conference showed clearly that Sinn Fein had confidence in Midleton's good faith and in his good standing in British politics. It would not be difficult to imagine the reception that would have

69. Gallagher, *The Anglo-Irish Treaty*, p. 47.
70. Midleton, *Records and Reactions*, p. 261.

awaited Macready had he rolled up to Mansion House to talk about a truce unaccompanied except by armoured cars; but when he was accompanied by those whose credentials and good faith were established, discussion was possible.

Midleton evidently enjoyed his role as intermediary, despite the fact that he was ill-used by the cabinet which kept him waiting round in London, whence he had gone to obtain cabinet consent to the two conditions. The first was readily conceded—the cabinet agreed to direct negotiations with De Valera, even if Craig declined to be a party to negotiations. The second proved more difficult, and Midleton was told by the Prime Minister that the cabinet would not concede a truce with both sides relinquishing their arms. Thereupon the persistent Midleton threatened the breakdown of all negotiations: he said it was useless for him to return to Ireland without the promise of a truce, for unionist members would not attend the conference; and he warned the Prime Minister that 'our military authorities, apart from being suspected by the rebels, could not hold their troops if, as I fully suspect, in the absence of a truce, outrages continued'.[71] Lloyd George, who had been kept fully informed of the Mansion House conference by telegrams from the Irish Office,[72] could hardly afford such an immediate breakdown of negotiations; and since one of the main factors in causing the British government to open negotiations was that the Irish situation was getting out of hand, it is reasonable to suppose that Midleton's warnings swayed Lloyd George. At any rate, he was convinced and without recalling the cabinet 'sat down and wrote me a letter conceding the point'.[73] That night Midleton returned to Dublin to negotiate the terms of the truce. On 8 July he and his friends did the ground work acting at first as intermediaries between Mansion House and the army's headquarters who gave them precise instructions, but later Macready emerged from his headquarters which were protected by every conceivable device. In his motor he 'boldly came through the crowd' which had assembled in the morning, and 'was actually cheered, although his life had for months been in imminent danger', to deal directly with De Valera. The negotiations in which De Valera 'showed a business-like and

71. *Ibid.*, pp. 261–2; Midleton to Lloyd George, 7 July 1921, B.L., F/38/1/19.
72. See e.g. B.L., F/19/5/10, 11.
73. Midleton, *Records and Reactions*, p. 262.

reasonable spirit in regard to all the military details' led to the truce which was declared on 11 July.[74] It was obscure on some points and there were to be many alleged and actual breaches, but it was a fact and enabled negotiations to begin.

There was a third way in which Midletonites assisted the negotiations. Their willingness to work for a wide settlement enabled the British government to open and continue negotiations with Sinn Fein.

Midletonites did not, of course, force the government to contact Sinn Fein. The reasons that the government acted decisively in June 1921 were a matter of time and timing. By the summer of 1921, being less distracted by the problems of industrial relations,[75] it had more time to devote to Ireland, just at a time when the Irish question was approaching its own crisis. It was faced with a decision of withdrawal or outright war: the first was out of the question; the latter though possible was inconceivable without first a serious attempt at compromise.[76] In these circumstances, the King's appeal for peace at the opening of the Northern Ireland parliament on 22 June provided an opportunity which struck the imagination of cabinet ministers. A nice combination of necessity and opportunity thus brought forth the invitation to De Valera in June 1921.[77]

Neither did the southern unionists dictate the government's course in the negotiations. The days when they could exert a decisive influence even on a unionist dominated coalition had

74. *Ibid.*; Midleton to Lloyd George, 9 July 1921, B.L., F/38/1/21.
75. See e.g. the changing preoccupations of Austen Chamberlain in his letters to his wife and sisters in 1921, B.U.L., AC 6/1/391–470, 5/1/186–221.
76. See e.g. the letter circulated to the cabinet from Sir J. Anderson to Greenwood, 18 June 1921, *ibid.*, AC 31/2/3. Anderson held that 'we have now reached a crucial stage'. He thought that an all out war was needed by June 1921 to crush the rebels militarily; but that such an effort would need to have the full backing of opinion in Britain, which up until then had had a demoralising effect upon the army and police in Ireland. He wanted the passive majority to be stimulated into active support of the government's policy in Ireland, and had, therefore, 'come round to the view that if the government decide to go in for martial law on Macready's lines, it is essential that they should first announce the extreme limit of concession to which they are prepared to go in the direction of dominion home rule . . . I know that what I suggest is directly against the hitherto fixed policy of the cabinet. It also goes beyond anything I have previously urged. I now put it forward purely as a matter of expediency. But I no longer entertain any doubt on the point. General Macready is, I understand, of the same opinion, though I don't know whether he will think it right to say so. . . .'
77. Cabinet minutes, 24 June 1921, P.R.O., Cab. 23/26.

passed, largely because of changes in the personnel and nature of the coalition leadership. By the middle of 1921 southern unionist sympathisers such as Long and Lansdowne were no longer in the cabinet and the coalition was led by men such as Lloyd George and Austen Chamberlain who in March 1921 had succeeded Law as Lord Privy Seal and leader of the unionist party in the House of Commons. Despite appearances, Lloyd George and Chamberlain had much in common. Both were wont to think in terms of broad tendencies rather than in terms of a detailed adjustment of all the various interests involved in a particular problem; and neither had ever seen the Irish question in terms of Irish minorities. Lloyd George had never shown himself sympathetic to the Irish minorities,[78] and his view that all issues were capable of settlement by himself in broad terms is well known. What is less well realised is that Chamberlain was of a similar turn of mind. He too had a tendency to think that problems could be solved if not by a wave of the hand, certainly by the wave of large slogans. This was especially true of his attitude towards Irish affairs. He had long seen the Irish question in terms of the empire and had long thought that it was capable of solution in terms of federalism but he had never worked out a scheme to provide even the basis of discussion; indeed he saw little need to do so, for once the idea of federalism was generally accepted all problems would be solved.[79] Both he and Lloyd George could be decisive and adroit politicians when acting upon their large ideas.[80] Moreover, tendencies in British politics—the changing nature of issues facing parliament and the influx of new, inexperienced men into the House of Commons, adroitly exploited by the government[81]— allowed these leaders to dominate and their views to prevail, especially when developments in Ireland had produced a situation eminently susceptible to talk in large terms. The result was that

78. See e.g. *Parl. Deb.*, 4 ser., clxxvi, 26 June 1907, col. 1421.
79. See e.g. A. Chamberlain to Lansdowne, 29 Oct., 11 Dec. 1913, B.U.L., AC 11/1/46, 55.
80. For an example of Chamberlain's decisiveness when faced with the prospect of loss of office, see him asking his brother, Neville (13 Nov. 1921, B.U.L., AC 32/1/2), to 'see that Birmingham is fully represented by good men' at the Liverpool conference of the National Unionist Association, where the government's Irish policy was expected to come in for fierce criticism.
81. See e.g. Dawson to I.U.A., 17 Feb. 1920, P.R.O.N.I., D 989A/9/20, and E. E. Wild to Chamberlain, 24 Nov. 1921, B.U.L., AC 31/3/33.

British policy towards Ireland had little room to consider sectional interests in a matter of such wide and vital importance. The government reckoned that an Irish settlement was necessary to solve a crisis in British civilisation and that only the broadest limitations to a settlement could be considered, viz., the Crown and the empire. To men of expansive ideas, the views of southern unionists were of little importance.

Despite all this, the attitude of the A.P.L. remained important to the government. Firstly, the Midletonites provided that necessary bridge by which the preliminaries to negotiations were settled. Secondly, their attitude enabled the government to attempt a settlement without fear of significant opposition. The point is a shade negative, but it is important. In the past the active opposition of southern unionists had prevented the unionist party from compromising on the union, and had been one of the obstacles facing Chamberlain's 'plans' for a federal solution to the Irish question. Despite the changing condition of British politics, the elements of southern unionist influence remained, especially its strength in the House of Lords, as did a lively recognition of that influence in the minds of ministers.[82] Thus a united southern unionist opposition could have been a powerful deterrent to too sweeping government initiatives on Ireland. However, the division of southern unionist opinion, and the willingness of some southern unionists to work for a settlement which ministers exploited, gave the government virtually a free hand to carry out its Irish policy. The government was able to forestall and discount the opposition of the I.U.A. and its supporters, especially since the support of some southern unionists for home rule weakened the unionism of their older supporters of the Walter Long type.[83]

82. See below, pp. 261 n. 127, 263–5, 270.

83. See e.g. Long's memorandum on Ireland and the problems of a settlement, 26 Sept. 1920, B.L., F/34/1/46. 'The Irish position has no doubt become extremely difficult in many respects; but it is at all events easier in one, namely, the undoubted fact that all the old political difficulties have disappeared. If I may illustrate this by my own case, I would say that in the old days I felt bound by the just demand of the unionists in Ireland, north and south, to be protected by England against the nationalists. . . . I also believed that the granting of home rule would mean a real danger to the United Kingdom from the naval and military point of view. This now is universally conceded . . . [and] . . . The first of these difficulties has disappeared, as the unionists of the south have abandoned their old position, and are now demanding—though in somewhat vague terms—self-government for their country; and Ulster is fully satisfied with the provisions made for her in our bill.'

Moreover, the role that some Midletonites played in bringing about negotiations, and the split, prevented the A.P.L. from asserting itself effectively and from freely criticising the government, even though there was reason to be dissatisfied with the progress of the discussions.

It was sadly ironic. The lack of southern unionist opposition enabled the government to indulge its Irish policy, and to do so with little or no regard for the interests or views of southern unionists of any complexion. Though the Midletonites were consulted in the course of the treaty and constitution negotiations, the treaty contained few of the provisions that they had requested, and the constitution of the Irish Free State did not give them what they had hoped for. It is possible to regard the government's attitude to southern unionists in a very cynical light. In pursuit of their larger object, ministers used the Midletonites to further government policy, and then threw them aside. This is not wholly true. There are signs that ministers felt some responsibility for the southern minority, and regarded their Irish policy as the one calculated to serve best the minority's long-term interests. However, that concern had only a marginal influence on the British representatives to the conferences with Sinn Fein, and they were careless of the detailed points on which southern unionists sought reassurance. A review of the negotiations in 1921 and 1922 not only demonstrates the role of southern unionists; it also shows that the government, while wary of their influence, paid little attention to their views and fears, and that when it consulted them it did so as much for tactical reasons as out of genuine concern for the plight of the minority.

FIVE

From the very beginning it was clear that the government intended to keep a tight rein on the negotiations, regarding the Crown and empire as the paramount objectives to be safeguarded.[84] Having allowed Midleton to complete the preliminaries, it proceeded to disregard the views of southern unionists. Straight away, Chamberlain was able to handle hostile critics.

84. For the course of the negotiations, see F. Pakenham, *Peace by Ordeal . . . the Negotiation and Signature of the Anglo-Irish Treaty, 1921* (1935, New English Library, Mentor, ed. 1967).

One such critic, Howell Arthur Gwynne of the *Morning Post* who was sympathetic to unionists of the I.U.A., opposed negotiations and demanded martial law in the twenty-six counties. He wrote that he intended 'to fight with all heart and strength to prevent Ireland being given the means towards independence and to help all I can to save our loyal fellow subjects now under the Sinn Fein harrow from further outrage and murder' and to 'plead with you for the loyalists of the south and west of Ireland'.[85] The split enabled Chamberlain to rout such critics and force them to destroy their own case. His reply begged Gwynne 'to remember that those unionists are by no means unanimous in support of your views. You speak as if southern unionist opinion were unanimous. I have the best reasons for knowing that they are not [*sic*]. There are many who would go greater lengths than the government in their anxiety to secure peace at almost any price'.[86] This line of defence, or attack, caught the sympathisers of the I.U.A. on the wrong foot. In order to meet it the southern unionist case became weaker: Gwynne was forced to discredit these so-called southern unionists and to urge Chamberlain that

the attitude of the southern unionists should not govern you in your action, partly because they are not free agents and act under terror and also because the question is much bigger than the safety of the southern unionists—it is the safety and welfare of the kingdom.[87]

This unfortunate response enabled Chamberlain to reply triumphantly: 'I quite agree that the opinion of the southern unionists cannot be decisive or even a principal factor in the decision which lies before the country.'[88]

The course of the negotiations made it perfectly clear that the southern unionists were neither a decisive nor principal factor in the government's view. Its attitude towards the Midletonites was governed almost entirely by tactical considerations. The critics of the government's policy could be disregarded for they were without leaders; and (playing on the undoubted faith that Midleton and his friends had in pledges made by the government

85. H. A. Gwynne to A. Chamberlain, 23 July 1921, B.U.L., AC 31/3/5.
86. Chamberlain to Gwynne, 25 July 1921, *ibid.*, AC 31/3/4.
87. Gwynne to Chamberlain, 27 July 1921, *ibid.*, AC 31/3/3.
88. Chamberlain to Gwynne, 28 July 1921, *ibid.*, AC 31/3/2.

at times when ministers had been too preoccupied to consider Irish problems themselves and had been quite willing to allow others, particularly the southern unionists in the convention, to handle them) the government not only disregarded the A.P.L.'s view of negotiations but also handled the Midletonites in such a way as to ensure that the opponents of government policy remained without leadership. Ministers consulted the A.P.L. at critical moments, holding out promises of guarantees; and they ensured that the safeguards for southern unionists contained in the treaty and the constitution, plus promises, though not sufficient to satisfy southern unionists, were sufficient to make it difficult for the A.P.L. to oppose the settlement with any vigour or any hope of success.

Southern unionists were themselves partly responsible for this failure to achieve adequate guarantees in the treaty. The unionists of the A.P.L. were insufficiently assertive. Having negotiated the truce, they expected that negotiations would be speedy and would concern the safeguards they had been promised for some time and which had been included in the 1920 act. It soon became clear that neither of these conditions would be met. Instead of swiftly concluding negotiations, as Kitchener had done at Vereeniging, talks were allowed to drag on, and outrages again occurred. The extent of violations of the truce should not be exaggerated, but there can be no denying that Sinn Fein was reasserting itself in some areas, much to the distress of southern loyalists. Such developments were made all the more unbearable because the drift of negotiations was towards far larger concessions than many Midletonites had considered possible, and it seemed that the 1920 safeguards for minorities would be whittled away. By October Midletonites as well as unionists of the I.U.A. were sorely distressed.[89]

Their response to this deteriorating situation was to place themselves at the government's mercy. In the first place, they refused to approach De Valera directly about the situation and the insertion of safeguards. When Chamberlain told Midleton that he and his friends, having been called in council by De Valera, had a perfect right to approach the Irish leader, Midleton reminded

89. Midleton, *Records and Reactions,* pp. 262–3; and letters from Desart, 25, 30 Sept. 1921, Mayo, 30 Sept., and Longfield, 22 Oct.. P.R.O., 30/67/46, ff. 2723–6, 2727–9, 2735–6, 2769.

him of the government's pledges and retorted that it was for the government, before making any settlement, to desire De Valera to come to terms with the minority, and that any suggestions the government should make as to the future of Ireland should be made dependent upon his doing so. Moreover, it would be difficult to hold unionists together, for some would feel deserted if Midleton and his friends approached De Valera for a settlement without the intervention of the government. Midleton told Chamberlain that 'any action by us must be part of our general contention that we had yielded throughout to *force majeure* in the question of the giving up of the union'.[90] Secondly, they did not press for direct and full representation when in October discussions really became earnest. Then a high-powered Sinn Fein delegation headed by Griffith and Michael Collins came over to London for a conference with an equally high-powered British government delegation. Southern unionists were divided over the question of representation at this conference, due to hold its first meeting on 11 October. In a letter to *The Times* on 5 October, Bernard, now Provost of Trinity College, Dublin, urged with a great deal of foresight that southern unionists should be represented on two grounds: that certain irrevocable decisions might be arrived at in the conference, which could affect southern unionists, without giving them an opportunity to put the case for and against; and that, since the conference was not one between two governments, it would be quite open for De Valera to say that he or his nominees attended the conference as representatives of southern Ireland, which included southern unionists, if no southern unionist representatives were present.[91] Others disagreed, thinking that southern unionist representation would be anomalous, and preferring a concurrent conference or a separate conference after the government and Sinn Fein representatives had agreed upon essentials. Some went further and said that southern unionists could do themselves more harm than good by seeking representation by the grace of the British government. They argued that in the conference to sit on 11 October the question to be discussed between avowed republicans and the British government would be as to whether the republicans become loyal subjects on the

90. Midleton's memorandum on 'Southern unionists and the conference', n.d. but *c.* 11 Oct. 1921, P.R.O., 30/67/46, ff. 2763–6.
91. *The Times,* 5 Oct. 1921.

terms offered to them by the British government, and in this discussion the presence of southern unionists would seem out of place; but once this question was settled and the general conditions agreed upon, it would lead to a discussion of the final terms to be granted to Ireland within the empire. 'Then southern unionists would have a genuine place within the conference and . . . their assistance would be asked for on account of their known financial and commercial abilities.'[92]

Instead, therefore, of asserting themselves, southern unionists contented themselves with protesting to the government and accepting a government suggestion to ensure that their views would be available to the conference. On 7 October, Midleton and Lord Wicklow tried to see the Prime Minister: he was not available and so they put their views to Edward Grigg, the most devoted of Lloyd George's private secretaries.[93] Midleton was particularly distressed for he felt 'he carried a very grave responsibility for the part he has played in getting southern unionists to abide by the consequences of negotiations with Sinn Fein' and 'went on to a long diatribe about "pledges" '. He reckoned that the government had gone to indefensible lengths in attempting to meet Sinn Fein and demanded two things. First, he demanded reassurances on the issue of sovereignty, the question of a separate territorial force for Ireland, and the question of pledges, particularly regarding taxation and the composition of the second chamber. Secondly, Midleton demanded that southern unionists should be heard during the conference on all questions affecting the security of minorities and the powers given under the 1920 act before any concessions in advance of that act were given. Grigg was not exactly tactful, telling Midleton that the government could not go to war again save on a vital issue such as the empire, but the government wanted to avoid the open hostility of the Midletonite section, and thus, in view of what Midleton said, Grigg sent him along to Chamberlain. The unionist leader was out, but eventually, on 10 October, he met Midleton.

92. Thompson reporting the views of members of the A.P.L. to Midleton, 4 Oct. 1921, P.R.O., 30/67/46, ff. 2739–42.
93. Grigg to A. Chamberlain, 7 Oct. 1921, B.U.L., AC 31/2/44. Ralph Francis Howard, 7th Earl of Wicklow (1877–1946); ed. Eton and R.M.C., Sandhurst; served with Life Guards in South African war; lt-col., South Irish Horse, 1909–22, serving in 1914–18 war; Irish representative peer, 1905–46; senator, Irish Free State, 1921–8; Shelton Abbey, Arklow, Co. Wicklow.

Midleton repeated what he said to Grigg, stressing the British government's responsibility towards southern unionists, and Chamberlain 'undertook to report very earnestly' to the Prime Minister his views.[94] There is, indeed, something pitiable about southern unionist reliance upon the government's good-will. At about the same time as Midleton was putting forward his views, the Protestant Archbishop of Dublin, John A. Fitzgerald Gregg, was pressing for some southern unionist representation at the talks and urging the maintenance of the safeguards contained in the 1920 act: he asked for special consideration for them, not only because they were a politically unrepresented minority, whose 'stake in the country is substantial to a degree altogether out of proportion to their numbers', but also because they were British citizens loyal in peace and war.[95]

Despite this lack of assertiveness, they remained a significant force. Though it had no intention of allowing southern unionists to interfere with the negotiations, the government could not ignore their appeals. Stressing the difficulty of admitting to the conference the spokesmen of bodies other than those officially entitled to speak for the electorate, the British representatives to the conference decided, after discussion on 10 October, upon an arrangement convenient to the government. Midleton and the archbishop were told that 'the Prime Minister would certainly be glad to receive a properly constituted delegation of southern Ireland unionists before any final settlement is arrived at'.[96]

This proposal was accepted. Midleton immediately took steps to arrange for a delegation.[97] He had hoped to consult the I.U.A. and make it as representative as possible, but was discouraged by Bernard and Oranmore,[98] with the result that the delegation consisted of associates of the A.P.L.: Midleton (representing peers and landowners), Bernard (church and education), and

94. Midleton's memorandum on 'Southern unionists and the conference'.
95. J. Dublin to Lloyd George, 8 Oct. 1921, B.L., F/38/1/22.
96. Conclusion of a meeting (the first) of the British representatives to the conference with the Sinn Fein delegation, held at 10 Downing Street, S.W., on Monday, 10 Oct., 1921, at 5 p.m., B.U.L., AC 31/6/1; Lloyd George to Dublin, 11 Oct. 1921, B.L., F/38/1/22.
97. Midleton's memorandum on 'Southern unionists and the conference'; Dublin to Midleton, 13 Oct. 1921, P.R.O., 30/67/46, f. 2753; Midleton to Lloyd George, 12 Oct. 1921, and Dublin to Lloyd George, 20 Oct. 1921, B.L., F/38/1/22.
98. Oranmore and Bernard to Midleton, 13 Oct. 1921, P.R.O., 30/67/46, ff. 2755–5B, 2756–7.

Jameson (business). They were repudiated by the I.U.A.,[99] and came to be regarded as 'representative southern unionists . . . rather than representatives of the southern unionists'.[100] They were to be available for conference with the government if required, and intended to insist upon six chief points, 'with unfaltering resolution'.[101]

Midleton need not have hurried. Having momentarily satisfied and occupied the Midletonites, the government was able to get on with the talks with little thought of the southern unionists. It was only when a critical point was reached in November that Midleton's delegation was consulted. At that time opposition to the government's Irish policy was mounting, and it was based largely upon the position of southern loyalists and rumours of the government's intention to 'persuade' Ulster to enter an all-Ireland parliament. The unionist members of the government feared a crisis, for it was possible that opposition to the government's policy would show itself in an adverse vote at the annual conference of the National Unionist Association to be held at Liverpool between 17 and 20 November.[102] The government took energetic steps to counter this opposition, and in doing so made use of the southern unionists. One part of the plan was to use the position of southern loyalists to bring moral pressure to

99. Resolution of the standing committee of the I.U.A., *Dublin Daily Express*, 27 Oct. 1921.

100. Quoted in O'Sullivan, *Irish Free State and its Senate*, p. 75. Since these were A.P.L. unionists, who kept in touch with the executive committee of the League—they explained the proceedings to the committee on 23 November and 12 December, O'Sullivan is incorrect in saying (p. 75) that 'southern unionists were not organised in a political sense'. However, the split in southern unionist ranks did affect the position of Midleton and his associates. That they were regarded as 'representative southern unionists' by the Irish negotiators was significant; as was the fact that in 1922 they stated 'quite clearly [to the Irish negotiators] that they had no definite mandate from any particular body, and were simply there as fairly representative of a class' (p. 85).

101. Midleton's memorandum on 'Southern unionists and the conference'. The six points were: that any military force should be an imperial force raised in concert with the two governments of Ireland, and not a local force raised by the governments separately one against the other; that the Senate must be maintained on approximately its present lines; that freedom of religion and religious bodies should be secured; that income tax should be restricted to Irish possessions; that the clause from the American constitution preventing discrimination against any class or creed should be included in the Irish constitution; the settlement of land purchase. Bernard included a seventh: the security and finance of Trinity College.

102. Pakenham, *Peace by Ordeal*, pp. 173-4, 185-8.

bear upon the Ulstermen. Lloyd George appeared to have accepted the A.P.L. viewpoint when, appealing in vain to Craig on 14 November to accept a parliament for all Ireland, he asked him to abandon the idea of two parliaments for Ireland on four grounds: the well-being of the empire, of Great Britain, and of Ireland, and for the sake of minorities in the north and south. 'In both parts of Ireland', he wrote,

there are considerable communities cut off from the majority of those to whom they are bound by faith, tradition and natural affinity. The majority in southern Ireland have a strong sense of responsibility for their co-religionists in the six counties. The minority there have an equal interest in your sympathy and support.[103]

Evidently another part of the government's plan to frustrate its opponents was to keep the Midletonites in line. The opposition could be handled as long as it remained leaderless. The government determined that it would, for on 11 November the Prime Minister invited the southern unionist delegation to meet the British representatives on the fifteenth.[104]

The meeting took place as arranged, Midleton, Bernard and Jameson representing southern unionism.[105] It was superbly handled by Lloyd George, but completely mishandled by the southern unionists. Lloyd George gave a full account of the negotiations, emphasising those aspects, particularly the Ulster difficulty, likely to appeal to the southern unionists. The latters' handling of the meeting was less happy. Whatever may be said in mitigation (the pressure of events and the disconcerting aspect of being confronted with such skilled and experienced negotiators as undoubtedly the British representatives were), the fact remains that the southern unionists missed their opportunity. Allowed free rein to state their case to the British negotiators

103. Copy of the letter to Craig in B.U.L., AC 30/3/26.

104. Note by Tom Jones, 11 Nov. 1921, *ibid.,* AC 30/3/23.

105. The following account is based upon a cabinet paper, 'Conclusions of a meeting of representatives of the southern unionists with the British representatives to the conference with Sinn Fein delegation, held at 10, Downing Street, S.W. on Tuesday, 15th November 1921 at 11.30 a.m.', copy in B.U.L., AC 31/6/16; and Bernard's memorandum of the same meeting, 15 Nov. 1921, B.M., Add. MS 52781, ff. 33–4. The British representatives were Lloyd George, Chamberlain, Sir Laming Worthington-Evans (War), Winston Churchill (Colonies) and Greenwood (Ireland).

anxious for support, they stated only part of it. Midleton confined his remarks to stating his objections to an Irish territorial force on the grounds of principle and cost, and expressing the hope that 'any armed forces permitted would have been under the British War Office'. Bernard asked for security for church property and educational and university institutions, and reiterated his objections to partition; while Jameson confined himself to breaches of the truce and to asking the government to put pressure on the Sinn Fein delegates to ensure its better observance. While Bernard called attention to the importance of securing in any settlement protection for the minority in southern Ireland on the lines of certain clauses in the 1920 act, issues such as land purchase, double taxation and the composition and powers of the second chamber were not raised in detail, and the government was given an easy passage. Lloyd George, while giving southern unionists a free rein, did not encourage them to raise issues and was therefore able to win over the delegation. He met Midleton's objections to an Irish territorial force by playing down its size and its role—he said it was necessary to reinforce the police; and was able to assure Bernard that the government was willing to work for security for church property and educational and university institutions, and that Sinn Fein would probably be willing to grant such security, since they had already accepted the need for a second chamber. He was thus able to give the southern unionists the impression that he was working for their interests, and even suggested that the deputation should meet the Sinn Fein representatives to discuss the whole position, including breaches of the truce. On reflection, it is clear that this suggestion could be interpreted to mean that the British government was washing its hands of the southern unionists and telling them that it was up to them to make the best terms with Sinn Fein on their own. But this interpretation does not seem to have occurred to the deputation which 'accepted this suggestion and the secretary was instructed to make the necessary arrangements'.

The delegation met Griffith on 16 November at 20 Cavendish Square for 'an informal discussion as to certain matters about which southern loyalists were anxious' in an optimistic spirit, and flattered by the attention given to them in the press.[106] Griffith,

---

106. This account is based upon a memorandum by Bernard, B.M., Add. MS 52781, f. 36. Bernard also kept press cuttings from *The Times*, 16 Nov. 1921.

who was sympathetic to the Anglo-Irish case,[107] agreed that land purchase should be cleared out of the way before an Irish government was set up; said he was in favour of a second chamber; promised he would consult loyalists before an agreement on taxation was reached; and said he would not object to clauses 5 and 64 of the 1920 act which forbade religious discrimination and the transfer of church property; and promised protection of the independence of universities and provision for university finance. Again, though, the southern unionists had mishandled and misjudged the situation: they had, it is true, obtained promises from Griffith to respect their wishes; but they had obtained no promise that these safeguards would be embodied in an agreement between the government and Sinn Fein and had not even discussed the proposed safeguards properly. For example, the composition of the second chamber does not seem to have been adequately discussed, and the southern unionists were too ready to accept vague assurances. As Griffith told De Valera,

They strongly argued there should be a senate. I said I was in favour of a second chamber and I believed my colleagues would be. If it comes to a point, when we were erecting the machinery I would propose that they be consulted as to the constitution of the senate. They said they were satisfied with this.[108]

If the southern unionists had misjudged and mishandled the situation, the government had not. Its manoeuvres kept the Midletonites on its side and a vote in favour of its Irish policy was passed at the Liverpool conference, despite strong efforts by die-hards to achieve an adverse vote.[109] The extent to which the government's consultation of the deputation was governed by tactics was underlined by events after the signing of the treaty, by which southern Ireland was to become a self-governing

107. A man of statesman-like breadth of vision, Griffith realised that a self-governing Ireland could exist only through the full and willing co-operation of all classes and creeds, and intended that memories of old wrongs and recent differences should be gradually effaced in the joint effort to rebuild the nation. Despite his work for the revival of the Irish language, he did not believe that unity should be achieved through the intense gaelicisation of English speaking Ireland, with the hegemony of the Gael as the ultimate ideal. He fully recognised the validity and essential Irishness of the Anglo-Irish tradition.

108. Quoted in O'Sullivan, *Irish Free State and its Senate*, p. 75.

109. Pakenham, *Peace by Ordeal*, pp. 185–8.

dominion within the empire under the style of the Irish Free
State.[110] Before publication its terms were communicated on 6
December to the southern unionists, who met government
representatives on the seventh.[111] Three points about the government's attitude are worth noting. In the first place, there were
many omissions as far as the southern unionists were concerned.
There was no provision for the completion of land purchase; no
indication as to the composition of the second chamber; no
safeguard against double taxation; and no provision for compensation for losses incurred in the recent unrest. Admittedly,
certain clauses of the treaty provided protection for church
property and some protection for universities; and compensation
for losses could possibly have come under article 5 requiring the
Irish Free State to contribute towards the public debt and war
pensions; but the nature of these provisions showed how little
thought the government had given to them. For instance, under
the 1920 act Trinity College was entitled to £30,000 per year
subsidy. This had not been secured under the treaty: when
Bernard pointed this out,

the Prime Minister, after reflection, admitted that he had not appreciated that point, for which he was sorry; but that he did not doubt that
the Sinn Fein majority would act in accordance with the repeated
promises which they had made to deal impartially with all classes and
creeds.[112]

110. The treaty applied formally to the whole of Ireland, but Northern Ireland
could, and did, request to be excluded from the Free State and retain its status
under the 1920 act. The Free State was to enjoy the same constitutional status as
Canada, with, for example, fiscal autonomy and the power to raise its own
military defence force. There was to be no Free State representation at Westminster but members of the Free State parliament were to take an oath of allegiance to the Crown. Britain was to remain, for the time being, responsible for
coastal defence, and was to be allowed to maintain naval establishments in certain
Irish ports.
111. L. Curtis to Midleton, 6 Dec. 1921, P.R.O., 30/67/48, f. 2819. O'Sullivan,
basing his account on information from Jameson (p. 76), says the meeting took
place on 6 December; but the contemporary documentary evidence relating to
the meeting says the seventh. These are: Bernard's [?] memorandum of the
meeting between southern unionists and the British representatives, 7 Dec. 1921,
B.M., Add. MS 52781, f. 38; conclusions of a meeting of the representatives of
the southern unionists with the British representatives to the conference with
Sinn Fein delegation, on Wednesday, 7 December 1921, at 2.30 p.m., S.F.B.
21st conclusions, copy in B.U.L., AC 31/6/21.
112. Bernard's memorandum, 7 Dec. 1921.

In the second place, the government was anxious to get the support of southern unionists for the treaty. Thus it was that this meeting was arranged between ministers and Midletonites. During the meeting Lloyd George not only mentioned the impossibility of altering the treaty, but was also at great pains to urge its advantages and to flatteringly acknowledge the British representatives' debt to the deputation's advice during the negotiations. So keen was the government to secure southern unionist support that, in the indignant words of Midleton,

Curzon, who was leader of the House of Lords, and who, although he had obtained admission there by favour of the Irish peers, now left hopelessly in the lurch, actually invited me to act with John Morley, a life-long home ruler, as mover and seconder of the 'settlement', when it was brought forward in the House of Lords.[113]

Midleton refused, and in order to indicate the extent of the support for the treaty among southern loyalists, Curzon telegraphed to Dunraven, who accepted.[114]

In the third place, if the government could not get the ungrudging support of the Midletonites, it was determined to avert their opposition. It did so by stressing their responsibility for the negotiations and for certain omissions, and by producing a tactful and carefully worded letter from Arthur Griffith—the product of an interchange between Lloyd George and Griffith—which promised full security for minority interests.[115] When Midleton complained that the government had given too many concessions and that the treaty included little protection for the interests of southern unionists, Lloyd George had his answer ready. There were safeguards for southern unionists on the only issues which had been raised in previous conferences between the British representatives and the southern unionist delegation: religious and educational rights were amply safeguarded in article 16; and article 2 provided for an appeal to the Privy Council if the treaty were violated. On the other hand, in answer

113. Midleton, *Records and Reactions*, p. 264.
114. Dunraven, *Past Times and Pastimes*, ii. p. 82.
115. Lloyd George to Griffith, 2 Dec. 1921, Griffith to Lloyd George, 4, 6 Dec. 1921, B.L., F/21/1/2–4. It appears that Lloyd George asked for a more tactfully worded letter concerning southern unionists. The letter was published in *The Times*, 8 Dec. 1921.

to Midleton's complaint that there was no provision for compensation for destroyed property, the completion of land purchase, or double income tax, Lloyd George retorted that these issues had not been raised at previous interviews. It was no help for the southern unionists to point out that the issues had been raised in their interview with Griffith, for Lloyd George was able to say as to other points 'not raised at previous interviews the unionists should obtain from the Sinn Fein representatives for themselves the securities they desired in the Irish constitution'. The government would of course give southern unionists its good offices, but would 'in no case do anything which looked like interference with the right of the Irish government to settle their own affairs',[116] and which would prejudice the success of the treaty. Thus the southern unionists were again handed over to Griffith, whom they saw on the afternoon of 7 December and who evidently reiterated the promises contained in his letter.[117]

SIX

Despite the failures of 1921, southern unionism remained a significant factor in discussions of the Irish question. The last chapter in the history of the union and the Irish question in British politics was the negotiations in 1922 over the constitution of the Irish Free State, and again, as long as they wished to be, southern unionists were a force to be reckoned with.

Though they resented its omissions, Midleton's followers in parliament had not voted against the treaty in December. This was not because they had given up the ghost, but because they were determined to make good the omissions, particularly when it came to framing the constitution of the Free State. What encouraged them to further action was Griffith's letter holding out the hope that southern unionists would not be reduced to political impotence in the new state. The letter promised southern unionists their 'full share of representation in the first chamber of the Irish parliament' and that they would be consulted as to the constitution of the upper chamber where their interests would be

116. S.F.B. 21st conclusions, 7 Dec. 1921.
117. O'Sullivan, *Irish Free State and its Senate*, p. 76.

'duly represented'. Moreover, Griffith thought that southern unionists would be able to play a large part in the new state, for he said:

that we desire to secure the willing co-operation of unionists in common with all other sections of the Irish nation in raising the structure and shaping the destiny of the Irish Free State. We look for their assistance in the same spirit of understanding and good-will which we ourselves will show towards their traditions and interests.[118]

Such promises encouraged unionists of the A.P.L. to continue political action through Midleton in 1922.[119]

They had high hopes of the provisional government of the Free State set up on 14 January 1922 under article 17 of the treaty and headed in effect by Collins, the chairman, and Griffith, who on 10 January had succeeded De Valera as President of the Dail. On several occasions they put their views to the new Irish ministers on a wide range of issues, the most important of which was the proposed constitution.[120] At the beginning of the year they were quite optimistic about achieving a satisfactory settlement, but as the Irish situation deteriorated with the ever-widening rift between the pro- and anti-treaty parties, they found the outlook less promising. In April and May Midleton was in close touch with the provisional government over the proposed constitution of the Free State. On 28 and 29 April he and Jameson had two interviews with Darrell Figgis, a prominent member of the standing committee of Sinn Fein and deputy chairman of the committee appointed by the provisional government to draft the constitution. In a conversation lasting several hours, Figgis outlined a scheme and had its many 'noteworthy defects' pointed out

118. *The Times*, 8 Dec. 1921.
119. R. G. K. Leonard to Midleton, 12 Dec. 1921, enclosing a memorandum on the treaty and prospects reflecting the views of the Dublin committee of the A.P.L. (which had met that day to hear Bernard's comments on the situation), P.R.O., 30/67/48, ff. 2836–9.
120. For instance, in February Midleton saw Griffith, who received his suggestions 'very warmly' (Midleton to Bernard, 27 Feb. 1922, B. M., Add. MS 52781, f. 105); and on 13 and 14 March he and Jameson met Griffith, Duggan, Hogan and O'Higgins—Collins joined them on the fourteenth (memorandum of meeting, P.R.O., 30/67/49, ff. 2891–6). The Irish Landowners Convention also kept the provisional government informed of its views on the speedy completion of land purchase.

to him. He was not very accommodating,[121] and although Midleton was able to follow up his criticisms in correspondence,[122] he was scarcely optimistic. On 30 April, he wrote to the King that he and Jameson had noticed 'a considerable hardening of the ministers in their attitude as compared to three months ago', and that they feared that serious difficulties would arise on the questions of the office of Governor-General, the Crown's representative in Ireland, and 'securing the minority against an unfettered democracy'.[123]

In these circumstances, Midletonites came to rely once more on the help of the British government to secure satisfactory safeguards. Despite Lloyd George's disclaimer of 7 December, they still thought that the British government had a moral obligation to assist in the settlement of outstanding issues, in view of past pledges and the position of the new Irish government. Though he recognised it was sensible to discuss the situation with Griffith, Midleton did not think it fair to Griffith and the new government to put on them the responsibility for points which the British government had undertaken to settle before any transfer of powers was made.[124] Thus southern unionists were careful to put their views before the British government, and did so with increased urgency, as they found the Irish situation deteriorating and the constitution being developed in an unsatisfactory manner.[125]

This persistence made southern unionism a real factor in the constitution negotiations that took place between representatives of the British and provisional governments in London at the end of May and the beginning of June. These discussions, concerned to bring the draft Free State constitution into line with the spirit and letter of the treaty, provided a real chance for the A.P.L. to

121. Memorandum of meeting with Figgis, 28 and 29 April 1922, P.R.O., 30/67/50, ff. 2935-40.

122. *Ibid.,* ff. 2960, 2969, 2976.

123. Midleton to H.M., 30 Apr. 1922, *ibid.,* ff. 2943-6. Midleton kept in close touch with the Irish ministers largely through the good offices of A. Belton, an investment banker and broker with offices in London, who had kept him informed of Sinn Fein attitudes in the previous year.

124. Midleton to Churchill, 16 Jan. 1922, P.R.O., 30/67/49, ff. 2873-4.

125. Cabinet minutes, 5 Apr., 10 May 1922, P.R.O., Cab. 23/30; Midleton to H.M., 30 Apr. 1922, P.R.O., 30/67/50, ff. 2943-6; Midleton to Churchill, 25 May, enclosing a letter from Bernard, *ibid.,* ff. 2977-8.

secure, with the aid of the British government, formal safeguards and to justify the position it had taken up. Again, the Midletonites were not entirely successful, though they did have some influence on the final form of the constitution.

That they did not achieve all they hoped was due mainly to the British government's attitude to the negotiations.[126] It had been increasingly embarrassed by developments in Ireland since the signing of the treaty. Apart from the fact of opposition to the treaty, particularly distressing had been the growth of disorder and its effects on loyalists, incidents on the Northern Ireland-Free State border, and then the electoral pact between the pro- and anti- treaty parties. Nevertheless, the British government felt that it could intervene again in Ireland only if a vital issue such as the Crown or empire were at stake and that all these incidents were minor points compared to the proposed constitution of the Free State. This was considered to be the keystone of the situation. Two things about it concerned the British government: the relations between Ireland and Great Britain, and the position of southern unionists.[127] The former was the crucial issue, because it could bring up again all the vital issues which had apparently been settled in the treaty negotiations. Should the constitution aim at establishing an independent republic, war and economic sanctions against the Free State were strong possibilities. But since the government had staked its reputation on an Irish settlement, it was determined to go to great lengths to fulfil the treaty and to use events such as the electoral pact as bargaining

126. The following account of the negotiations over the constitution is largely based upon a number of cabinet papers: the conclusions of meetings of the British representatives, B.U.L., AC 31/6/23–32, hereafter cited as S.F. (B); 'The record of the negotiations relative to the draft Irish constitution', compiled, it seems, by Churchill, *ibid.*, AC 30/2, hereafter cited as Constitution negotiations; and miscellaneous Irish papers contained in the Bernard, A. Chamberlain, Lloyd George and Midleton papers. Churchill's record of the constitution negotiations was based upon an impressive range of cabinet sources, most of which are also available in the P.R.O.

127. Churchill, at 23rd meeting of the British representatives, 26 May 1922, Constitution negotiations, B.U.L., AC 30/2/36. '. . . the constitution was the keystone of the situation. If it was a fair document, the British government could wink at the subterfuges indulged in by the provisional government. He was not sure that it would take so long to examine as Lord Birkenhead thought. The British government were only concerned with the relations between Ireland and this country and with the position of the southern unionists.' See also cabinet minutes, 16 May 1922, P.R.O., Cab. 23/30.

K

counters to persuade the provisional government to modify its proposals.[128]

On 27 May the draft constitution was presented to the British government. The product of a confused and difficult Irish political situation, the draft was considered unsatisfactory by British ministers, for it failed to give adequate weight to the vital concepts of Crown and empire. In fact, they said that the constitution proposed a thinly veneered republic 'with the King as lackey': the monarchy was stripped of all its powers; there was no appeal to the Privy Council; the proposed Irish parliament was to have the power to make treaties; there was no oath of allegiance.[129] As far as the British government was concerned, a grave situation had arisen. The empire was in danger; there was talk of a reversion to Crown colony government; and the next few days were spent in negotiations between representatives of the two governments in an attempt to alter the constitution to conform with the British view of the treaty. The position was complicated by outbreaks in Ulster,[130] but the British were not going to be outmanoeuvred on this point and determined to 'keep on the high ground of the treaty—the Crown, the empire'.[131] There Lloyd George considered the government 'unassailable', arguing that if the Free Staters 'insisted on a constitution which repudiated Crown and empire and practically set up a republic, we could carry the whole world with us in any action we took'.[132] This confidence not only enabled the British representatives to more or less present an ultimatum to Griffith,[133] but also enabled Lloyd

128. Lloyd George, 26 May, Constitution negotiations, B.U.L., AC 30/2, *passim.*

129. Meetings between some British and Irish representatives, 27 May 1922; and 24th meeting of the British signatories, 27 May 1922, *ibid.,* AC 30/2/46–67.

130. Cabinet and other British meetings, 30, 31 May, 1 June 1922, *ibid.,* AC 30/2/71–2, 75–7, 77–8; joint meeting of the provisional government of Ireland committee and the sub-committee on Ireland of the Committee for Imperial Defence, 1 June 1922, at the outset of which 'Churchill impressed on the meeting the need for the most scrupulous secrecy', *ibid.,* AC 30/2/79–82.

131. Lloyd George to Churchill, 8 June 1922, B.L., F/10/3/3.

132. *Ibid.*

133. Cabinet and other British meetings, 31 May, 1 June 1922, Constitution negotiations, B.U.L., AC 30/2/75–8; Lloyd George to Griffith, 1 June 1922, copy, *ibid.,* AC 30/2/78a–c. Lloyd George informed the Irish signatories in what respects the draft constitution of the Irish Free State was inconsistent with the treaty and stated that 'the British government and people are entitled to be expressly informed where Ireland stands in relation to the treaty and they are

George to temper a firm determination with judicious concession when he met the leaders of the Irish delegation on 1 June.[134] This combination apparently had its effect upon the Irish representatives. Having explained the reasons for the divergence between the treaty and constitution,[135] Griffith replied with a very conciliatory memorandum, conceding most points and narrowing differences on others.[136] Although it still left the position of the Crown and the Privy Council obscure, the reply was considered in general satisfactory and certainly no ground for breaking off negotiations.[137] The next few days were spent in clearing up these outstanding points and by 9 June an agreement, reasonably satisfactory to the British government, had been reached.[138]

Only then, when the government was virtually satisfied with the constitution, were southern unionists brought into the picture. At first sight, it might appear that the British government was beginning to show a more proper concern for southern unionist interests than it had done in 1921, but it can also be argued that its attitude had not changed. Knowing that the re-drafted constitution did not sufficiently safeguard southern unionists, the government tried to prevent them from becoming a centre of formidable opposition to its Irish policy. The main problem was to ensure the smooth passage through parliament of the bill embodying the constitution as agreed between the two governments.[139] Since southern unionists could interrupt that smooth passage and generally make life uncomfortable for the government, especially in the House of Lords, they were again brought into the discussions for largely tactical reasons. They were consulted, not so that the constitution could be modified to conform to their wishes, but so that the British government could ascertain

---

entitled to be informed at once . . . His Majesty's government must, therefore, press for an early and explicit declaration that the draft constitution will be amended so as to conform with the treaty in the several particulars in which as shown in the memorandum the present draft differs from it, and in particular for a clear answer to each of the following questions . . .'

134. Interview between Lloyd George and Griffith and Collins, asked for by the Irish leaders, 1 June 1922, *ibid.*, AC 30/2/83–7.

135. *Ibid.*

136. Griffith to Lloyd George, 2 June 1922, *ibid.*, AC 30/2/90–5.

137. Cabinet meeting, 2 June 1922, *ibid.*, AC 30/2/95.

138. *Ibid.*, AC 30/2/95–131, but especially cabinet meeting, 9 June 1922, *ibid.*, AC 30/2/122–31.

139. *Ibid.*

their views and secure a few concessions that while giving away
as little as possible would nevertheless undermine their opposition
to the settlement.

Thus on 29 May Churchill had been instructed to see Midleton
about the provisions in the draft constitution for the protection
of minorities.[140] Midleton was very critical of the provisions and
expressed himself forcibly. He said the constitution did not differ
materially from that outlined earlier by Figgis and that proportional representation and the 'travesty' of a Senate provided no
security for the minority. In fact, he concluded, 'The present
proposals form no basis for a settlement, and are a violation of
Mr Griffith's pledge'.[141] These observations on the representation
and protection of southern unionists were sent to the Irish
representatives as well as to the British,[142] but they were considered only after the British government was satisfied that the
rest of the constitution conformed to British ideas of the dignity
of Crown and empire. Only then were the southern unionists
properly brought into the discussions, and even then they
were not consulted on the constitution as a whole, only, as
promised earlier by Griffith, on those articles affecting the composition and relations of the two chambers of the proposed Irish
parliament. Such consultation was necessary not only to redeem
Griffith's pledges, but also because the British government thought
that 'it was most important to placate parliamentary opposition
in this country by including in the constitution adequate safeguards for the southern unionists'.[143]

The British representatives took energetic steps to forestall any
such opposition, and on 9 June Churchill was requested to
arrange a meeting between the southern unionists and the Irish
representatives.[144] Realising that the meeting would be a tricky
one, they tried to prepare the ground by briefing Griffith on the
position of the southern unionists. They warned him that they

140. Twenty-fifth meeting of the British representatives, (11 a.m.) 29 May
1922, *ibid.*, AC 30/2/69.
141. 'Conference on Ireland. Memorandum by Lord Midleton', S.F. (B) 58
(copy in P.R.O., 30/67/50, f. 2979–80). In particular Midleton objected to the
composition and limited delaying power of the proposed Senate.
142. Twenty-seventh meeting of the British representatives, (3.30 p.m.) 29
May 1922, Constitution negotiations, B.U.L., AC 30/2/70.
143. Twenty-eighth meeting of the British representatives, 9 June, *ibid.*, AC
30/2/129.
144. *Ibid.*

were 'honestly anxious about the parliamentary situation, unless southern unionist opinion was satisfied that it had been met reasonably as Mr Griffith had promised'; and they made specific suggestions for safeguarding the position of southern unionists under the constitution, based upon Midleton's earlier criticism of the draft and mainly relating to the power and composition of the second chamber.[145] This concern should not be misunderstood, however. The British representatives were in no way acting on behalf of the southern unionists or inclined to force concessions on the Irish. As far as they were concerned, it was up to Griffith and the southern unionists to reach agreement.

Meetings between the Irish negotiators and the southern unionists took place on 12, 13 and 14 June.[146] At the first meeting Griffith was accompanied by Kevin O'Higgins and Hugh Kennedy, and Collins joined them on the thirteenth. The southern unionist delegation of 1921 was now joined by a distinguished member of the House of Lords, Lord Donoughmore.[147] Churchill and Lionel Curtis, secretary to the British delegation, were also present. It was a difficult meeting on the twelfth. This was due in

145. Meeting between Churchill and A. Chamberlain and Griffith at Colonial Office 10 June 1922, *ibid.*, AC 30/2/131–6; and 29th meeting of the British representatives, 10 June 1922, *ibid.*, AC 30/2/137–9. Chamberlain suggested a reduction in the elective element in the first Senate and an increase in the numbers and length of tenure of the nominated element; that the period of delay should be increased above the 180 days in the draft; that the Senate should have the right to demand a referendum; the alteration of the provision that election to the Senate should be from men nominated by the lower chamber, since it would deprive minorities of the chance of voting for suitable candidates; and that the provision, that the lower chamber should dissolve only on a motion supported by a majority, be reconsidered.

146. This account is based upon: a record of the meetings between the Irish signatories and southern unionists, 12, 13 June 1922, Constitution negotiations, B.U.L., AC 30/2/158–67 (reproduced in Appendix C); and O'Sullivan, *Irish Free State and its Senate,* pp. 76–82 (based on O'Higgins's statements in the Dail debates). Donoughmore and Jameson also met, at Churchill's suggestion, Kennedy, O'Higgins and Curtis, after the large meeting on the twelfth; no details of this meeting appear to be available, but it is likely that it was concerned with drafting up heads of agreement which were discussed the next day. (Constitution negotiations, B.U.L., AC 30/2/164).

147. Richard Walter John Hely-Hutchinson, 6th Earl of Donoughmore (1875–1948); ed. Eton and Oxford; private sec. to Governor of Hong Kong, 1898–1900; Under-Sec. for War, 1903–5; member of London school board, 1903; chairman of committees and Deputy Speaker of House of Lords, 1911–31; P.C., 1918; chairman of special commission on Ceylon constitution, 1927–8; Grandmaster of Irish freemasons, 1913; member of Southern Ireland Senate, 1921; Knocklofty, Clonmel, Co. Tipperary.

part to events in Ireland since the treaty, especially the electoral
pact which had undermined southern unionist confidence in the
sincerity of Griffith and Collins;[148] and these natural difficulties
were increased, as Chamberlain had feared, by Midleton's
personality. At first he lived up to Chamberlain's description,
'one of the "sot" kind, without elasticity and difficult to do business
with'.[149] He complained that there was little point in taking part
in further discussions, because 'nothing he had said at previous
interviews appeared to have had any weight'. However, he was
eventually persuaded to take part by Churchill and his own
colleagues, notably Jameson. His colleagues living in Ireland took
a more flexible view of the situation, being prepared to accept
almost any concession in order to justify the position taken up
by the A.P.L. and anxious to avoid an open and fruitless conflict
with the existing powers in Ireland. Progress was difficult, but
owing to the energy of Churchill and the conciliatory spirit of
Griffith, discussion was kept going. These two tried to persuade
the southern unionists that new parties would be formed in the
new state so that 'loyalists' interests would have nothing to fear
in the future', but they were not satisfied with this general
assurance. Less optimistic than Churchill and Griffith about the
Irish situation, southern unionists feared above all else legalised
despoliation: Midleton believed that the provisional government
had to have money quickly and easily to satisfy men who wanted
work and land on their own terms. In these circumstances,
southern unionists demanded specific and permanent safeguards
against 'hasty legislative proposals at the expense of the 350,000
loyalists who will be practically unrepresented [in the lower
chamber] but who pay most of the taxes'.[150] In particular, they
demanded the establishment of a powerful and nominated second
chamber to offset their lack of representation in the lower
chamber, and wanted in effect to assert the supremacy of an
unrepresentative Senate over the elective chamber. As Bernard
said, 'They wanted a strong Senate in Ireland: they were apt to
pass resolutions first and repent afterwards'. Griffith readily
assented to a number of points, but since he had his own political
problems and had to be wary of jeopardising the whole treaty

148. Bernard to Midleton, 23 May 1922, B.M., Add. MS 52781, ff. 106–7.
149. A. Chamberlain to Hilda Chamberlain, 10 June 1922, B.U.L., AC 5/1/242.
150. Midleton to Lord Suirdale, 24 Nov. 1922, P.R.O., 30/67/52, ff. 3112–14.

position by making too many concessions to the minority point of view,[151] he resisted other, scarcely democratic, suggestions. In particular, he opposed demands that the Senate should be elected on a severely restricted franchise, based on a high property qualification; that it should be able to delay measures sent up by the lower chamber for one year; and that disputes between the two chambers should be resolved by joint sittings at which there should be joint voting. In this resistance he was fully supported by Churchill, for the British government agreed that within limits the elective chamber should be supreme.

Midleton was highly critical of Churchill's attitude. In discussion the latter had been quite scathing about the high claims made for the Irish Senate, particularly in respect of joint voting and the delaying power, the suspensory veto, and had kept referring to what would or would not be regarded as acceptable or desirable in English politics. After the first meeting Midleton took him severely to task for applying English criteria to the Irish situation, thereby deterring the Irish representatives from offering further concessions. In a letter on the thirteenth,[152] he urged Churchill to support the southern unionist demands for joint voting and a one year suspensory veto, arguing that there was no comparison between the political situations in England and Ireland:

. . . Ireland is a different proposition; the people are exceedingly ignorant, and as regards political organisation, they have had none of the experience which has been gained here in the last thirty-seven years. There has been no genuine political fighting in the south during that period.

This inexperience underlined the need for strong safeguards, for

There is now great intimidation. The Irish are morally cowards. It will be years before the force of an army numbered by tens of thousands is forgotten. Greatest extravagancies will probably be proposed and the proceedings in the Dail Eireann show you how the government are likely to have their hands forced. The fact that Griffith was indicted by a vote of censure while engaged in solemn conclave with you in London speaks for itself. For a generation to

151. O'Sullivan, *Irish Free State and its Senate,* p. 77.
152. Midleton to Churchill, 13 June 1922, P.R.O., 30/67/50, ff. 2981–2.

come, if Ireland is to be prosperous with a constitution of adult suffrage, the safeguards ought to be exceptionally strong.

Midleton's urgings were to no avail. The heads of agreement were drawn up at the second meeting, on 13 June, and finalised on the following day.[153] Of the ten provisions, six could be considered concessions to the southern unionist viewpoint. The size of the Senate was to be increased from 40 to 60 and two members were to come from each of the universities. A more restricted electorate for the Senate was conceded: only persons of 30 years and upwards were to vote in senate elections. The Senate was to be given the power to require a referendum; voting at the referendum to be by ballot and its decision final. The definition of money bills was to be decided by the Speaker, subject to an appeal to a committee of privileges to be drawn from both chambers, instead of being left to the Speaker's sole discretion. Concessions were also made on the question of the composition of the first Senate. The first but not any subsequent Senate was to be half nominated and half elected, the nominated element being chosen so as to represent minority and other interests and on the advice of certain interested bodies.[154] Finally, although southern unionists were not unanimous on this point, the constituency for elections to the Senate was to be the whole of the Free State, instead of the provinces.

This was as far as the Irish representatives would go to meet the southern unionist case. They would not give way on what southern unionists regarded as vital points to secure a strong Senate. In the first place, though willing to extend the Senate's suspensory veto from 180 to 270 days, the Irish would not concede the year demanded by Midleton. Secondly, while willing to concede joint debate in case of disagreement between the two chambers, they would not permit the joint vote asked for by the southern unionists who thought that a referendum on its own 'would be no protection if the majority wanted to despoil the

153. O'Higgins's notes on the conclusions of this meeting are reprinted in O'Sullivan, *Irish Free State and its Senate*, pp. 79–80, but there are copies of the heads of agreement in the Bernard and A. Chamberlain papers, B.M., Add. MS 52783, ff. 137–8, and B.U.L., AC 30/2/164–6 respectively.

154. This latter provision was not to be part of the constitution but to be embodied in a resolution of the new chamber.

property owners'. Thirdly, the request for open nomination or Senate candidates instead of nomination by the lower chamber was not conceded; though Griffith did suggest that one-third of the panel of 158 candidates for the 56 open seats should be nominated by the Senate. Lastly, there was the question of the composition of the Senates, other than the first. Midleton demanded a permanent and strong nominated and *ex-officio* element in all Senates, arguing that nomination in the first Senate was insufficient, for 'that was only a transitory provision; they wanted permanent provision'. But Griffith would not concede this point: the nominated element was to disappear gradually, one half to retire at the end of nine years, the other half after twelve years. His attitude on these points meant that only slight gains had been made over the 1914 act in respect of minority safeguards. That act had proposed a Senate of forty members, each serving a five year term: the first Senate was to have been nominated by the imperial government, but subsequent Senates were to have been elected, on the basis of proportional representation, by parliamentary electors in the four provinces as separate constituencies. The 1914 Senate was to have had no power over money bills, but disputes between the two chambers were to have been settled by their voting together at a joint session. The Free State Senate, as it emerged from the June negotiations, was not much different. It was larger, its electorate was more mature, and it had a suspensory veto; but the price of these improvements was a reduction by half of the nominated element of the first Senate and the loss of joint voting, a loss which offset the advantage to be gained from an enlarged Senate. In sum, apart from hollow victories in the convention and the 1920 act, five years of Midletonite agitation had achieved little by way of increased formal safeguards.

This realisation upset Midleton and his colleagues. As far as they were concerned, Griffith's refusals were more important than the concessions so engagingly made. They appear to have thought that the more limited their demands, the more likely they were to be conceded *in toto*: and expressed their dissatisfaction forcibly in a letter to the Colonial Secretary on 14 June.[155] No copy of this letter appears to be available (the one published in

155. Thirtieth meeting of the British signatories, 15 June 1922, Constitution negotiations, AC 30/2/171.

the *Irish Times* on 16 June was a revised version[156]), but the reception given by the British representatives to this 'very grace-less answer' illustrates the essentially unsympathetic attitude of the government to the claims of southern unionism. Ministers were very put out by the letter: Birkenhead, remarking that the answer was that no democracy in the world would have tolerated the Senate provided for in the 1920 act, thought that Churchill should tell them that they 'could very well go further and fare worse'. The annoyance also reflected the government's estimate of the power of the southern unionists. Although Churchill thought that 'it would no doubt help the provisional government that the southern unionists should be dissatisfied', it 'added to the difficulties of the British government'. It was therefore decided that he should try to obtain from the southern unionists 'a more satisfactory comment on the Irish constitution'.[157] The revised note was forthcoming, and feeling thus reassured Churchill made a statement in the House of Commons.

SEVEN

The government's tactics paid off. Despite a sense of grievance, the unionists of the A.P.L. were reluctant to act upon it by attempting to use their influence in the House of Lords to amend the constitution and extend the powers of the Free State Senate. A meeting of Irish peers, held on 16 November 1922 at Oranmore's London house and also attended by Bernard and Jameson, decided, with only Midleton and their host dissenting, that it would be inexpedient and unwise to oppose the Free State constitution bill in the House of Lords.[158] Thus the bill

156. The revised note was hardly an enthusiastic one. Though recognising 'the desire to meet our views' and the fact that concessions had been made, in accordance with previous pledges that they should be 'given the opportunity of seeing and discussing those articles of the Irish constitution which affect the composition and relations of the two houses'; they pointed out that other articles had not been submitted to them; expressed regret that 'the precedent of the Senate now in existence for southern Ireland under the act of 1920 has not been followed'; and concluded 'we are not satisfied that any Senate constituted as proposed by popular election, and with powers so strictly limited, can afford protection to minorities in Ireland'.

157. Thirtieth meeting of British signatories, 15 June 1922, Constitution negotiations, AC 30/2/167–77.

158. See below, pp. 292–6, for a discussion of the episode.

passed smoothly through the Lords with criticism but without amendment, and on 6 December 1922 the new constitution came into force in the Free State.

Southern unionists had abdicated their position. For the first time since 1885 they had not seriously attempted to influence a discussion of the Irish question, and the passing of the constitution bill through the Lords thus marks in more ways than one the end of an era.

X

Phase Eight: The End, 1922

THE signing of the treaty ushered in the final phase in the history of unionism in the south of Ireland. In the last month of 1921 and the first of 1922 the southern Anglo-Irish ceased to hold out against the new Ireland and bowed to the political aspirations of the majority of their countrymen. In view of the establishment of the Free State and the attitude of the British government, it is not surprising that the decline of southern unionism begun in 1914 was completed by 1922. More disappointing, however, in view of the habit of political agitation that had grown up since 1885, is the fact that the year 1922 also saw the end of significant Anglo-Irish political activity in the south. Despite hopes early in 1922, neither the I.U.A. nor the A.P.L. could adjust to changed political conditions. By the time the Free State was formally proclaimed at the end of the year, Anglo-Ireland's political determination and strength had evaporated. The disintegration in train since the split in 1919 was complete.

TWO

By the end of January 1922 unionism had ceased to exist as an effective movement in the south of Ireland. For this disappearance of unionist sentiment and organisation, Anglo-Ireland's assessment of the changing British and Irish situations was responsible.

Most obviously, the establishment of the provisional government on 14 January 1922, and the ending of British rule in the south with the 'surrender of Dublin castle' on the sixteenth, made impossible the continuance of unionism and unionist organisation there. Unlike Ulster unionism, southern unionism had always been essentially a constitutional movement; it could never contemplate resistance to the legally established government. The settlement embodied in the treaty was broader than that many had envisaged and contained few formal safeguards for the southern minority; but immediately the treaty was signed, most southern unionists accepted it as a *fait accompli,* an acceptance made easier by Griffith's conciliatory spirit. There was no question of a rearguard action on the part of southern unionists or Protestants to subvert the treaty: as the Protestant Archbishop of Dublin put it, 'The new constitution will claim our allegiance with the same solemn authority as the one that is now being constitutionally annulled.'[1] Public and private declarations of support for the new Free State were forthcoming from unionists and unionist institutions. The *Irish Times* responded quickly on 8 December, and was soon followed by the board of Trinity College, which passed a resolution accepting the treaty and expressing the belief that the 'true interest of Trinity College can only be furthered by Irish peace, and in the building up of happier conditions in Ireland'; and that 'Trinity men should take an active and sympathetic part'.[2] The most formal declaration came on 19 January 1922, at a meeting of southern unionists in the Engineers' Hall, Dawson Street, Dublin, organised by Mayo on his own initiative. The A.P.L. had tried to dissuade him from organising such a meeting, arguing that the time was inappropriate.[3] The result was that there was only a moderate attendance, but it included a number of peers (Cloncurry, Dunraven, Powerscourt and Headfort) and the idea was supported by the Protestant Archbishop of Dublin and Lords Kenmare and Dunsany, among others. A resolution was unanimously passed to the effect that the meeting, recognising that a provisional government had been formed, desired to support their fellow-countrymen in that government in order that peace might be brought about and the welfare of the country secured. Mayo suggested that election committees should be formed in Dublin, Cork, Limerick and Galway to get in touch with other local organisations, such as farmers' unions, Sinn Fein clubs, chambers of commerce, and all who intended to support the Free State. Dunraven, seconding the resolution, said that he approved, more perhaps than other southern unionists, of the terms of the treaty, but that even if he disapproved of them he

1. Quoted in Lyons, 'The minority problem in the 26 counties', p. 96.
2. *The Times,* 12 Dec. 1921.
3. Mayo to Midleton, 13 Jan. 1922, and Dockrell to Midleton, 14 Jan. 1922, P.R.O., 30/67/49, ff. 2868–9, 2871–2; and *The Times,* 17 Jan. 1922, for the text of the A.P.L.'s letter to Mayo.

would consider it his duty to put his views on one side and to do everything in his power to support the provisional government, which alone stood between them and chaos.[4] The A.P.L. had not been opposed to acceptance of the Free State, only to such a public declaration: it had accepted the inevitable at a meeting of the executive committee on 12 December,[5] and some reckoned that there was a 'great future' for their party in the new state.[6] Perhaps, however, the firmest recognition of the new system lay not in public or private declarations, but in the use made of it by the Anglo-Irish, as the unionists of the A.P.L. and the Irish Land-owners Convention began to put their views to the provisional government after the transfer of powers.[7] There was very little sympathy for the old unionist position persisted in by Jellett and the standing committee of the I.U.A. who were strongly critical of the treaty.[8] One of Midleton's supporters reckoned that

if anyone does not intend to be a loyal subject of the lawful and recognised government of the country, let him leave it and not jeopardise the position of the thousands who must remain and who intend to work for the common good.[9]

These fears were unfounded, for the I.U.A. lost ground still further in 1922. Members began to resign from the old organisation on the grounds that its objects were at variance with the establishment of the new state: one member wrote resigning 'in view of the fact that the Free State has been set up, and that so to work for the union would be to put myself in opposition to the established government of our country'.[10] Moreover, in these changed conditions and after its initial pique, even the I.U.A. seriously considered adapting itself. Some of its more calculating advisers reckoned that, though the old unionism was now impossible, if former unionists played their cards correctly, they

4. *Irish Times*, 20 Jan. 1922.
5. Leonard to Midleton, 12 Dec. 1921, P.R.O., 30/67/48, ff. 2836–9.
6. J. Tweedy to Midleton, n.d. but *c.* 12 Dec. 1921, *ibid.*, ff. 2843–4.
7. See e.g. memoranda relating to deputations waiting upon Irish ministers, 14 Feb. 1922 (Irish Landowners Convention), and 13–14 Mar. 1922 (Midleton and Jameson), *ibid.*, 30/67/49, ff. 2879–80, 2891–6.
8. See below, pp. 275–6.
9. Tweedy to Midleton, n.d., P.R.O., 30/67/48, ff. 2843–4.
10. Rev. H. S. Verschoyle to I.U.A., 22 Mar. 1922, P.R.O.N.I., D 989A/8/30A.

could play a decisive and prominent role in the new Irish state. The precipitate action of men like Mayo was deplored. On the one hand, it was thought that members of the I.U.A. should wait upon events and ought not to make profuse advances to the provisional government. Apart from any considerations of political honour and consistency, precipitate action was tactically unwise. If Irish unionists were ever driven to make a bargain with the new rulers of Ireland, they would get all the better terms from having been steadfast in their faith. Moreover, it was considered premature to make professions of friendship and allegiance to the new government, for there was no guarantee that it would be the government of the day in six months' time, and time was necessary to judge the trend of the policy and the force of opposition to the Griffith-Collins government. On the other hand, while abstaining from any public declaration of policy, the I.U.A. should not be completely passive. It should adopt other aims and form the nucleus of a conservative party which would represent the stable interests of the country and which would concern itself with social and economic questions, avoiding purely political questions in order that it might elicit the sympathy of the property-owning classes irrespective of politics. 'Purity and efficiency of administration, protection for property and civil rights, the maintenance of personal freedom, these would be the main planks of the platform of such a party.'[11]

If, on the one hand, the Irish situation encouraged the final acceptance of the new Ireland, the British situation did nothing to prevent it. What is less obvious than the constitutional objection to continued unionism is the point that there was little will to carry on any fight for the re-imposition of the British connection. The treaty and the events that arose out of it only confirmed the impression that had grown up of the uselessness of the British connection.

About the same time that Midleton was protesting to the government about the deficiencies of the treaty, Jellett on behalf of the I.U.A. was making frantic efforts to persuade British politicians to ensure that the government took a firm line over Ireland. Just before the treaty was announced Jellett wrote to Law, assuring him that unionists in the south of Ireland were firm

11. Dawson to I.U.A., 24 Jan. 1922, *ibid.*, D 989A/9/20.

in their unionism but lacked leadership, and asking him to urge the government to adopt a firm policy to suppress rebellion since the granting of independence would lead to civil war.[12] And after the treaty, Jellett found his worst fears confirmed: no protection for loyalists and indirect coercion of Ulster: 'in short, it is an abject surrender of every essential which the government has hitherto insisted upon'. The obvious division of opinion among Sinn Fein did nothing to lessen these fears. Jellett found that 'the prospect for Irish loyalists is truly appalling',[13] and the standing committee of the I.U.A. vainly urged caution upon Lloyd George on the ground that with the conflict of opinion among Sinn Feiners themselves and between Labour and Sinn Fein 'no provisional government that could be established . . . would be powerful enough to maintain any semblance of law and order. No reliable force could possibly be organised on the spur of the moment, and meanwhile the outlook for those who have any stake in the country would be appalling'.[14]

This feeling of being thrown to the wolves was soon widespread. It was all very well for politicians to explain that the settlement was the best that could have been achieved without continued fighting between the British government and Irish rebels; but southern unionists did not always see it in this light and can be excused for being dismayed at the substitution of the nugatory authority of the provisional government for the organised authority of the Crown. They thought that their loyalty and service to the empire deserved some better reward, and were bitterly disappointed when it received none. The feeling of almost heartbreak 'at the duplicity, mendacity and cowardice of our former friends',[15] of dismayed, sorrowful, even plaintive anger, is apparent in a letter written by a member of 'one of the most consistently unionist families in the south of Ireland' to Chamberlain.[16] In a speech to the Scottish Conservative Club on 19 January, Chamberlain had asked whom he had wronged by the Irish settlement and went on to say that he had not wronged

12. Jellett to Law, 7 Dec. 1921, B.L., 107/1/88.
13. Jellett to Law, 21 Dec. 1921, *ibid.*, 107/1/106.
14. Jellett (on behalf of the standing committee of the I.U.A.) to Lloyd George, 21 Dec. 1921, *ibid.*
15. J. M. Wilson to Carson, 14 Dec. 1921, P.R.O.N.I., D 1507/1/1921/284.
16. R. J. Uniacke Penrose Fitzgerald to A. Chamberlain, 24 Jan. 1922, B.U.L., AC 30/1/24.

the southern unionists. Commander R. J. Uniacke Penrose Fitzgerald, R.N., was quick to disillusion Chamberlain:

I happen to know a good many families of southern unionists, and I doubt if you would find one member amongst them who shares your view.

The people of whom I speak are not those who conciliated Sinn Fein, on the contrary they are those who have invariably opposed England's enemies uncompromisingly—Fenians, the Land League, Boers and Germans and Sinn Feiners alike.

Some of these families (in common with their English and Scotch contemporaries) now consist principally of women, due to the toll taken by England's wars.

Some of them are farmers who own nothing but their farms, who, because they would not subscribe to Sinn Fein, have had their cattle, horses and pigs stolen and hayricks burnt, and themselves have suffered boycott.

It is these whom the British government has now handed over to their enemies and whom you say you have not wronged. I submit that, by the same standard, it would have been no wrong to have left the British army in north Russia to the mercy of the Bolsheviks.

Had events in Ireland immediately vindicated the government's policy this sense of grievance might have died. Chamberlain argued that southern unionists would have fared badly had the Anglo-Irish war continued, for however complete the success of the government forces may have been in the end, 'nothing could have protected the unionists of the south of Ireland from great losses both in life and property in the course of the civil war which would have followed.'[17] On the other hand, he continued, the treaty would bring to Ireland peace and a new alignment of political parties with the result that southern unionists would feel a greater security than any that the British government could have offered to them had it continued the struggle. But events did not immediately vindicate that view; instead Jellett's forecast had been fulfilled. As soon as the treaty had been signed there had been a split in Sinn Fein. Some supported the treaty as giving southern Ireland the substance of independence, but others condemned it as a betrayal of the

17. Chamberlain to Fitzgerald, 26 Jan. 1922, B.U.L., AC 30/1/25. For his speech, see *The Times*, 20 Jan. 1922.

Republic, and on 7 January 1922 the Dail narrowly ratified the treaty by 64 votes to 57. Although the Dail's decision was in accordance with popular feeling, the dispute soon degenerated into violence. De Valera resigned as President of the Dail and some of his supporters denied the right of the Irish people to disown the Republic. The pro- and anti-treaty parties became almost military organisations as civil war gathered momentum with murders, raids, house-breaking, intimidation, cattle-driving, land grabbing, and in some places attempts to establish soviets.[18] As in the Anglo-Irish war, some areas, like Tipperary, were worse than others, but, equally, some places, like Markree Castle, Co. Sligo, which had emerged unscathed from the former, suffered in the civil war. Markree was occupied by Free State troops to prevent its being seized and perhaps destroyed by the republican Irregulars, but suffered £10,000 of 'wanton, mischievous and filthy' damage from the raw and often undisciplined government troops.[19]

Once again, the Anglo-Irish had become prominent targets for outrages and raids, and this time there was not even the hope of government protection. In May a deputation of southern loyalists complained to Churchill that the massacre of all Protestants and loyalists 'is a moral certainty . . . in the near future', because

the Sinn Feiners are armed, the loyalists are not. There are no effective police. There are no county courts or benches of magistrates. There is no machinery to put into force the warrants of the high court.[20]

There was more than an element of truth in this complaint. One night Sir Henry Robinson's home, Foxrock, was raided. After an exchange of fire, the raiders entered the house and, having filled their pockets with loot, told Robinson and his son, Lynch-Robinson, the R.M., that they would be 'court martialled next day for "resisting the soldiers of the Irish Republic in the execution of their duty" '. The next morning Collins came out to Foxrock

18. For an Anglo-Irish view of the civil war, see Phillips, *Revolution in Ireland*, pp. 247–312, but for a more impartial history, see Calton Younger, *Ireland's Civil War* (1968).

19. Lennox Robinson, *Bryan Cooper*, pp. 138–9.

20. 'Memorial handed in by a deputation of southern loyalists who waited on Mr Churchill on 25 May 1922', circulated to cabinet, copy in B.U.L., AC 30/3/52.

in an armoured car, but not to protect the Robinsons: as he explained, the provisional government was in no position to protect anybody and Robinson and his family 'had much better clear out, and come back later when things had settled down a bit'.[21] This is not to suggest that there was any definite nationwide campaign deliberately organised against the Anglo-Irish, but it does mean that they and their property were particularly vulnerable. The strategic position of their houses and the usefulness of their possessions meant that they were likely to be casualties in the battle between the Free Staters and Irregulars, and in the middle of 1922 many historic mansions and their contents went up in flames during the Free State operations against the republicans.[22] One of the most beautiful mansions in Ireland, Woodstock House, Inistioge, Co. Kilkenny, for centuries the family home of the Tighe family, was burned to the ground by armed men, and with the house were destroyed valuable and historical furniture and treasures.[23] Fortunately, Woodstock House was not occupied at the time, but other houses were.

Though on occasion not without a touch of humour, the experience for the occupants was not a pleasant one. In May 1922, Kilkenny castle, the home of the fourth Marquess of Ormonde, was burned and occupied by republicans who were then besieged by Free State troopers. After two days the republican garrison surrendered, but both sides were evidently proud of having 'defended' and 'rescued' Lord and Lady Ossory, who were then in residence. Despite the humorous potential of the situation, the experience was an unpleasant one: the *Irish Times*[24] reported that Lady Ossory was 'rather shaken by her trying experience during the latter days of the past week', and she and her husband retreated to England while Kilkenny castle was being

21. Lynch-Robinson, *Last of the Irish R.M.s,* pp. 170–3.
22. There is an interesting article in the *Morning Post,* 9 Apr. 1923, tracing 'the campaign of fire in Ireland', and listing and mapping the private residences and clubs burned between 6 Dec. 1921 and 22 Mar. 1923. The list, being based upon press reports, is, of course, incomplete, as not all burnings were reported in the press. There were some 192 burnings; 89 occurring between 6 Dec. 1921 and 5 Dec. 1922, the remaining 103 taking place in the fifteen weeks between 6 Dec. 1922 and 22 Mar. 1923. Tipperary was particularly badly hit, but nearly all counties suffered; only Queen's county and Carlow escaping.
23. *Irish Times,* 12 Aug. 1922.
24. *Irish Times,* 8 May 1922. For Ossory's account of the siege, see *Blackwood's Magazine* (Sept. 1936), pp. 414–28.

made habitable once more. Moreover, there was in the prevailing disorder ample opportunity for paying off private scores, for bolshevist-type organisations to put into practice their communistic principles, and for less law-abiding citizens, like those who raided Foxrock, to indulge their lawlessness. As Lynch-Robinson put it:

The police and soldiers were withdrawn, and officials like myself were left at the mercy of any thugs that happened to take a dislike to us. No doubt Winston Churchill and others who signed the peace treaty thought that they were doing a fine thing. I am not saying they weren't; but I felt that they were a little late in doing so. I was not such an optimist as to expect that much solicitude would be shown us by our late masters. Neither had we anything to fear from the new Irish government. But you cannot start a campaign of murder and outrage—however pure your motives may be—and then call off the killers with a stroke of the pen. The habit of taking what you want at the end of a revolver is not got rid of as easily as that and, treaty or no treaty, there were a whole heap of private vendettas to be settled up, and there was quite a lot of loot available for bandits without any police to interfere with them. It takes time to organise an efficient army and police force.[25]

Such insecurity made the British government's predictions about an Irish peace very hard to swallow. A sense of betrayal at being exposed by the British to more violence is very evident among southern unionists in 1922; and what is interesting is that—to judge from the memoirs they have left—it remained very much in their minds. Henry Robinson, writing in 1922, commented thus on the tragedy of the loss of young life in Ireland:

. . . It is even sadder to think that a Prime Minister of England should openly avow that the act of his life in which he takes the greatest pride is this peace which now leaves the country at the mercy of armed marauders who spare neither man, woman, nor child, who lay waste the country, burn and pillage the houses of the loyalists, rape their women, and shoot unarmed, defenceless men at sight.

One hears the government's apologists ask what alternative was open to them short of a war of extermination. The country was no

25. Lynch-Robinson, *Last of the Irish R.M.s*, p. 170.

doubt unprepared for this, but one might have thought that, as the government disarmed the whole of the loyal and law-abiding people and debarred these unfortunates from taking measures to protect themselves, they ought to have left sufficient police and military in the country to protect them until it was clear that the Free State government were in a position to do so. But day after day the robbery, murder and arson went on, before the Free State army were able to organise a sufficient defence force to cope with the rebels. We, who suffered, felt very bitterly that, if the government must stand aside and give us no succour in our danger and tribulation, they might at least keep silent over the pride and honour which they declare they have gained, until this peace, which is drowned in the blood and tears of the defenceless loyalists, is replaced by a peace of civilisation and christianity.[26]

As this was written so near to the event it almost had to be so bitter, but the same bitterness is evident in Midleton's reflections, published in 1939, when he refers to the treaty as 'one of the most deplorable desertions of their supporters of which any ministry has ever been guilty . . .'.[27]

This may appear a harsh judgement. After all, the British government had consulted Midleton on its Irish policy since 1916; it did make some provision for the compensation of victims of outrages in Ireland, establishing the Irish Grants Committee;[28] and it helped to ensure that certain minority safeguards compatible with modern democratic notions had been included in the Free State constitution, almost all the concessions made by Griffith on 12–14 June being those urged upon him by Chamberlain and Churchill at their meeting on the tenth. Yet as far as Midleton was concerned, the government could have done much more to protect loyalists and to prevent the whittling away of the safeguards proposed at the convention and contained in the 1920 act. It was all very well for ministers to point out that with the establishment of the Free State the *raison d'être* of unionism in the south had come to an end and that it was difficult to see how unionists as such could be represented in the Free

26. Robinson, *Memories Wise and Otherwise,* pp. 323–4.
27. Midleton, *Records and Reactions,* p. 264.
28. Set up in May 1922 and until April 1923 known as the Irish Distress Committee. See *Irish Free State. Compensation for Injury to Persons and Property* (1923), Cmd 1844.

State parliament. It was all very well to say that the provisions of the 1920 act were intolerable under modern democratic conditions. This may have been fair comment, but it did nothing to lessen southern unionists' sense of grievance. Many of the Irish peers sat in the hereditary British House of Lords with its two-year suspensory veto, and southern unionists did not think in democratic terms. They were essentially aristocratic, and, given their assumptions, their demands were reasonable. The whole southern unionist case was based on the assumption that superior wealth, training and social standing entitled people to precedence in the government of the country. The reason that they had supported the union in the first place was to protect their position as against the majority of their countrymen, and the reason Midletonites had later begun to work for Irish self-government was that they thought that nationalists, with a little pressure from the British government, would give them a place in the government of the new Ireland commensurate with their own estimate of their importance and influence. Not being democrats, they felt they had every reason to be indignant when the British government refused to press for the inclusion of undemocratic provisions in the Free State constitution.

Justified or not, this sense of being left in the lurch was real and had at least two consequences. In the first place, southern unionist bitterness found vent in a hatred of Lloyd George and all his works, developing and heightening feeling against the coalition government felt by southern unionists of all complexions. (There is, for example, an interesting typescript among the papers of the I.U.A., detailing the grounds on which Lloyd George could be tried and even executed for high treason.[29]) A second consequence of this sense of betrayal was to complete that diminishing confidence in the British connection. It snapped the emotional bond between loyalists in Ireland and Great Britain. Irish loyalists had

29. P.R.O.N.I., D 989A/8/30B. This document suggested that Lloyd George should be proceeded against under the treason and felony statutes on at least six grounds: he published at the King's expense under the royal arms a manifesto of De Valera denying the royal title; he declined to prosecute those denying such title and pardoned those condemned for treason; he entertained publicly men openly denying such title; he entertained privately in a private house in Scotland a man who had waged war against such title; he made an agreement with rebels to 'disturb' such title; he refused the protection of the law to those who maintained such title. It advocated the death penalty.

come to look almost naturally to Britain for protection and had come to identify their and Ireland's interests with those of the empire. Most would never do so again, even some of the stalwarts of the I.U.A., as is illustrated by an interesting episode in 1922. Professor William A. S. Hewins, the British economist and tariff reformer, had hoped to gain southern unionist support in regularising commercial and economic relations between Ireland and Great Britain. Though this plea was published in *Notes from Ireland*,[30] it met with little sympathy from southern unionists who now thought that it was up to Great Britain to look after her own interests and to sort out her own problems without aid from Irishmen. This is how Fane Vernon, one of the staunchest of southern unionists and honorary treasurer of the I.U.A., commented on the request for help:

Great Britain has, through her responsible ministers, given the case away, and nothing is left but to make the best of a bad bargain. Can Irish business-men do more than look after their own interests, when the English government has thrown them to the wolves in order to get out of the political difficulties which it has itself created? Irish business-men have been left to shift for themselves, and all they can do is to endeavour to help the rulers of the new Free State to build up the economic fabric in the way that will be most beneficial to itself . . .[31]

By the beginning of 1922, therefore, the old unionist position, which had been gradually declining since the middle of 1914, was completely abandoned. A distinctive movement which had been in existence since 1885 ceased to exist, as the Anglo-Irish finally accepted the political system desired, or at least accepted, by the majority of their fellow countrymen. For some the final decision must have been irksome, but many felt that southern unionists could 'without loss of dignity reconcile their willingness to bow to the inevitable now, with their opposition to all the home rule measures of the past'.[32] On the one hand, the union had failed, not through any inherent defect, but because of circumstances which resulted in the government of Ireland under the union being carried on in an atmosphere of distrust between Great Britain and

30. *Notes from Ireland* (1922), p. 69.
31. Vernon to Walsh, 27 Jan. 1922, P.R.O.N.I., D 989A/9/30B.
32. Leonard to Midleton, 12 Dec. 1921, P.R.O., 30/67/48, ff. 2836–9.

Ireland and between different classes and creeds in Ireland; circumstances which would have been remedied but for the course of party politics in Britain. On the other hand, whereas opposition to previous home rule schemes had been fully justified, acceptance of the treaty offering wide powers was also justifiable. Previous home rule schemes would have 'merely altered the direction of the current of patronage in Ireland without securing any material benefits for the country', and would have directed Irish politics 'into courses prejudicial to both Great Britain and Ireland'.[33] The present scheme, however, gave hope that all classes and creeds could co-operate for the good of Ireland.

THREE

Not only did the year 1922 see the end of unionism in the south of Ireland, it also saw the end of significant and united Anglo-Irish political activity. Since one of the bases of such action had been a pre-disposition to favour the British connection, this may not seem surprising in view of the weakening, politically and emotionally, of that connection. However, a promising habit of political action had developed since 1885, and at the end of 1921 unionists had expressed a willingness to adjust to new political conditions, those of the A.P.L. in particular being optimistic about their political future in the Free State. But in the event neither the I.U.A. nor the A.P.L. could adjust as a body and form the nucleus of a conservative party in the new state, for Anglo-Ireland's political strength and unity evaporated in the south in 1922. An amalgam of several interests, broadly speaking, southern unionism and Anglo-Ireland had comprised three parts: the ultra-conservatives—the smaller landed gentry and businessmen; the progressive conservatives—the more substantial landowners and businessmen; and the British orientated conservatives—those with large British interests. At the height of its power and influence, southern unionism had been a combination of these elements. The dispute over the convention had broken down this threefold combination, and the renewed violence of Irish life in 1922 completed this disintegration. The deteriorating Irish situation undermined completely the cohesion and political

33. *Ibid.*

ambition of Anglo-Ireland, preventing the old unionist groups and organisations from adjusting *en bloc* to play a significant political role in the Free State. It did so in three ways. It weakened Anglo-Ireland numerically. It shattered the confidence of those who remained in Ireland and undermined their determination to continue distinctive political activity. Lastly, the disorder reacted upon the provisional government's attitude to southern unionists' claims for a powerful Senate. The government's refusal to concede to all these demands, when taken in conjunction with Anglo-Ireland's diminishing confidence, split the old unionist groups still further, breaking down that influential combination between Irish progressives and British conservatives in the A.P.L. and leaving Anglo-Ireland leaderless.

One consequence of the threatening Irish atmosphere in 1922 was to weaken Anglo-Ireland in absolute terms. It drove from Ireland many of the Anglo-Irish, like the Lynch-Robinsons who left immediately after the raid on Foxrock: 'I have not got the temperament that feels it exciting and exhilarating to go about with one's life in one's hands, and under the constant threat of being shot. . . . I longed for a little security and peace, and to get out of the atmosphere of killing'.[34] Exactly how many left Ireland because of the developing and actual civil war is difficult to say. One guide, however, is the rapid decline in the Protestant population between the census of 1911 and that taken by the Free State in 1926 (for obvious reasons, there was no census taken in 1921). In 1911 there were 327,000; but by 1926 there were only 221,000; a loss of 106,000 or about 32.5%, compared with a decrease in the Roman Catholic population of 2.2%. Part of this Protestant decrease, perhaps a quarter, can be attributed to the withdrawal of the British army and the disbandment of the R.I.C. The rest was due to several causes. Some families died out but part of the decrease must have been the result of emigration. The ordinary rate of emigration must not be forgotten, but it is reasonable to assume that the quality of life for southern unionists before and just after the treaty increased the ordinary rate of emigration and accounts largely for the decline of the Protestant population.[35]

Although no reliable figures are available the tendency is clear, and some examples will show that unionists of all shapes and sizes

34. Lynch-Robinson, *Last of the Irish R.M.s.,* pp. 174–5.
35. *Saorstat Eireann Census Report* (1926).

were leaving the south of Ireland in 1922 because of the troubles. One of the most interesting examples of an Irish unionist official in flight is Sir Henry Robinson, who retired to Eastbourne and inflicted upon the reading public a second volume of recollections, because they helped to shut out 'much of the ignominy and humiliation we endured when we were driven out of the country as part of the English garrison'.[36] It is difficult not to feel sympathy with a man who in a poignant introduction dedicated his book to the

lovers of Ireland who had been driven from their country by stress of circumstances, but whose affection for Ireland nothing can wholly obliterate, and who still find a pleasure in recalling the early years spent in their old homes among the Irish people. . . . Many of us who have not a drop of English blood in our veins, and who realise that there is no future in Ireland for us, still look back on the country with deep affection.

Perhaps the most striking case of a staunch unionist in flight is that of the faithful Wilson. His brother, Field Marshal Henry Wilson, was assassinated; his beautiful and picturesque mansion, Currygrane House, Longford, the old home of the Wilsons, was burned to the ground, the raiders putting families of their own selection into some of the outer buildings;[37] and there is no reason to think that Carson was exaggerating, when he told the Lords in December 1922:

The brother of that gallant soldier is now living in humble lodgings in an English village, shattered in health and broken in spirit. I saw him lately, and I assure you it was hard to bear—the wreckage which all this had brought about.[38]

Less spectacular was the plight of Protestant farmers in Co. Leitrim. There seems to have been a regular crusade against Protestants in that county, particularly near Manorhamilton where a number of Protestant residents were given notice to quit and where the Protestant school and teacher's residence at

36. Robinson, *Further Memories of Irish Life* (1924), p. 10.
37. *Irish Times*, 18 Aug. 1922.
38. *Parl. Deb. (Lords)*, 5. ser., lii, 4 Dec. 1922, col. 224.

Lurganboy were destroyed by fire.[39] Thus the *Irish Times* was able to report on 16 June 1922 that Protestant refugees were daily pouring into Enniskillen from north Leitrim, instancing the case of Thomas Sanders who arrived with his family, having been compelled to leave his farm, contents and all stock at Manorhamilton, following a raid by armed men who stole money and valuables and threatened the family with death if they did not immediately leave the place.[40]

Their flight usually entailed a final severance of their connection with Ireland. Wilson died in Sussex in 1933, leaving effects to the value of only £510 8s. 5d.,[41] and others, like Edward Beaumont Nesbitt, formerly of Tubberdaly, King's County, had not the heart to return, even though later on the opportunity offered.[42] They still cared for their former tenants and labourers, but the future was too uncertain to persuade them to return: the demands of the landless men meant that a return was not worthwhile, for it only needed one person to stir up the people.[43]

The second way in which the deteriorating Irish situation reacted upon Anglo-Ireland's political aspirations in 1922 was by undermining the determination and independence of those who remained in Ireland. Not all allowed themselves to be stampeded out of the country, but those remaining found that they had to maintain good relations with either of the political parties just to be able to exist in Ireland, and this dependence

39. See e.g. *Freeman's Journal,* 19 May 1922; *Irish Times,* 8 June 1922; *Irish Independent,* 16 June 1922.

40. *Irish Times,* 16 June 1922.

41. *Landed Gentry of Ireland* (1958), p. 767; his will, proved 28 Feb. 1934, P.R.O.I., 1A–14–128.

42. E. Beaumont Nesbitt to Mrs Savage Armstrong, 19 Jan. 1925, P.R.O.N.I., D 618/172.

43. The flight of the county families has been called 'the flight of the earls', but it should be noted that some of the country gentlemen were, like Lynch-Robinson, glad to leave. According to Lennox Robinson, 'the war had thinned county society and many families were glad to exchange the loneliness of some big house in Kerry or Mayo for a small villa in Ealing or Bournemouth. Many country gentlemen had married English wives and for them it was a homecoming, though oddly enough it was sometimes the English wife who minded most the change of home, and one knows of a couple from the distant west who were burned out and retired to Brighton—to the great delight of the Irish husband, whereas his English wife was desolate and heartbroken for the Connemara she had learned to love.' (*Bryan Cooper,* pp. 139–40. For a view of the position of an Anglo-Irish family, see Lennox Robinson's play, *The Big House* (1928)).

inhibited them from any distinctive political action. Some loyalists, even members of the I.U.A., living in areas where the authority of the provisional government was weak, found it necessary to come to terms with republicans in order to safeguard their lives and property. The Galway unionists were at the mercy of the republicans—Major William Arthur Persse, for example, was arrested and held hostage, while his home, Roxborough, was taken over as a refuge for Belfast Catholics[44]—and they had to keep on good terms with them to save their homes. The more usual reaction, however, was for unionists to identify themselves with the provisional government. The most pathetic and symbolic instance of this new dependence on the part of men hitherto unselfconsciously arrogant occurred on 12 May 1922. Then a deputation appointed by some 230 members of the general synod of the Church of Ireland and consisting of the Archbishop of Dublin, the Bishop of Cashel and Sir William Goulding, waited upon Collins and asked 'to be informed if they were to be permitted to live in Ireland or if it was desired that they should leave the country'.[45]

Such a course of action was made less distasteful by the generally conciliatory attitude taken by the provisional government towards the minority in public and in private. Griffith had impressed southern unionists in 1921 and the early part of 1922, and the disenchantment over the electoral pact and the beginning of hostilities in May was soon overcome. Although not always willing or able to accept southern unionist suggestions, the Irish ministers were always frank with southern unionists and anxious to secure their co-operation. This had been clear in the constitution negotiations, and was true after the deaths of Griffith and Collins, on 12 and 22 August respectively. After their deaths the main burden of responsibility for the Free State passed to William T. Cosgrave, who became head of the government, and Kevin O'Higgins, the Minister for Home Affairs. These new men made a considerable impression upon many southern unionists. Not only did they seem determined to restore law and order, they also showed consideration towards the minority. They adhered loyally to the June agreement and defended southern

44. *Irish Times,* 3 May 1922; ed. Lennox Robinson, *Lady Gregory's Journals 1916–1930* (1946), pp. 21, 173–5.
45. Colvin, *Life of Lord Carson,* iii. 429; *Irish Times,* 10, 13 May 1922.

unionists, as the constitution went through the Dail.[46] They were ready to listen to southern unionist representations, and were engagingly frank even under close questioning, as on 18 October when for two hours Desart talked over the Irish situation with Cosgrave.[47] It was an exploratory talk, preparatory to a more formal interview which Cosgrave was anxious to have with leading southern unionists including Midleton. The topics covered were land purchase, double income tax, the safeguarding of Trinity College, the composition and powers of the Senate, the magistracy, the problems of the restoration of law and order, the administration of justice and the sentencing of criminals, and the effect of the escapes of prisoners on the *bona fides* of the government.

Desart reported that Cosgrave was 'an educated man of about 45 or 50, of good appearance and manners, very quick and intelligent—genuinely anxious to restore order and create stability, while his recent experiences have given him a conservative outlook', who took plain talking in good part, and that

46. O'Sullivan, *Irish Free State and its Senate*, pp. 77, 84–95. The June agreement was faithfully carried out; the only exception being that by universal consent the university representation to the Senate was transferred to the Dail. The two universities were each given three seats in the Dail instead of two each in the Senate. The nominated element in the Senate was drawn up after consultation with various representative bodies, as promised; and of the thirty nominated members in the first Senate, most could be said to have come from the old ascendancy class, though not all had been active unionists and one, Granard, had been a lifelong home ruler. O'Sullivan reckoned that 'sixteen of the thirty might be described as belonging to the class formerly known as southern unionists . . .' (pp. 90–1). Of course, the minority was not well represented in the elective element. Nevertheless, the Senate was disparaged by allegations to the effect that it was predominantly a Protestant and freemason body; but the first Senate consisted of 36 Catholics and 24 non-Catholics, not all of whom were episcopalians. (Lady Desart, for example, was a Jewess, and no less than three senators were members of the Religious Society of Friends.) The proportion of non-Catholics to Catholics decreased as time went on (p. 95).

Speaking on the minority problem shortly after Griffith's death, O'Higgins, who had accompanied Griffith in the June negotiations, said: 'We now know no political party. We have taken quite definitely a step forward in our evolution towards completion of nationhood. These people are part and parcel of the nation, and we being the majority and strength of the country . . . it comes well from us to make a generous adjustment to show that these people were regarded, not as alien enemies, not as planters, but that we regard them as part and parcel of this nation, and that we wish them to take their share of its responsibilities.' (*Dail Debates*, i. 482).

47. Desart to Midleton, 22 Oct. 1922, enclosing a memorandum of his meeting with Cosgrave, P.R.O., 30/67/51, ff. 3065–75.

'no summary can really convey the tone and character of the conversation which was courteous and friendly throughout'. His memorandum on the interview does, however, convey some of the tone of the meeting. Cosgrave expressed himself very anxious for a formal conference with Midleton and other prominent Irish peers, and was very forthcoming over all issues, particularly over the Senate and the problems of law and order. As regards the Senate, he was willing to keep the number at sixty, despite the transfer of university places to the Dail, and would have liked to include representatives of the landed gentry in the nominated element of the Senate, 'as he desired eagerly to keep them in the country and thought it essential to do so'. Cosgrave was even more forthcoming over the urgent questions of law and order, upon which Desart spoke uncomfortably plainly. Cosgrave said that the government was fully aware that the escapes of prisoners were affecting the *bona fides* of the government, but that it was doing its best against overwhelming difficulties. As in so many other matters the government had many in its services who were not reliable, prisoners and gaolers— now 'fighting on different sides had been friends, had fought together in old days'; the old good-natured tolerance of Irishmen to breakers of the law and sympathy with anyone who was punished remained; moreover, there were not enough places for prisoners. Ministers were also trying to improve the efficiency and level of the government forces. The difficulty was the availability of officers: '. . . the best old soldiers were accustomed to serve under officers who were skilled and of a class they respected and that officers of this class they could not get and were difficult to create'; but ruffians were being weeded out, and in the more peaceful areas great hopes were had of the new civic guard, who were a 'good class of men'.

In such confusing circumstances there was no political role for the I.U.A. to play, and its ambitious plans for reconstitution came to nothing. The state of Ireland provided little opportunity or incentive to embark upon a new departure: even the difficulties of travel made impossible the convening of the general council to alter the aims and objects of the association.[48] The I.U.A. thus

48. Circular letter issued by the standing committee of the I.U.A., Mar. 1926, copies in P.R.O.N.I., D 989A/9/32.

abandoned its political activities in the early part of 1922. *Notes from Ireland* continued publication (from London), but it did not criticise the new state; instead it confined itself, in the main, to emphasising the blackest aspects of the life of Irish loyalists under the new régime. Even the stalwarts behind this publication saw that political activity was impossible, and in 1922 the I.U.A. dropped its old role and gradually adopted a new, harmless, non-political role. Henceforth, it devoted its activities to relief work among the loyalist classes, 'trying to relieve cases of acute distress among members and other loyalists, suffered in consequence of loyalty to the Crown'.[49] The standing committee was formed into an advisory committee and, working with the other Irish loyalist relief organisations which sprang up about the same time, did invaluable work among distressed loyalists. Grants of money, food and clothing were obtained and administered to 'a large number of cases bordering on destitution'. The committee also assisted claimants, who were unaware of the procedure, to obtain advances from the Irish Grants Committee in London, 'in foot of their claims or decrees under the Compensation Act'. Moreover, the committee 'procured and administered relief in a very large number of cases of destitution amongst British ex-service men'.[50] An ignominious end for the oldest unionist organisation in Ireland, but, financed by subscriptions from old loyalists and their sympathisers in Great Britain, it carried on relief work until 1957. That it was able to function for such a long time is not a testimony to the political courage of southern unionists, yet it is a testimony of their sense of social solidarity.

More disappointing was the failure of the unionists of the A.P.L., the Midletonites, to adjust as a body to play an influential role in the new state. This failure was related to the third consequence of the Irish situation for Anglo-Irish political activity.

49. *Ibid.;* and minutes of a meeting held at the House of Commons, 30 May 1922, to form the Southern Irish Loyalists Relief Association (*ibid.*). It was through the S.I.L.R.A. that the I.U.A. seems to have worked. The new association also invited the various other organisations that had sprung up in the Anglo-Irish war— the Southern Irish Loyalists Defence Association; the R.I.C. Relief Committee; and the Irish Registration Bureau—to amalgamate. The I.U.A. also co-operated with the Duke of Northumberland's Fund, which carried on a propaganda on behalf of the empire and which represented distressed Irish loyalists as having held to the last and with the utmost gallantry the distant outpost of the empire in Ireland.

50. I.U.A. circular, Mar. 1926.

The dispute over the treaty made the provisional government resist renewed southern unionist demands for a strong Senate. Midleton had been very dissatisfied with the Senate that had resulted from the June discussions, and on 9 November he tried in vain to convince Cosgrave, Patrick J. Hogan, the Minister for Agriculture, and O'Higgins, of the need to grant the Senate wider powers. When he pointed out that the present delaying powers would only irritate opinion, Cosgrave made no attempt to justify the provision, but said that the position in Ireland was a barrier to a reconsideration of the matter, for the concessions that had been made in the June discussions had been agreed to in the Dail only by frequently threatening resignation and appeals to 'Griffith's memory and the good faith which should be kept with him'.[51] Such remarks persuaded Midleton that the Irish ministers were not free agents and determined him to try other means to extend the Senate's powers. His motives were not unmixed, however. Not only was he more than ever convinced that a lengthy suspensory veto on British lines was essential to protect minority interests, his interviews with the provisional government having made it 'clear that *persuasion* goes for little with no power behind it'.[52] He also wanted, by trying to obtain the fullest paper safeguards, to justify the position he had taken up since 1917 and to re-establish himself in the right wing of British politics from which he had been separated by his recent progressive attitude on the Irish question.[53] He, therefore, without consulting the A.P.L., set about organising a movement in the House of Lords to obtain adequate compensation for distressed loyalists and to amend the Free State constitution bill due to come before that House at the end of November.

The attempt to obtain better compensation was harmless enough, but his attempt to extend the powers of the Senate provoked a crisis in the A.P.L. Its more Irish orientated members, led by Jameson and Wicklow, not only resented Midleton's failure to consult them but also were strenuously opposed to any provocative action by Irish peers in the House of Lords. They

---

51. Memorandum of a meeting between Midleton, Donoughmore and Desart, and Cosgrave, Hogan and O'Higgins, 9 Nov. 1922, P.R.O., 30/67/52, ff. 3087–8.
52. Midleton to Suirdale, 24 Nov. 1922, *ibid.,* ff. 3112–14.
53. Midleton to Jameson, 17 Nov. 1922, *ibid.,* ff. 3101–14; to Bernard, 14 Nov., 4, 16 Dec. 1922, B.M., Add. MS 52781, ff. 108, 110–12, 113–14.

doubted whether the peers could succeed in extending the Senate's powers in view of the British government's opposition to amendments. Although Law's conservative government, formed on 23 October on the break up of the coalition, was sympathetic to southern unionists, it was as determined as its predecessor not to jeopardise the Irish settlement and to see that the British parliament passed the constitution bill in exactly the form agreed upon by the June conference and subsequently ratified by the Irish parliament.[54] Attempts at amendment would not only be futile; they would also be positively harmful to the southern minority. Unlike Midleton, Jameson and Wicklow were concerned solely with the Irish situation and did not now share his faith in paper safeguards. They now argued that the only safeguard of any value to the southern minority was the good will of their fellow countrymen: 'granted that good will, no paper safeguards are necessary, without it they are useless'.[55] That good will existed, but would certainly be alienated should the Irish peers try to amend the constitution as it passed through the House of Lords. Such an attempt would be regarded as a hostile act towards the provisional government which placed much emphasis on the early completion of the treaty and constitution in order to establish itself firmly; and it would play into the hands of the republicans who would 'like nothing better than to be able to say that the treaty was only a dodge to rehabilitate unionist ascendancy'.[56] Finally, its more Irish orientated members denied that any gesture was necessary to justify the position taken up by Midleton and the A.P.L. They did not feel, as Midleton did, that he had failed. On the contrary, they thought that he had done a

54. For the conservative government's attitude to the Free State constitution see minutes of the conference of ministers, 22 Nov. 1922. Since the treaty had statutory force, and since no responsible opposition to it had been raised in the recent general election, ministers felt that they had no alternative but to carry through the policy of ratification of the Irish bills, and would do so not only in the letter but also in the spirit. This meant that the constitution had to be passed without amendment, since it could not violate the treaty. 'Even if expressions can be found in some articles which, taken by themselves, might seem inconsistent with the treaty, the defect is cured by clause 2 of the Irish act, which gives to the treaty force of law and invalidates any provision of the constitution in so far as it is repugnant to the treaty.' Nevertheless, it was resolved that government speakers should adopt a 'sympathetic attitude towards those who had suffered from events in Ireland' (P.R.O., Cab. 23/32).

55. Wicklow to Midleton, 11 Nov. 1922, P.R.O., 30/67/52, ff. 3097–3100.

56. *Ibid*.

lot for southern unionism, successfully clearing away much class misunderstanding, and that had it not been for him,

> we should have been in a far worse position—and come what may your efforts have brought us into touch with the best of the Sinn Fein party and have let them know that we are willing to co-operate with them.[57]

In fact, it was felt that 'the position of none of us . . . will be improved by excuses for what we have done'.[58] In sum, they were less concerned than Midleton about British politics and precedents. They were not prepared to assert themselves but were willing to make the best of a bad job and rely on the good will of the Free State government.

An open rift threatened among unionists of the A.P.L. As Jameson wrote:

> We business men and others who live in Ireland and who have not been consulted by our president in the action he proposes to take would feel the disastrous effects of a false step at the present time. From a business man's point of view it would be unwise and might be dangerous. Our influence on the future depends a great deal on [our] position in the Senate and we are dependent for that on the goodwill of the government. Action would probably be taken to dissociate sundry of our provincial people from the proposal and a most regrettable difference of opinion disclosed. A published difference between the few of us who acted on behalf of southern unionists would bring ridicule and discredit on all of us.[59]

To meet this situation, Bernard and Jameson were invited to attend a meeting of Irish peers, which Midleton had arranged to address at Oranmore's London house on 16 November. There was 'a good attendance'.[60] Midleton reported his recent interview with members of the provisional government and his intention to move amendments to the constitution bill in the Lords, to increase the power of the Senate. A long discussion followed. Oranmore spoke in favour of some action in the Lords. Jameson

57. Sir John Arnott to Midleton, 8 Dec. 1922, *ibid.*, ff. 3129–30.
58. Jameson to Bernard, 22 Nov. 1922, B.M., Add. MS 52783, ff. 146–7.
59. Jameson to Bernard, 13 Nov. 1922, *ibid.*, ff. 142–4.
60. This account is based upon Midleton's memorandum of the meeting, P.R.O., 30/67/52, ff. 3089–90. There is a briefer memorandum in the Bernard papers, B.M., Add. MS 52783, f. 145.

strongly advised against any further attempt to improve the constitution bill, as did Bernard, Dunraven, Desart and Lansdowne, and communications were read from Lord Iveagh and Walter Guinness, who owing to their commitments to others commercially felt great difficulty in taking action. Desart thought that the results obtained would not be commensurate with the difficulties that might result. In a subsequent letter to Midleton he explained that he was confident that they would not get their amendment in the Lords and that they should 'run a grave risk of prejudicing the very people we desired to help'.[61] It would have been represented as an attempt to wreck; Cosgrave and his friends would not have dared to accept it; and the British government would not have helped the loyalists. Even had the amendment been passed by the Lords and Commons, the Dail would have refused to accept it; the date of the commencement of the constitution would have had to have been extended; and 'probably everyone in Great Britain except a group would have called us wreckers'. Moreover, any attempt would have led to an unseemly dispute among southern unionists. The Dublin committee of the A.P.L. would have dissented and very possibly dissociated themselves from the peers' action, and then there would be a difference of opinion as to what Griffith promised and 'you three accepted—really a question of what each of three people understood at an interview'.

Such opinions swayed the meeting against Midleton.[62] The feeling was that any attempt to extend the powers of the Senate would be unsuccessful and would jeopardise the good relations that existed between southern unionists and the provisional government, as the former would be charged with having broken the treaty. It was, therefore, decided not to move amendments to the constitution bill in the House of Lords.

Although a public controversy was avoided, this episode and the failure to extend the Senate's powers broke up the Midletonites. On the one hand, a number of prominent Irish peers, Desart, Donoughmore, Iveagh and Midleton, declined to serve in the Free State Senate which they regarded as a puppet assembly.[63] On

61. Desart to Midleton, 26 Nov. 1922, P.R.O., 30/67/52, ff. 3117-9.
62. Midleton's memorandum, 16 Nov. 1922.
63. Lord Granard to Bernard, 1 Dec. 1922, B.M., Add. MS 52783, f. 40.

the other hand, the A.P.L. was wound up. Midleton was very depressed by the Irish peers' decision. While bowing to the feeling of the meeting, he would have preferred to have gone down fighting, even if only to redeem what he considered to be his pledges to his followers. He refused to accept the validity of the arguments against rejection, believing that 'we are going to abandon, against my better judgement, a permanent advantage from the fear of jeopardising temporary good will'.[64] Resigning his position as chairman of the A.P.L., he decided 'to drop for the future the very close connection which I had had with Irish politics for fifteen years'.[65] The organisation was wound up but in such an atmosphere of restrained mutual recrimination that there was no effort to remodel it to meet the demands of the new Ireland.

Thus by 6 December 1922, when the provisional government came to an end and the Free State was formally proclaimed, Anglo-Ireland found itself weakened and politically impotent. Not only was it deprived of the services of a number of distinguished men, including its most active champion of recent years. It was also, with the dissolution of the A.P.L. and the altered role of the I.U.A., left without an organisation and a firm basis for effective political action.

FOUR

The events and circumstances of 1922 thus vitiated a developing tradition of organised and united political activity on the part of the southern Anglo-Irish. Henceforth, they made little impact on politics in either Great Britain or the twenty-six counties.

The activity they undertook in British politics was pathetic. The Midletonites had their last fling in the mid-1920s, when some of them made a last despairing effort to implement at least a fragment of the Irish convention's findings. Twice in the years 1926–27 southern Irish peers defeated the conservative government in the House of Lords on the question of the completion of land purchase. A group of unionist peers, including Mayo, Oranmore

64. Midleton to Suirdale, 24 Nov. 1922, P.R.O., 30/67/52, ff. 3112–14.
65. Midleton, *Records and Reactions,* p. 265.

and Midleton, argued that the British government was morally bound to meet the difference between the price paid to landlords under the 1923 Free State Land Act and that contemplated by the convention. Despite strong government opposition, the House of Lords endorsed this view, without, of course, influencing the government.[66] The unionists of the I.U.A. were more consistent but just as ineffectual. Between 1925 and 1939 the London branch of the I.U.A. was revived by 'exiled' loyalists such as J. M. Wilson. At first not only did the revived branch try to bring home to the British public the republican tendency of the Free State and the 'monstrous' treatment meted out to southern Irish loyalists, it also hoped to bring about the restoration of the union. This last object was soon abandoned, however, and in 1933 the London branch, with its fluctuating membership of between one and two hundred, became the Irish Loyalist Imperial Federation, 'to safeguard the constitutional rights and liberties of south Irish-born loyalists', a part of the futile die-hard imperial movement in Great Britain.[67]

The Anglo-Irish were even less effective in the Free State. To politics as to other areas of Irish life they contributed little after 1922. Many families continued to leave Ireland and those that remained 'withdrew into a kind of ghetto'.[68] Nowhere was this more evident than in politics, despite the substantial representation given, as promised, to the minority in the Senate. Deprived of political organisation and the guidance of such leaders as Midleton, the Anglo-Irish did not respond boldly to new political opportunities in the Free State. Instead, they contented themselves with sneering at the education and brogue of the new ministers and wondering whether 'they understood the ordinary conventions of polite society, did they know how to tackle an oyster, was it true that they eat peas with a knife?'[69]

Henceforth, Anglo-Irishmen engaged in Irish politics only as individuals interested in politics, not as representatives of a distinctive party or class committed to political action. A number did play an active role in the new state, some in the Senate, and others, such as the representatives of Trinity College and Bryan

66. McDowell, *Irish Convention,* pp. 212–13.
67. I.U.A., minute book of the London committee, *passim.*
68. Lyons, 'The minority problem in the 26 counties', p. 99.
69. Lennox Robinson, *Bryan Cooper,* pp. 147–8.

Cooper (unsuccessful in the first elections to the Senate but returned as independent member for south County Dublin in 1923), in the Dail.[70] But, though as individuals they may have offered each other their political support, as when Jameson appeared on Cooper's campaign platform in 1923,[71] and formed a loose independent group in the Senate, they did not act or even try to act as a party.[72] Perhaps this was a sensible course, but it was not the only one open to such independents. Jameson acted as a mediator in the civil war,[73] and considerable courtesy and respect was afforded to Cooper, not only on his own merits but also as a representative of the old ascendancy willing to help bridge the old minority and the new ascendancy.[74] Such evidence suggests the position of influence that might have been open to former southern unionists had they been united and organised. As it was, unorganised and unsupported by a formal party, the range of political manoeuvre of these individuals was severely

70. The number of independent candidates, though not all were from the Anglo-Irish class, varied from election to election; but generally only a handful, between six and twelve, were elected. See O'Sullivan, *Irish Free State and its Senate, passim*.

71. Lennox Robinson, *Bryan Cooper*, pp. 145–6.

72. In the Dail Cooper was considered the sole representative of the old. ascendancy; the members for Trinity College represented only that College. (See e.g. *Dail Debates*, i. 1152, 1153.) There was in the Senate an independent group, under the chairmanship of Jameson, but it was only very loosely knit. A body of senators who habitually consulted together in regard to measures which came before the Senate, they were not bound by any pledge and they frequently voted on opposite sides in divisions. Though the majority were ex-unionists, the group had other adherents, such as Senators Douglas and Mrs Stopford Green. It was an exclusively Senate group and no member of the Dail belonged to it or attended its meetings. Twelve strong in 1928, 10 in 1931, and 7 in 1934, it did not encompass all ex-unionists, some of whom, like Sir John Keane, remained independents but not of the independent group. Not only was the old ascendancy unorganised, the attendance of some ex-unionist senators was bad; though it is only fair to say that the two senators with the poorest record of attendance were not southern unionists, and a number of them lived in England—their Irish homes having been burnt or otherwise destroyed by the republicans. On the independents and independent group see O'Sullivan, *Irish Free State and its Senate,* pp. 154, 242, 266–8, 278, 302, 317, 359–62, 384, 389, 417, 428, 447, 448, 514–5.

73. *Ibid.,* pp. 112–15. On 30 April 1923 De Valera asked Jameson and another independent senator, Douglas, to meet him with a view to discussing practical steps for the conclusion of immediate peace. They acted as intermediaries between the two sides, but their efforts did not result in a compromise because De Valera's terms were considered too high by the government.

74. *Ibid.,* pp. 93, 221; Lennox Robinson, *Bryan Cooper,* pp. 153, 160–1, 171.

limited, and eventually they were forced to identify themselves completely with the pro-treaty party.

The case of Bryan Cooper illustrates this point well.[75] Having adopted what was in effect the programme of the A.P.L. and convention unionists, he managed to maintain his position as an independent member until 1927, acting on his own initiative in the Dail, and in the main supporting the government, though not uncritically. Regarding himself as a representative of a virtually unrepresented minority, he acted as one might have expected an ex-unionist brought up in the country gentleman tradition to act. In some ways he had large ideas, insisting that Ireland should become more international and opposing the view that Ireland could best express herself by 'hugging herself tighter and ever tighter and accepting nothing from outside'; but on concrete issues, such as the Shannon scheme, he was unadventurous, being concerned with peace and stability, economy and 'the individual'. This concern for the 'individual' can be seen either as the benevolent landlord's concern for his tenantry, or as the attempt of a misfit or aristocrat trying to prove his versatility by championing the working man in various matters. Less mistakeable was his insistence upon economy in administration: his contribution to the formulation of the procedure of the public accounts committee, his pitiless criticism of government expenditure, and his concern for taxation, can be seen as an aspect of the paternalist's suspicion of the profligate nature of central government. And most characteristic was his insistence upon stability and law and order. It was on this issue that Cooper found his independence compromised. In 1927 the Free State party, Cumann na nGaedheal, was under considerable electoral pressure from the opponents of the treaty. As far as Cooper was concerned the issue was the stability and good government of Ireland, and in the circumstances he had no other way of indicating his firm support of the government's policy and his distaste of its critics than by abandoning his position as an independent and becoming a member of Cumann na nGaedheal. (Incidentally, his adhesion to the Cosgrave party gave the republicans a great electoral weapon, and De Valera's followers tried to inflame nationalist opinion

75. The following appreciation is based largely upon information contained in ch. VIII of Lennox Robinson's *Bryan Cooper.*

against the government 'by throwing the mantle of unionism over it, and dead walls were plastered with the offensive slogan, "Cooper's dip for Free State sheep".')[76]

FIVE

This abdication by the Anglo-Irish of political responsibilities at a national and a local level was disappointing but understandable. Their view of Ireland was different from that of the nationalists now in control of the government of the new Ireland. The Anglo-Irish attitude to political activity was governed by more traditional and imperial considerations rather than by a particular view of the Irish nation. The key to understanding southern unionism and the political activities of the Anglo-Irish is Anglo-Ireland's responsiveness to events, its ability to judge its interests, as the possessing class, in the light of changes and to gauge the political potentialities of any situation. At a local level, the diminished importance of the Anglo-Irish was as much a consequence of a changed social structure as of a lack of will to act, and their failure to participate in national politics was equally complex. It was not just that the shock of the transition in 1921-23 had broken their confidence and poise. Rather, once the initial crisis had passed, there was for most of the time little incentive to take up the threads of political organisation broken in 1922; while at other times there were strong disincentives to any Anglo-Irish political initiative. For most of the time Anglo-Irish interests were not in any immediate or obvious danger; and at other times of renewed crisis, particularly for a short period after 1932, the Anglo-Irish found it impossible to act without jeopardising their interests. To take Professor Lyons's analogy of the dog that did not bark at night in the Sherlock Holmes story, the southern minority has not barked since the treaty, because at times it was afraid to and at other times it had no reason to.[77] With these fluctuations between moods of almost total alienation and periods of relative tranquillity, it is not surprising that the Anglo-Irish took the line of least resistance, reverting to that localism and apathy that had characterised their political life before 1885.

76. O'Sullivan, *Irish Free State and its Senate,* p. 221.
77. Lyons, 'The minority problem in the 26 counties', p. 92.

How far Anglo-Irish interests were adversely affected by this withdrawal and lack of distinctive political organisation, it is difficult to say. In more peaceful times their interests were respected. The Free State had every interest in encouraging business concerns in Ireland and the dominant element in the new Irish parliament, the farmers, had every reason to try and restrain agitation of any kind. And in times of political crisis the minority was bound to suffer owing to their political tradition and their peculiar position in Ireland. In any violent dispute over the treaty, they found their lives and property in jeopardy, whichever side they sympathised with. Economic war affected the larger agrarian and grazier interests irrespective of politics; in the troubles, Lady Gregory, a republican sympathiser who had always been on good terms with the surrounding countryside, could keep the peace in her district only by virtually surrendering to republicans her right to do as she pleased with her possessions;[78] and many of the unionist senators paid 'dearly, both in their property and persons, for their patriotic temerity in daring to serve their country'.[79]

It is difficult to see how a strong position in the Senate or an independent party organisation could have lessened the effect of a clash of principle over the treaty once it had occurred or reoccurred. But it is possible that a strong position in the Senate or an independent party might have altered events. Admittedly, a strong position in the Senate resulting in a clash between the two houses of parliament might have led to untold disasters. But, equally, had the Anglo-Irish shown more political courage and less pique in 1922, and more political energy and cohesion after 1922, the course of Irish politics since the treaty might have been different and to their advantage. Not only might they have provided the basis of a real conservative party in the Free State, but they might also have avoided some of the future emergencies which found them so impotent by leading Irish politics away from barren controversy over the treaty.

78. Lennox Robinson, *Lady Gregory's Journals 1916–1930*, pp. 25–8.
79. Phillips, *Revolution in Ireland*, p. 311. For these incidents, see O'Sullivan, *Irish Free State and its Senate*, pp. 102–8.

Appendix A

INITIAL MANIFESTOS OF THE I.L.P.U.,
OCTOBER 1885.
(from the *Irish Times*)

1. *Issued 16 October 1885 and announcing the existence of the Union:*

An association has been in existence since the 1st of May, under the name of the 'Irish Loyal and Patriotic Union', the object of which is to uphold the true interests of Ireland by affording to those Irishmen of all creeds and political opinions, who believe that their country can best prosper as a part of the imperial system, an opportunity of uniting in an organised opposition to the efforts being made by the party led by Mr Parnell to sever the legislative connection between Ireland and Great Britain; and of thus asserting and maintaining by their votes the integrity of the empire, the general supremacy of the united parliament, and, not least, the social freedom of the individual, of which, in the opinion of the association, these are essential bulwarks and guarantees.

The association is entirely unsectarian in its character, and is composed of members of both great political parties in the state. It will support indifferently those candidates—whether liberal or conservative—who, while standing on the principles of the association, will be likely to be most acceptable to the electors in each constituency. While expecting from them a firm adhesion to the main lines of the existing constitution, it would desire that they should approach, in a fair and candid spirit, the consideration on their merits of any proposals for the reform of Irish institutions or the promotion of Irish industries that may be submitted to the imperial legislature.

The marked and cordial approval with which the movement has been met by many influential members of the two great political parties, and the wide and hearty support with which it has been received have already placed it on such a firm and established basis that the public announcement of its existence and aims need no longer be deferred. The association now appeals with every confidence to all those throughout the United Kingdom of Great Britain and Ireland who believe that the best interests of both countries are bound up with their permanent union, to support them in carrying out the objects which it has in view, and by so doing to aid in upholding the authority of the imperial parliament, and maintaining its dignity and efficiency.

The operations of the association will be confined to the three southern provinces—Leinster, Munster, and Connaught—and its endeavour will be to put it in the power of every voter in these provinces to record his vote at the coming election for a candidate pledged to oppose every proposal aimed at the severance of the parliamentary and imperial connection.

In these provinces there are seventy constituencies, and it is intended to oppose the election of 'separatist' candidates in each of these, in so far as may be found practicable, and to such an extent as the funds of the association will permit.

A considerable sum of money has already been subscribed for this purpose, but a much larger amount will be required to give full effect to the scheme of the association.

Subscriptions forwarded for this object will be devoted exclusively to the purposes of the elections, and should any balance remain over it will be disposed of in accordance with the wishes of the subscribers to the association.

Further details and information regarding the hon. treasurers can be had on application (by letter only) to the secretary, Mr Ed. Caulfield Houston, 33 Leinster Road, Dublin.

October, 1885.

2. Second manifesto issued 23 October 1885:

You are earnestly requested to note that the objects of the association are:

1. To give to all Irishmen who support the legislative connection between Great Britain and Ireland an opportunity at the general election of recording their vote in its favour, if they so desire, and to this end.

2. To subscribe, within strictly legal limits, and in proper cases—but without directly interfering in any election—towards the payment of the lawful election expenses of parliamentary candidates who support the legislative connection between Great Britain and Ireland.

3. To secure the freedom, purity, and legality of elections in Ireland by disseminating correct information as to the laws relating thereto.

It will thus be seen that it is left to local organisations in every case to avail themselves of the advantages at the disposal of the association, and that it is of the utmost importance that no time should be lost by the constituencies in setting such organisations on foot.

Where suitable local candidates cannot be found, the association will be prepared to recommend, for the consideration of the constituency, gentlemen of ability and character who will be in a position to stand.

The association hopes to have in hand funds which will enable it to subscribe to the election expenses of candidates in every constituency in the three provinces of Leinster, Munster, and Connaught, to the amount which the candidates would be required by law to pay for the expenses of the returning officers.

It is suggested that it would be desirable that candidates selected by constituencies, whether liberal or conservative, should be men of moderate views and known to the constituencies, as well as of high personal character.

The executive committee beg to impress upon you that it is of the utmost consequence to remove the impression unfortunately, but not unnaturally, very prevalent in England that, outside Ulster, those Irishmen who are in favour of maintaining in essentials the existing parliamentary connection with Great Britain will do nothing to help themselves.

A display of apathy on their part at the coming elections will greatly strengthen this impression, and most seriously endanger their interests.

It is also in the opinion of the executive committee very desirable that the combined strength of those who hold these views should be fairly gauged at the polls. They believe that the great development of the so-called 'National' League is no true indication of the feeling of the people, and are confident that there are very many amongst those that have hitherto gone with the extreme party who, disgusted with the tyranny of the local 'National' Leagues, and alarmed at the prospects of the social chaos which would inevitably result from the establishment of a separate Irish legislature, would gladly embrace an opportunity of recording their votes in favour of a policy of gradual, moderate, and peaceful reform consistent with the maintenance of the legislative connection between Great Britain and Ireland.

3. *Election manifesto issued 26 October 1885:*
To the free and independent electors of Ireland.

FELLOW-COUNTRYMEN!—

You are now on the eve of the general election, and in a short period an opportunity will be given you to record that vote, which thousands of you are about to exercise for the first time.

Two courses are open to you, and two only. You must either vote for Mr Parnell and separation from Great Britain; or you must vote for those who have the best interest of our country at heart, and who seek its future prosperity by upholding the connection with the empire. Which will you do?

You are asked to submit to a continuance of the bondage of the so-called 'nationalists!' Recall the events of the last five years during which the Land and National Leagues have embittered your home life, have coerced your individual liberty, have extorted your hard-earned gains, and have permitted, without condemnation, the infamous outrages which have spared neither age nor sex, neither class nor creed.

Consider the result of those years! Is your condition better? Is the labourer better paid? Is the artisan more prosperous? No! The social life of our country has suffered, our constitutional freedom is now imperilled.

You are called free and independent electors! Where is your freedom and where is your independence? Does your freedom and your independence find expression in those conventions, where representatives are foisted upon you for acceptance—untried, unknown, of no weight, standing, or repute, and in many cases without local connection—men who now boast they are 'simply machines' in the hands of a dictator. It does not. Your freedom and your independence are thrust aside. Your vote, given to you by the imperial parliament, is sought to be made of no value, and your liberty of action of no possible account.

You have had experience of how these men would govern your affairs. In your poor law boards and committees they have shown you how they consider your interests should be dealt with. Are you satisfied with their treatment of you? Surely not!

These men have been lifted by you to positions of responsibility and trust. They have abused your confidence and added to your burthens. Your unions are rapidly becoming bankrupt, rates increase, and only those who hold the League ticket can obtain relief or be assisted under the Labourers Act. Thus you are deprived of rights conferred upon you by the united parliament, and worse coercion is practised towards you than ever the most despotic government permitted.

PEOPLE OF IRELAND!—

Consider what separation from the empire would mean for you. Remember how many thousands of our fellow-countrymen find employment in the factories and workshops of England, and the thousands more who procure ever recurring work in the harvest fields. Are you willing that the cry of 'No Irish need apply' should be raised by our justly irritated fellow-citizens? Are you prepared for the cutting off of those sympathies which now exist between Great Britain and our country, and the removal of that share in the public employments and offices of the state which so many of our brothers now enjoy?

The party which Mr Parnell leads claims to be representative of the people of Ireland! But who are the people of Ireland? Are they those cliques of petty traders, bankrupt farmers, and idle loungers which throughout the country form themselves into League branches and coerce their fellows—are these the people of Ireland? They are not! These are the men who now seek to intimidate you, that they may boycott you the more hereafter. These are not the people of Ireland, nor have they authority to speak in their name.

The people of Ireland are those hundreds of thousands of labourers who have been enfranchised; those artisans whose handiwork and labour support our country's progress; those farmers whose care and thrift have given them a stake in the land; those merchants and traders whose business is being ruined by reckless and self-seeking agitators; and those other classes and other men whose welfare is bound up with the country's prosperity. These are the people of Ireland—the representatives of our nation—who now possess the power of the vote, whose will and whose desires must find expression at the polling booth.

It is to these men the responsibility now attaches. They are the persons who must consider the enormous importance of the issue with regard to which they are called upon to decide. Capital is flying from our shores! Must credit go too? How are the industrial resources of our country to be developed? If we cut ourselves adrift from the imperial credit, what can we offer as security to investors? Who will invest where credit is gone? Who will lend when the exchequer is bankrupt? Do not be deceived by high-sounding statements regarding prosperity under a separate parliament. Prosperity in such a sense as the separatists use it, is simply another word for beggary! A national exchequer could only be sustained by highly increased burthens and enormous general taxation.

CITIZENS OF THE EMPIRE!—

You are still connected with the strongest power in the world! You have still the protection and the privilege of citizenship! The united parliament of the empire has given you your vote. See that you exercise it rightly and well.

As citizens of a world-wide empire you are not called upon to renounce your patriotism or to forget your native land. Her needs and her necessities should be your present care. Submit to no dictation! Reject all tyrannous proposals! Remember your responsibility, your position, and your country! Support those who will advance her prosperity! Give aid to those who oppose her ruin!

Hundreds of thousands of pounds have been subscribed by you and yours to the League funds both here and in America. Have you the remotest idea of how all this money has been spent? Have you benefited by the thousands squandered in law suits, the thousands demanded from you for testimonials, the thousands spent on luxurious living? Are you satisfied with this outlay of it? Have you and yours benefited by the thousands subscribed for the relief of those who suffer and are distressed amongst you? Are you satisfied with the paltry sums which are given, while the thousands are withheld? Banquets, testimonials, and the expensive living of parliamentary filibusters are but poor returns for the extorted contributions of a nation.

Your purses have been drained—you and your children suffer—your poverty has been preached for many a day by the League—but the muzzle of the revolver still demands that money which you are told to refuse to all lawful claims.

Your tyrants sit in judgment on you and your fellows. Taking to themselves the powers which should only attach itself to law and justice, they hold their 'National' League courts throughout the country. They extort fines heavier and more severe than the law of the land would ever inflict, and they seek to make independent men grovel in the dust before them, and undergo as great humiliation as ever did the slaves of ancient times. They would fain paralyse commercial enterprise, and endeavour, reckless of all consequences, to ruin homes and country, so that their petty despotism should gain sway. Their war is not a war with landlordism; it is a war with those who refuse obedience to the League Star Chamber in Dublin.

IRISHMEN,—

You shall not be deprived of that privilege of expressing your individual opinion which the coming election seeks to place within your power. The voice of the so-called nationalist conventions is not the voice of the people. The people must speak at the polling booths. These men who endeavour to deprive you of your just rights will not be returned to parliament unopposed. Candidates of different mould, and of full knowledge of you and your affairs, will also seek your suffrages. They will seek to revive freedom of opinion, and to prove to the world that you will no more be slaves. They will not seek to dictate to you or ask for money. They will oppose the organisation of coercion, ruin, and fraud. Their sole object will be to further the best interests of our fatherland. Your destiny is in your hands. Be just and fear not! No man on earth can know how you vote, unless you yourself disclose it. Your duty is plain! The traditions of our ancient race forbid the prostitution of your liberty! Let not the chains of slavery now bind you! Your best interests and your domestic ties demand a recognition at your hands. Cast aside all that which now holds you down! Fear nothing, but act for yourself and those you love! Give social tyranny and petty despotism its death blow! Strike the blow now! Vote for your country and your home! Bring to this land that time of peace and progress she so sadly needs!

God save Ireland and the empire!!!

By order of the executive of the I.L.P.U.

Appendix B

MEMBERS OF THE HOUSE OF LORDS WITH IRISH INTERESTS

1. *Irish representative peers and members of the House of Lords with property in Ireland or the sons of Irish families* (based upon *Dod* and G.E.C., *Complete peerage*):

Key: † Irish representative peer; ' minor; " liberal before, conservative or unionist after, first home rule bill; S interest in the three southern provinces; U interest in Ulster; B interest in Britain—where there are multiple interests, the letters are arranged in an order of apparent priority.

Abercorn	UB	Clanricarde	"S
Albermarle	"BS	Clanwilliam	U
Annaly	"S	Claremont	SBU
Annesley†	UBS	Clifden	"SB
Ardilaun	S	Clonbrock†	S
Arran	"SB	Cloncurry	S
Ashbourne	S	Clonmell†	SU
Ashford	BS	Congleton	"S
Athlumney	S	Conyngham	USB
		Cork and Orrery	"SB
Bandon†	S	Courtown	SB
Bangor†	UB	Crofton†	S
Belmore†	U		
Bessborough	SB		
Boyne	S	Darnley	SB
		Dartrey	"US
Cairns	U	De Clifford	"S
Caledon†	UB	De Freyne	S
Carew	"S	Deramore	US
Carlingford	"SU	De Ros	US
Carysfort	"SB	De Vesci	"SB
Castlemaine†	S	Devon	SB
Castletown	"SB	Devonshire	"BS
Charlemont	US	Digby	SB
Clancarty	S	Donegall	U

Sandwich	BS	Talbot de Malahide	"SU
Seaton	SB	Templemore	US
Shaftesbury	BU	Templetown†	U
Shannon	S	Trevor	UB
Sheffield	BS	Vaux of Harrowden	SB
Sligo	"S		
Stanhope	SB	Ventry†	S
Strafford	"UB	Waterford	SU
Strafford (bar.)	"UB	Wolseley	S

Note: Although the politics of some peers are difficult to ascertain, it is clear that before 1886 most of the above were conservative and that only a few of those who were liberals in 1885 remained so after the first home rule bill. Those remaining liberals, often with reservations and not necessarily committed to home rule, included: Bessborough, Clermont, Cork and Orrery, Greville (a home ruler), Leinster, Russell, Shaftesbury and Vaux of Harrowden.

2. *Irish representative peers and members of the House of Lords with residences in Ireland, December 1920* (list based upon *Dod,* Hansard and *Who's Who, 1920*):

Key: † Irish representative peer; ' minor; S interest in the southern provinces or the three included counties; U interest in the six counties; 1 voting on government of Ireland bill, generally with Midleton; 2 ditto, but acting selectively with Midleton; 3 voting consistently against Midleton on the bill.

Abercorn	U3	Clancarty	S	De Vesci†	S1
Annaly	S	Clanwilliam	U2	Devonshire	S
Arran	S1	Cloncurry	S1	Digby	S
Athlumney	S	Congleton	S	Donegall'	U
Bandon†	S	Conyngham	S	Donoughmore	S1
Bangor†	U2	Courtown	S1	Downshire	U
Barrymore	S1	Crofton†	S1	Drogheda†	S1
Bellew†	S1	Curzon†	—3	Dufferin	U3
Bessborough	S1	Darnley†	—	Dunalley†	S
Carew	S	Dartrey	S	Dunleath	U
Carrick	S	Decies†	S	Dunraven	S1
Castlemaine†	S	De Clifford'	S	Ely	US
Castletown	S	De Freyne	S	Emly	S
Cavan†	—	Deramore	U3	Enniskillen	U
Charlemont†	U2	Desart	S1	Erne'	U

Farnham†	S2	Lanesborough†	S1	Ormonde	S1
Fingall	S1	Lansdowne	S		
Fitzwilliam	S1	Leinster	S	Pirrie	U
		Leitrim	S2	Plunket	S
Gormanston	S	Limerick	S	Powerscourt	S
Gosford	U	Listowel	S1		
Gough	S1	Londonderry	U3	Ranfurly	U2
Granard	S	Longford'	S	Rathdonnell†	S1
Greville	S1	Lucan†	S3	Roden†	U3
		Lurgan	U	Rossmore	S
Harlech	S1				
Headfort	S1	Manchester	U	Shaftesbury	U
Hemphill	S1	Massereene	US3	Sandon	S1
Holm Patrick	S1	Mayo†	S1	Shannon'	S
Huntingdon	S	Meath	S	Sligo	S1
		Midleton	S1		
Inchiquin†	S1	Monck	S	Talbot de	
Iveagh	S1	Monteagle of		Malahide	S1
		Brandon	S1	Templemore	S
Kenmare	S1	Mountgarret'	S	Templetown†	U3
Killanin	S1	Muskerry†	S		
Kilmaine†	S1			Waterford'	S
Kilmorey†	U3	O'Neill	U	Westmeath†	S1
Kingston†	S1	Oranmore†	S1	Wicklow†	S1

Appendix C

SOUTHERN UNIONISTS AND SAFEGUARDS

1. *Memorandum, circulated among the cabinet 20 July 1916, of safeguards proposed by southern unionists and notes upon them by Sir Arthur Thring* (B.U.L., AC 14/5/41):

We, the unionists of the south and west of Ireland, renew our opposition to the contemplated proposals of the government upon the grounds so fully stated by us in our memorandum to the Prime Minister and to the unionist members of the cabinet. But in deference to the strongly-expressed desire of ministers, we beg to put forward the following suggestions, which we think should be embodied in the proposed bill in the interests of justice and good government and for the protection of minorities in the southern provinces.

We understood from Mr Lloyd George that the contemplated bill was intended to be effective as a temporary measure for the government of Ireland during the period of the war and for a year afterwards, and it is upon this basis that we put forward these suggestions.

We presume that the safeguards provided in 'The Government of Ireland Act, 1914' will be generally preserved and enacted in the new bill. But we desire to direct very especial attention to the following provisions, which should be also incorporated in the new bill, and some of which have been partly dealt with in 'The Government of Ireland Act, 1914'.

1. Differentiation in taxation

The Irish parliament shall not by any law or regulation of trade, commerce, revenue, taxation, or otherwise give preference to or differentiate between any classes or class of corporation, persons, or property, real or personal.

Note. The proposed provision goes further than the heading, as it would prevent any legislation which gave a preference to, or differentiated between, classes of persons or property.

So far as the question of free trade and protection is concerned, the matter is dealt with by section 2 (7) of the act of 1914, which prevents the granting of bounties on the export of goods, and by section 15 (1) (c) and (f), which, as respects customs duties, prevent discrimination, and prevent customs duties being imposed which are out of proportion to the corresponding excise duties.

The powers of the Irish parliament as respects taxation are very limited; but it would be, of course, absurd to impose this further restriction on these already limited powers, as it is impossible to impose any sort of taxation without differentiating between classes of property. A tax which does not tax all property and all persons must inevitably differentiate between classes of property or persons.

The same remark applies to the powers of the Irish parliament with respect to trade or commerce. These powers are limited most materially by section 2 (7) of the act of 1914, but it would be impossible to exercise such powers as the Irish parliament have got without some sort of discrimination between persons and property. For instance, the general regulation of railway and local harbour rates must involve discrimination between classes of persons and property.

Presumably it is intended to provide against the Irish parliament imposing a tax on some named corporation or person, e.g., a special excise duty on Guinness. But the whole question of discrimination is one of degree, and it is impossible to assent to a proposition which, in order to prevent the abuse of a power, makes the exercise of the power impossible.

It will be noticed that discrimination on religious grounds would be prevented by section 3 of the bill.

2. *Suggested clause in lieu of section 3 in Home Rule Act*

In the exercise of their power to make laws under this act, the Irish parliament shall not make a law so as either directly or indirectly to establish or endow any religion, or prohibit or restrict the free exercise thereof, or give a preference, privilege, or advantage, or impose any disability or disadvantage, on account of religious belief or religious or ecclesiastical status, or make any religious belief or religious ceremony a condition of the validity of any marriage, or affect prejudicially the right of any child to attend a school receiving public money without attending the religious instruction of that school, or alter the constitution of any religious body except where the alteration is approved on behalf of the religious body by the governing body thereof, or divert from any religious denomination the fabric of cathedral churches (or other churches or places devoted to worship or to religious, educational, or charitable purposes, or glebes or glebe lands or burial grounds), or divert or take from any religious denomination or educational authority any funds or property, real or personal, belonging to, held by, or administered by such denomination or authority, or hitherto administered for the benefit of persons belonging to the Church of Ireland or any other Protestant denomination, or make any law which may contravene the provisions of the Irish Church Act, 1869; and no training college, school, teachers or pupils connected with or under the management of persons belonging to any Protestant denomination shall be placed in a worse position in respect of the right to receive grants or assistance from public moneys than they enjoy at the time of the passing of this act under the system of education in Ireland as administered by the Board of National Education and by the Intermediate Education Board for Ireland or otherwise, howsoever.

Any law or regulation made in contravention of the restrictions imposed by this section shall, so far as it contravenes these restrictions, be void.

Note. The suggested new clause, down to the words 'cathedral churches', follows the existing section.

It is then proposed to leave out the provision of the present section which prevents the diversion of property from religious denominations except for public purposes upon payment of compensation, and to substitute special restrictions, the effect of which will be that churches, places devoted to worship, or to religious, educational, or charitable purposes, or glebes or glebe lands, or burial grounds, cannot be diverted from any religious denomination for any purpose whatever. Other property can be.

It seems impossible to have an absolute restriction of this sort covering so many classes of property. There is no reason why a religious denomination should not have its property taken away for public purposes by the authority of the Irish parliament just as much as any other corporation, so long as compensation is paid.

The new clause then goes on to enact that no property, of any sort whatever, is to be diverted from any religious denomination if it is administered for the benefit of persons belonging to the Church of Ireland or any other Protestant denomination. The effect of this is to take away from any non-Protestant church the benefit of the wide exemption which is given by the closing words of the present section 3, and to give a wider exemption to the Protestant church. Such a proposition can hardly be defended in a clause the object of which is to prevent preference being given on religious grounds.

The clause then goes on to preserve for the Protestant educational institutions and staff the same right to receive grants out of public money as they have at present. From a practical point of view this seems an impossible provision, as it would prevent any limitation or alteration of the present grants for education, and would so tie the hands of the Irish parliament as to make the provisions of the act giving them power with respect to education a mere farce. The object of such a provision can only be accomplished by making education a reserved subject.

3. Tenure of judicial office

During the period of the war and for a year afterwards the provisions of the Government of Ireland Act, 1914, with respect to the appointment of judges in Ireland and their tenure of office, and substituting for the appeal to the House of Lords from courts in Ireland, an appeal to the judicial committee of the Privy Council shall not have effect, and all judges of the Supreme Court or other superior court in Ireland and the law officers shall be appointed by His Majesty, and shall hold office by the same tenure as that by which the office is held at the date of the passing of the Government of Ireland Act, 1914, and the existing appeal from courts in Ireland to the House of Lords shall continue as at that date.

Note. The proposal is that during the period of the war and a year afterwards all appointments to judicial offices, including the law officers, should be made as now, and that the tenure of those offices should be as now. It is also proposed that the existing appeal from courts in Ireland to the House of Lords should continue.

As a purely temporary proposal there seems to be little to be said against this, so far as it affects purely judicial appointments, if the nationalist party are ready to agree to it.

The proposal seems, however, almost absurd as regards law officers, inasmuch as they have been, and always will be, purely political appointments. It does not the least follow that the United Kingdom government would appoint the same men as the Irish government, and it is clear that the law officers of the Irish government should be persons not opposed to the views of that government.

It is proposed that the present practice of appeals to the House of Lords should continue for a time.

4. Reservation of the subject-matter of the Land Law (Ireland) Acts and Congested Districts Board Act

The general subject-matter of the Land Law (Ireland) Acts and any legislation relating thereto or dealing with the tenure or ownership of land in Ireland, including matters relating to the Congested Districts Board of Ireland, shall be included among the reserved matters as defined in paragraph 12 of section 2 of 'The Government of Ireland Act, 1914'.

Note. The question of the reservation of the Land Law (Ireland) Acts was argued at every stage of the home rule bill. It is difficult to see how any reservation of the subject-matter of these acts is consistent with any scheme of home rule.

The reservation of the Land Purchase Acts is, of course, quite a different question. The subject matter of those acts is reserved, as the security of a vast sum of money advanced by the United Kindgom is involved. It would, of course, be impossible for the Irish government to carry out land purchase without the United Kingdom credit.

It seems clear that the Congested Districts Board's work, as a whole, should not be reserved. Their general work in relieving congestion and of improving congested districts should certainly be under the control of the Irish government. So far as they exercise powers under the Land Purchase Acts, their powers must, of course, be controlled, and will be controlled, to some extent by the United Kingdom government.

5. Compensation for criminal or malicious injuries

The existing law relating to compensation for criminal injuries or malicious injuries shall not be altered except by the parliament of the United Kingdom.

Note. It is suggested that the existing law relating to compensation for criminal injuries or malicious injuries is not to be altered except by the parliament of the United Kindgom.

It is, of course, absurd to suggest that the government of Ireland, if they are to have any power, should not have power to alter the law relating to malicious injuries. This was practically admitted on the part of the opposition when the amendment was moved in the House of Lords and withdrawn. The withdrawal of the amendment was advised on the grounds that, 'if we are to assume, as we must assume, for the purposes of this argument, that there is to be a local legislature, it will be very difficult to preclude that legislature altogether from dealing with changes of law such as this. I do not see how, under the system—which again we must assume—it will be possible to throw the whole of the responsibility for such matters upon the imperial parliament at Westminster.'

6. Civil service appointments

The appointment of all offices and employments in the civil service of the Crown in Ireland, which at the time of passing of this Act is made after an examination by the civil service commissioners of the United Kingdom, and to offices and employments in the civil service of the Crown in Ireland which may be authorised by Irish act (other than the appointment to offices and employments which are excluded by His Majesty by order in council from the operation of this section) shall be made only after such competitive examination as may be prescribed by regulations made by the civil service commissioners of the United Kingdom.

Note. It is proposed that all civil service appointments which are now made after examination should continue to be made after examination, and that the examination is to be by the civil service commissioners of the United Kingdom.

It is obvious, of course, that the Irish government would probably require an examination, possibly harder than our own examination, for civil service appointments. But to take out of the hands of a responsible government the power of prescribing the qualification of their own servants and of conducting any examination which may be required for their own servants seems absurd.

Something of the sort might possibly be accepted as a purely temporary provision if it was agreed to by the nationalist party.

7. Income tax and death duties

The power of the Irish parliament with reference to the imposition of income tax (including supertax) and death duties shall only be exercised in respect of income arising or property situate in Ireland.

Note. It is suggested that the power of the Irish parliament with reference to income tax (including supertax) and death duties shall only be exercised with respect of income arising from property situate in Ireland.

As far as death duties is concerned, the object of the amendment seems to be amply attained by the provisions as to death duties in section 15 (1) (c) of 'The Government of Ireland Act, 1914', and by the ordinary law as to the incidence of death duties.

As far as income tax is concerned, the suggestion is absolutely contrary to the principle of the Income Tax Acts, which charge the tax on a man's income wherever it arises; that is to say, income tax follows the residence of the taxpayer, and not the residence of the property, except so far as schedules A and B are concerned.

Further than this, it will be noticed that, except as respect supertax, the powers of the Irish parliament with respect to income tax are very limited, and are restricted by section 15 (1) (c) to the alteration of the conditions under which exemptions, abatement, or relief from the tax may be granted.

2. *The British government's record of the meetings, on 12 and 13 June 1922, between southern unionists and the Irish signatories to the treaty to discuss minority safeguards in the new Irish constitution* (B.U.L., AC 30/2/158–64):

At 11 a.m. on Monday, June 12th, a meeting was held at the Colonial Office between the Irish signatories and the representatives of the

southern unionists. Mr Churchill was in the chair and the following
were also present: Mr Griffith, Mr Kevin O'Higgins, Mr Kennedy,
Lord Midleton, Dr Bernard, Lord Donoughmore, Mr Andrew
Jameson and Mr Curtis. The following record was made by Mr
Curtis:—

Mr Churchill submitted to Lord Midleton and his colleagues clauses
extracted from the constitution relating to the Senate, observing that
they were, of course, strictly confidential.

Lord Midleton complained that nothing he had said at previous
interviews appeared to have had any weight. The Senate was constituted with no safeguard to minorities. There was the strongest objection
on his side to the nomination of candidates by the lower house and to
taking the whole of Ireland as one constituency.

Mr Churchill remarked that the government had thought that this
last revision would suit the interests of loyalists.

Lord Midleton objected that commercial representatives would have
little chance.

Lord Donoughmore observed that they had not the organisation to
cast a solid vote; the 180 days period of delay did not give enough time
for the formation of public opinion. There was no provision for joint
meetings of both houses. As in the present Dail, the loyalists' case
would never be voiced in the lower house. No adequate provision
had been made for a large stable element in the legislature.

Lord Midleton said that he had represented all these facts to Mr Figgis
on the 26th April without effect, and he did not see much use in taking
part in further discussions.

Mr Churchill begged him not to close the consideration of the
question and Mr Jameson pointed out that no finality had yet been
reached and the matter was still open for consideration.

Lord Midleton reiterated his complaint that his representations had
met with no response.

Mr Griffith analysed the provisions of the constitution relating to
the upper house and said that the provisional government were now
ready to nominate half the first Senate with a view to securing the
representation of loyalists.

Lord Midleton said that was only a transitory provision; they
wanted permanent provisions.

Mr Churchill said that the government had discussed these provisions
with the Irish representatives and had expressed the view that the
selection of candidates by the chamber would exclude loyalists; they
might have no candidates in whom they would have confidence as
spokesmen. It was the essence of popular government that people of
unpopular views should be able to make their voices heard. The

minority ought to have its own candidates. The provisional government had now met the second point raised by the government by increasing the nominated candidates to 20; the government also held that 10 of these candidates should sit for 6 years instead of 3. The Senate should be strong enough to put into operation the constitutional checks; after six years the old party lines might be changed. The period of six months after which the bill became law automatically was too short. The government thought that the referendum was the security from the point of view of property. In England, unionists had wanted the referendum as a conservative provision. The signing of a petition for a referendum with no protection for secrecy was objectionable and it would be difficult to get enough signatures. The government thought that the Senate should be able to demand a referendum without the petition.

Lord Midleton thought that the referendum would be no protection if the majority wanted to despoil the property owners.

Mr O'Higgins drew attention to the Senate of Northern Ireland which was wholly elected by the lower house. Lord Midleton had made no criticism of this in the Lords.

Lord Midleton replied that Ulster did not want a Senate and said that if they must have one it must be wholly elected. The result had been an utter failure as a check on the lower house.

Mr O'Higgins said that the minority must not think of themselves as a stereotyped minority. Sinn Fein was now divided, new parties would form, most important the landed party. He illustrated the position from his own constituency. The Farmers' Union would seek as representatives the best spokesmen of their interests who should be drawn from the loyalists; so also in commerce. Dockrell would have been elected if he had stood for Dublin; loyalists' interests would have nothing to fear in the future.

Dr Bernard thought the upper house would simply reflect the lower. An upper house should contain unpopular people.

Lord Donoughmore observed that everyone condemned a similar proposal made in this country by the Bryce committee.

Lord Midleton said that Ireland was subject to violent fluctuations of opinion, and they must have stability in the upper house.

Mr Churchill asked whether it was possible for an upper house to make final decisions against the majority of the people. He had always regretted in England that there was no chance of discussion between the two houses, which would tend to release party deadlocks, but a joint sitting of Lords and Commons was impossible unless the number of the Lords was greatly reduced.

Lord Midleton said that a Senate of 40 with a chamber of 200 was

too small. The chamber was elected on the most democratic constituency ever proposed.

Mr Jameson asked if the election of the Senate was on the same
constituency.

Mr Griffith replied that it was.

Both parties then withdrew for 20 minutes to confer.

The meeting was resumed at 12.45, the Secretary of State still being
absent.

Lord Midleton said he would sketch out a proposal on behalf of his
colleagues. They urged that nominations by the chamber should be
dropped. The Ulster arrangement had all been fixed up in an hour's
controversy. The Senate should be enlarged. In a small house the
lobbying for three or four odd votes was intolerable. The Senate
should be one-third of the lower house, 75 would be fairer.

Mr Griffith explained that the lower house would not be 200 but
more like 120; 40 had been chosen because it was a third.

Lord Midleton said that if it was 120 a Senate of 60 would be a
fair thing.

Mr Jameson thought 120 in the lower house was too small for the
reasons given above by Lord Midleton.

Mr Kennedy said it would be 128 with the present house. The
number was based on the Government of Ireland Act, they had taken
200 for the whole of Ireland including Ulster, which contained
1,200,000 people; the basis was one member to every 30,000.

Lord Midleton asked them to consider a Senate half the size of the
chamber. The government here would have jumped at such a proposal.

Dr Bernard complained that there was no university representation.

Lord Midleton asked who was to decide what was a money bill?
Could it not be the High Court?

Lord Donoughmore thought that the Speaker might give the first
certificate and there should be appeal to some judicial tribunal. He
instanced the land purchase bill; here the Speaker had decided that
old age pensions and safeguarding of industries bill were money bills.

Lord Midleton said that he greatly preferred the Senate of the 1920
act; in appointing members to the Senate he hoped that they would
consider consultation with chambers of commerce, educational bodies,
the legal profession, the landed interest, of which the Irish peers were
the natural custodians. He took note of Mr Griffith's desire to nominate
men acceptable to loyalists. The electorate for the Senate should be
people over 30. The constituencies should be the provinces, not all
Ireland. Commercial candidates in Dublin would get little chance in
the west and south. He would also like a property qualification for
the electorate for the Senate.

Dr Bernard said they wanted a strong Senate in Ireland; they were apt to pass resolutions first and repent afterwards.

Mr Churchill re-entered at this point and remarked that the decision of the Speaker on money bills was difficult to defend.

Mr Griffith explained that under the constitution all money bills had to go to the Senate who could discuss them and return them to the Chamber within 14 days with a recommendation.

Mr Churchill thought they might have a special tribunal instead of the Speaker.

Lord Midleton thought that the minimum time for suspending a bill should be a year, then let the Senate and lower house vote together and if one-third of both houses vote against the bill let there be a referendum.

Mr Churchill thought this too stiff, two out of three of these checks would suffice.

Mr Griffith said that joint voting was inadmissible. In England liberal government would have been impossible under the system.

Mr Churchill agreed that the House of Lords would be solid against Labour. The popular will must rule in the end. He suggested (1) a joint session, (2) a year's delay failing agreement in the joint session. In England two years gave a tremendous bargaining power to the upper house. He objected to a majority in the Commons being outvoted in a joint meeting.

Dr Bernard preferred a joint session to a referendum.

Mr Griffith said that they might agree that a two-thirds vote of the Senate may require a referendum by secret ballot.

Lord Midleton hoped the two houses might vote as well as discuss together.

Mr Churchill said he would never agree to this in England.

Lord Midleton replied that the Irish Senate was not hereditary but was elective.

Mr Griffith said that he had no objection to the provinces as constituencies, but thought that the loyalists would prefer the whole country. He saw no objection to increasing the number of the Senate. A larger vote might be less open to corruption.

Lord Midleton pleaded for *ex officio* members.

Mr Griffith objected.

Lord Donoughmore urged that the nominations for the election should be open.

Mr Griffith said that he had no objection but thought that the selection of candidates by the lower house would help the loyalists.

Mr O'Higgins said they wanted to admit men like George Russell who were not politicians.

Dr Bernard said that the selection of candidates by the chamber was most objectionable.

On Mr Churchill's suggestion it was then agreed that Mr O'Higgins and Mr Kennedy should meet Lord Donoughmore, Dr Bernard and Mr Jameson at 4.30 that afternoon and that the discussion should be resumed at 5 o'clock on the following day.

The discussion between the Irish signatories and the representatives of the southern unionists was continued at 4 p.m. on Monday, June 12th, in the Colonial Office. Lord Donoughmore, Mr Andrew Jameson, Mr Kennedy, Mr O'Higgins, and Mr Curtis were present. No record was prepared of the discussion.

On Tuesday June 13th, Mr Collins returned to London and at 10.30 a.m. that day Mr Churchill met him and Mr Griffith at the Colonial Office.

A further meeting took place between the Irish signatories and the representatives of the southern unionists at 5.30 p.m. on Tuesday, June 13th, at the Colonial Office. There were present Mr Churchill, Lord Midleton, Dr Bernard, Lord Donoughmore, Mr Jameson, Mr Griffith, Mr Michael Collins, Mr Kevin O'Higgins, Mr Kennedy, and Mr Curtis. Agreements were arrived at on the following points (22/N/4):

1. The Senate to consist of 60 members of whom two are to be elected by the National University of Ireland and two by the Dublin University.

2. The remaining 56 are to be elected from a panel consisting of three times the number of members to be elected, of whom two-thirds are to be nominated by the Chamber and one third by the Senate.

3. The electorate for the Senate to be persons of 30 years and upwards.

4. The period between the first presentation of the bill to the Senate and the day upon which it shall be deemed to be passed is extended from 180 days as provided by article 37 to 270 days.

5. Three-fifths of the members of the Senate may require a referendum during the 90 day period mentioned in article 44 without a petition as there provided. The demand by petition to remain as an alternative.

6. In the case of disagreement provision to be made for joint debate of the two houses but not for joint voting.

7. On the referendum being taken the decision to be final without further delay. Voting at the referendum to be by ballot.

8. Whether a bill is a money bill to be certified by the Speaker subject to appeal to a committee of privileges drawn equally from both houses and presided over by a judge of the Supreme Court who shall have a casting vote but no other vote.

9. The first Senate to be one-half nominated and the other half elected by the chamber, the whole to be divided into four classes, of whom half of the nominated members retire from office at the end of 12 years, half of the elected members at the end of 9 years, the remaining half of the nominated members at the end of 6 and the remaining half of the elected members at the end of 3 years. The nominated members to be nominated by the president of the executive council in a manner calculated to represent minorities and interests not represented adequately in the chamber and such nomination to be made on the advice of the following bodies: chambers of commerce, College of Physicians and College of Surgeons, Benchers of King's Inns, and Incorporated Law Society, Corporations of Dublin and Cork. The stipulation as to consultation not to be embodied in the constitution but to be contained in an undertaking to be embodied in a resolution of the new parliament.

10. The question whether the constituency of the election of senators was to be the Irish Free State taken as a whole or the separate provinces was left to the decision of Lord Midleton and his colleagues, such decision to be communicated by Lord Donoughmore and Mr Curtis on the following day.

Appendix D

SOUTHERN UNIONISTS AND THE PARTITION OF IRELAND

Memorandum by Lord Desart, 22 November 1919, submitted to the cabinet committee on Ireland (P.R.O., Cab. 27/69/2/41):

I send you a disquisition about the advertised policy of the government regarding this country, more especially with regard to the question of partition, which I personally should oppose in any form and in any circumstances which I can contemplate.

I myself believe it to be impossible politically, and, if imposed, that it would turn out to be impracticable in working, both economically and socially, and would not alleviate, but would promote trouble both inside and outside Ulster. It would also involve what, as it seems to me, would be a base desertion of the 300,000 to 350,000 southern unionists who have not only maintained their loyalty through years of agitation, in the face of great temptation from home rulers, spoliation from Gladstonian legislation, and little regard from any government—and who in this war have given their all for the empire—I don't believe any record in that respect is brighter than that of the gentry and sons of the Protestant clergy of the south and west of Ireland.

First politically

Ulster or the six counties (sometimes the claim is for the first, sometimes for the second) do not wish for partition, but have lately categorically stated they would accept it in the last resort. In fact they did so when they accepted the amending bill in 1914.

Southern unionists are all opposed to partition but some are much influenced by the attitude of Ulster—others, like myself, regard the Ulster attitude as selfish, and to put it quite plainly as a betrayal of their old friends in the south. But I think it is certain that all southern unionists are opposed to partition. They would be lunatics were it not so. An Irish parliament without Ulster would leave southern unionists without any representation at all—while they would provide the larger part of all taxes and rates.

The nationalists are bitterly opposed to it—and I do not believe that such of their leaders as remain in public life could make any compromise which would be accepted by their followers. It would merely throw all these into the ranks of Sinn Fein.

Sinn Fein demands what I hope I may safely call the impossible—an independent republic—and to this the whole of Ireland is essential and any weakening of nationalists on this point would add to their influence.

Lastly the R.C. hierarchy. They cannot, if they would, abandon their people in the north and are therefore another force against partition.

I may say that in my opinion they are a force and very probably a deciding force against any form of home rule, which I am convinced they are determined to avert—mainly I think because they fear education rates which would lead to school boards.

Thus, if my diagnosis is correct, you have as regards partition:

An unwilling Ulster—or six counties.

A hostile body of southern unionists.

Bitter opposition from nationalists.

Scornful rejection by Sinn Fein.

A hierarchy which will make no concession.

I can myself conceive no possible workable solution of which partition in any shape would form a part.

Some people urge (notably the *Spectator*) that temporary exclusion would lead the Irish parliament to behave well, so as to induce Ulster to join later on. My prognosis would be very different.

If you take the whole of Ulster you will have there a large nationalist and Catholic majority. If you take the six counties you would have a considerable nationalist and Catholic minority,—and the most bitter and violent in Ireland.

There would be continuous agitation by these people, suppressed by the Protestant majority, probably by strong measures. That agitation would be fostered and supported by every nationalist organisation in the south and west. That seems to me to be inevitable.

One probable result would be that every act of oppression (so called or real) by the Protestant rulers in the north would be met by reprisals on the unfortunate Protestants in the south. The methods of the north are not very tender and the replies of the south would probably be even less so.

It might ultimately mean the re-conquest of Ireland—after intense suffering of the population and perhaps economic ruin.

In detail I believe it would be unworkable. Trade and commerce is one and interdependent in the whole island and different laws or different regulations on each side of the Boyne would seriously impede the progress and affect the prosperity of the whole country. I will not labour this, though it might be developed, as for the moment it is a subsidiary point.

Probably there is one thing on which all unionists in Ireland whether north or south are in agreement, which is that to hand over Ireland in its present condition to an Irish parliament would mean the persecution and ostracism of all loyalists, and almost certainly an immediate demand for complete separation, with an executive working to make things impossible so long as that was refused.

I am not so sure about British unionists. Many of them without knowledge have adopted the convenient belief that any form of self-government would pacify Sinn Fein, which, though I do not myself believe it to contain a numerical majority, is by its wonderful organisation and direct purpose predominant and able to work its will by intimidation.

Though I suppose you will never get Englishmen to believe it, it would be a betrayal of the respectable farmers and others, of whom there are many, who would be only too glad to dissociate themselves from Sinn Fein if they believed the government would protect them, and of old soldiers who have fought for the empire.

To say that conditions under the union are satisfactory would be absurd, though I still believe it is the best, perhaps the only possible, government—but I submit there never was a moment less opportune for experiments in independent self-government here. I have no doubt that nationalists agree in this though they dare not say so.

My belief is that in present circumstances the government can produce no scheme which has any chance of acceptance here.

Certainly it would seem that a condition precedent to bringing any form of self-government into actual operation should be the abandonment of the claim to independence and the cessation of political murders and outrages. Even if a measure were passed, it should be held in suspense till this happens.

Home rule is not, I think, very near, for I do not believe a scheme imposed by Great Britain will in present conditions be accepted here. It can only as I think come from agreement of some sort in Ireland and you can judge as well as I as to the chance of that at the present time.

Whatever it is to be, it cannot be given a dominion or other label— geography and history alike must make any settlement different to the one regarding new countries many thousand miles away. State rights as in America are I think the nearest possible precedent—though not very suitable. If it comes, and some day it may do so, it will have to be adapted to Ireland and the United Kingdom. There is no existing parallel.

Strategically the harbours and coasts of Ireland are as vital to the state as those of Great Britain, and an obstructive or hostile parliament and executive in Ireland might be a grave peril to the empire. Do not Englishmen recognise this?

I very much hope your view will be that self-government in existing conditions would be as fatal to Ireland as perilous to England, and that partition will not be any way an alleviation—but the contrary—and that unless and until Irishmen can themselves formulate something possible of acceptance it is useless to endeavour to impose British-made schemes on Ireland.

Nothing would induce me personally to do otherwise than oppose partition. To me that is a point of principle—and I have given you some of my reasons for holding this opinion.

I cannot however dismiss as impossible the acceptance by parliament of some scheme involving some form of partition—and I venture to urge with all the force at my command that this would be fatal to Ireland and its prosperity, and a betrayal of loyal men in the south (which includes many who are neither unionists nor Protestants), would create a running sore and a perpetual bitterness between north and south and would at once establish what would practically be a Sinn Fein government on the flank of England, unchecked by the influence or power of representatives of loyal elements from the north.

To my mind nothing could be more disastrous to both islands than this.

Bibliography

THIS bibliography contains items cited in the text and others which were found particularly helpful for an understanding of the subject and period under review.

This book was based largely upon primary sources. By far the most important collection was that relating to the I.L.P.U. and I.U.A. in the P.R.O.N.I. Hitherto unused, it covers the period 1886–1922, and comprises a large collection of printed material, various minute books, mainly for the period up to 1914, and some correspondence, mainly for the period after 1914. This collection, together with Midleton's account of his activities after 1914 in his memoirs (*Records and Reactions*), provided an outline of southern unionist ideas, activity and effectiveness, a good foundation which was built up from other sources. Broadly speaking, the primary sources fell into two sections. On the one hand, there were those primarily giving evidence of the motives and aims of southern unionists and their organisation. The description and identification of southern unionists was based upon the usual standard reference works, supplemented by what few biographies and memoirs were available, and obituaries; and these sources were substantiated and enlarged upon by reference to imaginative literature and to some estate papers, both of which gave a vivid picture of what the Anglo-Irish stood for. As for motivation and aims, for the period up to 1914 interesting information was found in printed works, notably the various pamphlets issued by southern unionists and their organisations, parliamentary debates, particularly in the Lords, and reports of meetings organised by the I.L.P.U. and I.U.A. Any gap between private thought and public utterance was guarded against by reference to certain private correspondence, including the Pennefather, Hannay and Lecky papers, and the published letters of Dowden. Such collections contained, *inter alia*, comments on the southern unionist position by correspondents such as Bryan Cooper, unionist M.P. for South Co. Dublin in 1910. After 1914 there was more private correspondence conveniently available. The changing views of southern unionists were documented from the Midleton and Bernard papers, both of which contain a considerable correspondence between the more eminent southern unionists. Such evidence was supplemented by reference to the press controversy that surrounded the Midletonites' new departure, parliamentary debates and various memoranda, particularly for 1916 and 1920, in the Lloyd George and Law papers. The descriptions of the views of the Midletonites' opponents were based largely upon material available in the P.R.O.N.I., including various pieces written by that staunch Longford unionist, J. M. Wilson, and the press controversy in 1918. The picture of southern unionist organisation up to 1914 was based largely upon the various minute books and annual reports of the I.L.P.U., I.U.A., and U.A.I. After 1914, however, few such books were available, and the description of southern unionist organisation was based upon more scattered sources. For the period 1914–16 Wilson's observations were useful; the developing split in the I.U.A. was traced from the S.U.C.'s viewpoint in that committee's own minute book and in the papers of that sympathetic Tyrone unionist, H. de. F. Montgomery; and the Midleton and to a lesser extent the Bernard papers threw light upon how the Midletonites reacted to the challenge presented by the S.U.C. The activities of the I.U.A. after 1918 were traced in its periodical publication, *Notes from Ireland,* and those of the A.P.L. in the Midleton and Bernard papers, particularly the circumstances that resulted in the winding up of the A.P.L. without any attempt to modify it to meet the challenge of the Free State. The *Irish Times* proved generally the most useful newspaper and was consulted regularly for its correspondence columns and reporting. It was particularly helpful in tracing the emergence of the I.L.P.U. and its editorials were generally representative of southern unionist opinion until the split. After the split, the other Dublin unionist newspaper, the *Dublin Daily Express,* which supported the S.U.C., was consulted more frequently.

The second broad category into which the primary sources fell was those illustrating the impact made by southern unionists upon British politicians and their importance in discussions of the Irish question. The Balfour and Law papers showed their influence in the unionist party before 1914. For the period after 1914 the Lloyd George, Law and Asquith papers were useful, as were the Austen Chamberlain papers which contain many cabinet papers relating to the 1916 crisis and full cabinet records relating to the Irish treaty negotiations in 1921 and the constitution negotiations of the following year. The cabinet minutes proved disappointing. The southern unionist activity in the convention is well described in the confidential report by the chairman to H.M., copies of which are in the Irish convention papers in Trinity College and the Midleton papers.

Such primary sources were supplemented by various secondary works, the most useful of which were: R. Blake, *The Unknown Prime*

Minister, a biography of Law, invaluable for the controversy over the third home rule bill; D. Gwynn, *Life of John Redmond;* S. Gwynn, *John Redmond's Last Years* and R. B. McDowell, *The Irish Convention 1917–18,* both useful for the convention; F. S. L. Lyons's article on Irish unionists and the devolution crisis in *Irish Historical Studies* (1948); D. McCartney's article in *Irish Historical Studies* (1964–5) on Lecky's *Leaders of Public Opinion in Ireland,* a useful case study of a unionist being born; and D. O'Sullivan, *The Irish Free State and its Senate.* Good's brief book on *Irish Unionism* was disappointing, being concerned mainly with Ulster unionism and giving unionism in the south short shrift.

Time and other circumstances prevented the extensive use of Irish local newspapers and the assiduous tracking down of correspondence in private hands, but it is contended that the sources consulted are representative of those necessary for a study of southern unionism.

A. PRIMARY SOURCES

I. Manuscript materials

1. Beaverbrook Library
Andrew Bonar Law papers.
David Lloyd George papers.

2. Birmingham University Library
Joseph Chamberlain papers.
(Joseph) Austen Chamberlain papers.

3. Bodleian Library
Herbert Henry Asquith papers.

4. British Museum
Arthur James Balfour papers, Add. MS 49683–49962.
John Henry Bernard papers, Add. MS 52781–52784.

5. National Library of Ireland
Five account books relating to the Butler estate, Castle Crine, Co. Clare, MS 4253–6.
F. S. Bourke collection, MS 10723.
Diaries of Lady Alice Mary Howard, 1 Jan. 1874–25 Nov. 1922, MS 3600–25.

Seven duplicate letter books of Arthur Brook of Killybegs relating to
the Murray Stewart and Musgrave estates in Co. Donegal, 1866–1903,
MS 4273–9.
Rev. James Owen Hannay (pseud. G. A. Birmingham) papers, MS
8271.
O'Neill Daunt's journal, MS 3042.
Frederick William Pennefather letters, MS 3249.
John Redmond papers, MS 15,164–15,280.

6. *Public Record Office, London*

Cabinet minutes, 1918–22, Cab. 23/5–32.
Cabinet papers, 1916, Cab. 37/150–2; 1919–20 (Cabinet committee on
Ireland), Cab. 27/69/1 and 2.
Midleton (St John Brodrick, 1st earl of . . .) papers, P.R.O. 30/67. The
Irish material for the period up to the end of 1922 is in vols 29–52.

7. *Public Record Office of Northern Ireland*

(a) Major collections:
Lord Carson of Duncairn papers, D 1507.
Erne papers, D 1939.
Hugh de Fellenburg Montgomery papers, D 627/428–38; T 1089.
I.L.P.U. and I.U.A. (including the James MacKay Wilson) papers,
D 989. The more important items include

i. minute and other books
Executive council m.b., 1886–9 (D 989A/1/3).
M.b. of the executive (general) council, 1889–1920 (D 110/Mic and
D 989A/1/4).
Organising sub-committee m.b., 1886 (D 989A/1/2).
Executive committee m.b., 1893–4 (D 989A/1/5).
Speakers' committee m.b., 1893–4 (D 989A/1/6).
Parliamentary consultative committee m.b., 1894–1900 (D 989A/1/7).
Finance committee m.b. (including the minutes of all other com-
mittees of the I.U.A.), 1907–12 (D 989A/1/10).
Subscription book (D 989A/3/3).
M.b. of the London committee of the I.U.A., 1919–39 (D 989A/1/11).

ii. *Annual reports* (D 989A/7)

iii. correspondence etc.
File of 'in' letters (P–S), 1892–3 (D 989A/8/2).
Correspondence with Sir Edward Carson, 1913–14 (D 989A/8/4).
MS material relating to the split in the I.U.A., 1918–19: minutes of

meetings of the S.U.C. (D 989A/1/10 and 8/16); assorted correspondence (D 989A/9/6A, 8/17, 9/11C, 11/10).
Richard Dawson of the London committee of the I.U.A. reporting to the Dublin committee on movements of English opinion on home rule, 1919–22 (D 989A/9/20).
Memoranda, circular letters etc. relating to incidents affecting loyalists in the Anglo-Irish and civil wars (D 989A/8/23).

iv. miscellaneous writings of J. M. Wilson

Letters and memoranda relating to his activities in the Irish crisis, June–July 1916 (D 989A/8/10, 9/5).
Letters and vouchers relating to his tour of the Irish counties, 1915–17, with draft ms and typescript notes reporting, on a county by county basis, local feeling with regard to current issues, the war, conscription, Redmond's position, Sinn Fein etc. (D 989A/9/7).

(b) Smaller collections:
Unionist Clubs of Ireland, D 1327/1.
Unionist Associations of Ireland, D 1327/2. This collection comprises the minute books of the Joint Committee of the U.A.I., 19 Dec. 1907–15 Jan. 1915 (D 1327/2/1, 2); an agenda book (D 1327/2/3); a register of speakers and canvassers (D 1327/2/4).

(c) miscellaneous items:
Minute book of the Kingstown and District Unionist Club (founded 13 Feb. 1911), D 950/1/147.
Various press cuttings, pamphlets etc., including some relating to the U.A.I., D 1327/7/6–8.
T. Comyn Platt (British League for the Support of Ulster and the Union) to Dawson Bates (U.U.C.) 6 Apr. 1914, D 1327/4/2.
E. Beaumont Nesbitt to Mrs Savage Armstrong, 19 Jan. 1925, D 618/172.

8. *Public Record Office of the Republic of Ireland*
Various wills.

9. *Trinity College, Dublin*
John Henry Bernard correspondence.
Irish convention papers, 1917–18—two boxes (one of official papers) from the collections of John Pentland Mahaffy and J. H. Bernard, MS 2986–7.
William Hartpole Lecky correspondence.

II. Printed materials

1. PARLIAMENTARY AND OTHER OFFICIAL PUBLICATIONS

Census reports (U.K., 1911), (Saorstat Eireann, 1926).
Dail Debates.
Irish Free State. Compensation for Injury to Persons and Property (1923),
Cmd 1844.
Parliamentary Debates.
Report of the Proceedings of the Irish Convention (1918), Cd 9019.
*Return showing by monthly periods the number of murders of members of the
Royal Irish Constabulary and of the Dublin Metropolitan Police and of
soldiers, officials and civilians, and the number of political outrages on persons
and property in Ireland from the 1st day of January 1919 to 30th April 1920*
(1920), Cmd 709.
*Return showing the number of serious outrages in Ireland reported by the
R.I.C. and the Dublin Metropolitan Police during the months of October,
November and December 1920* (1921), Cmd 1165.
*Special Commission Act, 1888; reprint of the shorthand notes of the speeches,
proceedings and evidence taken before the commissioners appointed under the
above-named act,* 12 vols, 1890.
*Summary of the returns of owners of land in Ireland, showing, with respect
to each county, the number of owners of land below an acre, and in classes of
up to 100,000 acres and upwards, with the aggregate acreage and valuation
of each class.* Parliamentary paper, lxxx (1876).

2. NEWSPAPERS AND PERIODICALS

*Belfast News-Letter; Blackwoods Magazine; Contemporary Review;
Dublin Daily Express; Dublin Evening Mail; Freeman's Journal; Glasgow
Herald; The Globe; Irish Bulletin; Irish Independent; Irish Times;
Leinster Leader; Morning Post; National Review; Nineteenth Century;
Notes from Ireland; Quarterly Review; The Scotsman; The Times;
Yorkshire Herald; The Witness.*

3. MEMOIRS AND OTHER CONTEMPORARY NARRATIVES

(Including some of the more important of the early pamphlets published by southern unionists.)

Ball, Sir Robert, *Reminiscences and Letters of . . . ,* ed. W. Valentine
Ball, London, 1915.
Battersea, Constance, *Reminiscences,* London, 1923.
Churchill, W. S., *The World Crisis. The Aftermath,* London, 1929.
Colles, Ramsay, *In Castle and Courthouse: Being Reminiscences of Thirty
Years in Ireland,* London, 1911.

Cooper, Bryan, *The Tenth (Irish) Division in Gallipoli*, London, 1918.
Desart, Earl of, and Lady Sybil Lubbock, *A Page from the Past. Memories of the Earl of Desart*, London, 1936.
Devas, Nicolette, *Two Flamboyant Fathers*, 1966. Readers Union ed., London, 1967.
Dunraven, Lord, *Past Times and Pastimes*, 2 vols, London, 1922.
Ewart, Wilfrid, *A Journey in Ireland, 1921*, London, 1922.
Good, J. W., *Irish Unionism*, London, 1920.
Gwynn, Stephen, *John Redmond's Last Years*, London, 1919.
Hamilton, Elizabeth, *An Irish Childhood*, London, 1963.
Hussey, S. M., *The Reminiscences of an Irish Land Agent*, compiled by Home Gordon, London, 1904.
I.L.P.U., *A Guide to the 'Eighty-six'*, Dublin, 1886.
I.L.P.U., *Prospectus*, London, 1886.
I.L.P.U., *Statement Submitted to the Prime Minister by the I.L.P.U.: Part III: the Union Vindicated. Ireland's Progress, 1782–1800–1886*, Dublin, 1886.
I.L.P.U., *Union or Separation*, Dublin, 1886.
I.L.P.U., *A Year of Evictions in Ireland*, Dublin, 1887.
I.L.P.U., *The Plan of Campaign, Illustrated. Extra-No. IV. Correspondence on the Clanricarde Estate*, Dublin, 1889.
I.U.A., *Annual Reports, 1887–1920*. (There is a gap between 1914 and 1919.)
I.U.A., *The Irish Unionist Alliance: Its Work and Organisation*, Dublin, 1893.
I.U.A., *The Irish Priest in Politics: as Revealed in the Evidence Given on the Hearing of the Meath Election Petitions*, Dublin, 1893.
Le Fanu, W. R., *Seventy Years of Irish Life*, London, 1893.
Long, W., *Memories*, London, 1923.
Lynch-Robinson, Sir Christopher, *The Last of the Irish R.M.s*, London, 1951.
Macready, Sir Cecil Frederick Nevil, *Annals of an Active Life*, London, 1924.
McNeill, R., *Ulster's Stand for Union*, London, 1922.
Maguire, Thomas, *The Effects of Home Rule on the Higher Education*, Dublin, 1886.
Midleton, Lord, *Ireland—Dupe or Heroine?*, London, 1932.
Midleton, Lord, *Records and Reactions 1856–1939*, London, 1939.
Montgomery-Cuninghame, Col. Sir Thomas, *Dusty Measure. A Record of Troubled Times*, London, 1939.
Nicholas, Rev. William, *Why are the Methodists of Ireland Opposed to Home Rule?*, Dublin, 1893.
Pakenham, Francis, *Born to Believe*, London, 1953.

Plunkett, Sir Horace, *Ireland in the New Century*, London, 1904.
Plunkett, Sir Horace, *The Irish Convention: Confidential Report to H.M. the King by the Chairman* (printed, though not published, copies in T.C.D. convention papers and Midleton papers, P.R.O.).
Ponsonby, Sir Frederick, *Recollections of Three Reigns*, London, 1951.
Robinson, Sir Henry Arthur, *Memories: Wise and Otherwise*, London, 1923.
Robinson, Sir Henry Arthur, *Further Memories of Irish Life*, London, 1924.
Somerville, E. Œ. and Ross, Martin (V. F. Martin), *Irish Memories*, London, 1917.
Somerville, E. Œ. and Ross, Martin, *Some Irish Yesterdays*, London, 1906.
Trench, R. Steuart, *Realities of Irish Life*, London, 1869, 5th ed., 1870.
Webb, Thomas E., *The Irish Question: a Reply to Mr Gladstone*, Dublin, 1886.

4. CONTEMPORARY WORKS OF REFERENCE

A Concise Dictionary of Irish National Biography, ed. John S. Crone, Dublin, 1928.
Annual Register 1885–1922.
Bateman, John, *The Great Landowners of Great Britain and Ireland*, London, 1883.
Burke's Landed Gentry of Ireland, London, 1912, 1958.
Burke's Peerage, Baronetage and Knightage, London, several eds., but especially 1967.
De Burgh, U. U. H., *The Landowners of Ireland*, Dublin, 1878.
Dictionary of National Biography.
Dod's Parliamentary Companion, 1832—work still in progress.
G.E.C., *Complete Baronetage*.
G.E.C., *Complete Peerage*.
Thom's Irish Almanac and Official Directory, Dublin, 1844—work still in progress.
Thom's Irish Who's Who, Dublin, 1923.
Walford, E., *The County Families of the United Kingdom: the Titled and Untitled Aristocracy. A Dictionary of the Upper Ten Thousand*, London, 1879, 1882, 1896, 1906 and 1912 eds used especially.
Who Was Who (1897–1916), London, 1920. *Who Was Who (1916–1928)*, London, 1929. *Who Was Who (1929–1940)*, London, 1941. *Who Was Who (1941–1950)*, London, 1952.

5. PUBLISHED COLLECTIONS OF LETTERS ETC.

Letters of Edward Dowden and his Correspondents, eds E. D. and H. M. Dowden, London, 1914.

Fragments of Old Letters, E.D. to E.D.W., ed. E. D. Dowden, 2 series, London, 1914.
Lady Gregory's Journals, 1916–1930, ed. Lennox Robinson, London, 1946.
A Victorian Historian. Private Letters of W. E. H. Lecky, 1859–1878, by H. M. Hyde, London, 1947.
'Lord Milner's Irish Journal, 1886', by T. H. O'Brien, *History Today*, xiv (Feb. 1964), pp. 43–51.
Intelligence notes 1913–16, ed. B. Mac Giolla Choille, Dublin, 1966.

6. IMAGINATIVE LITERATURE
Birmingham, G. A., *The Bad Times*, London, 1908.
Corkery, Daniel, *The Hounds of Banba*, Dublin and London, 1920.
Farrell, M. J., *Mad Puppetstown*, London, 1931.
Farrell, M. J., *The Rising Tide*, London, 1937.
Robinson, Lennox, *The Big House*, London, 1928.
Somerville E. Œ .and Ross, M., *Experiences of an Irish R.M.*, Everyman ed., London, 1944 (incorporating *Some experiences of an Irish R.M.*, 1899, and *Further Experiences of an Irish R.M.*, 1908).
Somerville, E. Œ. and Ross M., *In Mr Knox's Country*, London, 1915.

B. LATER WORKS

1. BIOGRAPHICAL
Beckett, J. C., 'Carson—unionist and rebel', in *Leaders and Men of the Easter Rising: Dublin 1916*, ed. F. X. Martin, London, 1967, pp. 81–94.
Blake, Robert, *The Unknown Prime Minister*, London, 1955.
Bowen, Elizabeth, *Bowen's Court*, London, 1942, 1964.
Calwell, C. E., *Field Marshal Sir Henry Wilson . . . His Life and Diaries*, 2 vols, London, 1927.
Colum, Padraic, *Arthur Griffith*, Dublin, 1959.
Colvin, *The Life of Lord Carson*, see Marjoribanks.
Cummins, Geraldine, *Dr. E. Œ. Somerville. A Biography*, London, 1952.
Digby, M., *Horace Plunkett, an Anglo-American Irishman*, Oxford, 1949.
Dugdale, B. F. C., *Arthur James Balfour*, 2 vols, London, 1936.
Gollin, A. M., *The Observer and J. L. Garvin*, London, 1960.
Gollin, A. M., *Proconsul in Politics*, London, 1964.
Gwynn, D., *The Life of John Redmond*, London, 1932.
Holland, B., *Life of Spencer Crompton, 8th Duke of Devonshire*, 2 vols, London, 1911.

Jenkins, R., *Asquith,* London, 1964.

Lecky, Elisabeth, *A Memoir of W. E. H. Lecky,* London, 1909.

Lucas, R., *Colonel Saunderson M.P. A Memoir,* London, 1908.

McCormick, D., *The Incredible Mr Kavanagh,* London, 1960.

Majoribanks, E. and Colvin, I., *The Life of Lord Carson,* 3 vols, London, 1932–6.

Marrecco, Anne, *The Rebel Countess. The Life and Time of Constance Markievicz,* London, 1967.

Murray, R. H., *Archbishop Bernard, Professor, Prelate and Provost,* London, 1931.

Newton, Lord, *Lord Lansdowne. A Biography,* London, 1929.

O'Brien, R. B., *The Life of Charles Stuart Parnell,* 2 vols, London, 1899.

Petrie, Sir Charles, *Walter Long and his Times,* London, 1936.

Petrie, Sir Charles, *The Life and Letters of the Rt Hon. Sir A. Chamberlain,* 2 vols, London, 1939–40.

Robinson, Lennox, *Bryan Cooper,* London, 1931.

Steele, Sarah L., *The Right Honourable Arthur MacMurrough Kavanagh. A Biography,* London, 1890.

Taylor, Monica, *Sir Bertram Windle. A Memoir,* London, 1932.

Taylor, R., *Michael Collins,* London, 1958.

Thornley, D., *Isaac Butt and Home Rule,* London, 1964.

White, T. de Vere, *Kevin O'Higgins,* London, 1948.

Young, K., *Arthur James Balfour,* London, 1963.

2. GENERAL AND SPECIAL STUDIES

Arensberg, C. M., *The Irish Countryman. An Anthropological Study,* London, 1937.

Beckett, J. C., *A Short History of Ireland,* London, 1952.

Beckett, J. C., *The Making of Modern Ireland, 1603–1923,* London, 1966.

Bennett, R., *The Black and Tans,* London, 1959, Four Square ed. 1961.

Bolton, G. C., *The Passing of the Irish Act of Union,* London, 1966.

Boyce, D. G., 'British conservative opinion, the Ulster question and the partition of Ireland, 1912–21', *Irish Historical Studies,* xvii (1970–1), pp. 89–112.

Boyce, D. G., 'How to settle the Irish question: Lloyd George and Ireland 1916–21', in *Lloyd George: Twelve Essays,* ed. A. J. P. Taylor, London, 1971, pp. 137–64.

Buckland, P. J., 'The unionists and Ireland: the influence of the Irish question on British politics, 1906–14', Birmingham University M.A. thesis, 1966.

Buckland, P. J., 'The southern Irish unionists, the Irish question and British politics, 1906–14', *Irish Historical Studies,* xv (1966–7), pp. 228–55.

Buckland, P. J., 'Southern unionism, 1885–1922', Queen's University, Belfast, Ph. D. thesis, 1969.

Buckland, P. J., *Irish Unionism, 1885–1923: Select Documents*, Belfast, 1972.

Curtis, L. P., *Coercion and Conciliation in Ireland, 1880–1892. A Study in Conservative Unionism*, Princeton, 1963.

Fanning, R., 'The unionist party and Ireland, 1906–10', *Irish Historical Studies*, xv (1966–7), pp. 147–71.

Gallagher, F., *The Anglo-Irish Treaty*, ed. T. P. O'Neill, London, 1965.

Guttsman, W. L., *The British Political Elite, 1832–1935*, London, 1963.

Holt, E., *Protest in Arms: The Irish Troubles 1916-23*, London, 1960.

Lynch, P. and Vaizey, J., *Guinness's Brewery in the Irish Economy, 1759–1876*, Cambridge, 1960.

Lyons, F. S. L., 'The Irish unionist party and the devolution crisis of 1904–5', *Irish Historical Studies*, vi (1948–9), pp. 1–22.

Lyons, F. S. L., *The Irish Parliamentary Party, 1890–1910*, London, 1951.

Lyons, F. S. L., 'The minority problem in the twenty-six counties', in *The Years of the Great Test, 1926–39*, ed. F. MacManus, Cork, 1967, pp. 92–103.

Macardle, D., *The Irish Republic*, 1937, Corgi ed., London, 1968.

McCartney, D., 'Lecky's *Leaders of Public Opinion in Ireland*', *Irish Historical Studies*, xiv (1964–5), pp. 119–41.

McCracken, J. L., *Representative Government in Ireland*, Oxford, 1958.

McDowell, R. B., *British Conservatism, 1832–1914*, London, 1959.

McDowell, R. B., *The Irish Convention 1917–18*, London, 1970.

MacKenzie, R. T., *British Political Parties*, London, 1955.

Mansergh, N., *The Irish Question, 1840–1921: a Commentary on Anglo-Irish Relations and on Social and Political Forces in Ireland in the Age of Reform and Revolution*, London, 1965.

O'Brien, C. C., *Parnell and his Party*, 1957, corrected impression, Oxford, 1964.

O'Sullivan, D., *The Irish Free State and its Senate. A Study in Contemporary Politics*, London, 1940.

Pakenham, F., *Peace by Ordeal: an Account, From First-Hand Sources, of the Negotiation and Signature of the Anglo-Irish Treaty, 1921*, London 1935, New English Library (Mentor) ed. 1967.

Palmer, N., *The Irish Land League Crisis*, New Haven, 1940.

Phillips, W. A., *The Revolution in Ireland, 1906–23*, London, 1923.

Pomfret, J. E., *The Struggle for Land in Ireland, 1800–1923*, Princeton, 1930.

Savage, D. C., 'The origins of the Ulster unionist party, 1885–6', *Irish Historical Studies*, xii (1960–1), pp. 185–208.

Smith-Gordon, L. and Staples, L. C., *Rural Reconstruction in Ireland. A Record of Cooperative Organisation*, London, 1919.

Stewart, A. T. Q., *The Ulster Crisis*, London, 1967.

Taylor, A. J. P., *English History, 1914–1945*, Oxford, 1965.

Thompson, F. M. L., *English Landed Society in the Nineteenth Century*, London, 1963.

Thornley, D., 'The Irish conservatives and home rule, 1869–73', *Irish Historical Studies*, xi (1958–9), pp. 200–22.

Whyte, J. H., 'Landlord influence at elections in Ireland, 1762–1885', *English Historical Review*, lxxx (1965), pp. 740–60.

Younger, Calton, *Ireland's Civil War*, London, 1968.

Index

(s.u. = southern unionist; 1914 bill = third home rule bill; 1914 act = Third Home Rule Act (1914); 1920 bill = Government of Ireland bill (1920); 1920 act = Government of Ireland Act (1920).)